AMERICA INSIDE OUT

ALSO BY DAVID SCHOENBRUN

As France Goes
The Three Lives of Charles de Gaulle
Vietnam: How We Got In, How to Get Out
The New Israelis
Triumph in Paris
Soldiers of the Night: The Story of the French Resistance

AMERICA INSIDE OUT

by David Schoenbrun

McGRAW-HILL BOOK COMPANY

New York • St. Louis • San Francisco
Hamburg • Mexico • Toronto

1 2 3 4 5 6 7 8 9 DOCDOC 8 7 6 5 4

ISBN 0-07-055473-0

LIBRARY OF CONGRESS CATALOGING IN PUBLICATION DATA

Schoenbrun, David.
America inside out.
1. Schoenbrun, David. 2. Journalists—United States—
Biography. I. Title.
PN4874.S332A31 1984 070'.92'4 [B] 84–3868
ISBN 0–07–055473–0

Book design by A. Christopher Simon

for
Dorothy, Lucy, and Noémi

CONTENTS

PROLOGUE

A PERSONAL HISTORY

This is a story that spans some fifty years of American and world history. It is not a work of fiction. It is a true story of a half-century of extraordinary events that would not have been believed if any author had tried to invent them.

No laudanum-crazed ravings of a Baudelaire could have imagined the crematoria of Dachau and of Auschwitz. Flowers of evil blossomed across Europe in the forties. Six million people died in torture and in flames only because they were Jewish. Many were not even practicing Jews. They merely had Jewish parents. As a war correspondent, walking a pace behind General Patton, I saw the living dead of Buchenwald and the piles of bodies stacked like cordwood, some of the limbs still twitching. I saw tough General Patton turn green and vomit. Who would have believed that the Jews would rise like a phoenix out of their ashes and realize the seemingly hopeless dream of resurrection in their own homeland in Israel? This I witnessed as a young reporter in Palestine.

I saw men and women as devils, and men and women as angels. Germany gave us Adolf Hitler and Heinrich Himmler, but also Albert Einstein and Thomas Mann. I saw Ilse Koch, the Bitch of Buchenwald, who decorated her barracks rooms with lampshades made of human flesh, a female Satan. But I also knew a female saint, Irène Curie, daughter of Pierre and Marie Curie, Nobel Prize discoverers of radium. Irène also won a Nobel Prize, with her husband Frédéric Joliot, for proving that when an atom splits, a chain reaction occurs, a landmark discovery ushering in the atomic age.

One day in Irène's laboratory at the Collège de France, she saw a vial of deadly radioactive salts begin to slide off a table. Before it could hit the floor, she dived across the room and threw her body over the vial, screaming to her lab fellows to run for their lives. They did and they lived. Irène Curie died, her body rotted through with cancer from the radioactive fluid.

When I look upon the world I have lived in, I renew my faith and hope in human progress by remembering Irène Curie, and my classmate Jonas Salk and my friend Isaac Stern and all the men and women who have made this world a better place in which to live. Despite all I have seen, I remain an optimist, albeit a disenchanted optimist, for I know too much of evil, greed, and selfishness to ignore their constant threat, but an optimist nonetheless, for I have lived through the worst of times and have often seen the eventual triumph of the good.

In a long career as a globe-trotting correspondent, I have learned a great deal about how decisions are made, some by accident and sometimes by misconception, sometimes brilliantly with the most unexpected results. I have seen American foreign policy at its most enlightened, in the Marshall Plan, and came to know and admire George Catlett Marshall as one of the greatest and most modest of Americans. But I have also seen American policy at its most arrogant and ill-conceived, in Vietnam, a cruel disaster architected by men whom David Halberstam described as the "best and the brightest."

I discovered that brilliance of mind and depth of learning are not always positive qualities, and that knowledge, by itself, is not a guarantee of good thinking or correct decisions. I came to respect character, integrity, and common sense as more valuable than brilliance and erudition. Jean Monnet, "Mr. Europe," creator of the Common Market, technocrat supreme, who did more than any statesman or general to bring peace to Europe's millions, never went to college. He was a wise man, an honest man, a man of character. He did not have the education or the intellectual tools of a Henry Kissinger, but he was ten times the creator.

Dwight D. Eisenhower was graduated near the foot of his class at West Point but he was a better man who did more for his country and the world than the brilliant Douglas MacArthur, who stood at the head of his class. Monnet, speaking of Eisenhower, once told me: "He consistently makes the right decisions without understanding all the elements of a problem, while a hall full of Harvard professors are proposing the wrong decisions knowing all the elements of the issue."

Harry Truman was no intellectual giant but he was worth a hundred Richard Nixons. Nixon was a first-rate law student, near the top of his class at one of the nation's finest schools, Duke University. His failure was not a failure of knowledge or brains. He knew the law. But Nixon did not respect the law he knew.

I learned as a reporter that knowing law or history is not enough, not nearly enough. Georges Bidault, prime minister and foreign minister of France, had been a teacher of history at one of France's most famed lycées, Louis-le-Grand in Paris. But he never could understand that a new moment of history had arrived in the midcentury, when the people of Algeria, long stateless and colonized, had been stricken with what Thomas Jefferson had called "the infectious disease of freedom." Bidault did not have the common sense to realize that the African peoples wanted no more empire. Bidault was a French nationalist, arrogant and egotistical, faults of character that undermined his learning.

My story does not only deal with world-shaking decisions, great leaders, holocausts, wars, and politics. It ranges across the spectrum of human enterprise. In my youth I was a student of Latin and the Latin languages and became a teacher of French. I was not more than sixteen when I came across a volume of Cicero's essays *De Officiis.* In it, Cicero quoted a thought by a philosopher he admired, Heauton Timoroumenos: "I am a man: nothing human is alien to me." From that moment on, this thought motivated me to give free rein to my curiosity in every form of human endeavor. It has been the strongest drive in my career as a reporter, broadcaster, lecturer, and author.

An example of that broad-spectrum drive came one day in Paris in 1950 when I was conducting interviews on the occasion of the midcentury year with four men of totally different professions, each a man who was making important contributions to our culture: Professor Nguyen Buu Hoi, a Vietnamese scientist who headed the prestigious Curie Research Institute in Paris; Jean Monnet, head of the Action Committee for a United States of Europe; Christian Dior, premier couturier of the world; and General Pierre Gallois, military advisor to General Eisenhower, Supreme Commander of the Atlantic Alliance's armed forces.

Dr. Buu Hoi was one of the first world scientists to insist upon the link between cigarettes and cancer. He had also found cures or palliatives for dozens of tropical diseases, from herpes to leprosy. He had a fine sense of humor and told me that smoking and drinking alcohol were both highly dangerous but if you had to smoke and drink, "do it simultaneously. Smoking tightens up the arteries and impedes the blood circulation but alcohol opens up the arteries and stimulates circulation."

Christian Dior joked about the fact that the most famous dressmakers were men but mainly homosexuals. "Our female chromosomes give us the taste and fashion sense to create for women. Male chromosomes give us the strength to work hard and survive the mad rush and chaos of every new fashion season."

Jean Monnet, one of the most extraordinary men to arise in postwar Europe, was in the process of changing the history of Europe with his grand plan for unity, which led to the creation of a Coal and Steel Community, an Atomic Energy Community, and an Economic Community, better known as the Common Market. He told me: "Reporters talk about my complex schemes of unity, those complicated communities and my grand, visionary concept of a United States of Europe. It is not complex or visionary at all, nor is my main aim to improve Europe's energy and industry. The idea is to integrate the efforts and planning of European nation-states so that they will learn to live together in peace. In fact, they will be so integrated that they cannot make war upon each other again. That is the simple idea, the best kind of idea, the core of my thinking." Later we will examine the extraordinary success of Monnet's "simple idea."

The most interesting interview, and still fresh thirty years later, a rarity, was the talk with General Pierre Gallois. The atomic age was only some five years old but Gallois had an understanding of some of its consequences that was startling and prophetic. "The atomic bomb has changed warfare fundamentally and forever. It has also changed traditional thinking about alliances. Twice in this century, you Americans came to our shores to rescue us and win the final victory, first over the Kaiser, then over Hitler. But you will never come again to liberate us in another war. One cannot rescue radiated rubble."

Gallois went on to explain why General de Gaulle had called for an independent French atomic force. "We do not doubt the goodwill and loyalty of our American allies. But we cannot believe that you would risk the destruction of New York or Washington to defend Paris. You cannot be that quixotic. If Russia threatens an invasion of France tomorrow, what would you do in retaliation? Nuke Russia? Soon they will have a titanic atomic arsenal and they will be able to nuke you. Before the age of atomic bombs, jet planes, and missiles, America lived safely behind its Atlantic and Pacific ocean moats. You are no longer safe from attack. You can't save us without committing suicide. So we need our own atomic force in our own defense. What would Russia profit from invading and occupying France if we could knock out Moscow, Leningrad, and other Russian cities? France isn't worth five or six Soviet cities. It will be too costly for Russia to attack us. They know that you won't defend Paris again but they damn well know that we French will."

Gallois's analysis remains today the best rationale for the independent French atomic force. This is one of the most explosive issues today in the controversy between the Western nations and Russia over the deployment of missiles in Europe. This will lead, later in this report, to a full discussion of the consequences of the atomic age.

Of all the many extraordinary people that I came to know, perhaps the most extraordinary, destined to make a powerful and costly impact upon America, was a tiny, almost unknown wisp of a man whom I met at Fontainebleau, in the spring of 1946. He was the newly proclaimed president of a small country about which I and most Americans then knew nothing. His name was Ho Chi Minh, his country, Vietnam.

I was, at the time, Paris correspondent for a small but highly regarded news agency, the Overseas News Agency (ONA), and radio "stringer," that is, part-time newscaster, for CBS. I had met Ed Murrow during the war and he told me to be patient, for an opening on the CBS News staff would come soon enough and he wanted me to be his Paris correspondent. It was a dream that came true a year later, in 1947.

When I left ONA, I was replaced by a brilliant young reporter who was to become America's most famed and successful reporter-author, Theodore H. "Teddy" White. He was one of a remarkable group of young American newsmen, the finest corps of reporters ever assembled in one capital at the same time. Among them were a young Boston Brahmin, Harvard classmate of John F. Kennedy, Ben Bradlee, who would become executive editor of *The Washington Post* and oversee with skill, integrity, and courage the great Woodward-Bernstein exposés of Watergate that would blast Nixon out of the White House. There was a pudgy, cigar-smoking youngster, a stringer for *Variety* covering show business news, named Art Buchwald, today the premier humor writer and political satirist in the world, published around the world. And many others the reader will meet in a chapter about life in Paris in the 1950s.

They were then little known, just as Ho Chi Minh, president of a newly independent, small, remote land, Vietnam, was little known to reporters and to the world. Ho first came to my attention when I read a dispatch in the French press agency Agence France-Presse (AFP) about a conference scheduled to be held in Fontainebleau to create new relationships between the former French colonies of Indochina and the newly liberated country of Vietnam.

I talked with Ho a number of times in Fontainebleau and at his country's offices in Paris. One day, I asked him if he had ever been to America and what he knew about our country. Ho told me that as a merchant seaman he had once spent a week or so in New York, had discovered that the streets were paved with garbage, not gold, and that he had seen "the horrors of your black ghetto called Harlem."

I knew that Ho was a communist, and I knew all about Harlem, having been born and raised there, but his words startled and depressed me. I didn't want him to think of America as garbage and ghettos. I was proud of my country. As a soldier I had just come through a war that was for me and for millions of Americans a true crusade for freedom. I felt we had turned back the darkness of the Nazi night and brought to the world the dawn of a new hope for freedom and for equality of all peoples. I was a naïve idealist in 1946. I am still an idealist today if no longer naïve.

Impulsively I said to Ho: "I'd love a chance to tell you about

America. I'm living here in Saint-Cloud, just at the gate of Paris, with my father, stepmother, and wife. I have American friends, fellow reporters, good men. Would you like to come to dinner, spend an evening with us, tell us about your country and your dreams, and listen to us talk about our country and our dreams and goals?" To my astonishment and delight, Ho Chi Minh said he would accept the invitation. Neither of us could have guessed what that night would eventually lead to.

Whenever anyone asks, "What is going to happen in Poland, or Lebanon," or wants to know if Walter Mondale or Howard Baker would make a good President, I think back to the twists, turns, and surprises of the past fifty years and refuse to answer. Who would ever have believed that that tiny, frail, obscure Vietnamese would defeat the modern army of France, and then frustrate mighty America, which failed, after a giant effort, to crush his small band of guerrillas. It was as though a swarm of mosquitoes had made an elephant run away.

Who can possibly foresee the magic alchemy of the White House which can turn midgets into giants and giants into pygmies? In his early years, Franklin Delano Roosevelt gave no sign of his great courage, commitment, and compassion that would make him one of the greatest Presidents in our history. Harry Truman, a small-time politician from a corrupt city gang, met the challenge of greatness. General Eisenhower, a military man, gave us eight years of peace, whereas our civilian Presidents plunged us into war. Richard Nixon, who had made anticommunism a theology and a career, entered the White House and then held out his hands in reconciliation to Moscow and Peking. Who knows what a man can become or what the future may bring? There is an ancient Chinese curse: "May you know the future."

But we do know the past. And by looking deeply into the past, free of the passions of the moment, we can perceive the roots of the present. The past is present today in many areas. No issue is so hotly debated in the 1980s as Social Security, the historic act of the 1930s. We suffer from a "Munich syndrome," a fear that any concession to a dictator is appeasement. We suffer from a "Pearl Harbor syndrome," the fear of a "sneak attack," which is the main rationale behind the controversial MX missile, forty years after Pearl Harbor.

So, our exploration of American events, from Roosevelt to

Reagan, is not only history. It is contemporary, in that it shows us how we got to where we are. This is not a formal history, for I am a reporter and a student of history, not a historian.

I doubt that even a professional historian could document and evaluate the exploding world of our times in a single volume. This is, rather, an examination of the world we live in, with close-up portraits of the men and women who made this world, as I saw the events and the world-makers, as I experienced the unfolding dramas, lived in them and learned from them, lessons that I can share with my generation and pass on to our children.

In my lifetime, I have seen America come full circle from Franklin Delano Roosevelt and his New Deal to Ronald Wilson Reagan, once a New Dealer, now the leader of those who blame Roosevelt and the New Deal philosophy as the root of our evils. Reagan and America today are as different from Roosevelt and America yesterday as they could be and still remain the same nation. Indeed, there are those who wonder if it is still the same nation.

We shall examine that question and many more in this chronicle of a changing America and a changing world, from Roosevelt to Reagan and hundreds of extraordinary characters around the globe in every major field of human enterprise. I have been an observer and at times a participant in the events that shook our world, so, inevitably, albeit reluctantly, I myself have become a character in this chronicle.

CHAPTER 1

REAGAN AND ROOSEVELT

For drama, joy, color, beauty, there had never been an inauguration like it.

After a long career in B-films, Ronald Reagan starred in the greatest role any American could ever hope to play: President of the United States. Nature and Fate were both smiling upon the fortieth President on a clear, sunny January day in 1981, the first time in American history that the inaugural ceremony was being held on the West Front of the Capitol, facing a magnificent vista overlooking the open mall with its monuments to the great men of American history. Directly in front of the new President was the monument to George Washington. Off to one side, the stately memorial to Thomas Jefferson, and beyond the Reflecting Pool, the columns of the Lincoln Memorial. These were the men who founded, shaped, and gave a soul to the government of the United States, conceived in freedom with liberty and justice for all, a government dedicated to the promotion of the general welfare of all its citizens.

At the moment that Ronald Wilson Reagan arose to deliver his inaugural address in the monumental presence of these giants, Americans were also cheering the sight on TV of fifty-two men and women, held hostage in Iran for more than a year, released at last, flying out of Teheran, heading home, like doves of peace to celebrate the inauguration. Poor Jimmy Carter, on the reviewing stand, valiantly smiling, had tried so hard, through sleepless nights and long prayers, to free the hostages, only to see them freed just in time to crown the man who had defeated him, in part because he could not obtain their release. What a bitter moment for Carter.

What a glorious moment for Ronald Reagan, in whose person one of America's most cherished dreams had been realized: anyone born in the United States, of the most humble origins, could aspire to be President. Well, almost anyone, male, white, and Christian. One day perhaps a woman, a Jew, a black could aspire to the American dream. In our times, John F. Kennedy had become the first Catholic to enter the White House, Thurgood Marshall the first black to don the robes of a Supreme Court justice, and Sandra Day O'Connor the first woman to enter the male sanctuary of the court. She would be put there by President Reagan, the first sports announcer and film actor to attain the White House.

What noble thoughts would inspire Ronald Reagan on this auspicious occasion? To what great cause would he dedicate his new Administration? Standing in the crowd, feeling the pulse of hope generated by the ceremony, I felt fairly certain of what Reagan would say. For the past fifteen years I had observed him develop his major themes in dozens of speeches and hundreds of syndicated columns and radio talks: government is too big, spends too much, provides welfare that takes away the motive to work, diminishes the value of the dollar, and piles up huge deficits that steal the heritage of future generations. These were the themes he had put forward in his successful electoral campaign. Perhaps the magic of the White House would eventually work its alchemy on him as it had on other Presidents in our time, but on Inauguration Day Ronald Reagan was still the campaigner, not yet the President subjected to the exigencies of his office.

Those who had voted for Ronald Reagan and who shared his political views were not to be disappointed by his inaugural address. All his well-known themes were there. After a traditional reference to the orderly transfer of power, the "miracle" of our democracy, and a courteous bow to President Carter for his "gracious cooperation" in the process of change, Reagan lost no time in launching a familiar theme. "For decades, we have piled deficit upon deficit, mortgaging our future and our children's future." Then, the benchmark of his Presidency, an assertion never before made by any other President: "Government is not the solution to our problem, government is the problem."

We had heard this idea before but never put forward so tersely, so concisely, and, above all, on the highest level of government, by the man who would shortly take the oath of office and have in his hands levers of enormous power to turn his idea into a reality. It was a bid to turn back to another century, a simpler day in a smaller America, isolated from the world, growing inwardly as it expanded across its continent with new frontiers beckoning. In this sense of turning back, Ronald Reagan revealed that he was not a conservative, preserving the heritage of years of growth, but a reactionary, and a radical one, reacting against the history of the United States in the twentieth century, a period of extraordinary expansion of American power and a new role in the world, all requiring a bigger, stronger government. Could that really be reversed? Was government really our problem? These would be among the most heated, controversial questions of the Reagan Administration.

Within two weeks of his inauguration, President Reagan moved to keep a campaign pledge to his supporters and financial backers in the oil industry, and to make good on one of his themes: to end government "interference" with business. On January 28, 1981, President Reagan abolished controls on the price of oil. Inside a week, on February 4, gasoline prices and prices of home heating oil were raised by Exxon, Texaco, and Shell. The other oil giants would follow quickly.

There was no talk, to be sure, of cutting subsidies of all kinds to farmers, industries, and business. For Reagan and his supporters, government is there to put a floor under their prices, not a ceiling over them. When government helps business it is, of course, not interfering. A loan to bail out a failing Lockheed or Chrysler is not "interference" in private enterprise, but a high-profits tax or an antitrust suit is intolerable. When government underwrites industries and farms, government is not a problem. Government becomes a problem only when it seeks to restrict or police business.

Granting tax concessions and other advantages to business is helping America become strong, but granting welfare to the poor or the victims of the marketplace economy weakens America, saps its morale. In short, welfare for the rich is good for America but welfare for the poor is bad for America, bad even for the poor themselves, for it encourages them to be shiftless and lazy. Somehow, loans to the inefficient managements of American corporations would not similarly encourage them in their inefficient methods.

Reagan's thinking on these issues brought America full pendulum around, ending a fifty-year cycle that had begun with the New Deal of President Franklin Delano Roosevelt in 1933. For a half-century, the political philosophy and economic measures created in the New Deal had dominated American society. Certain elements of the New Deal had come under sharp criticism, the Supreme Court ruled some of its provisions unconstitutional, but its fundamental principles went unchallenged and became a permanent part of our national life, principally the proposition that the government must intervene in political and economic crises to help the poor and defend the minorities from repression of their civil rights.

As I flew back to New York to report on the Reagan inauguration, my mind went back to that other inauguration, the first I had ever attended, when Franklin Roosevelt, standing painfully on steel supports that held his withered legs, crippled by polio, tossed his great head and smiled his dazzling smile and pledged himself to pull America out of the morass of the Depression. I remembered as though it were only yesterday the surge of hope that lifted me out of my own depression, my fears of a ruined life before it had really even started. I thought of the irony of a Reagan who, like myself, had been a youngster supporting Roosevelt, a Reagan who had then cast his first vote in a Presidential election for Roosevelt, now pledged to undo what Roosevelt had done in the New Deal. I thought, too, of the tens of millions of Americans in the 1980s who had not lived through the Depression or the New Deal and who knew little or nothing about it. They were being told that the New Deal was a "giveaway program," the start of a welfare state, encouraging the shiftless and the cheats, and that welfare was out of control, so costly that it was wrecking our economy and was responsible for the economic crisis that once again was threatening our well-being in the 1980s.

There is no doubt that welfare costs have rocketed but so has almost everything else, including the price of oil and the ever-expanding military budget. That the welfare programs need constant reexamination and rethinking is unarguable. That they should be cut to the bone or scrapped, that the basic philosophy of the New Deal, which is rooted in the finest American traditions, be abandoned is unthinkable. As I pondered on this issue that day, it seemed to me that the time had come to look back to the source of this fifty-year cycle of American life, to explain to generations who had not experienced those times exactly what the New Deal really was, so that we can understand in today's perspectives what America needs, what kind of a people we are, or should be. Instead of paying mere lip service to the American ideal of liberty and justice for all, we must make certain that in the conduct of our public affairs we are faithful to those principles that have made this country great, the envy and admiration of the world.

From my teens to age thirty, the impressionable years of early manhood, there was only one President of the United States, Franklin Delano Roosevelt, FDR. No other man has so dominated the life of a great nation, so reversed the course of its history. Roosevelt gave America new goals, new directions, a new social system, and a new role for its government, carrying out a campaign promise to give all Americans a "New Deal."

Franklin Roosevelt was convinced that democratic capitalism could only survive and prosper if the basic principles of democracy were applied to achieve economic and social justice as well as civil and political freedoms. He was aware, as banker J. P. Morgan and his fellow tycoons were not, of the growing rebelliousness of the American people, who had come to perceive that there were two Americas, one rich and privileged, the other exploited and taxed, with one set of laws for the rich and another for the poor.

As the election campaign of 1932 got underway, America was sinking into the quagmire of a hopeless breakdown of the nation's financial and industrial structures. In September 1931, 305 banks closed their doors. The next month 522 banks closed down. Hysterical depositors, their life savings wiped out, were hammering on the locked doors hopelessly. Among them was my father.

I was sixteen years old, on the brink of manhood, in my second year of college, at City College in New York. I wondered what would happen to me. Would I get a job on graduation, what kind of life was I facing in a ruined America? Only Roosevelt offered me any real hope for the future. I was sickened by the impotent bleatings of Herbert Hoover and his empty promises of "prosperity just around the corner." I was horrified by the scene of General Douglas MacArthur leading American army troops in a brutal assault upon the Washington encampment of war veterans who had come to demand financial help and jobs.

Young as I was, not old enough to vote, I nonetheless threw myself with all my strength into the election campaign of 1932, as a volunteer for Roosevelt. My role was insignificant, licking envelopes at Democratic Party headquarters, delivering flyers and ads, stuffing them into mailboxes. But I went about my duties with all the zeal of a campaign manager. I sensed that my future, my life, depended on a Roosevelt victory.

I was thrilled when I heard on the radio, on July 1, that Roosevelt had won the nomination of the Democratic convention on the third ballot. On July 2, breaking with precedent, FDR flew to Chicago to deliver his acceptance speech in person. Like so many things that Roosevelt did, this became a new precedent and every nominee thereafter has delivered that speech in person.

In his acceptance speech, Roosevelt coined a phrase that would live in history: "I pledge you, I pledge myself, a new deal for the American people." He proceeded to launch a stirring appeal. "Let us all here assembled constitute ourselves prophets of a new order of competence and courage. This is more than a political campaign; it is a call to arms."

I felt that he was appealing to me personally. I worked in a frenzy, neglecting my studies. I must have broken all records for envelope- and stamp-licking. My tongue was furry with glue but I was exalted, a young man with a mission. My efforts were rewarded when my district chief informed me that Governor Roosevelt, on the campaign trail, would be delivering a fund-raising speech at the Commodore Hotel, and that, after his speech, he would meet in the greenroom with some of us young volunteers to thank us for our efforts on his behalf. I rode a pink cloud down to the Commodore to meet and listen to my hero.

Roosevelt was already seated when we entered the conference room. He did not want us to see him being wheeled into the room. He was exhausted from the campaign tour and his legs could not support him for long. He grinned at us, with his famous smile, his long cigarette holder cocked up at its jaunty angle between his teeth, his massive head tossed back. My heart jumped when I saw his radiant, confident smile. He thanked us and went on to tell us of his hopes for America, assuring us that we would all find jobs and raise our children in a strong and healthy America. Then, to our surprise, he asked whether we had any questions.

It was a bright and not a shy crowd of young people and the questions came swiftly. I sat there quietly at first, not quite daring to ask the embarrassing question that was on my mind. But, I was a brash youngster. I have changed over the years. Now I am a brash oldster. I finally worked up my courage and raised my hand. "Governor, sir, please do not take offense, but I am troubled by having seen you last week across the river, in Jersey City, arm in arm with Mayor Frank Hague. Everyone knows he is a crooked political boss. What were you doing arm in arm with him?" No sooner had I asked the question than I flushed red and looked around for the nearest door to make a quick escape.

Roosevelt looked at me as his broad smile narrowed and then disappeared. He took his cigarette holder out of his mouth and balanced it on an ashtray. I tensed for the storm that was about to break over my head. But Roosevelt's face was serious, not angry. The room was hushed as everyone watched the governor and waited for his reply.

"I've been told that you all have been working hard for me. That means, I take it, that you think I'll make a good President." I just managed to squeak out an apologetic "Yes, sir" as he continued. "But hasn't it occurred to you that before I can become a good President, I first must get elected President?" He paused briefly for us to digest this and went on. "Now, to win this election, I must win a great number of important states with big electoral votes. One of those states is New Jersey. And it is a fact of political life today that New Jersey is largely controlled by Mayor Frank Hague.

"Mayor Hague has an efficient organization. It can get the voters to the polls in November. Unless Hague gets behind me, I could lose New Jersey. I must have his support whether I like his ways or not. That's why I crossed the river to see him last week. Now, there is a lesson in this for all of you. It is a basic lesson in politics which you probably won't learn in your political science classes. To put it bluntly: if ever you see someone you admire arm in arm with someone you mistrust, ask yourself this fundamental question: Who is using whom?"

I was so young and naïve that my first reaction was shock, a kind of chill, to learn that my hero was a cynic. His policy of expediency did not enchant me. Later, I would find myself angrily opposed to Roosevelt's policy of expedience when he maintained close relations with the pro-Nazi regime of French Marshal Pétain during the war. It was ironic that my personal contacts and links to Roosevelt were unpleasant, even hostile, although I never stopped revering him as one of the greatest Americans of all time. It was a useful lesson I had to learn and that I pass on to the readers of this book and to my children: Very few men are all good and very few men are all bad.

One must be tolerant of the faults of our leaders if, on balance, overall, they serve the national interests well. I loved Roosevelt and still do but I recognized that he had his faults and weaknesses. I never liked Richard Nixon and still don't but I recognize that he was a strong President and had a positive, highly successful foreign policy.

The American people, back in the thirties, were not concerned about deals with political bosses like Mayor Hague. They wanted a leader who could pull them and the nation out of the depths of the Depression. If Roosevelt allied himself with Hague for that purpose, it was quite acceptable to the voters. They swept Roosevelt into office by an overwhelming margin: more than a seven-million vote plurality and an electoral college landslide of 472 to 59. FDR carried all but six states. His record would be equaled forty-eight years later by Ronald Reagan. Nothing else links the two men. They were nothing like each other in origins, education, and ideologies.

Ronald Reagan had graduated in June 1932 from Eureka College, in Illinois, a small Disciples of Christ school. He was a football player and sports addict who would get his first job as a sportscaster for the NBC affiliate in Des Moines, Iowa, station WHO. He admitted to biographers later that he was undereducated, not interested in his studies or in politics. But he was acutely aware of hard times, for his own father had suffered reverses.

John Edward Reagan had gone bankrupt and lost his small shoe store in the Depression. Unemployed, he was paid a small salary as a campaign worker for Roosevelt in Illinois. He worked hard, voted for FDR, and was rewarded with a job administering the meager relief rolls then in existence. Later he was put in charge of a local Works Progress Administration (WPA) after FDR had created the agency. Reagan's father was part of the "Big Government social welfare system" that his son Ronald has been denouncing and cutting out of the budget in his current tenure at the White House. But back in the hungry thirties, Ronald Reagan was happy to see Washington take care of his desperate father.

In the long interim from the election of November 8 to Roosevelt's inauguration on March 4, 1933, a long lame-duck period that Congress would soon cut down, FDR labored late into the night preparing his program. He knew he would have to act swiftly and that a shock effect was needed to boost the morale of the American people and get the machinery of government and of industry going in a fast start.

A number of steps in a new direction were taken even before Roosevelt's inauguration. A Twentieth Amendment abolished the long interim, and changed future Presidential inaugurations to January 20. Then, on February 16, the Senate voted to repeal Prohibition. Four days later the House followed the Senate vote.

On March 1, only three days before FDR took office, six states declared a bank holiday. By March 4, as Roosevelt was set to deliver his memorable address, telling the American people that "The only thing we have to fear is fear itself," bankruptcies had hit a peak. At four-thirty that morning, Governor Herbert Lehman ordered all New York banks closed, and the Governor of Illinois, the Reagan family's home state, followed suit, ordering a bank holiday.

In his inaugural address, Roosevelt pledged that one of his first Presidential acts would be to ask Congress to grant him "broad Executive power to wage a war against the emergency as great as the power that would be given me if we were in fact invaded by a foreign foe." The President asserted: "This nation asks for action, and action now!"

Roosevelt's words inspired millions of Americans of every class and milieu: Harvard professors of economics and law, Boston ditchdiggers, New York's ethnic minorities, even small-town Babbitts, and two remarkable young men, an Illinois sportscaster and an East Texas grade-school teacher, both of whom later, in their own

Presidencies, would lift phrases and ideas from Roosevelt's historic first inaugural address.

Lyndon B. Johnson would call for a "war on poverty," in almost the same terms as FDR had called for emergency war powers in a peacetime economic crisis. Johnson was a disciple of Roosevelt, whom he revered.

Ronald W. Reagan, with a very different goal in mind, would nevertheless borrow other phrases from FDR. Where FDR had called for a "new deal," Reagan, in his inaugural address of January 20, 1981, would call for a "new beginning." Where FDR had said that this nation "asks for action, and action now!" Ronald Reagan asserted that "We must act today in order to preserve tomorrow. And let there be no misunderstanding—we're going to begin to act beginning today."

Reagan had never forgotten what has become known in American history as Roosevelt's "first hundred days," when the President, facing a demoralized and dazed Congress, had rushed through the major parts of his program. Later we shall take a close look at Reagan's hundred days, the first major attempt in almost fifty years to reverse the directions and philosophy of Roosevelt's hundred days.

FDR was quick off the mark. The day after his inaugural address, March 5, Roosevelt issued a proclamation imposing a four-day bank holiday and calling on Congress to meet in special session on March 9. He wanted immediately to stop the panicky run on banks which threatened to bankrupt all of them. He also issued an executive edict halting all transactions in gold.

On March 9, Congress went into extra session. It took seven hours to put through Roosevelt's omnibus banking bill which would facilitate the reopening of liquid banks under government regulation. From March 9 until Congress adjourned on June 16, FDR legislated his New Deal in fifteen major proposals that were speedily passed by representatives and senators who had virtually no ideas of their own and were only too glad to have a forceful leader who seemed to know where he was going. Right or wrong, many congressmen felt that at last some action was being taken. The Hoover days of optimistic but essentially empty rhetoric were over.

On March 12, FDR delivered the first of many "fireside chats," intimate, informal radio talks that would literally bring the President into everyone's living room and make each citizen feel that he was close to his government. My own family would check the radio schedules each day to see if FDR had a talk that evening. Then, when he did, we would huddle around the console of our Atwater Kent, one of the few treasures of an affluent life we had managed to keep. When we heard that patrician voice drawl out the words "my friends," we would look at each other and smile and know that everything was going to be all right.

No President has ever been able to duplicate Roosevelt's ability to communicate one on one with millions of people. Ronald Reagan, a professional actor with a natural affinity for the television camera, is a superb Presidential performer, the best broadcaster since FDR himself. But circumstances and his own policies prevent him from matching Roosevelt's mass appeal.

Reagan knows very well, having lived through it himself, the power of Roosevelt's words. He has often borrowed some of them. In speeches throughout the campaign of 1980, Reagan referred repeatedly to the "forgotten American." But Reagan's "forgotten American" was not Roosevelt's "forgotten man." FDR's American had been forgotten by men of wealth and power who hired "goons" to beat up workers and break up strikes, who foreclosed farms and bought them cheaply at auction. FDR's forgotten man was a man who needed help and Roosevelt would give it to him.

Reagan's "forgotten American" is not unemployed or landless. He is, in Reagan's words, in hundreds of speeches from his 1966 gubernatorial campaign in California on through his inauguration in 1981, "the man in the suburbs working sixty hours a week to support his family and being taxed heavily for the benefit of someone else." The "someone else," of course, was the poor family on welfare. Reagan's phrase may have been borrowed from FDR but he was not talking to or about the same Americans.

In 1933, my family was that "someone else." We were not on welfare, for there was not yet any real welfare program, but we urgently needed help. There was private charity and some meager federal and state relief funds. Throughout New York there were soup kitchens, doling out a watery brew and chunks of bread to jobless, hungry men. The day I was delivering a package in the garment center and suddenly saw my father, in a worn overcoat, shivering in the cold wind, standing in a soup-kitchen line, was the blackest day of my life. He was not unemployed that day. He had a temporary job assisting a diamond merchant grading his goods. But he went to the soup kitchen to keep as much of his pitiful wages as he could for his wife and children.

I suppose today there are some who would call him a welfare cheat, for going to a "handout" while employed. I still get furious when I hear overweight Americans, with two cars, and a TV set in every room, talk about welfare cheats and food stamp "abuses." I pray that each of them would, just for a week or two, have to stand in line for a handout, for a job, stripped of their dignity, of their very identity. Let a congressman watch his wife and children grow thin and pale and weak before his eyes and then see if he will vote to cut down food stamps and to cancel free lunches for schoolchildren, while approving tens of billions of dollars for a Pentagon which would waste more than any poor person could "cheat."

Franklin Roosevelt's fireside chats strengthened public morale. His very first chat was aimed at restoring public confidence in the banks. Some one thousand banks had already failed. He promised that he would impose government scrutiny of their operations and would insure their deposits. He asked the people to trust him and told them it was better to put their money into safe banks, with interest, than to hide it under their mattresses or bury it under their barns.

The very next day, March 13, 1933, the banks began to reopen. By the end of the month seventy-five percent were again operating and deposits exceeded withdrawals, although the banks were still shaky. Over and over again in my career, I was to learn that perception can be more powerful than reality. Nothing had yet improved in America but the people trusted FDR. They brought their monies back on his word, and the banks strengthened. This was a lesson in the power of genuine leadership.

On March 31, the Congress passed FDR's proposal for a Reforestation Act which created the CCC, the Civilian Conservation Corps. It was aimed at conserving our natural resources but also was used as a device for putting thousands of men to work at once on a useful project.

On April 19 an embargo was placed on all gold shipments by executive order. In effect, this took the United States off the gold standard. A few weeks later, on FDR's urgent proposal, Congress canceled the gold clauses in all government and private obligations, making all debts payable in legal tender. America's most influential columnist, Walter Lippman, wrote that Roosevelt had recaptured public morale. And the *London Observer,* in a prophetic comment, said that "America has found a man. In him, at a later stage, the world must find a leader."

On May 12, Congress passed the Agricultural Adjustment Act, the AAA. It authorized creation of a Farm Credit Administration to refund farm loans at very low interest rates, and provided more than one hundred million dollars of federal money for new mortgages and the adjustment of farm debts. It was one of the most urgently needed answers to a crisis growing violent. In the previous five years as much as ten percent of the nation's farms had been foreclosed at auction. In self-defense, farmers had formed vigilante bands that showed up at auctions armed with pitchforks, two-by-fours, and scythes, threatening prospective purchasers. Farmers would march into courts to break up foreclosure cases. In one case, in April, a mob dragged an Iowa judge off his bench and might have lynched him if sheriffs had not driven up to rescue him.

As important as the AAA was an appropriations measure also passed on May 12: the Federal Emergency Relief Act. It provided half a billion dollars for relief of the thirteen million unemployed who could no longer be taken care of by states, local communities, or private charities. It also made available funds for the recovery of business and agriculture. The President asked Harry Hopkins, his most loyal and intimate friend, his very shadow, to oversee relief operations for him.

Within two years, total "emergency" relief expenditures had rocketed to more than five billion dollars. The public debt was piling up and conservatives began a battle cry of opposition that would go on for the next fifty years until they finally elected a President who not only agreed with them that future generations would be bankrupted by this debt and its heavy annual interest, but would begin to put into effect demands for drastically reducing federal spending, particularly social spending, not military spending. The voice of the Republicans and of the financiers, the New York *Herald Tribune,* daily denounced "extravagant federal spending" which it claimed had produced "an economic chaos with no end in sight."

The people of the United States once again refused to believe

Republican protests. In the midterm elections of 1934, the first chance the people had to vote on the New Deal, they gave FDR a triumphant victory by voting into office 322 Democrats out of the 435 seats in the House and a total of 69 senators out of 96. The President had complete party control of both houses in the Seventy-fourth Congress. Taking advantage of his victory, FDR obtained from Congress at its opening session, in January 1935, 4.8 billion dollars to be used virtually at his own discretion. The public debt passed the thirty billion mark, some four billion greater than the First World War debt at its highest.

One of the most severely criticized yet most successful of Roosevelt's innovations was passed on May 18: the Tennessee Valley Act. It was designed to control Tennessee River floods, but even more importantly it initiated federal financing of vitally needed rural electrification. Nationalization is a four-letter word in America but TVA was an outstanding example of a successful nationalization project.

Wall Street went into hysterics only nine days after TVA when the New Deal, galloping ahead, passed a Federal Securities Act requiring registration and approval of all issues of stocks and bonds. FDR had remembered Cousin Theodore Roosevelt's attacks on the "money trusts" and the manipulative financiers, the "robber barons" of America. On May 27, with the enthusiastic support of a radical senator from Wisconsin, Robert La Follette, Jr., he persuaded Congress to impose a whole series of checks on Wall Street and the corporations. All new securities offered or advertised for interstate sale had to be registered with a government agency. Every offering had to contain full details on the condition of the corporation. The act also stipulated that the directors and officers of the corporation be held criminally liable for any deliberate omission of facts or any willful mistatements of the details of the stock offering.

The Securities Act was carried out more fully in June of the following year with the creation of the Securities and Exchange Commission. The commission, now a permanent part of American financial life, no longer challenged by anyone, licensed stock exchanges, registered all their securities, prohibited the formation of pools and other means of cornering and controlling the market. Roosevelt, in a brilliant tactical move, appointed Joseph P. Kennedy of Boston as first chairman of the commission because, as FDR dryly remarked, "Joe knows all the tricks of the trade," a polite way of saying "It takes one to catch one."

In June 1933, Congress moved to help small home owners as it had helped the farmers. It created the Home Owners' Loan Corporation to refinance small mortgages of privately owned homes. It provided within a year almost a billion dollars of federal funds that were used to approve more than three hundred thousand loans that saved American homes from being foreclosed as farms had been. No source other than the federal government could have provided the legal power or the funds to carry out this rescue operation.

On June 16, 1933, the Congress ended its now historic hundred-day session (in actual count it was only ninety-nine days, but "the hundred days" was a catch title for the press and it lived on). Two important pieces of legislation completed the New Deal programs. One was the Emergency Housing Division Act that provided funds for the Home Owners' Loan Corporation. It would finance private construction of low-cost houses in urban slum-clearing projects. It was a boon to the moribund construction industry as well as to lower-class Americans in desperate need of housing. But conservatives, overlooking the fact that the federal money was going to private construction firms, blindly denounced "government handouts and excessive spending." The second act of June 16 was perhaps the most controversial and far-reaching of the hundred days. It was the National Industrial Recovery Act, NRA.

Like the Housing Act, it was proclaimed to be only an emergency measure, scheduled to expire in June 1935. In fact, it did expire a few days ahead of time, on May 27, 1935, just as the Administration was planning to extend it. It expired permanently by a rare, unanimous decision of the Supreme Court, which declared NRA to be unconstitutional. The unanimous decision, coming on top of other decisions declaring New Deal measures to be unconstitutional, infuriated FDR and induced him to a grave error. He mounted an assault on the Court, asking Congress to increase its membership by six new justices to permit him to "inject new life into the nine old men." It was one of the few severe defeats that Roosevelt suffered. His majority in Congress, alarmed by the attempt to upset our traditional checks and balances by an Executive Department assault on the Judiciary, voted against his proposal.

Seven months after his hundred days, in January 1934, FDR

was still on the move. He pushed through Congress the Gold Reserve Act and devalued the dollar to 59.06 cents of its former gold parity. Then, in August of 1935, just a year before his reelection campaign, Roosevelt succeeded in winning approval of two important pieces of legislation that had been on his agenda for a long time: a Utilities Act to control holding companies, in the tradition of Theodore Roosevelt's fight against J. P. Morgan; and the most important and enduring legislation of his career, the Social Security Act.

The Social Security Act created two federal-state systems for old-age insurance and unemployment compensation. It introduced a social principle that again became an issue of heated controversy in the summer of 1981, by granting a minimum old-age insurance payment to every American who had reached sixty-five years of age, whether that citizen had worked the minimum quarters of the year required by the act or not. Roosevelt argued that there were some unfortunate citizens who would never completely qualify except as human beings in dire need. Something had to be given to them. The benefits proposed were truly minimal, ten dollars a month.

Inevitably, with inflation, the level was raised until, by 1981, it had reached $122 a month. It was hardly a princely sum in 1981 but it amounted to several billions a year nationwide, and the Republican-controlled Senate voted to abolish it. Conservative Democrats in the House broke with their party's majority leaders and joined with Republicans to follow the Senate's lead. Then, in a later vote, they reversed themselves after a strong public protest. Many political observers early in 1980 and through 1981 predicted that Social Security would become the Reagan Administration's Achilles heel. Reagan suffered his first major defeat in his hundred days when he tried to cut Social Security and force early retirement at lower rates. Even his own Republican majority in the Senate, plus the conservative Democrats, voted against him. The vote was a sharp slap in the face to President Reagan, 96 to 0, with four senators not voting.

Roosevelt had his setbacks too, of course, but never of those dimensions, and more often from the Supreme Court than from the Congress. In his first term, particularly, FDR's control of Congress was almost absolute. His most radical measures were passed with minimal debate and opposition. In June 1935, he prevailed upon Congress to legislate a series of acts designed to bring about a more equitable distribution of wealth and to prevent too great a concentration of money and its powers in a few hands.

Heavy inheritance taxes were imposed to prohibit the accumulation of great fortunes. Surtaxes were levied on high incomes and tax-exempt securities were abolished. Corporations were hit by graduated income taxes, holding-company taxes, and taxes on surpluses. Over the years many of these measures were amended or rescinded and clever lawyers found loopholes in every law. Despite their howls, the rich got richer and more and more money found a way to perpetuate itself and to concentrate power.

It was by acclamation, without a vote, that FDR was renominated for a second term on June 27, 1936. On November 3 of that year, FDR won the most sweeping majority vote in American history: a popular margin of victory by eleven million ballots and an electoral landslide of 523 to 8. His Republican opponent, Governor Alfred M. Landon of Kansas, only won two states, Maine and Vermont.

FDR went on to break a precedent as old as the nation when he defied George Washington's dictum that no man should serve more than two terms. World War II had erupted near the end of Roosevelt's second term, in September 1939. By the summer of 1940 the German dictator Adolf Hitler had already gobbled up Austria, Czechoslovakia, Poland, and France. Americans who had, at first, laughed at Hitler and his funny little mustache and called him Charlie Chaplin began to take him very seriously. Roosevelt, understanding the prejudice against a third term, said nothing about his own desires or intentions, avoiding what could have become a dangerous accusation of dictatorship.

On July 18, 1940, the Democratic Party, with no other possible leader in sight, nominated Roosevelt again. FDR was then in a position to accept a call to duty and break an historic precedent without the onus of having sought to do so, although we all knew that was what he wanted and that was what the American people wanted. There is a time-tested American aphorism, "Don't change horses in midstream," and the people decided to ride again with FDR after war had broken out in Europe.

On November 5, 1940, Roosevelt was elected again, by a greatly reduced but still impressive margin of victory over Republican attorney Wendell Willkie: 27 million against 22 million. It would then become easier to go from a third term to a fourth term, once the two-term barrier had been breached.

By 1944, the United States was the Allied leader in a world war on three continents, Europe, Africa, and Asia. The American people would not change Presidents, particularly a winner, while a war was raging. Roosevelt would thus go on to defeat New York's Governor Thomas E. Dewey by a three-million vote plurality but a massive electoral college majority of 432 to 99.

Roosevelt's fourth term would be a brief one. Inaugurated on January 20, 1945, Franklin Delano Roosevelt, the man whom historians today rank with Washington and Lincoln as one of the greatest of all our leaders, died in Warm Springs, Georgia, on April 12. George Washington had founded our nation, Abraham Lincoln had preserved its unity, and Franklin Roosevelt had given it its soul and its conscience.

He was not a saint. Roosevelt was, as all humans are, fallible. He made errors, some of them grave. He betrayed his own moral code. This man who promised to remember the "forgotten man" and care for the "common man," this President of soul and conscience, personally ordered the cruel, unjust internment of Japanese-Americans. Tens of thousands of innocent men, women, and children were herded off to camps, guilty only of having yellow skin and being descended from a people whose planes had destroyed most of our Pacific fleet. They were automatically listed as potential spies and enemies.

Members of the German community and the Italians, against whose ancestral lands we were also at war, were not interned. The internment of the Japanese was clearly a racist reaction. Racism grows out of ancient tribal fears of any who are not members of the same tribe and who are markedly different in size, shape, or color. It was unconscionable of Roosevelt to yield to panic and racism. Some compensation to the interned Japanese was paid to them in 1948, but it was not until February 1983, more than forty years later, that the American government officially conceded its original sin and restored honor to the Japanese-American community. This was and remains a black mark on Roosevelt's record, along with his lack of concern about the Jewish victims of Hitler.

Fifty years after Roosevelt was elected on his pledge to give

Americans "a new deal," it is now fashionable to say, "The New Deal is dead." Ronald Reagan's spectacular triumph in Congress after his inauguration won him approval of his programs to cut social services and taxes. Cuts of some thirty billion dollars in social programs, to be cut even more deeply in the future, we were told, marked the end not only of FDR's New Deal but of Harry Truman's Fair Deal and Lyndon Johnson's Great Society. Almost alone in the Congress at first, Senator Edward Kennedy fought to stem the conservative tide, without success during Reagan's first year.

The witty, literate columnist of *The New York Times* Russell Baker, in August 1981, commented that Kennedy's convention speech in 1980 had been absolutely perfect "to get him elected in 1936." Loyalty to the principles of the New Deal had become funny.

But is the New Deal really dead? And if it is, what does it tell us about America today?

The New Deal was a set of principles and of programs to carry them out. The principles are simply stated: that government must do for the people what the people cannot do for themselves; that powerful private interests must be made subservient to law and to government; that people must be paid a livable wage for a maximum hours of work; that Americans have a right to look forward to at least a modest income in their old age and protection against ill health and crippling accidents.

One might quarrel with the programs that were designed to carry out those principles. But should one quarrel with the principles of the New Deal? FDR held that American democracy was incomplete, that it concentrated on political rights but not enough on economic and social rights.

If that is now just a joke, if all that is dead, then an important part of what made America the world symbol of a better society is also dead.

I do not believe it.

CHAPTER 2

DAYS OF INFAMY

The New Deal was not an overnight success, not a quick fix for the Depression. It was, however, a booster shot of morale and hope for millions of suffering Americans. We could see light up ahead, beyond the gloomy pits into which we had sunk. Banks reopened; a modest welfare program, which would, inevitably, spread wide and deep, was underway; bankruptcies were arrested; some jobs opened up. We were beginning to recover. There would be slips and slides, progress and new recessions, but the worst was over.

I could stop worrying about my future. On graduation, I had taken and passed the New York City teaching examination and had begun a career as a teacher of French, at Townsend Harris High School, my alma mater; at John Adams; and then Far Rockaway. By then our family had moved from Harlem to the Bronx to Washington Heights, finally to Belle Harbor, at the tip of the Rockaways, across Jamaica Bay from Brooklyn, following a climb up the social ladder of many middle-class Jewish families.

It was in Belle Harbor that I met a girl, a neighbor living a few blocks away in the more affluent district of Neponsit. Her name was Dorothy Scher, daughter of a successful, wealthy local dentist. She was one of the most brilliant and gifted students in Far Rockaway High School, one of three students in the state of New York to get a grade of 100 percent on the statewide Regents exam in math. In addition to being a math wiz, Dorothy was a talented young artist-illustrator. She went from high school to the leading commercial art school in New York, Parsons. There she more than fulfilled her promise by graduating at the top of her class, winning the Parsons scholarship for a one-year study abroad, in France and Italy.

If I take time and space here to tell the reader briefly about Dorothy, in a book devoted to major world events, it is simply that wooing and winning this splendid woman was and remains the most important event in my life. Recently we celebrated our forty-fifth wedding anniversary, a rarity in today's world.

In this book the reader will meet some of the most creative, important men and women in modern history. But of all the extraordinary personalities I have met and known, there is for me none to compare with this beautiful, talented, commonsensical, kindly, wise woman who has shared her life with me and made my own life richer than it could ever have been without her. From time to time the reader will meet her again in this story of my life with Uncle Sam, for she was an actor in it, albeit keeping offstage and in the wings.

We were happy in a dreadful world. Roosevelt may have given us all hope but the rest of the world was going rapidly to a flaming hell. Benito Mussolini in Italy brutalized his opponents by pouring castor oil down their mouths on the streets of Rome. He had his admirers in America, who boasted that the fascist dictator had "made the trains run on time," an achievement held to be magnificent. Perhaps he greased the rails with castor oil.

Then the horrors of Adolf Hitler and his Nazi thugs and torturers became more widely known. He tore up the Versailles Treaty, renouncing its harsh terms imposed on Germany by the victorious Allies at the end of the First World War. Hitler rearmed Germany, marched into the Rhineland while France and Britain, which had been bled white in their Pyrrhic victory in the war, watched him with the frightened eyes of a rabbit paralyzed by the approach of a snake.

Hitler, emboldened by his success, sensing the paralysis of the democracies, swallowed up Austria in an Anschluss, an imposed union with Germany. He then claimed that the Czech government was crushing the German-origin peoples in the Czech province of the Sudetenland. The leaders of France and Britain, Premier

Edouard Daladier and Prime Minister Neville Chamberlain, flew to Munich the last week of September 1938 to meet with Hitler and try to avoid war over the Sudetenland.

On September 30, they signed the Munich Pact with Hitler, one of the most disgraceful surrenders to a dictator in the history of the democracies. They gave Hitler the Sudetenland, warned the Czechs not to fight the excision of their province. They hoped to "appease" Hitler, satisfy his appetite so that he would finally be glutted and no longer threaten his neighbors. The appeasement merely whetted his appetite for more conquests.

I saw it coming from the start, not because I was particularly expert or prophetic about world affairs but because I had excellent sources of information. My mother was a Cassirer, one of the leading intellectual families of Germany. Many members of the family had fled Germany with the advent to power of Hitler, who had become chancellor the same year that Roosevelt had become President. Among them was one of the leading philosophers of those days, an eminent professor of world renown, my granduncle Ernst Cassirer.

Ernst Cassirer held the chair of philosophy at Hamburg University. He was a close friend of Albert Einstein. Einstein urged him to come to America and he was offered the post of professor at Yale, and then professor emeritus at Columbia. One day I asked Uncle Ernst to explain Hitler's successes, his intuitive, almost magically prophetic ability to foresee what he could grab without serious opposition from powers much stronger than Germany was at the time. I have never forgotten his answer and it has proved applicable to so many international crises of the past fifty years.

Cassirer said: "It is not a matter of intuition or instinct. There is a very simple rule of international life that has few exceptions. Those who are willing to risk everything, even death and destruction, to attain their ends will prevail over more responsible and prudent men who have more to lose and who are rational, not suicidal." I have seen this truism time and time again, in the dangerous, cruel games played by a Stalin, a Castro, a Khomeini, a Qaddafi, an Idi Amin, and such macho generals as George Patton and Ariel Sharon of Israel, or Hussein of Iraq, Assad of Syria, and countless others.

So convinced was I that the appeasement at Munich would only stimulate Hitler's appetite, and that war would come rapidly, that

I asked Dorothy to marry me the week of Munich. By then, I was earning $37.50 a week as a substitute teacher but she was earning $42 a week as the art director of a small but well regarded advertising agency. Her career was on the rise, for she had won the prestigious Art Directors' League award for the best advertising design of the year. Almost $80 a week was a princely sum for a young couple in 1938.

We had been in love, "keeping company," in the quaint phrase of those days, for six long, frustrating years, an agony of sexual repression for healthy young people. Those were the days of virgin brides when good girls didn't "go all the way." And my Dorothy, bless her soul, was the "goodest" of good girls. We married on September 23, 1938, just a week before the disgraceful appeasement at Munich and just a year before my gloomy predictions of war came about.

The war went even more badly than I had anticipated. Hitler had rearmed Germany with the most modern weapons. He was a gambler, totally reckless. The French were defeatist with no appetite for fighting. They crouched behind defensive positions in their supposedly impregnable Maginot Line, a series of fortifications built in the thirties to protect France's eastern frontiers bordering on Germany. Unfortunately, the Maginot Line did not extend beyond France. It left open the invasion plains of Belgium, north of France, and was easily bypassed by Hitler's Tiger tanks and screaming, terrifying Stuka dive-bombers, in what became known as a blitzkrieg, a lightning war.

Hitler's lightning war blazed first over Poland and destroyed those brave, quixotic fighters, who charged on horseback against armored tanks. Then he turned to the west. The world watched with astonishment as Hitler's legions destroyed the "world's finest army," the French, in a month, more quickly than they had overrun Poland. They sent the British fleeing for their lives in the evacuation of Dunkirk, which has lived on in history as a glorious flight from an ignominious defeat.

The jackal of the Nazi-Fascist "Axis," Italy's dictator Benito Mussolini, waiting to be sure of a German victory, then struck in an invasion of southeastern France. President Roosevelt lashed out at the fascist hyena closing in on the lion's kill: "The hand that held the dagger today plunged it into his neighbor's back."

By then I was working afternoons, after teaching, in a little cubbyhole on the seventeenth floor of 485 Madison Avenue, site of the CBS News offices. Five men, earphones glued to our heads, a look of intense concentration on our faces, pounded on old, upright Underwood typewriters, the keys hitting the drums with the noise of a herd of wild horses at full gallop. It was the newly created monitoring room, an idea conceived by Paul White, the innovative news director. He had to be innovative, for radio news was still in its infancy, and White had to make up its procedures as the new medium developed.

We were listening to shortwave broadcasts from Europe's capitals, from London, Paris, Berlin, Rome, Warsaw, Moscow, some in English, but most in the language of the transmitter. My listening post was Radio Paris. Sitting next to me, listening to Radio Berlin, was one of my ubiquitous German cousins, Reinhold Cassirer, known in the family as Heiner, and to his American friends as Henry, which became his legal name. He had won his doctorate in history at London University.

Our job at the monitoring station was to type summaries of the newscasts we were listening to—no easy task, going from German or French into English at broadcast speed on a stiff old typewriter. Our summaries and comments on what we had heard were then given to the newswriters and on-air broadcasters, men like Elmer Davis, Ned Calmer, John Charles Daly.

When our work was over, Heiner and I would have a coffee and talk about what we had heard. One day I casually mentioned to him that I had read an editorial in the New York *Daily News* that sounded familiar but I could not quite place it and it was troubling me. I handed it to him. He read it, wrinkling his nose and chewing his lips, a habit that made him look like a giant rabbit. Then he exclaimed, "Why, no wonder it is familiar! I typed that out three days ago and showed it to you. That is almost word for word from a Goebbels speech on Radio Berlin."

We talked excitedly about what it could mean. Was someone on the *Daily News* slipping Nazi propaganda into the paper, or was it a coincidence? Or an unconscious plagiarism? We agreed to start checking the *News* regularly to see if there were any more "coincidences." Within a month, we had come up with a half-dozen more.

Every Saturday for months, we would go to the New York

Public Library and read back copies of the *News.* We also checked the editorials and columns of the Chicago *Tribune* and the Washington *Times-Herald.* The owner and publisher of the New York *News,* Captain Joseph Patterson, was a cousin of the newspaper titan of the Midwest, Colonel Robert McCormick, publisher and owner of the mighty Chicago *Tribune,* the dominant voice in some ten states of the Middle West. Still another cousin, "Cissy" Patterson, owned and operated the influential Washington *Times-Herald.* They were all highly contentious and extremely vocal critics of Roosevelt, as well as being anti-British and isolationist.

After many months of careful, exhaustive research, we sat down to reread and review our material. It was considerable and left us with no doubt that someone, with or without the knowledge of the owners, was inserting material that paralleled too closely for accident or coincidence Nazi propaganda. It was not just a case of two people having roughly the same opinions. It was, very often, a word-for-word identical articulation of those opinions.

We agreed that Heiner, with his scholarly training, would arrange the material in documentary form and that then I would take it and write it up as an article. I had come up with a provocative title: "A Newspaper Axis in America?" We knew that we were playing with dynamite. The papers in question, and their owners, were giants who could crush us. We wondered if anyone would believe us. We ourselves had doubted the authenticity of our thesis and thus had worked long months and many hours to check it out painstakingly.

Finally, we were ready to submit the finished article. I took a deep breath and telephoned a crusading newspaper editor, one of the biggest names in journalism, Ralph Ingersoll, former editor of *Life* magazine. Ingersoll had launched a noble experiment in journalism, the daily paper *PM,* the only paper in America to refuse all advertising. Ingersoll was trying to prove that a paper could operate successfully on its sales alone and throw off what he felt was the undue influence of advertisers. He had a powerful financial backer, willing to give him the money to get started until he could prove his point. The backer was Marshall Field, another giant name in Chicago, as big if not quite so powerful as the "Colonel" of the *Tribune.*

I told Ingersoll briefly that I had evidence of some kind of a

Nazi propaganda plant inside the *Daily News.* He drew in his breath; I could hear his gasp as he shouted into the phone, "Who the devil are you, some kind of nut?" I assured him that I was no kind of nut and suggested that he call Dean Gottschalk at CCNY to check me out. Ingersoll replied, "No, that won't be necessary. Bring your material down here right away, leave it with my secretary with your telephone number. I suppose I ought at least to look at it."

The next morning my phone rang. It was Ingersoll. "Young fellow, this material is sensational. You have both done a splendid research job. Call Cassirer, then come on down, the two of you, I want to talk to you."

Heiner and I walked into Ingersoll's office, shook hands. He said: "You've made your case. We're going to publish this. I want you fellows to go to the newsroom and ask for our foreign editor, Alex Uhl. You'll be working with him."

Ingersoll explained that he could not run the article the way I had written it. "We are not a magazine, we're a newspaper, and we don't do big takeouts. Your piece is a long article—very good—but not what we want. We want to milk this, get a dozen or more short pieces out of it, hit it every day, with a front-page banner. Uhl knows how to do that. But don't worry. It's your story and you'll get bylines on it."

We thanked him again and began to leave his office, when he said: "You haven't asked me what you want for this?"

Heiner and I looked at each other for a moment. Then I turned to Ingersoll and said, "Sir, we are teachers, not journalists. We haven't a notion what this is worth as a fee. We'll trust you and leave it to you."

Ingersoll laughed. "Uh-oh, this'll cost me more. Look, talk to Alec, come back, and I'll have a check. By the way, one check or two, and how?"

Heiner answered, "Two, split it half and half, we are partners."

Uhl was brisk but courteous, a real pro, with no time to waste. He told us just how he was going to run the piece, with side-by-side boxes of Goebbels's quotes and *Daily News* editorial excerpts. In between the boxes would be copy commenting on and explaining the story. The byline would read: by Alex Uhl, with David Schoenbrun and Henry Cassirer.

He asked us to be available for conferences from time to time to give him needed background on the story, congratulated us, and asked us to give his secretary our addresses and phone numbers. He would let us know when the series would roll. I thanked him but then said we wanted to see the articles before they were set in type. "It's our story, and our names will be on it. We want to clear it." Uhl looked at us sharply. "Okay, fair enough, but don't be a pain in the butt about it."

We went back to Ingersoll's office still not quite believing that our brainstorm had become reality. Ingersoll handed us two envelopes. "Hope this will do it. It's the most we've ever paid." We tore open the envelopes. I flushed when I saw the check: one thousand dollars! It was a fortune in those days. I did not know what to say. I glanced at Heiner who looked cool but had a little smile at the corner of his lips. His jaw was working and I knew he was as moved as I. Ingersoll watched us, grinned and said: "That's not much for six months' work. Thanks and good luck!"

In the street I let out a war whoop that almost stopped traffic. Heiner, always more restrained than I, wiggled his nose, chewed his lips, looking more than ever a rabbit, but a rabbit who had just seen a mountain of tender, sweet carrots. We shook hands and hurried home.

It was two weeks before the series was ready to appear.

The day the article appeared, I paced back and forth in front of the kiosk on my corner until it was delivered, snatched the first copy, and then stood aside to see who would be buying it. I had to control myself not to point to the banner "Axis Press in America," and tell someone that it was my story, my first byline in a major metropolitan paper.

That afternoon some of the newswriters at CBS came to the monitoring room to congratulate me, and one of them said that Paul White would like to see me. I went to the news director's office wondering what was on his mind. He looked up and said: "Great story, but why didn't you bring it to me?"

"Well, it's really a print story, hard to tell, too long to tell on the air. I didn't think it would be useful to you."

"Well, next time you get a big idea, don't make my decisions for me. Tell me about it."

I left his office, wondering whether all this might lead me into a career in journalism. But then I thought that this was a kind of freak story. I had no idea how I would go about finding something else.

The series caused a lot of talk in New York, particularly when Captain Patterson of the *News* gave it prominence in his own paper. He wrote an editorial, entitled "You're a liar Mr. Ingersoll!" His readers, several million of them, would never have heard about our charges had he not led his editorial page with an attack on *PM* and a denial of our story.

Ingersoll met me for lunch some time after the series to tell me that he was turning over the paper to John Lewis. "The world is going to hell," he said, "and I'm tired of fighting and losing. Now I'm going to do something that is healthful and amusing and make enough money to stay out of the rat race."

When I asked him what he intended to do, he told me, "Buy a ranch, under a big sky, ride a horse, and raise cattle." He went on: "Let me tell you something that may be useful in later life. I went to see a friend, a financial wizard on Wall Street and told him I was quitting the paper and wanted to earn some money and enjoy life. He told me that was easy to do. But before he would advise me I would have to tell him how much money I wanted to make. He warned me to think carefully of my answer. I laughed and said, 'Oh, a million dollars would be just right.'

"My friend nodded in assent and said: 'That's okay, but let's keep it strictly to a million or less. You see, Ralph, a million is a sum that a man can control and use. But, beware about money; if it gets too big, it controls you. The men of great fortunes are prisoners of that fortune. The money takes on a dynamism of its own. It carries great responsibilities. You begin to work for your money instead of the other way around. So, don't be greedy, a lot of money is another kind of rat race.' "

His friend had gone through his dossiers after asking Ingersoll what he knew best in the way of a product that could be sold. Ingersoll, after some thought, said printing presses. His friend handed him a report on second-hand printing presses, where they could be found and marketed. He told Ingersoll that he would help him finance a printing-press business. "You ought to be able to earn enough to sell out with about a million-dollar profit in five years. Then, go buy your ranch and ride under the big sky."

Ingersoll shook hands with me and said good-bye. I never saw him again but I did hear that he had made his million, bought his ranch, and was riding under the Big Sky.

I never had a yearning to ride a range or make a million. In any case I would not have been any good at either. My only yearning has been to understand the world in which I live and to do something to make it just a little better, if I could.

The world certainly was in need of improvement in the forties. Hitler controlled western Europe and Goering was blasting London in a "blitz" of massive air raids on its population centers. Hitler put in motion his plan Operation Sea Lion, for the invasion of Britain as soon as the Luftwaffe had destroyed the air defenses and the morale of the British people. Every day at our listening posts we followed news of the Battle of Britain.

On June 18, 1940, Prime Minister Winston Churchill addressed Parliament stating that Britain was facing a mortal threat and that all of its resources must be rallied to stop the Nazis. He promised that Englishmen would fight every step, on the streets, in the country, on the beaches, and that "if the British Empire shall live a thousand years, this will be its finest hour."

We all thrilled to Churchill's brave eloquence. I also rushed into the newsroom to tell the writers about another speech beamed by radio from London to France that very same June 18, a speech that very few people heard that day but one which would be repeated many times and would rival Churchill's for courage and drama. It had been made by an obscure brigadier general of the French Army, who had been appointed under secretary of war in the last days before the French collapse and surrender to Hitler.

The brigadier was Charles de Gaulle. He told his countrymen that all was not lost, that this war was a world war,* that France had powerful allies in England and in America with limitless resources, that France still had an empire that stretched around the world. With a powerful voice that ranged from deep baritone to a cracked tenor, a voice vibrating with emotion, General de Gaulle

* Reporters, summarizing the talk, wrote that de Gaulle had said that France had lost a battle not the war, which was a world war. The phrase "France has lost a battle, not the war" was never spoken by de Gaulle, yet it is often quoted in France as his famous message of June 18. De Gaulle's aides liked the phrase and had posters printed putting the words in quotes, solidifying the myth that de Gaulle had uttered them.

exclaimed: "Has the last word been spoken? Must hope die now? Is our defeat decisive? No, nothing is lost for France!" He went on to proclaim: "Whatever happens, the flame of French resistance must not and will not be extinguished!"

The few people who heard de Gaulle on June 18 soon spread word that there was a French general in London who had formed a new movement called Free France, and who called upon his countrymen to join him in resisting the abject surrender to the Nazis, refusing to join Hitler's "New Europe." Some Frenchmen and women, who had not heard de Gaulle, had reached the same conclusion as he, that the French had to fight against fascism, fight for the eventual liberation of their land and restoration of democracy. They began to form underground resistance movements.

Hopes for freedom were kept alive by the magnificent courage and skill of young Englishmen who rushed into their Spitfire fighter planes at the first alert of a German air raid and flew into the sky to challenge the powerful Luftwaffe. The Battle of Britain started on August 8, 1940. It ended in a victory for the Royal Air Force which defeated, in thousands of aerial "dogfights," the greatest aces of the German Air Force. The cost was tremendous, losses going beyond fifty percent of RAF squadrons. By October 31, when the blitz ended, British civilian deaths were 14,281, with another 20,325 wounded. The end of the blitz did not mean the end of German air attacks on Britain. But it ended the Battle of Britain. Goering could not destroy British air defenses or British civilian morale. Operation Sea Lion was canceled.

Later, when I got to London and lived through German air raids, I saw for myself the incredible strength and even humor of the British under the worst attacks. I was broadcasting in a BBC studio when suddenly our building shook, windows shattered. We thought we were hit, but the bomb had struck just across the street. We all grabbed pails of sand that were alongside all desks and rushed to the street to help fight the fires that were blazing.

The building had been sheared away on three sides as though a giant hand had sliced them off. One side of the building was, incredibly, intact. On a third-floor landing we could make out the figure of a man. The fire captain was told by a neighbor that it was Rupert Jones, an old war veteran. The captain shouted, "Mr. Jones, sir, Mr. Jones, we're coming for you, are you all right?"

Back came a peal of laughter. "Yuss! I'm foyne!" And another cackle of laughter. Someone whispered, "Poor old Jones, 'es gorn crackers!" Another shout from the fire captain: "Now, easy does it, Mr. Jones, stand back, the ladder is coming up." Jones leaned over and waved. "I was sittin' on the pot and I pulled the chain and the 'ole bleedin' buildin' came down."

The crowd exploded with laughter. It did not last long. All around us were burned bodies, dead bodies, ambulances, fires. There was rescue work to be done. I thought to myself that Churchill was right. This was Britain's finest hour. Britain stood alone in the world and faced down Hitler. France had fallen, along with Belgium and Holland. Spain and Italy were in fascist hands, Russia suffered under the tyrant Stalin, America still nursed isolationist dreams. Britain alone defended democracy, and if we are free men and women today we all owe a debt to the British.

I was certain as early as that magnificent June 18 that men like Churchill and the French general, de Gaulle, would be able to rally their slim forces for the long fight back to freedom. We were among the first, at CBS, to tell Americans about the de Gaulle and Churchill speeches that day. I prayed that my own great country would wake up soon and join in the battle.

There were not many occasions for rejoicing, however. The news was almost regularly bad. The Vichy government, under German control, arrested and interned leaders of the French Republic. The British, justifiably worried about the French fleet, attacked their former allies at Mers el-Kébir, sinking many ships and inflicting heavy casualties. It embittered the French, gave propaganda ammunition to the Nazis, and weakened the cause of General de Gaulle. However, if the French fleet had fallen into the hands of the Germans, the result would have been worse.

Soviet troops took over Lithuania, Estonia, and Latvia. Stalin swallowed them up and made them Soviet states. Hitler named Gauleiters—governors with absolute powers—for Alsace and Lorraine and took final steps to take them back from France and incorporate them into the German Reich. Italian troops in Libya went on the offensive against Egypt. Japan issued an ultimatum to Vichy France to cede bases in Indochina. After Vichy agreed to let Japanese troops enter Vietnam, they attacked French posts in several districts: Lang Son, Dong Dang, Than Moi.

In September, at long last, the Congress in Washington passed a bill instituting obligatory military service. Our army was dangerously undermanned and poorly armed. Roosevelt, on the verge of recognizing the German satellite regime of Marshal Pétain, on the grounds of "expediency," sent Pétain a warning message, telling him that "the fact that France is under German occupation cannot serve to justify any aid to Germany in its war with Britain."

Roosevelt's policy on France rapidly became an issue of heated controversy in the United States. Many Americans, alert to what was happening in Europe, were sharply critical of the Vichy regime's subservience to the Nazis. We considered that Pétain's chief of government, Pierre Laval, was himself a fascist, a more than willing creature of the Nazis. We admired General de Gaulle's refusal to accept the French surrender and we appealed to FDR to recognize and give support to de Gaulle. He thought that de Gaulle was a potential dictator, a man on a white horse, an ambitious right-wing adventurer. It was one of FDR's most grievous mistakes, which was to affect adversely French-American relations right up to today.

Hitler's persecution of the Jews spread to France. One of the most infamous acts in French history occurred on May 14, 1941, when French police in Paris arrested more than ten thousand European Jews, who had been granted refuge in France, and turned them over to the Nazis. Honorable Frenchmen and women—and there were many—sickened by the shameful spectacle, created new underground escape routes for Jews. French nuns hid Jewish children in their convents. A French Jew, Jean-Pierre Lévy, chief of a resistance network, Franc-Tireur, redoubled his group's attacks on German installations and on the Vichy regime of Marshal Pétain.

Then, on June 21, 1941, German troops launched an offensive against the Soviet Union. Hitler, frustrated in the west, unable to bring brave England to her knees, had turned his full fury on the Russians, in Operation Barbarossa, a campaign he had hoped to launch after defeating the British. It was a major turning point in the war. If Hitler could defeat the Russians, he would virtually be master of the world. If he failed, he had sealed his own doom. Most of us, giving expression to our desires rather than any rational analysis, celebrated the aggression as the first big step toward Hitler's destruction.

Our optimism was cooled off rapidly when German troops cut

through Russia as they had in Poland and France. In less than a week they had captured Riga and Vilna. Stalin, early in July, proclaimed a "national war" requiring the efforts of every Soviet citizen, ready to fight even with handguns and knives as partisans in small groups wherever Germans had penetrated. Churchill had already told Parliament that Britain was ready to aid the Soviet Union. Churchill had no love for communism or for Stalin, but Hitler was the main enemy and had to be stopped.

A news item on July 25 did not receive the attention it merited. All Japanese assets in the United States were blocked. And another bit of "small news" escaped our attention a few days later when Roosevelt's right-hand man, Harry Hopkins, went to Moscow to see Stalin. His mission was to set up conditions for a device that would permit FDR to send aid to Stalin, without a bitter fight in Congress. It was called Lend-Lease, a pretense that it was not an outright grant of materiel without any plan for payment. It was designed to supply weapons and trucks to the Russians without payment but hiding that fact from Congress, still angry about unpaid war debts from the First World War.

News from the eastern front continued to be bad. The Germans captured Kiev in mid-September and were assaulting the gates of Kharkov. Soviet troops were falling back all along the line. At the end of September, American, British, and Soviet officials met in Moscow to study ways to send aid to Russia.

Stalin, frightened by the German advance, proclaimed a state of siege in Moscow and transferred his government to Kuibyshev in the province of Samara. He put Marshal Zhukov in charge of the defense of Moscow and appointed himself commander in chief of all Soviet armed forces. Roosevelt sent him a message of support and announced that he had given the American Navy the "mission of carrying aid to Britain, Russia, and China," and promised that it would not fail in its task.

Congress, abandoning, little by little, its neutralist policies, agreed to arm the merchant marine. There was no protest against a Roosevelt declaration that the American Navy had received orders to fire on any German or Italian ships that penetrated the perimeter of the American coastal defense zone.

It was a sunny crisp Sunday in December. Dorothy and I were having brunch in the drugstore in our apartment building. We were talking about plans for the day—ice-skating in Central Park, hot chocolate at Rumpelmayer's, a movie, a Chinese dinner, a perfect, inexpensive New York day. On the radio we were listening to the music of the Philharmonic Orchestra on CBS. Suddenly, the music was cut off and we heard an announcer saying: "We interrupt this program to bring you a news bulletin." Then the familiar voice of John Charles Daly: "Japanese planes this morning attacked the American naval base at Pearl Harbor, in Hawaii. . . ."

America had paid a heavy price for the long years of isolationism, of refusal to recognize the threat of power-hungry dictators. Not only were we ill-prepared to fight a global war, our commanders at Pearl Harbor were caught completely off-guard. Our military posture was criminally negligent. Most of our planes were destroyed on the ground, our battleships sunk or badly damaged at anchor. We were not on war alert, to be sure, but the negotiations with Japan had gone badly, the situation was at best unhealthy, and our High Command in Hawaii failed to take even minimal precautions.

Admirals denounced the Japanese aggression as a "sneak attack." I wondered what kind of an attack they expected, one with bugles blowing and pennants flying, as in the days of chivalry? FDR called it "a day of infamy," and the phrase has lived on in American history. The attack on Pearl Harbor was only one of many days of infamy throughout the world in the 1940s; the appeasement of Hitler at Munich, the rape of Czechoslovakia, the dismemberment of Poland by Hitler and Stalin, Hitler's invasion of Russia, Japan's invasion of Southeast Asia and the Philippines. Many more infamous days were ahead, after Pearl Harbor, all leaving their mark on future generations.

The Japanese sneak attack is as much alive in the 1980s as it was in the forties. Americans took a vow more than forty years ago never again to be caught unprepared. The terrible losses and shame of Pearl Harbor have entered into the American psyche and are present in our current debates on nuclear policy. The Pearl Harbor trauma is the prime motivating factor in proposals to produce the MX missile to counter a potential Soviet first strike.

Equally alive in current debates is that day of infamy, September 30, 1938, when Britain's prime minister, Chamberlain, and France's premier, Daladier, bowed to Hitler's demands on the Czech Sudetenland at the Munich Conference and the word "appeasement" etched itself into the minds of Western leaders forever after. Today, any suggestion for any kind of concession to or compromise with the Soviet Union provokes the cry "Munich! Appeasement!" This has happened time and time again, all through the forties and fifties in the Cold War between Russia and America. The very word "détente," meaning only a relaxation of tensions, became confused with appeasement.

Because of this trauma, Europeans, particularly the French, who have a long-standing love-hate relationship with the United States, become exceedingly nervous any time an American secretary of state or President flies to Moscow talking about détente or coexistence. They are immediately suspicious of a "sell-out of Europe." On the other hand, when America, as is the case today with President Reagan, takes a hard, anti-Soviet stand, our European allies complain that we are too provocative and are endangering their security.

The Soviet Union has its own traumas, its own memories of infamy that affect current policies. June 22, 1941, the day of the Nazi invasion of Russia, will never be forgotten. Twenty million Russians died in World War II. The men who run the Soviet Union in the eighties were soldiers in the forties. For them, Germany is a dangerous enemy. Russia has occupied ancient Prussia and the eastern German lands and installed a particularly dictatorial communist regime in the state of East Germany which it created. Never will the Russians permit the reunification of the two Germanies, other than under complete Soviet control. Even then, it is doubtful if the Russians would dare create a greater Germany, given the skills and energies of the German people.

Russian memories go back even farther than 1941, to the Bolshevik Revolution of 1917 when British, French, and American troops invaded Russia to support the White Russia proczarist forces in an attempt to crush the revolution and the newly created communist state, the Soviet Union. That, for the Russians, is a day of infamy. Russians today mistrust the Western Europeans and the Americans. Events of 1917 and 1941 are not history in the Soviet Union. They are an integral part of today's psychology and strategy.

One of the most quoted of aphorisms is the comment of philosophy professor George Santayana: "Those who do not know the lessons of history are condemned to relive them." It might also be said that the opposite is true: Those who remember too rigidly, applying old lessons in changed contexts, are likely to make new errors. It is safer to keep in mind another aphorism: History never repeats itself. If that is true, then what happened in the past is not an absolute guide forever. History's lessons are valuable only if they are reinterpreted in the light of new realities.

CHAPTER 3

THE WAR OF WORDS

There was some good news as 1941 came to an inglorious end. There were the first signs of a turning point in the seemingly unstoppable march of the dictators. Marshal Zhukov truly earned his medal as a hero of the Soviet Union when he rallied Moscow's defenders and halted the Nazi forces at the very gates of the Russian capital. By December 20, Soviet troops had forced the Germans back more than a hundred miles from Moscow. It was Hitler's first failure. Soviet marshals, courageous Soviet soldiers, and one of Russia's greatest assets, old General Winter, conqueror of Napoleon, had stopped Hitler in the snows of Russia. The Red Army song jumped to the top of the hit parade.

As the new year dawned, my life came in for a sudden change. It began with a telephone call, early in January 1942. It came at seven in the morning and jarred me out of a deep sleep. "David? It's Dean Gottschalk."

I tried to gather my wits, wondering if at last my long-awaited appointment to CCNY had come through.

It hadn't. The dean apologized for waking me so early but said it was urgent. "A man named Donovan, a government official, called on me yesterday afternoon. He is recruiting, but I don't know what the jobs are. He asked me to recommend former students who speak foreign languages and are familiar with the history and politics of foreign lands. I gave him your name, among others. He said he knew who you were and would like you to call upon him between nine and eleven this morning if you could."

I thanked the dean, noted down the address—a Wall Street law firm—and sat down to breakfast with Dorothy, speculating excitedly on this sudden development. We guessed it must be some State Department or War Department research and analysis project. Pearl Harbor had caught the government short-staffed on Americans with knowledge and a feeling for foreign nations. Now that we were at war with Germany my special knowledge of that country, and also of German-occupied France, might be of value in Washington.

Mr. Donovan was a strongly built man, radiating authority, yet soft-spoken. I did not know then that he was Wild Bill Donovan, America's most decorated World War I hero, then a millionaire Wall Street lawyer. A Republican, sharply critical of Roosevelt's New Deal, he went to work for the President enthusiastically when FDR called him to Washington to work in the war mobilization.

Donovan began by throwing a barrage of questions at me. What did I know about French underground movements? What did I think about de Gaulle? Had Pétain been playing a double game, pretending to collaborate with the Nazis but protecting the French people? Would he be willing secretly to provide information to the Allies? He threw out questions as though he were back behind a machine gun at Belleau Wood.

I held up my hand and said, "Mr. Donovan, please, hold it. I'll try to answer your questions, but don't you think you ought first to tell me what this is all about? What kind of personnel are you looking for? What kind of job?"

He grinned at me and said, "Spies."

I gulped. "Spies? I wouldn't be worth a damn as a spy."

"Why not?"

"Well, I'm talkative and argumentative. I've got a short fuse. I'd never get away with it."

Donovan laughed. "Well, you're also frank and honest and seem to know yourself. Those are good qualities."

"Maybe so," I replied, "but not for a spy. Thanks a lot, but I'm really not interested."

He looked at me for a long moment. "Okay. When you walk

out of here, you'll forget this conversation ever took place. But there is something else cooking that may be more to your taste. It's not ready yet. We'll let you know about it soon."

For the next two weeks friends started calling and telling me about strange men asking all sorts of questions about me. I was clearly undergoing a security check by J. Edgar Hoover's FBI investigators.

Some of the questions and observations in that early investigation were so ludicrous that I could hardly believe it. One investigator noted that he had staked out a position near my apartment and observed the comings and goings of people who rang my bell. At least half of them spoke "foreign tongues," he somewhat quaintly noted. But his most significant observation reported that only two out of twenty "male visitors wore hats." I could not fathom the significance of that report until a friend at the Justice Department told me with a smile, "All good, patriotic, loyal Americans wear hats. Only liberals, leftists, and strange characters go hatless. That was the point against you."

There were full accountings of the frequent evenings that my wife, her sister, and I spent down in Sheridan Square at a Latin-American dinner-dance club called the Café Latino. The reports noted: "They continually danced the rhumba, the mambo, and the paso doble. Everyone talked Spanish and ate Spanish dishes." This was clearly suspicious behavior.

Suddenly there was a demand for my services. News was flooding in from all the war fronts, from Russia, the Far East, the Pacific, and from North Africa, where British troops were engaged in action against the enemy on the Egyptian-Libyan frontier. Editors were overwhelmed and out of their depth. John Lewis of *PM* called me in and asked for more pieces about the methods of Nazi propaganda.

The "American Axis" articles had been a great success. Now he was interested in the propaganda story in itself. He had heard about my work at the CBS monitoring station and wanted to see the material. Paul White, at CBS, also called me in. He had no job in the newsroom for me, but he did offer generous fees for background and analysis pieces that I could submit to his broadcasters. There was enough coming in for me to give up my other odd jobs and become a full-time freelance writer. I was finally on my way to a career as journalist.

Then a Japanese victory hit with profound impact upon the geopolitics of Asia, an event that signaled the end of the "white man's burden," of white, Western colonialism in the Orient. General Perceval, of the British Imperial Staff, surrendered the "impregnable" fortress of Singapore, symbol of British might in Asia. The Japanese took more than seventy thousand prisoners, the worst defeat in a single battle that the British had ever suffered. It was a lesson to all the subjugated peoples of Asia, as well as to those of Africa, that the white man was not invincible.

Singapore's cannons controlled every approach by sea. No invading armada could possibly have entered the harbor and put down a landing force. But the Achilles heel of Singapore was its undefended rear area, lush with green jungle thought to be impenetrable by an invading army. The British had made the same mistake that the French had made with their Maginot Line and their confidence that large enemy units could not penetrate through the Ardennes forest without being spotted in time and cut to pieces.

Among those who watched these developments with concentrated and passionate interest was a Vietnamese named Ho Chi Minh. He saw the Japanese troops enter his country and brush away French static outposts as they might brush away flies. He noted the Japanese infiltration of the jungles behind Singapore. Ho formed small guerrilla units of his Vietnamese followers deep in the jungles and in the mountain caves of his country and began hit-and-run attacks on the Japanese invaders. His guerrillas were far more successful in their harassment of the Japanese than the French who had set up fixed "strongpoints" in the jungle. Ho and his people were receiving invaluable training for the war they would one day launch against the French and the Americans. But in World War II, Ho was a valued ally of the Americans, praised by General Douglas MacArthur for the help he gave in the fight against Japan.

The Japanese had already captured Manila and were closing in on Bataan. General MacArthur begged Washington for help but there was none to send him. America was very far away, its factories still gearing up for war production. Then, for the first time since our Civil War, the territory of the United States came under attack. The coast of California, just below San Francisco, was bombarded by shells from a Japanese submarine.

The nation was shocked. Were the Japanese preparing for an

invasion of America, or for a Pearl Harbor on American continental territory? California blacked out at night. The police and civil defense officials received hundreds of phone calls from hysterical citizens and from those of unstable mind "reporting" Japanese patrols and paratroopers around their homes.

I called John Lewis at *PM* and told him that the submarine shelling was just a stunt, a clever tactic of "nerve warfare." The Japanese wanted to panic us into diverting money and efforts to civil defense at home instead of a counterattack in the Pacific. I had talked with Pentagon and State Department specialists on Japan and they all assured me that there could be no invasion or sustained bombardment of the United States. Japanese forces were totally committed in Asia and the western Pacific. Lewis told me to write the article quickly. He wanted to get it into print and alert citizens to the maneuver before a German submarine would lob some shells into New York.

The day after my piece appeared in *PM,* explaining that there was no reason to be panicked by the Jap nerve-war stunt, I received the phone call that Donovan had told me would come. It was not Donovan in person, but someone speaking on his behalf. He would be flying up from Washington on March 1 and would like to see me that same day.

Donovan had no time to waste. He told me that two new government agencies were being formed. One would be called the OSS, the Office of Strategic Services. He grinned. "That's my cloak-and-dagger operation, my spy center, the one you would not work for." He said that the other would be the OWI, the Office of War Information, including the Voice of America.

"The Voice will be the American equivalent of the BBC. It will broadcast in more than twenty languages to begin with and then expand as we find fluent broadcasters in many more languages. The OWI also will have a desk for analysis of enemy propaganda. Your background is perfect for that operation. Your piece in *PM* about the Japanese submarine was first-rate. You're just the man we need for the OWI propaganda-analysis desk and for some broadcasts in French to occupied France."

As I left Donovan's office, I don't think my feet touched ground. I was overjoyed. At last I would be making a contribution to our fight against the Nazis. Propaganda was a potent weapon in warfare.

We Americans had a lot to learn, but we were eager, and Roosevelt had managed to attract an extraordinary collection of brilliant men to operate the OWI. At the top, in Washington, was Elmer Davis of CBS. At the head of the Overseas Division in New York was one of America's leading playwrights, Robert E. Sherwood. Chief of the News Division was Ed Barrett, an editor of *Newsweek* magazine. One of the top men under Sherwood was Joseph Barnes, editor of the New York *Herald Tribune*.

No organization outside government in time of peace could have afforded the payroll of the men and women who ran the OWI, each of whom had taken a big cut in income to serve the country. There were many Europeans who had fled Hitler and were eager to serve the United States. Among them was one of France's most competent newsmen, Pierre Lazareff, prewar editor of *Paris-Soir*. He was named head of the French broadcasting service of the OWI.

They had a tough job in mind for me at the Voice, but it was so exciting, provided so much invaluable training, taught me so much, that I never minded for a minute. It was the shift that newsmen hated, the "lobster shift." I don't know why it was called that, but duty began at midnight and lasted until 8:00 A.M. It was a killer. Around about three o'clock an overwhelming desire to sleep would hit me hard in the first weeks, until I adjusted to the schedule. Worst of all, Dorothy would be leaving for her studio just as I came home to bed at 9:00 A.M. We would meet again at six in the evening. She would have dinner, while I had breakfast. Best of all, we would then go to the Café Latino and dance the rhumba and mambo from about seven to ten at night, when I would have to go to my desk at the OWI. Although my shift began at midnight, I would have to spend at least an hour beforehand going over all the news of the day, bringing myself up to the minute before taking over the desk.

At first, my assignment was to go through the news files and select items that had a high propaganda content, that is, which either lent themselves to enemy propaganda that had to be countered, or gave us an opportunity for an offensive of our own in the war of words.

Our planes, trying to hit factories turning out materiel for the Germans, missed their targets in the industrial area outside Paris, in Boulogne-Billancourt, and caused heavy civilian casualties, more than 600 killed and 1,500 wounded. Nazi propaganda writers in Berlin inflamed French opinion against the Anglo-Americans. We had a most difficult time explaining what had happened, pointing out that the Nazis deliberately installed their war production in centers of dense population where it was difficult to strike at them without hitting innocent civilians. It was an argument that would be made many times in the next forty years. It was hotly debated in the summer of 1981, when Israeli planes struck heavily against PLO bases in Lebanon and caused severe civilian casualties.

What we decided to do, after a spirited debate at the highest levels of the OWI and State Department, was to tell the truth about our failures. Sherwood, Barnes, and other top men insisted that it was important to build up the Voice's reputation for integrity and truthfulness. We could better prove to people listening in Europe that the Nazis were liars if we first established ourselves as truth-tellers. It would also be easier to convince people of our propaganda themes if they knew that our news broadcasts were accurate and reliable.

There were, and still are today, many men in Washington in the civil service and the Congress who did not think that honesty is necessarily the best policy, and who wanted to suppress the worst news of American setbacks. But the highly professional staff of the OWI resisted the would-be censors. The professionalism of the staff equaled that of the best newspapers, networks, and national magazines, mainly because the executives, producers, and writers came from the best of the media. In addition to Barnes of the *Tribune* and Barrett of *Newsweek,* there was Adrian Berwick of the *Reader's Digest,* C. D. Jackson of *Life,* S. M. Bessie of *Look,* and a host of Harvard Nieman Fellows and Pulitzer Prize winners.

Staffers did not come only from press and radio. Connie Ernst, one of the young OWI editors, had been a theater stage manager. Her father, Morris Ernst, was one of America's most distinguished attorneys, a civil libertarian, prominent in the work of the Civil Liberties Union, and a close friend and advisor of President Roosevelt. One of London's and America's top theatrical producers and directors, John Houseman, supervised production of Voice broadcasts. Today, in his eighties, Houseman has been enjoying a new career as a television performer. He has had great fun and earned more doing commercials than producing the plays of Shakespeare, which may tell us something about our values. He is the somewhat overbearing and pompous character who glares out of the tube and says haughtily: "Smith, Barney make money the old-fashioned way—they earn it!"

We all earned our money—very little—the old-fashioned way in 1942, with ten-hour shifts or more, six days a week, and seven if there was any kind of emergency—and emergency was almost routine during the war.

The Japanese repeated their stunt of shelling the American coast from a submarine by bombarding the Canadian port of Vancouver, just north of Seattle, Washington. But the propaganda value of that tactic had lost its force, particularly since the American fleet had scored smashing victories over the Japanese in the Pacific. The aircraft carrier *Yorktown* had been lost, but not before its planes and sister ships had sent another dozen Japanese warships to a Pacific graveyard. The Japanese had lost mastery of the Pacific to the Americans within six months after Pearl Harbor and by the first anniversary of Pearl Harbor the Americans had reversed that defeat and had the Japanese on the run.

Britain's General Bernard Montgomery had held the line against Rommel all through the summer of 1942, halting his advance into Egypt at a village called El Alamein. He waited until he had built up huge supplies of tanks and artillery shells. Monty was a careful commander and would not go on the offensive until he had a large margin of firepower over his adversary.

He went on the offensive against the Desert Fox, Rommel, on September 23, recalling for me the memorable day of my marriage and the shameful capitulation at Munich. We had come very far from September 23, 1938, to September 23, 1942. Monty's opening artillery barrage caught Rommel by surprise. He had no idea that the British had amassed so much power. British tanks came looming up out of the smoke. Thousands of "Tommies" walked alongside and behind the armor, plodding determinedly across the sands to the Nazi lines. The press would later call those tankmen and that heroic infantry the Desert Rats, conquerors of the Desert Fox. It was a glorious victory for the British against a redoubtable foe. Marshal Rommel suffered his first defeat. From then on General Montgomery, later promoted to Field Marshal, and then knighted by his king, would be known as Sir Bernard Law Montgomery, and then Lord Montgomery of Alamein.

While Rommel was falling back in North Africa, the Germans had begun a massive offensive on the eastern front. The Sixth Army, under Field Marshal von Paulus, was striking south and east toward the Volga River and the great prize of the Caucasus oil fields beyond. On October 6, 1942, Radio Moscow broadcast an Order of the Day to Soviet troops: "The Germans are approaching the Volga. Not a step backward! Fight as the soldiers of Alexander and Kutuzov fought for Russia."

The Soviet communists were appealing to their soldiers, not in the name of Marx or Lenin, but in the mystical names of Mother Russia. We did not, of course, use that comment on the Voice, but we did pick up the exhortation "Not a step backward," and compared it to the historic French order at Verdun: "*Ils ne passeront pas!*" We told our listeners, more in hope than in conviction, that the Germans would not pass the Soviet lines at Stalingrad as they had failed to break the French defenses at Verdun. Large-scale maps of the Volga region and of Stalingrad were hung in the OWI newsroom and the Voice, to follow the fighting day by day, finally street by street.

OWI chiefs had, by then, come up with a genial, new device and I was assigned to work it out on the overnight shift. It was called the Propaganda Man. Someone, I never found out who it was, had pointed out at a top staff meeting that we could work German broadcasts and press editorials backward to uncover the directive that had been written by the Nazi High Command in Berlin's Wilhelmstrasse. Once we had reconstructed the directive, we could analyze the strategy behind it and try to discover the motives and pressures weighing most heavily on our adversary. It was my job to prepare that analysis in a written report to the top brass.

My job was to go over the hundred thousand words and more that came in to us daily from London on the BBC teletype, culled from British monitoring and British intelligence reports. There was much invaluable material coming in also from underground groups in Western Europe, particularly the French, who were doing magnificent espionage work on the Germans as well as armed attacks on their bases and facilities.

All this material flooded my desk from midnight to 6:00 A.M., at which point I let the tapes pile up on the teleprinter while I began the difficult task of sorting through everything I had read and dividing it up into themes and lines. After that, I would look at my notes and try to draw the profile of the Propaganda Man. That took until 7:00 A.M., time to begin to write up a maximum two-page report, summarizing the main themes, and taking note of any significant differences in the orders that were given to the French, Spanish, British, and American broadcasting sections of the German networks. Someone else watched the Arabic and Asian broadcasts.

The most tension-ridden moment came at 8:00 A.M., when my report was distributed to the top-echelon executives of OWI and the Voice at their morning meeting. All the big men and women were there. Tired and pale, I would slink in and sit at the back, ready to answer questions based on my report. I knew, too, that once the report was cleared in New York, it would go on to Washington, to Army, Navy, Air Force, State Department intelligence services, as well as to Donovan's OSS and to the White House.

As a result of this work, I was informed one day before the end of the year that I had been approved for special training and would soon be given instructions about going to a camp on Long Island. An OWI team was being put together at the request of the Allied Supreme Commander, General Eisenhower, to report to his headquarters in Algiers.

American and British forces had landed in Algeria and Morocco on November 8, 1942. Roosevelt had sent a message to Marshal Pétain informing him that it was necessary to invade French North Africa in order to keep that strategic territory out of German hands. It was the first massive amphibian landing operation for the Americans in the war. It was successful, but, tragically, forces loyal to Pétain had resisted. Frenchmen had fired on Americans for the first time since they had fought side by side with us to help us win our independence. Casualties were heavy and the political situation was a mess.

The mess in Algiers thickened the day before Christmas when a young man, whose motives and associations could never be clearly determined, Fernand Bonnier de la Chapelle, shot and killed Admiral Darlan. Two days later, a military tribunal, meeting in secret, found de la Chapelle guilty of murder, condemned him to death, and had him executed, again secretly. No one ever had a chance to hear his testimony or to hear or read his answers to interrogation.

Was his the act of a crazed individual? Was it a conspiracy? Who were the conspirators?

Rumors were rampant in Algiers but it was, as in the case years later of Lee Harvey Oswald, impossible to answer any of the questions. The man who might have answered them was dead, executed before a firing squad. The secret execution by French authorities, under overall American command, led many reporters to believe that it was the French themselves, possibly with Consul General Robert Murphy's approval, who wanted to get rid of the fascist Darlan who had become an embarrassment to everyone. American reporters in Algiers, men like CBS's outstanding correspondent Charles Collingwood, were pressing Murphy to explain why a Pétainist and an ally of the Nazis had been put in political command of French North Africa.

The Americans had spent the year following the disaster of Pearl Harbor putting their gigantic industrial machine to work for war. Roosevelt had appointed Donald Nelson to be in charge of a Victory Program to plan the mobilization of the American economy for war. He put a Detroit automaker, William Knudsen, in charge of converting civilian production to military output. In addition, the President had conferred with a Frenchman, little known to the public but highly regarded by all world statesmen, one of the wisest, best organized, and most successful planners in history, Jean Monnet.

The name Monnet was best known to brandy drinkers, for Monnet cognac was one of the finest products of French vines. Monnet had been, in his youth, a salesman for his family cognac in Canada and the United States. But he was not interested in the brandy business. He soon went into banking and ran a financial investment house in New York. Then he joined the League of Nations as an international civil servant.

Short, stocky, with a high flush on his cheeks, and twinkling gray-blue eyes, Jean Monnet was soft-spoken but always clear, crisp, and in control of his facts, figures, and foresights on any problem he studied. He walked into President Roosevelt's office and told him: "Mr. President, American factories can turn out at least one thousand planes a week. With such an output, you can win the war."

Roosevelt called in Knudsen and asked him about the Monnet

proposal. Knudsen snorted and said that the Frenchman was mad and did not know what he was talking about. Roosevelt handed over Monnet's working papers and told Knudsen to have a look at them. A few days later, Knudsen and Donald Nelson both called on Roosevelt to say that Jean Monnet was right and they were ready to go ahead with his plan to produce at least 50,000 planes.

By year-end 1942, Washington published, with justifiable pride, the production figures of the year: 48,000 planes, almost exactly the number Monnet had predicted; in addition, 50,000 combat vehicles, and almost 700,000 machine guns. America had become the "arsenal of democracy" that General de Gaulle had promised the French people, on June 18, 1940, would help the Allies to defeat Hitler and restore freedom to France, with the help of a French planner.

I would meet Jean Monnet, in Algiers in 1943, and begin a close relationship that would last until his death in 1979. I reported on the Monnet Plan for French postwar rehabilitation and on his plan for a European Coal and Steel Community, forerunner of the Economic Community, or Common Market, of Europe. Monnet will go down in history as Mr. Europe, a man who never commanded an army, never fired a gun, never held elective office in any state, but who did more, by the power of his ideas, to change the nature of European politics than most of the generals of history.

The only country in which Monnet's genius went largely unhonored was his native land, France. Monnet's concept of Europe, based upon a merger of individual nationalisms into a "supranationalism," ran counter to the extreme chauvinism of the French people and, above all, of General Charles de Gaulle, who would tell me: "I have fought too long for the Tricolor of France to lower its standard now and run up the flag of Europe. I know no 'Europe.' Show me a country called Europe!"

It is characteristic of the many contradictions of French civilization that France should have given us in this century the proudest of nationalists, Charles de Gaulle, and the most committed of internationalists, Jean Monnet. Over the centuries, the French have given us the ultimate philosopher of reason, René Descartes—"I think, therefore, I am"—and the ultimate Christian philosopher of faith, Blaise Pascal—"The heart has reasons that reason does not know." It is for this, and many more reasons, that I have always found

France to be the most stimulating, the most inspiring, as well as the most irritating and provocative of all societies. The French are frequently infuriating but never boring.

Roosevelt and Churchill had constant problems with the French. It caused us much trouble at the Voice of America. To be fair, one should also say that the French had constant and vexing problems with Churchill and Roosevelt, particularly Roosevelt. Churchill, although he fought constantly with Charles de Gaulle on a broad range of policies, nevertheless was the first to recognize his superb leadership qualities, the first to give official government recognition to de Gaulle's Free French movement in London. Churchill provided de Gaulle with money and weapons, as well as diplomatic standing. This, Roosevelt refused to do.

Churchill and Roosevelt met in French-controlled Morocco, at Casablanca, in a conference that would last from January 14 to 28, 1943, to discuss policy toward the Axis and on how to deal with the impossible situation in French North Africa. Regarding the Axis, they finally agreed on a policy that would lead to great controversy and endless criticism by military men and historians. It was "unconditional surrender," no negotiations with Hitler, Mussolini, and Tojo. We would destroy their armies and sea and air fleets until they were forced to surrender to us without conditions—Roosevelt and Churchill would not sit down and negotiate an armistice with "liars, murderers and war criminals." We repeated the message every day, all through the day, in our broadcasts.

This policy was highly praised in the press of the world and extremely popular with the American and British people, for it was based on sound, moral principles. However, military men and historians have argued that morality is not the best justification of a war policy. Churchill and Roosevelt, they said, were forcing the Germans to fight on to the very last gasp, because unconditional surrender left no other alternative. This would lengthen the war and cause many more Allied casualties.

The decisions affecting France at the Casablanca Conference were the most difficult we had to deal with at the Voice of America. President Roosevelt, our leader, strongly opposed General de Gaulle. He was willing only to send him arms and financial support for the war effort. By 1943 the territories of the French Empire had rallied to de Gaulle's banner and adopted his emblem, the

Cross of Lorraine, the cross with two bars, one narrow, one wide, that had been worn on the standards of Joan of Arc. But Roosevelt would not recognize him politically and diplomatically as the head of a French government, only as the leader of a military movement.

Roosevelt was backing General Henri Giraud against de Gaulle, even for the military leadership of the Free French. It was a serious misjudgment by Roosevelt. The only thing Giraud had in common with de Gaulle was his height. Like de Gaulle, he towered six feet four inches tall. In almost every other respect, his intelligence, his political judgments, Giraud was a limited man, de Gaulle a giant. I would soon enough find myself in the middle of their rivalry, although during the conference my job was to try to plaster over the disagreements and write positive broadcast reports and analyses about their agreement at Casablanca to work together.

The Casablanca Conference produced a situation with serious consequences for French and American relations. Roosevelt called in de Gaulle for a confidential talk on their conflicts. General de Gaulle was infuriated when he entered FDR's office and saw two pairs of big brown shoes protruding from under the drapes behind Roosevelt's desk. The oversized brogans belonged to FDR's Secret Service bodyguards. De Gaulle was outraged, personally insulted, to see that the American President would not meet him alone without protection.

De Gaulle told Roosevelt that he ought to be recognized officially as representing French sovereignty. FDR flatly refused, telling de Gaulle that the French people were living under Nazi occupation and rule and were not free to choose their leaders. After the war, said FDR, France will restore the Republic and hold free elections. "If they choose you, general, as their leader, then so be it. We will be happy to recognize you. But not until then. Not now."

General de Gaulle, in reply, told Roosevelt that there are times in the life of a nation when its peoples are in chains and not free to express themselves, that a leader then emerges from the ranks and holds high the flag of the nation. After all, said de Gaulle, in what he meant to be no more than an historical analogy, "No one ever elected Joan of Arc." It was a very French, witty, and literate remark. And Roosevelt, a witty, literate man himself, familiar with the French character, knew that de Gaulle meant only to score a debater's point. But FDR, who did not like de Gaulle, pretended that the reference to Joan of Arc had been made in all seriousness.

After the talk with de Gaulle, FDR informed reporters "off the record," knowing full well how the story would spread, that de Gaulle thought he was Joan of Arc, that he had a "Joan of Arc complex." Reporters thought it was very funny. Some of them had long accused de Gaulle of thinking he was Napoleon. The story spread through Casablanca and eventually everywhere, enraging de Gaulle, whose sense of humor did not include being made the butt of a false joke.

To make things worse, Prime Minister Churchill, who admired de Gaulle and knew that he himself would be as stiff-necked as de Gaulle were Britain to be in the same circumstances, could not resist his own bit of fun. Churchill was famous for his sometimes savage, Swiftian humor. When reporters clustered around him on his way from his car to a meeting room and asked him if he had heard that de Gaulle thought he was Joan of Arc, Churchill let his spectacles slip down to the tip of his nose, peered over them, and said: "Yes, I know. Trouble is, my bloody bishops won't let me burn him." Reporters howled with laughter, as Churchill winked at them and cautioned, "That is not for publication, gentlemen, it will not be cleared by censors."

The Roosevelt–de Gaulle exchange has since been authenticated by de Gaulle himself and in the memoirs of those present. Robert Sherwood brought the story back to the OWI from Casablanca. I have never come across any proof of the alleged Churchill sally about burning de Gaulle. It may well be apocryphal. But it became real when it was repeated frequently and got back to de Gaulle. De Gaulle told me some years later that it did not anger him as Roosevelt had. De Gaulle admired Churchill and the British people, and Churchill had supported and supplied the Free France movement when it needed help most. FDR had originated the "Joan of Arc complex" story, was trying to promote Giraud as the leader of France, and it was FDR that he would not forgive.

If the Casablanca Conference caused us problems at the Voice, it also brought us a major victory in the war of words. Goebbels himself came to the microphones of Radio Berlin to denounce the Allies and their new policy of unconditional surrender. "The word surrender," he thundered, "does not exist in the German vocabulary." He went on to rant and rave, day after day, about the "Jew President, Rosenfeld," and his British "butler," Churchill. We were delighted and went around congratulating each other. There is no bigger victory in a war of words than to force your opponent to waste his air time denying and therefore circulating your charges.

Only a week after the Anglo-American final communiqué at Casablanca and its vow of fighting on until the unconditional surrender of the enemy, the most exciting news broke on February 2, 1943. The Soviets had launched a counteroffensive at Stalingrad against the bloodied and exhausted German troops. Field Marshal von Paulus had surrendered his once-proud Sixth Army. Along with the marshal, twenty-four generals were taken prisoner. German losses in the Battle of Stalingrad totaled three hundred thousand, including ninety thousand prisoners on the day of capitulation.

If the final German defeat seemed certain, the power of German arms had by no means been eliminated. General von Manstein launched a new offensive, after Stalingrad, and recaptured Kharkov. German submarines were taking a terrible toll of Allied shipping on the Atlantic. Churchill, in Commons, admitted to heavy losses, but was cheered by the members when he stated that Allied shipbuilding had exceeded losses by more than a million tons. In the Pacific, American soldiers and marines, suffering severe losses, were winning back the islands that Japan had taken the year before. The Japanese were well dug in and it took constant naval and aerial bombardment before our assault infantry could root them out in hand-to-hand fighting. The war was not over, not nearly.

For me it was about to begin in earnest. I opened my morning mail and read the first word in an official document: "Greetings." It was the traditional salutation in a draft notice. I was being called up for military service. In the draft lottery, I had drawn a high number and was due for relatively early induction into the army. It seemed to me to be most appropriate that I be called to the colors early, since I had been among the first young men to favor American participation in the war against Hitler. I had written articles, done broadcasts, participated in demonstrations calling for action. Now it was my time for action.

I went around the OWI office, and made my good-byes, collected my good wishes. The war of words was over for me. The real war was about to start.

So I thought.

CHAPTER 4

SERIAL NUMBER 32904876

Of all the tests and examinations I had to pass in my career, the easiest was the physical examination for induction into the army. It was almost impossible to fail if you were standing up and breathing. Millions of men would be needed for the invasion of Europe and the final assault on the islands of Japan. Doctors were instructed not to look too closely at anyone who did not bring in a medical certificate claiming exemption. They would herd inductees into a large, empty room, line them up, and say: "Drop your pants and your shorts, open your mouth, stick out your tongue." Then they would go down the line, put a stethoscope on a man's chest, take a quick eye-check for venereal disease, tap him on the shoulder, and say, "Okay, you're in."

The army in those emergency days turned out soldiers like a butcher putting beef into a grinder and turning it into hamburger. No individual cuts, just a big, collective hash. There was no attempt by the Selective Service System to distinguish among men of differing skills or levels of literacy. There was no time for fine-tuning of the military system, at least in the early days of induction. Linguists became cooks, chemists were assigned to the laundry, accountants to the motor pool. All was chaos, all was geared to destroy every element of personal independence, of individual thought, all the values of democracy. The army was definitely not a democratic state and felt it could not be. To survive in combat, men would have to become part of a team, reacting more by instinct drilled into them than by rational thought. At least, that was the theory in World War II.

The theory was faulty but it worked then. I saw the remarkable transformation of citizens into soldiers capable of holding their own against the most professional and experienced fighting men of the enemy. Almost overnight, America converted bookkeepers, clerks, machinists, salesmen, teachers, and short-order cooks into a formidable fighting force. The process was a painful one, the methods used, antiquated and of dubious psychological validity. But, under pressure of necessity, it worked. It was the miracle of democracy, a loose, often chaotic system, defying its critics by its success.

I am frankly not sure just what the best system is for the 1980s, but I suspect it would be more equitable, much more fair, safer, and cheaper to turn to universal military training than to stick with the all-volunteer force. Of only one thing am I sure, the American people will not accept either universal training or a draft unless they are convinced that it is fair to all income levels and social groups. They may go along with a volunteer force that is essentially composed of the lowest levels of society, just so long as it is voluntary, but if a draft is going to hit their own families, it will have to be fair and not loaded with exemptions or special privileges for the wealthy and educated.

There were few special privileges for anyone when I was drafted in 1943. There are, of course, always some clever manipulators, people of power and connections or cunning who can beat the system, but, by and large, the draft spread its net wide over the country and pulled in the able-bodied men from every level of society. And if mistakes were made at first, assigning expert accountants to motor pools, and sending German specialists to Guadalcanal, most of the mess would gradually be straightened out and maximum use of our manpower was achieved in the forties.

I did not think so in the first few days, when I lost my name, identity, and freedom of action to become a serial number—32904876—at Fort Dix, New Jersey, where the mosquitoes flew in dive-bomber formations and where the sergeants in charge of the recruits would have been more comfortable in the German army than in the American. They hated all species of man—"spicks," "kikes," "wops," "micks," "niggers"—and one catch-all category that covered everyone: "assholes." It is part of the mystery and miracle of democracy that we were able to build a great armed force out of camps like Dix.

The procedure for breaking down all civilian attitudes of individuality began by issuing uniforms that did not fit. I was a ridiculous sight. I could not march around the parade ground without tripping over my pants and falling down every ten yards. I was the very model for the original Sad Sack. The drill sergeant could not stand the sight of me, which was an advantage, for he finally sent me back to the quartermaster, with a note instructing him to give me a uniform with at least an approximate fit.

I was an ideal victim of every ancient army trick. Highly motivated to be a superachiever, gung-ho for the war against Hitler and Tojo, I would jump to carry out every order and was ignorant of the army maxim "Keep your mouth shut, your bowels open, and never volunteer." On my third day at Fort Dix, at morning roll call, the top sergeant strolled over to the parade ground with a clipboard in his hand. He roared out: " 'Tenshun!" He looked at the clipboard, pretending to study it, and then looked up. "Any college grads here?" he asked in a respectful voice. I raised my hand along with three other men.

The "top" turned purple and the veins swelled in his neck as he bellowed: "You're not in some kind of goddamned schoolroom. You're in the army and you don't raise your hands. You step forward, smartly, and come to attention." We proceeded to do so. With a grin of pure malice the sergeant then said: "Okay, college boys, shithouse duty this morning."

We were marched off by a corporal to the communal, evil-smelling toilets, handed pails, mops, and caustic liquid that made our eyes smart. For the next three hours we labored at cleaning up, getting ourselves filthy in the process. When the corporal came back to inspect our work, he said: "You did a good job on the shithouse, men, but you assholes sure stink. To the showers, on the double, one-two, one-two." I never slept so well as I did that night.

The next day, the top sergeant came back to roll call with his clipboard. I had no intention of being trapped again, so when he asked, with studied civility, whether any of us could speak Spanish,

I did not step forward. No matter, there was no escaping him. He pointed a finger right at me and shouted: "You, college boy, shithouse specialist! Front and center!"

I stepped out of the ranks at his order, took a snappy left turn to the center, then a crisp right turn to face him. He had his hands on his hips. "Not bad for a college boy. A real drillmaster, ain't you?" I said nothing but stood ramrod stiff. He put his nose to mine and roared: "Answer, when addressed!"

"No," I replied.

The sergeant bunched up his fists. "What the hell do you mean, 'No'?"

"I mean, no, I'm not a drillmaster."

"Wiseguy, eh? Buddy, you are up shit creek without a paddle. Report in to Cookie. He's got a job for you."

I went into the mess hall, where a giant from Alabama, a three-hundred-pounder, had my name on a list. "Y'all that smart feller from New Yawk, huh? Now, boy, just shuffle after me, got sumpin' y'all can do, seein's how yuh so smart."

It was a hot Jersey day, muggy, without air, but I was unprepared for the scene out of hell that Cookie pushed me into. He told me to stand in front of the open end of a huge missile, a doughnut machine. A blast of hot air from inside the machine almost made me faint. I looked in and saw that there were two metal trenches that ran around the inside of the missile. They were filled with hot oil that was being circulated around the machine. Cookie told me to look at two barrels, on either side of me, one filled with sugar, one filled with cinnamon. "Now, listen heah, boy. In one minute they gonna be poppin' rings of dough into them oil runnels. That dough gonna get a golden brown after one turn. When they reach this open nose in front of you, they gonna flip out and y'all are gonna catch them and roll 'em, one by one, first in the sugar, then in the cinnamon. Then stack 'em in those empty trays behind the barrels. Now, tell me this, college boy, did they learn yuh how to do that?" A deep rumbling sound, like the first warnings of an earthquake, began to resound. I realized it was Cookie laughing from his gut, which was round and deep as the barrels of sugar and cinnamon. He walked away, still laughing, while I stood there in dismay.

My trials began at once. The rings of dough were bouncing around in the hot oil inside the machine. Just as Cookie had told me, one came out, not flipping but sliding down an incline, and I had to grab it. I screamed with pain. Cookie had "forgotten" to give me the special gloves of the doughnut maker. "Ole" Billy-Joe was getting his revenge on me. I gritted my teeth and resolved not to quit or show pain. The doughnuts kept sliding out and I kept catching them and rolling them in sugar and cinnamon. I was thankful there was no chocolate sauce that day. I had to take my uniform jacket off and work in my undershirt which was already as wet through as though I had been swimming. Soon my hairy arms were covered from my wrists to my elbows in a sticky caramel-like syrup, while my fingers were burning and I was sure that the flesh was peeling off.

An hour later, the massive mess sergeant lumbered in, holding out his hamlike hands, dangling a pair of gloves in front of me. "Hey, perfesser, y'all done fergit yoah gloves."

As he stood there, roaring with laughter, I took a freshly rolled doughnut, red-hot, and shoved it down his gullet. "Hey, Sarge, taste this one and tell me if I'm making them right."

His face turned scarlet, as he tried to pull it out and scream at the same time. A baker grabbed me and pushed me toward the door. "Run for your life, you crazy bastard."

I ran as I had never run before. The three-hundred-pound red-neck did not have a chance to catch me. I did not stop running until I got to the commandant's office in the headquarters building. The desk sergeant stared in amazement at a half-naked, crazed soldier covered in caramel.

"What in hell . . . ?"

"Sir, I, I, I. . . ."

The next thing I saw was the face of a doctor. He said: "You okay, soldier?" I was on a cot in the base hospital, my two hands heavily bandaged, a cold cloth on my forehead.

"I guess so, Doc. My hands kind of hurt, though."

"They should. You've got a pretty bad burn. But they'll heal. Listen, the military police tell me you assaulted Cookie. How in the hell did a little runt like you assault old Man Mountain Toliver?"

"Assault him? Why, Doc, all I did was give him a doughnut."

The captain began to laugh. "Yeah, I heard the story. But soldier, you came close to being killed. If he had gotten his hands on you . . ."

I chuckled. "You should have seen that bastard's face when I shoved that red-hot doughnut down his gullet."

In my hospital bed I had a chance to listen to the radio and to try to catch up on all the developments in which I had been so completely engrossed at the OWI. When I had left the office, our Navy had just scored an impressive victory in the Pacific, destroying an entire Japanese convoy of twenty ships in the Battle of the Bismarck Sea.

We were still engaged in slow, costly liberations of islands earlier captured by the enemy. In a bloody battle we had retaken Guadalcanal in the Solomon Islands, in February 1943. In Africa the British were hitting Rommel hard, forcing him all the way back along the North African littoral, from his penetration into Egypt toward Tunisia, where Eisenhower's American forces could start hitting him. Rommel was trapped in an Anglo-American pincers and was being squeezed and hammered front and rear.

There was disturbing news on the home front. A black market had sprung up on gasoline. Shoes were rationed and Americans began to grumble. We are a self-indulgent people and do not take well to austerity, particularly after the lean years of the Depression. Black citizens were starting to mutter about a "white man's war, let 'em fight it." All the propaganda talk about the "Four Freedoms" and the fight against fascism meant little to blacks suffering from racism and discrimination in the "world's greatest democracy," a phrase that was a mockery to them.

Black leaders were furious about continued discrimination against Negro soldiers in the U.S. Army. The army of democracy practiced discrimination in its ranks, segregating Negro from white troops, using black Americans as cooks, servants, truck drivers. They did not grant them the equality of using them in combat units, as though blacks could not be trusted with a gun. Trouble was heating up in America's black ghettos, and not only in the South. Americans were about to discover that racism was not limited geographically in America.

Race riots would break out in Los Angeles on June 4, in Detroit on June 20, and on August 1, the worst of all, in New York's ghetto of Harlem, where I had been born and raised. The news was sickening in the midst of a war against the worst racist of all, Hitler.

I could not read the papers because of my bandaged hands and I soon discovered that radio, exciting and immediate though it was, could not match the press, particularly *The New York Times,* my secular bible, for depth of coverage. Radio merely gave headlines that stimulated the appetite for more information that could only be obtained in the papers.

Father O'Reilly, the chaplain, came to tell me he had exacted promises from the sergeants to lay off me. He was a devoted *New York Times* addict. He came in every morning, bringing his *Times* with him, and we spent an hour talking of American and world events. It was good to talk with an intelligent man and be free, even briefly, from the moronic and sadistic noncommissioned officers who were "breaking in" the recruits by breaking their backs and their minds.

The doctor finally removed my bandages and I could get a look at my hands. There were raw red patches where the blisters had broken and the skin had not yet grown back. They were tender and sore. "There's no infection. Your hands are fine. You've got to keep them clean and they'll toughen up again." He handed me a pair of white cotton gloves. "Keep these on to keep your hands clean. Rinse them in lukewarm water. Sleep with the cotton gloves on. You should be all right in about two weeks, but you can leave the hospital this afternoon."

I became a changed man, with a healthy attitude, determined to avoid confrontation with my tormentors. If they were as stupid as I thought, I decided that I could outwit them without provoking them. As it turned out, I did not get a chance to try my new strategy on my red-neck "superiors."

A messenger from headquarters came to my tent one morning and told me to report at once to the commanding officer. I reported in to the C.O., in a neatly pressed, clean uniform, my field cap tucked into my belt, in regulation style, threw him a snappy salute, and came to faultless attention three paces in front of his desk.

He looked at me and said: "Somebody important wants you urgently. These are travel orders in one envelope, and sealed, secret orders in another. In the first envelope, with your tickets, are instructions. You are not to break open the sealed envelope until you hand it over to a military police officer at the end of your journey. One of the jeeps will take you to the Newark station. Your train leaves at 1400. Pack your gear and be ready to be picked up at 1200. Good luck, soldier."

He handed over the envelopes. I saluted, did an about-face, and walked out of his office on eager legs. I did not have the slightest notion what this was all about but the thought that I was leaving Fort Dix lifted my spirits so that I wanted to sing and dance.

I did not have the faintest notion where I was going, or why, or who had sent through the orders. But I got on the train at Newark joyfully. The train arrived at Baltimore and I proceeded to the stationmaster's office, according to instructions in the envelope. There, a lieutenant of the military police met me, and tore open the sealed envelope.

He looked at me a bit strangely after reading the secret orders. "So, you're one of those Ritchie nuts, are you? Well, come with me."

CHAPTER 5

THE RITCHIE NUTS

I followed the lieutenant to a truck and he told me to hop in the back. He explained nothing. The truck moved off, made its way through Baltimore, then to the countryside, and slowly began to climb up mountain roads. I sat there pondering. I was a "Ritchie nut," it appeared. I wondered just what kind of a nut a Ritchie nut was.

The truck braked to a stop. The lieutenant came around to the back, dropped the flap. "All right, soldier, jump out."

I jumped onto a dirt road. The air was cool and sweet. To my left, the road curved through a forest of oak and birch, and higher up, pines. To the right, the same landscape, except for a big sign, protruding from a wooden house: "The Fox Hole." I could see soldiers loitering and chatting with girls. Without the uniforms, it might have been a summer vacation resort. I would learn later that we were in the Blue Ridge Mountains.

I walked around the truck and saw the entrance to the camp, a guard post, a barrier, and an ironwork gate with the words "Camp Ritchie." Now, at least, I knew what a Ritchie was. Very soon, I would discover what kind of nuts it contained.

We walked through the gate after our papers were inspected, and the lieutenant led me past a row of barracks to a central open square dominated by a three-story brick building, which housed the commandant and his headquarters staff. I ran up the steps swiftly, eager to find out what kind of a place it was and what my assignment would be.

The desk sergeant, to my surprise, was a human being not a gorilla. He greeted me warmly. "Welcome to Ritchie. Glad to have you aboard." I grinned, thanked him, and asked him what ship I would be on. He laughed and I felt good. Someone in the army had a sense of humor.

"You're in barracks B. When you leave here, turn right, cross the plaza, go straight ahead to a row of barracks. B is the second on your left. Someone will show you your bunk. Take your gear and stow it. You'll be told what to do next."

I thanked him again and then asked: "Sergeant, could you be kind enough to tell me where I am and what kind of camp this is?"

He looked up from his papers with surprise. "Haven't you been told anything?"

"No, I was given orders at Dix to go to Baltimore and an officer escorted me here."

"Oh. Well, it is supposed to be a secret camp, but frankly, there's nothing so really secret going on that you could not have been told. Camp Ritchie is an officer-training camp for G-2, the intelligence branch of the army. It's a special project, somewhat different from the normal G-2 of a regular army company. You'll be told all about it at a briefing session for newcomers at five this afternoon. Directions are posted on the bulletin board in your barracks."

I picked up my B-bag, the canvas bag with clothing for immediate use. A bag with winter uniforms and other gear would be delivered later. I slung the B-bag over my shoulder and headed toward my new "home." At least it was a building, a long narrow rectangle of wood and cement, not a leaky tent like the one I had been living in at Dix.

I saw the big red letter B that I was looking for and mounted three steps, threw open a screen door, and stepped in. Something long and white jumped at me over my head. I almost let out a scream as I fell back in self-defense. The creature reversed itself and went into another long, high leap. My eyes focused and I saw it was a man, naked except for the briefest white loin covering. He was lean and lithe and an incredible athlete. In three giant leaps, reaching a height of at least six feet, he covered the entire length of the barracks. As I watched open-mouthed, he landed and then stuck one foot backward, at right angles to his body, with one arm extended forward and another backward, in a perfect arabesque.

A voice called out: "Come on in. And close your mouth, there're a lot of flies around here."

A soldier, in an undershirt and shorts, resting on his bunk, waved me in and over to him. "That, sir," he said, pointing to the figure holding its arabesque pose, "is Georges Skibine, *premier danseur des Ballets russes de Monte-Carle.*"

I gaped at him. His French accent was pure Parisian. Skibine was a famous dancer. I was beginning to get an idea what kind of a nut a Ritchie nut was. As for me, I was delighted. I had gone from Billy-Joe and the Man Mountain to a ballet dancer and a bunkmate who spoke beautiful French.

I dropped my bag and walked over to the bunk of the man who had addressed me. I held out my hand. "Schoenbrun, David Schoenbrun."

"Friezell, Bernard Friezell, *mon vieux.* Are you Schoenbrun like the Hapsburg Palace in Vienna? With or without an umlaut?"

I could have cried with joy. He spoke French, and German, was familiar with Vienna, and was witty. What kind of a paradise had I stumbled on?

We shook hands and Friezell, with whom I would share many adventures in the years ahead, said, "I only just got here yesterday but I know enough to fill you in. This is a military intelligence camp of a special kind. It is organized by language groups and this barracks is one of two French barracks. That means that every man assigned to them is fluent in French.

"We are going to get some kind of training to get us ready for fighting in France. I don't know just what. I have heard rumors that we are going to be parachuted into France to make contact with the underground Resistance groups and maintain liaison between the Resistance and Allied headquarters in Algiers. We'll know more after a briefing this afternoon."

At the afternoon briefing session a lieutenant gave us word of what we were going to do.

"Gentlemen," he began, to my astonishment. I had not been

called a gentleman since I had become 32904876. Things were looking up at Ritchie, a most unorthodox army camp.

"Gentlemen, you are all divided into language groups. You will speak to each other in the language you are assigned to when you are on duty, and it is recommended that you speak in your particular language at all times, even in off-hours at the barracks or the camp PX. Some of you may be sent to France before the army invades. In any case you'll be among the first Americans into France or Italy or wherever you are assigned. You are already fluent in your language. We want you to be more than fluent, we want at least some of you to be able to pass yourselves off as natives of the country you're in."

He continued. "You will go to classes every morning and to military and other specialized exercises every afternoon. Your teachers will tell you on the opening day what the course is about and what you have to learn. You are all presumably well educated men. I don't have to give you every detail now."

Monday was reality day, the start of classes. The same expectant thrill that had always sent me to class early in college moved me at Ritchie. The first class was "Identification." The instructor told us that we would have to learn this so thoroughly that it would become "part of your being." "This" included all of the ranks and unit badges of all our enemy and Allied troops.

"Your life may one day depend on knowing whether the man who stopped you to check your papers is a *Leutnant* or an *Oberleutnant,* or a *Hauptmann.* You must learn the difference in the *galons* of a French lieutenant colonel and a colonel, each of whom wears on his epaulets a different number of alternating gold and silver stripes." From individual and unit identifications, we would then move on to weapons and airplane identifications. It would be no easy task to recognize and memorize the complicated list of identifications. The task was made a bit easier when, at the end of class, he distributed a brochure with color-plate examples of the items we would have to learn.

This was followed by a class in map-reading and map-making, the proper use of a compass, and the plotting of azimuths. Once again we were told that this was no ordinary classroom but that our lives would depend on how well we learned to make our way in hostile territory. "I am not going to give you grades. If you pass these courses you will be given the bars of a lieutenant. Your final marks will come on the battlefield and, if you have not really learned your lessons, the final mark may well be final."

In the afternoon, after a short lunch break, we had a class in the handling of prisoners. The young instructor was a fine-featured man, his nose and lips a bit too sharp, but his jaw strong and his manner confident and authoritative without strain. He told us how to order a prisoner to stand a few paces from a wall or car or tree, spread his legs wide, and then fall forward so that he was barely balanced on his fingers. Today every child of ten who watches television is familiar with this technique, but it was new in 1943.

"If you balance him properly, you can search him without his being able to attack you. But be careful to stand between his out-spread legs, for a man is most vulnerable in that position. If he makes the slightest movement, you can bring your knee up sharply to his crotch, and, I promise you, he will not be in a condition to do you any harm."

The lieutenant's accent was New York, not the New York of the streets, but the patrician New York of town houses. He did not sound like Roosevelt but he had the same tone and air of a kind of American aristocracy. I was not surprised when I asked a man sitting next to me what the lieutenant's name was and he answered: "Oh, that's David Rockefeller." Camp Ritchie was truly a treasure house of extraordinary men, from ballet dancers to bankers.

In addition to classes, we were given field exercises, weapons and combat training, not the combat training of regular troops but of special forces. That included hand-to-hand fighting, karate, and ways to kill silently with knives and fingers. We had all lost most of our civilian bloat and felt fit until we met our instructors. They were all made of granite and steel. They were not muscle men, not weight lifters with bulging biceps and pectorals. They were lean and moved so swiftly that our eyes could hardly follow their twists and turns.

They told us that two stiff fingers jabbed under the rib cage could stop a man's heart. They demonstrated and had us practice on dummies. They showed us where the carotid artery was located in the neck and how to press it quickly to make an enemy unconscious. We were told that the bridge of the nose was one of the most vulnerable parts of the body. One of the instructors told us with a straight face that "The nose is the body's Achilles heel." One of the most effective means of self-defense when attacked was to insert your fingers into the aggressor's nostrils as deeply as you could and then "Rip his nose apart."

They paired us off for rough-and-tumble sessions after they had demonstrated the right moves. One of their favorite means of attack was to turn the body at right angles to the opponent, to protect the genitals, then to bring the edge of the shoe with full force down the shin of the adversary, and grind it into the arch of his foot. They demonstrated on a few of us and the trainees would yelp with pain at the very lightest scrape of the instructor's heavy boot.

I worked hard at the lessons, thinking that if I never got into hand-to-hand combat the lessons might help me later in the streets of New York. When I mentioned this to one of the instructors he laughed at me. "Don't be a jerk. If muggers grab you and ask for your money, give it to them. They carry knives, razors, guns, and are a lot tougher and more experienced fighters than you. Use these lessons only if you absolutely have to, if someone is trying to kill you."

Weapons training was a serious affair. Other exercises at Ritchie turned out to be hilarious and, one night, almost as deadly as war itself. It was an exercise designed to teach us how to make contact with Allied units in enemy territory. Had I known that I would find myself in that kind of combat I might have paid more attention.

We were given maps with the topographical features of the Blue Ridge area around the camp. However, instead of using the names of the villages and roads, the maps had French names on them so that we could not find our way by reading road signs. They wanted us to learn to use coordinates and radio transmitters to locate our rendezvous point.

The instructors divided up our French-language contingent into two groups. One was to play the role of a French Resistance band hiding in the forest. The other was to be an American intelligence team whose assignment was to make contact with the Resistance unit. While we "Frenchmen" were being briefed, the instructors were also briefing the men in the German-language barracks. They would form a German patrol trying to locate and capture underground fighters.

To make the entire exercise more realistic we were issued combat uniforms. The "Resistance" team was given civilian clothing and berets. The Germans were issued German Army uniforms. Each group was told to report to an instructor at 10:00 P.M., faces blackened with burnt cork. We had our maps and coordinates, short-range radio transmitters and receivers. We were then put into trucks whose flaps were fastened down tightly so that we could not see out of them. The entire truck was blacked out and we were not permitted to use our flashlights and matches to read a compass. We would have no idea where we were going.

I was in the American team whose mission it was to find our French allies. I sat in the dark for what was an hour of twisting and turning. We could at least read the radium dials on our watches. Then, the truck stopped and we were told to hop out. The truck then took off and four of us were left in the blackness of a mountain forest at night.

We had handguns and M-1s, all loaded with blanks. Rubber knives coated with chalk were stuck into our boots. If there were hand-to-hand combat with the German patrol, the instructors would be able to judge by the chalk marks where we had hit. We would also be judged by the time it took us to make contact. Trucks were hidden around the area to be used as "prisons" if we captured anyone or were ourselves captured. It was a well-planned war game, very close to what we would be experiencing when our armies invaded France, or if we were parachuted into France to join the Resistance.

Johnny Gates was the radio man. I was the map reader and direction finder. Two other men were "point men," acting as scouts ahead of us to make sure the way was clear. Johnny picked up a Morse signal, very faint. We moved off the road and into the forest, following a dirt path. The signal grew stronger. One of the scouts came back and said that there was an open field and a farmhouse. He had not spotted any signs of Germans. We moved into the field and fell to the ground, propelling ourselves forward on elbows and knees. I checked my map to see if any of the features we were looking at corresponded to the map. They seemed to. If I was correct in my reading, we had to cross the field, enter the woods behind, and then move to our right, north by northeast, where there should be a brook to cross.

Suddenly we heard a cough and we froze. Then a deep grunt and some noise of movement in the grass about fifty yards ahead of us. One of our scouts came gliding back, giving a good imitation of a snake. "My God, men," he whispered, "it's a giant bull. We have stumbled into a bullpen, I think."

We did not dare move a muscle. City boys were not at home in a forest and certainly did not know how to cope with bulls. We heard a dull pounding of hooves off to the left. The bull was moving away from us. Suddenly shots rang out and men were shouting. It was the German patrol. The bull was after them.

We got up to run to the woods ahead of us. The farmer came rushing out with a shotgun and a flashlight. He saw our running figures silhouetted against the light and he opened fire. His shotgun did not have blanks in it. The pellets whistled over our heads and we literally ran for our lives. The farmer thought we were either vandals or thieves. Fortunately, he was a good man and he fired deliberately over our heads to chase us off. We did not know that, of course, and believed he was shooting at us.

We panicked and dropped our gear, the radio, the maps, everything but our guns. We knew that if we threw down our guns the punishment would be severe back in camp. We made the cover of the forest. But by then, shaken up and without maps or radio, we did not have the faintest chance of making contact with the Resistance group. Worse than that, we were thoroughly lost at midnight somewhere in the Blue Ridge Mountains.

We wandered around for another hour before stumbling on one of the instructor's trucks waiting for prisoners. We were only too happy to surrender. We got back to camp in disgrace and fell into our bunks exhausted at about three o'clock.

On following nights the exercises went somewhat better, and camp authorities learned that it was a good idea to warn farmers that we were going to prowl around in their fields. And all men were warned to look or listen for bulls before entering a pasture. I always had a lingering suspicion that the farmer had been tipped off to the war game and rushed out to frighten any clumsy soldiers.

A few days later, I was on the firing range when I received a message to report to headquarters. When I got there, I saw Bernie Friezell sitting on a bench opposite the commandant's office. He asked me if I knew what this was about and I told him I did not. Some five minutes later, we were sent in; the commandant had a telegram in his hand. He looked up at us and said: "This is somewhat unusual."

We looked back at him questioningly, waiting for him to continue.

"This telegram," he said, waving it in the air, "asks me to transfer Schoenbrun and Friezell immediately, Priority 3-A, to headquarters in Algiers. It is signed Eisenhower. You men know General Eisenhower?"

We were astonished. I finally found my voice. "No, sir, we don't know the Supreme Commander. But I can make a guess about that message." I told him about Eisenhower's original request to OWI about sending a French political intelligence team over as soon as possible. My former teammates at OWI had undoubtedly arrived and were now ready to bring me over. I doubted very much that Eisenhower had time to worry about such details but that they had persuaded his aide to send the telegram in his name to give it more weight.

Then Bernie said: "Sir, we are only three weeks away from completing our training and getting our lieutenant's commission. Can we finish it up?"

The commandant shook his head. "When General Eisenhower asks me to act immediately, that means yesterday. Sorry men, but as of right now you are restricted to quarters on twenty-four-hour alert. Your meals will be brought to you. I'm going to check out air transport and move you out as fast as I can."

We protested. "But that's not fair. We are still at the very bottom as buck privates. How can we do our job without rank?"

"That's not my problem, that's your problem." He paused and thought a moment. "I've got a flexible T.O.* here at headquarters. Tell you what, I'll promote you today and give you corporal stripes."

We both groaned. "Corporal!"

The commandant laughed. "That's right, same rank as Napoleon."

I muttered, "And Hitler."

He laughed more loudly. "Right! Just think how far you fellows

* T.O. stands for Table of Organization and lists the ranks available to the commanding officer for his men.

can go." Then he got up from behind his desk and came over to shake our hands. Commandants at Ritchie were more like genial schoolmasters than army officers.

"Good luck, men, and give my best to Ike. He's a great man."

We staggered out of his office and went to see the top sergeant. He called the commandant, verified our story, and handed us corporal stripes. "Sew them on tonight, corporals, and congratulations."

We mumbled our thanks and made our way to barracks, torn by conflicting emotions. We were thrilled to be called to Algiers but unhappy about our training course being cut off right at the end. I was thinking about Dorothy. How was I going to tell her or see her if we were being restricted to barracks?

Well, before going to barracks, I could get to a phone and break the news. She took it well, knowing that it was coming soon anyway. But she said that she was leaving at once for Ritchie, counting on me to find a way to see her, or perhaps persuade the commandant to let her come to say good-bye in the barracks. I warned her at once not to mention anything to anyone. The army had strict rules against any public revelation of troop movements. And although Bernie and I were not a troop, we were under military command and a flight overseas was secret information. Dorothy promised to be quiet but said she was coming to Ritchie anyway, hoping somehow to see me.

A fellow soldier told me what to do. "If you want to take the risk, David, go to the far eastern corner of the campgrounds. Some of us cut a big chunk out of the chain fence. You can wiggle through and meet Dorothy at the Fox Hole."

"Suppose I'm called for transport out of here while I'm at the Fox Hole?"

"Bernie can tell them where you are."

"Yeah, but won't I catch hell for busting out of camp under restrictions?"

"Yes, you'll catch hell. Technically speaking, a soldier under restriction for travel to a war zone who does not show up is guilty of desertion in time of war. You can be shot."

"My God, you're kidding."

"No, I'm not. That is the regulation. But there isn't a chance that this commandant will do much. After all, you're not really going over the hill. You told Bernie where you'll be. You can be ready to leave at once. All they'll do is bust you back to private, take your stripes away, and put a strong reprimand on your service record."

I thought it over. I desperately wanted to see my love and say good-bye. I did not know when, if ever, we would see each other again. I decided to take the risk. I asked a friend to go out to the Fox Hole and use a pay phone to call Dorothy and tell her to go directly to the Fox Hole.

That night, under cover of darkness, with the camp area deserted, I made my way to the hole in the fence and wriggled through. Dorothy was waiting in the Fox Hole, her eyes red but a big smile lighting up her face when she saw me come through the door. We went upstairs for privacy and tender farewells until the first light of predawn. Then we embraced a last time and I made my way back to barracks B, my heart heavy and beating rapidly. No one spotted me and I got into the barracks safely. I was relieved to see Bernie asleep in the lower bunk. They had not come for us during the night.

We sat in barracks for four of the longest days of our lives, playing chess and speculating about Algiers and the work to be done there. Finally the call came. A truck drove us to the airport in Baltimore, the first short lap on a long journey to Africa and General Eisenhower's headquarters.

CHAPTER 6

WITH EISENHOWER IN ALGIERS

We flew from Baltimore to Presque Isle, Maine, the army's jumping-off point for flights to Europe. Our first stop was Prestwick, Scotland, after an uneventful flight. At Prestwick we changed to a new, sinister plane with all its windows painted black. We would be flying to Marrakesh, Morocco, on a route that paralleled the French coast and was patrolled by German fighter planes. We could show no lights.

We bumped our way south toward Morocco, the pilot flying into every cloud he could find for cover against German patrols. As a result, our plane tossed quite a lot and we were happy to hear the announcement that we were coming in for a landing. We had flown late at night for additional protection and came down as dawn was breaking over Marrakesh. As we stepped out of the plane, we could see the dazzling African morning sky, lime green and pink. It was summer and would get blazingly hot, but at dawn the air was cool, fresh, and scented with the sweet blossoms of orange and lemon trees. A heavier, cloying scent was unfamiliar to me. I would discover it was a strange combination of orange blossom and dung.

We were met by military police who directed us to a transient camp to await new passage to Algiers. We had been flying quadrimotor planes across the Atlantic, but inside Africa there were two-engine planes, Dakotas, DC-3's, the "pack mule of the Air Force." They would take us over the Atlas mountains to the Mediterranean and then eastward over Oran, Algeria, and then down into Algiers. *Alger la blanche,* the French called it, white stucco villas in green hills, overlooking the white rooftops of the Casbah, the rabbit warren of Arab abodes, rising steeply from the harbor to the hills. Algiers was shaped like a bowl, the shops and ships at the bottom, the Casbah and the European residences rising up to the lips of the bowl. Everyone in Algiers had bulging calves.

We had been told to report to a building called the Maison Agricole on the Boulevard Baudin, at the bottom of the bowl, near the harbor. The OWI had changed its name in Algiers. It was known as the PWB, the Psychological Warfare Branch, a crazy-quilt patchwork of civilians, soldiers, English and American men and women, with local French secretarial and engineering personnel.

It was a wonderful moment when I walked into the newsroom. Mike Bessie was there, and his close friend William Royall Tyler, a Harvard instructor in fine arts, French-born, speaking an exquisite French. William Doerflinger, an editor with E. P. Dutton, was working over an ancient and cranky mimeograph machine which spit purple ink whenever he came near it. C. D. Jackson, of *Life* magazine, elegantly turned out in a Savile Row raw-silk suit, was chatting in the corner with crusty old Bill Byrd, a prewar reporter on the Paris *Trib,* an intimate of Hemingway and Scott Fitzgerald. Bill was one of America's most knowledgeable oenologists, and in his apartment behind the Chambre des Députés in Paris, then occupied by a German general, he had a fabulous wine cellar. They were a sophisticated, literate *confrerie* and I was overjoyed to be on the team.

They all made me warmly welcome and began filling me in on what they were doing. The most visible activity of the PWB was the daily preparation of a world-news file that would be distributed to the military command; the army proper; the army's newspaper, the *Stars and Stripes;* the Allied radio transmitter that sent out broadcasts to all troops and to the Nazi-occupied countries of Europe. It was the basic source of news for the entire Mediterranean theater, Morocco, Algeria, Tunisia, principally.

At first, my role was to familiarize myself with almost all aspects of PWB's work so that when I took over my assignments I would be able to function competently. I was somewhat dismayed to think that I would once again be back in the "war of words." But Mike Bessie assured me that propaganda analysis would by no means be my only role. I would be used in liaison with the French, also in broadcasts to France, and in political intelligence inside the Allied camp.

The political situation in Algiers was tense and bitter. The French were fighting among themselves, in a power struggle for leadership between General de Gaulle and General Henri Giraud, co-presidents of the CFLN, the French Committee of National Liberation, a situation that had a built-in conflict and would not endure. There was constant friction between the French and the Americans because the American consul general, Robert Murphy, who had become General Eisenhower's political advisor, was backing Giraud against de Gaulle. American interference with French affairs infuriated the proud French, bewildered the Resistance, and caused grudges that would carry over into the postwar world and still today have an underlying effect on French-American relations. One of my assignments would be to keep abreast of all those frictions and try to find ways to soften the blows.

One of the most immediate and urgent tasks was to bring myself up to date on the war over the two and a half months that I had been in Ritchie out of touch with the outside world. There had been many important developments over the summer of 1942.

By mid-May, the North African campaign had ended with a smashing Allied victory and the unconditional surrender of the German and Italian armies. Field Marshal Rommel had been thoroughly beaten. The Desert Fox flew to Europe, escaping capture, but his men did not. Almost three hundred thousand German and Italian prisoners had been taken, a huge loss for Hitler and Mussolini. Italy was being pounded by our planes and Mussolini had a very shaky grip on power. Il Duce was living his last days as a comic-opera figure.

Mussolini was summoned by Hitler to a meeting at Verona and warned that the Germans would move in if he could not stiffen his defenses. On July 25, Mussolini was forced by his generals to abdicate power and was immediately put under arrest. Marshal Badoglio, leader of the coup, took over the Italian government. He proclaimed that the war would continue. "Italy is faithful to its pledges." At the same time, secret messages were sent to the Allies, asking for terms of surrender. The Italians still hoped that they could salvage something out of their catastrophe. They hated Hitler, who had treated them with contempt. They suspected that the policy of unconditional surrender was addressed to Hitler rather than to Italy. They had made a shrewd guess and a number of *fascisti* would become "Allies."

A few days after I had arrived in Algiers, Marshal Badoglio surrendered unconditionally. General Eisenhower, adhering strictly to the principle proclaimed at the Casablanca Conference, would not give the Italians any terms and would not negotiate with them. However, Marshal Badoglio, playing a strong card, ordered Italian troops to cease all actions against the Allied forces, but to continue to fight against all other attacks. He knew that Hitler would order German troops to move into Italy and take it over. He wanted the Allies, after his surrender, to turn to him to fight the Germans with them.

Our troops landed in Naples on September 9 and, as expected, Hitler's forces occupied Rome, while Nazi paratroopers jumped on the Vatican and set up combat positions in Saint Peter's Square. Then, on the twelfth, in one of the most extraordinary individual coups of the war, Nazi paratrooper Otto Skorzeny jumped with a specially trained commando on the prison where Mussolini was being held at Gran Sasso, liberated him, and escaped to north Italy, which the Wehrmacht had just occupied in force. Marshal Badoglio, with Eisenhower's endorsement, formally declared war on Germany and called on Italians to fight faithfully at the side of the Allies. Never has a coat been turned so swiftly and deftly.

Having completed the war review, I turned to the files of PWB to bring myself up to date on what was happening in Algeria inside the French camp and in French-American relations. The winds of discord blew through the streets and alleyways of Algiers, and the Gaullists were angrily resentful of the Americans. On the highest levels there was almost daily friction between the Americans and General de Gaulle.

Robert Murphy, the American consul general in Algiers, had first appointed Admiral François Darlan high commissioner, although Darlan had collaborated closely with the Nazis and insisted that he was still the personal representative of Marshal Pétain. Then, after Darlan's assassination, General Henri Giraud had replaced him. Giraud had escaped from a German prison and made his way to Algiers with the help of General Eisenhower. He had never served Pétain or collaborated with the Germans. But he was an extreme reactionary and an egomaniac who made even General de Gaulle look modest.

The American press had attacked Giraud and criticized Murphy severely, particularly when Giraud set about installing a fascist-style regime in North Africa. Nazi decrees that had been forced on France were imposed on North Africa by Giraud and the pro-Vichy fascist officers he had maintained in power. Jews were made to wear the yellow star and were barred from practicing all professions. The American proconsul took no action against this Nazi outrage. Pro-Allied officers, who had turned against their Vichy-appointed superiors when the Allied invasion began, sabotaging coastal defenses, cutting cables and communications lines, to aid the Americans, were arrested by officers still loyal to Pétain and charged with treason. They were sent to concentration camps in the Sahara desert. The chief of intelligence for PWB, Ed Taylor, had gone to Murphy to protest the arrest of men whose crime was to help us. Murphy broke all records for sheer gall by telling Taylor that he could not interfere in French affairs.

President Roosevelt, embarrassed by the storm of press criticism, angered himself by evidence of fascist activities protected by American military force, issued a statement that events in Algeria were taking place under the pressure of war. He said that all political appointments and developments were only temporary and would be reviewed when security permitted. Murphy himself then began to put pressure on Giraud to correct the abuses of his regime. Pro-Allied officers were gradually released. The anti-Semitic decrees were lifted. But officers loyal to Vichy and Pétain remained in key positions and Giraud still controlled the levers of power until the summer of 1943.

In June, the CFLN had been constituted with Giraud and de Gaulle as co-presidents. A democrat loyal to the Allies, General Catroux, had replaced a fascist, Marcel Peyrouton, as governor-general of Algeria. Pro-Gaullists dominated the embryonic Cabinet posts in the CFLN. The only commissioner who was not a Gaullist was the man in charge of armaments, Jean Monnet. Monnet, however, was the most deeply democratic and pro-American of the whole CFLN. Although de Gaulle was only a co-president, he was able to dominate the National Committee. In any case, Giraud had no head or feel for politics and was easily outmaneuvered.

I set about learning everything and meeting everyone at French headquarters. Above all, I wanted to meet General de Gaulle. Ever since his call to resistance on June 18, 1940, and the creation of Free France, he had fascinated me. I had gone to French bookstores and to the library of the French consulate in New York and obtained his books. I was most impressed by *Vers l'armée de métier* (*Toward a Career Army*) and *Le fil de l'épée* (*The Edge of the Sword*), which provided insights into de Gaulle's character and mind, as well as his talent as a writer. His French was classical, very much in the style and cadences of Caesar's commentaries, colored by an occasional flair of romanticism that revealed passion beneath his austerity.

Vers l'armée de métier, a military treatise on a professional army, contains essays on the French and German people, with insights into their nature, and also revelations of the mind of the writer himself. There was a poet in de Gaulle who achieved in his writings the opposite of what Victor Hugo had once said of himself: "If I had not been a poet, I would have been a soldier." Charles de Gaulle was a soldier-poet.

De Gaulle knew the Germans well and had a love-hate relationship with them. He admired their efficiency, their musicians, and their poets; he despised their tendency to accept slave-master relationships, their base and coarse characteristics. Yet he could not help sighing: ". . . there are moments when each [French and German] dreams of the great things they could do together." He did not think, however, that it was possible for "Gauls and Teutons" to work together because "The way they think is so different that this keeps both peoples in a constant state of mistrust." De Gaulle then went on to describe the Frenchman and the German, with a kind of Olympian observation of strange breeds of men that interested him but were not his kin.

"This Frenchman," he wrote, "who takes so much pain to be orderly in his thinking and so little in his actions, this logician always torn by doubt, this careless hard worker, this imperial adventurer who loves nothing more than his hearth at home, the fervent admirer of alexandrine verse, tailcoats and royal gardens, who nonetheless sings popular songs, dresses sloppily and litters his own lawns . . . how can the German ever join, understand or repose his confidence in this unstable, uncertain, contradictory people?"

Surely no foreigner has ever written so biting a comment on the French character and its paradoxes. His rapier pen did not spare the Germans, either. His portrait of the Germans, etched in acid, could not conceal a grudging admiration for certain German qualities he wished the French possessed. He saw Germany as "an elemental force of nature, a matrix of powerful but confused instincts." But he slashed out at some of the more vulgar characteristics of Germans.

"These born artists without taste, these highly skilled technicians of a feudal society, these bellicose but loving fathers of families, whose dining rooms are designed as temples, whose toilets are Gothic palaces, who build their factories in forests, these oppressors who want to be loved, these servile warriors, these chivalrous knights who swill their beer until they vomit." Germany, wrote de Gaulle, "is a sublime but glaucous sea," filled with "monsters and treasures." It is a "multi-colored cathedral, whose transepts echo with the roars of barbarians and blind the eyes, the spirit, and the soul."

De Gaulle, I was to discover through the years, was himself a kind of sublime paradox, with the very contradictory nature that he ascribes to his fellow Frenchmen. He loved his country but not his countrymen. He was a nationalist with no illusions about his nation. He feared no foe, only his friends. He was a passionate iceberg, a hermit happy only in cheering crowds, a soldier who held militarists in contempt, a politician who refused to join a party or even let one join him. De Gaulle was a statesman who reigned over but did not serve a state, a dreamer who wished to be a man of action.

I was excited when I received my first appointment to call upon Charles André Joseph Marie de Gaulle. It was a surprise to see his modest villa, whereas General Giraud was sumptuously installed in a palace. De Gaulle made no protest over this rather petty attempt to diminish him. He carried his own stature, radiating a magnetism of leadership without need of the trappings. He paid no attention to his lowly rank as brigadier general, and refused to accept promotion which he was offered often, and could have given to himself when he was chief of state. In the manner of Stalin, Chiang, and Mao, he wore simple uniforms, unadorned with medals. Medals were for ordinary men, not for immortals.

He stood before me like a giraffe towering over a chipmunk. I am as short of the average as de Gaulle was above it. But he seemed not even to notice the difference and my discomfort. He shook my hand and led me over to a sofa in front of a coffee table. He was courtly in his polite welcome, showing none of the haughty aloofness that I had expected from his remarks in *The Edge of the Sword.* I came to understand his distinction between a public and a private posture. Not that he was warm or informal. He was still very much the chief, erect, unsmiling, but scrupulously correct.

De Gaulle began by telling me that his aides had informed him of my background. "You have taught French in New York," he said, "and you are a scholar of French literature. What is your favorite work?"

This was the last thing I expected to hear from him, but I was ready, hoping he would like my answer. "It is difficult to choose one favorite work in the richness of French literature, sir, but I greatly admire *Le Rouge et le Noir.*"

"Ah, yes, an excellent choice, Stendhal is one of our great writers. Have you read much of Chateaubriand? He is one of my favorites."

For about a half hour, de Gaulle talked literature, history, history as literature, and literature as history. I was frustrated. Before I had a chance to ask him the questions I had in mind, his aide came in, excused himself for the interruption and announced that a certain colonel had arrived.

General de Gaulle arose, ending our "conversation," which he had steered all the way. He gravely thanked me for coming and invited me to come by from time to time. "An American steeped in French culture! What a pleasant experience," he remarked, with just a hint of malice.

I left his office excited by his courteous welcome, impressed by his knowledge of French literature and history and his willingness to discuss it with me with no trace of condescension. Then, as I was walking down the hill I suddenly realized that he had completely manipulated me. It was a lesson I would not forget later when I entered upon my career as a journalist. Never let a chief of government or any other important person take charge of an interview.

They know how flattering it can be to treat a journalist as an honored guest, or an equal, how easy it is for them to trap one into answering instead of questioning them. I would take de Gaulle up on his offer to come by from time to time, but the next time I would be ready for him, and whatever question he asked me would be briefly answered and my own question asked before he had a chance once again to steer the conversation his way.

Back in the newsroom I began work on my current assignment. I wrote confidential background reports for PWB officials on the uncivil war between de Gaulle and Giraud, and between de Gaulle and Robert Murphy. I would check out the day-by-day incidents with PWB intelligence men and with French sources. The French had created an *Assemblée consultative,* a preparliamentary body to debate and vote upon a whole series of internal political, economic, and social measures affecting French citizens that were not properly in the domain of the American High Command or the State Department. This did not stop Murphy in Algiers or Secretary of State Cordell Hull and President Roosevelt in Washington from interfering whenever they pleased.

Most Americans never did understand or believe the highhanded, imperialistic behavior of our proconsuls in Algiers, Morocco, and Tunisia. They were thus shocked and angered when de Gaulle would publicly denounce "America's will to dominate." We saw ourselves as liberators, as fighters for freedom, which, indeed, in large measure, we were. But we were by no means as pure and dedicated to democracy as we would like to believe. Anyone with access to the official documents, or who lived through some of the stormier scenes in North Africa and later in French-American conflicts inside France, knew just how arbitrary, interfering, and dominating our officials could be. It is perfectly true that Charles de Gaulle had the unfortunate trait of always making the worst of a bad thing, but it is also true that if he was stiff-necked it was to some extent a result of so many kicks in the butt. Just a few samples from my files will illustrate his charge of American interference and "will to dominate."

On May 8, 1943, Roosevelt sent the following telegram to Churchill. "De Gaulle is, without question, taking his vicious propaganda staff down to Algiers to stir up strife between the various elements, including the Arabs and the Jews . . . He has the messianic complex . . . I am inclined to think that when we get to France itself we will have to regard it as a military occupation run by British and American generals . . . I do not know what to do with de Gaulle. Possibly you would like to make him Governor of Madagascar."

Churchill knew that that last line was simply Roosevelt's malicious sense of humor, but the rest of the telegram was not a joking matter. FDR really meant, and would later try, to occupy France as though it were an enemy country instead of an ally. De Gaulle never forgave him his hostile policies toward France which he resented more than FDR's personal slurs.

On June 1, Robert Murphy sent a telegram to Cordell Hull stating that he had talked with Anthony Eden and that the British foreign secretary was fed up with de Gaulle. Murphy claimed, incorrectly, that Churchill believed "De Gaulle is capable of a coup d'état" and that "Churchill has asked Murphy whether General Giraud was taking 'all necessary police measures.' " It was an incendiary message based on exaggerated interpretations of British complaints about de Gaulle. It is true that Eden and Churchill were often exasperated by de Gaulle. Churchill had said that "The cross I bear is the Cross of Lorraine." But Churchill never wavered for a moment in his support for de Gaulle as leader of Free France and never anticipated limiting in any way France's right to be a free ally and to choose her own leaders.

Churchill had no choice but to avoid any serious conflict with his more powerful partner, Roosevelt, but he would not follow Roosevelt's attempts to break de Gaulle. It was Churchill's view that the Anglo-Americans should try to "bend de Gaulle" but not to break him, for to break him would be to precipitate civil war in France and an unweldable breach in Allied relations. He did not share Roosevelt's view that France was a decadent nation. He also, from time to time, warned FDR that the alternative to de Gaulle might be the French Communist Party. That would give FDR pause to reconsider his acts.

As I observed these quarrels, my admiration and affection for Dwight D. Eisenhower grew. He was a man of tact, with an ability to get along with the most tempestuous characters. He told me a number of times that he understood de Gaulle's problems and actually liked the difficult French general. De Gaulle, too, despite his fierce fights with the Americans, never said an unkind word of Eisenhower. Like almost everyone, even de Gaulle "liked Ike."

Many years later, when both men were presidents, and I was

interviewing de Gaulle for the *Saturday Review,* I mentioned to him how fortunate a coincidence of history it was that two men who were wartime comrades and friends should now be presidents of their countries. De Gaulle sighed sadly and replied: "Yes, Eisenhower and I had affective feelings for each other. But, only men can have friends. Statesmen have only national interests."

De Gaulle was rationalizing his own temperament. He did not tolerate any close friendships. He failed to appreciate the importance of friendship even to a statesman. Friendship is a valuable ingredient in any alliance. Eisenhower understood this. Eisenhower was less educated, less brilliant than de Gaulle, but he had other qualities more valuable, above all, common sense. Education is, to be sure, a precious asset, but common sense, honesty, and integrity are more precious and Eisenhower had these fine qualities in good measure.

On June 17, 1943, in Telegram number 288, sent from the White House to London at 3:30 P.M., Roosevelt thundered: "I'm fed up with de Gaulle . . . there is no possibility of our working with de Gaulle . . . I am absolutely convinced that he has been and is now injuring our war effort and that he is a very dangerous threat to us. The time has arrived when we must break with him. It is an intolerable situation."

Churchill was appalled. He knew that de Gaulle had won the support of French officers in North Africa and even more so in the global French Empire, whose territories had all rallied to the standard of Free France. Churchill also knew, which FDR did not, that the underground resistance movements in France, with only insignificant exceptions, had also declared themselves in full support of General de Gaulle.

Churchill felt that it was imperative to have the utmost cooperation and coordination between the Allied High Command and the French Resistance when the moment came to open up a second front in France, which Stalin was demanding with ever increasing stridency. Any move to get rid of de Gaulle would provoke an outburst from the Resistance. If anything could damage the war effort, it would be FDR's foolish and dangerous threat to "get rid of de Gaulle."

Churchill's long reply to FDR was sent on June 18, 1943, File number 851.01/6/–43. As always, Churchill sought first to appear to be in agreement with FDR. If he had opposed him, FDR would have been more stubborn. So Churchill began by stating, "I agree with you that no confidence can be placed in de Gaulle's friendship for the Allies." That, of course, was very different from agreeing with FDR's charge that de Gaulle was a dangerous threat. The prime minister proposed that instructions be given to Murphy and Britain's consul in Algiers, Harold Macmillan, a future prime minister himself, to take a "number of steps" to make "de Gaulle fall into line." It would be wiser, Churchill said, to try this before any final break. The entire telegram seemed to agree with Roosevelt, whereas, in fact, Churchill was evading the issue of breaking with de Gaulle.

I found myself in the eye of these storms as I shuttled back and forth from our newsroom and studios to the headquarters of General de Gaulle and General Eisenhower. I only saw them rarely but each time it was exciting. Everyone knew that they were already figures who would live on in history as "immortals" of their countries. Meeting with de Gaulle was each time a challenge, but Eisenhower was always relaxed and friendly, seeming untouched by the awesome responsibilities of his Supreme Command.

General Eisenhower had a beautiful suite of rooms in the Hotel Saint George, high on a hill overlooking the city of Algiers and the Mediterranean. His staff had their meals on a wide terrace, whose railings were covered in purple bougainvillea. Every two weeks or so, some staff member would invite me to lunch at the officers' table. I had taken to wearing a uniform jacket with civilian U.S. buttons on it that Mike Bessie had given me.

It was strictly against regulations for military personnel to wear civilian insignia, and very much against regulations for a noncommissioned officer not to wear his stripes, yet I had to take the risk. I mixed regularly with officers up to field rank and above. It would not be possible, even in the easy informality of Eisenhower's headquarters, for a corporal to dine and talk freely with a major, a colonel, and, at times, with generals. General Patton would come by occasionally, and if he had suspected that I was a "non-com," he would have had me court-martialed. There was nothing informal about Patton except his habit of calling practically everyone a son of a bitch.

General Eisenhower was irritated by Patton's language and swagger but did not reprimand him. Patton's success as a commander made up for his behavior until the day, in Sicily, that he slapped a soldier suffering from a nervous breakdown at a hospital, calling him a coward and malingerer. There were American correspondents present who reported the incident. Outraged parents at home bombarded the White House and War Department with protests, forcing Eisenhower to reprimand Patton sharply.

Eisenhower was an easygoing commander but he also had a fierce temper if pushed too far. One of his aides told the story of an American staff meeting during which a colonel, involved in a dispute with a British opposite number, started to tell Eisenhower what "that British bastard" was doing. Eisenhower's face flushed red. He pounded the table and shouted, "That will be enough! Don't you ever say that again or I'll bust you down to private. There are no British, American, French, or any other national bastards at this headquarters. There are certainly bastards aplenty here, and I'm looking at one, but bastardy is NOT a national characteristic. Call a man a bastard, if you must, but don't blame his country for him." The outburst was Ike at his very best, a decent man who hated any form of bigotry.

One day, at the Saint George, I was delivering some papers to Eisenhower and he asked me how I was getting along with the French. I told him that I liked the French very much and got along fine with them, although they were always jumpy and tense about their conflicts with the Americans. They seemed to like me and trust me, I thought. I confessed to General Eisenhower that our conflicts with de Gaulle were seriously affecting morale. Eisenhower looked at me a bit sharply. He was not going to permit any disloyal talk about official policy. But when he realized that I was just answering his questions honestly, he relaxed. He grinned at me, that infectious, wide grin that charmed everyone. "Well, young feller, if you can get along with the French and make them think kindly of an American, it will certainly be a big help to all of us."

An aide came in to hand him a slip about his next appointment. I got up to leave, but he waved me down. "Stay on a minute, I think you'll be pleased to meet the man coming in, and I'd like him to know you and get briefed on what we are doing at PWB. He's a great broadcaster and one of the smartest men I know. Prime Minister Churchill consults him often. It's the CBS News correspondent Ed Murrow."

Murrow walked in, tall, elegantly groomed and darkly handsome. Eisenhower greeted him warmly and then introduced us. I had all I could do to restrain myself from gushing. Murrow was a special hero. His voice from London under the blitz had brought the war home to Americans and won much-needed sympathy for the brave British. After the introductions, Murrow told me that he was staying at the Hotel Aletti, in downtown Algiers, not far from my office on the Boulevard Baudin. He suggested that I meet him for drinks between six and six-thirty. I left the office eagerly awaiting the meeting with Murrow.

Murrow talked passionately about the British people and their magnificent sense of civism, their courage and readiness to accept sacrifices. He told stories of Churchill, his incredible capacity for French brandy and Havana cigars, his brilliant wit. Then he asked me about de Gaulle and the French. We spent a pleasant hour in which Murrow demonstrated a Churchillian capacity for Scotch and cigarettes. He had a dinner appointment and when he got up to leave he said: "I enjoyed our talk. The French puzzle me and I'd like to hear more about them one day. If you get to London, give me a ring. Or, perhaps we can meet again in the Ritz bar in liberated Paris." We would.

I had, by then, been given a new assignment. The "slot-man" had been moved elsewhere and Mike Bessie had offered me the post. It was tough but stimulating. A slot-man is a newsdesk editor who receives the raw news copy as it comes in on the teleprinters and then assigns items to a battery of newswriters, some generalists but some specialists in areas requiring expert knowledge and constant attention.

My job was to assign the copy, as it came in, to the appropriate writer, to tell him just how many words we would want for our news file, as well as to suggest certain "angles" on propaganda to work into the story. The writer, on finishing his piece, would return it to me for editing. The pressures were strong, we had to move copy quickly and beware of errors that the top PWB brass might jump on. Our writers were competent but, inevitably, errors would be made. Sometimes I would catch them and then get into an argument with the writer. It almost led to disaster for me one day.

It was a day on which I had sent my jacket out for cleaning and put on another one without noticing that the fresh jacket had my corporal stripes on it. I was tired and irritable and had just read a piece from our air-war writer that had boasted about "pinpoint" bombing, one of our more unfortunate propaganda mistakes. There was no such thing as pinpoint accuracy then, and I seriously doubt that even now, with all our technological advances, bombers are accurate from high altitudes.

The writer, poor fellow, was only following our official propaganda line. But I had told him several times not to talk about pinpoint bombing no matter what our directives said. We had killed hundreds of French people, innocent civilians, by off-target bombing of Boulogne-Billancourt and several other French towns and villages. The French people mourning their dead knew that we had not bombed accurately. They cheered Allied planes flying over France toward Germany but hated our attacks on German installations in France, for we often as not hit the French.

The British did a better job than we did, not necessarily because they were better pilots or bombardiers, although many of them were more experienced, but because British bombers would swoop in low over target and had a good accuracy record. In our faith in our new bombsights, we would let our bombs drop from high up. Sometimes it worked. When it did not, civilian casualties would be high.

Tired of the absurd boasting, particularly on a day when there were French casualties, I was bawling out the writer. Suddenly I noticed that, aside from my own voice, the room was strangely quiet. No one was typing. I looked at the writers and they were all looking over my head at something behind me. I turned around and saw a red-faced Colonel Hazeltine with a gentleman in khaki, whose red epaulets carried the markings of a British general staff officer. And here I was, a lowly American corporal, shouting at a gallant RAF flight-leftenant.

My blood chilled as I heard Colonel Hazeltine say: "Report to my office at once, corporal." He then turned and whispered an apology to his guest and took him by the elbow to continue his tour elsewhere.

Colonel Hazeltine looked at me and shook his head. "We're going to have to yank you out of that slot. We just can't let a non-com shout at an officer. PWB is a crazy mishmash and we have to close our eyes on some of our rules, but I can't let that happen again."

I quietly said, "Yes, sir," and left. I felt no guilt. That scene was not my fault. The fault was in an absurd system that mixed military ranks and civilians indiscriminately and put me into a post that should have been filled by a captain. If they had let me stay in Ritchie and obtain my commission, there would have been no trouble at all.

I went to see Mike Bessie and told him that Hazeltine wanted me replaced in the slot by an officer of sufficient rank. Mike just waved his hand airily and said, "Friend, forget it, I'll straighten it out. We've not long to wait, and then . . ." He stopped talking and gave me a knowing wink.

That was good news! We had all been waiting for a move out of Algiers into action in Europe. An advance guard had already gone on to open PWB offices in Rome. But my group was slated for France. So, an invasion was in the plans, if I understood Mike's wink.

The delay in opening a second front in France was one of the most controversial issues at headquarters, along with a controversy over the campaign in Italy, "the false front." Some of our men who had come back from the Italian front cursed Churchill for urging that campaign and for a speech he had made about cutting through "Europe's soft underbelly." Italy, with a spine of rocky mountain ranges, was anything but a soft underbelly. The fighting there was rugged and would get worse. In addition, rumors were rife that Churchill was now talking about a quick thrust to the Balkans, a diversion that could put off a western front indefinitely.

It was apparent that Churchill wanted to use our armies for political objectives that he considered vital to Britain's interests in the postwar world. Churchill was Clausewitzian in the sense that he believed that, if diplomacy were an extension of war by other means, war was a means of achieving diplomatic goals. He was constantly concerned with postwar zones of influence and knew that they would almost certainly be determined by the lands that the armies conquered. He wanted the Allies to get to the Balkans before the Red Army won it from the Germans and Stalin kept it for himself.

The only issue on which Churchill was prepared for a confrontation with his friend Roosevelt was the need to take into account political objectives when drawing up strategic plans. He even quarreled openly with FDR when the American President made it clear that he was not sending American boys to fight and die to maintain British colonies. Churchill publicly proclaimed that he "had not become the King's First Minister to preside over the liquidation of the British Empire." That was the one issue on which Churchill would oppose Roosevelt vigorously.

General Marshall and General Eisenhower both urged FDR not to let Churchill exploit the Allied war machines for his purely political goals. The Americans were only concerned with the best way militarily to defeat Hitler. Our generals had little knowledge or experience of European politics and wanted none of it. There were congressmen and editors in America who would agree with Churchill that, after Hitler, Stalin would become a dangerous adversary and that communism was a serious threat on the horizon. But Roosevelt and his senior commanders would not listen to such talk. Nor would they yield to the constant calls from General Douglas MacArthur to send more troops and arms to the Pacific.

President Roosevelt and General Marshall both felt that Western civilization and the survival of democracy required the fastest possible defeat of Hitler. Once Hitler had been beaten, there would be time and men for Japan. They adhered to this priority rigidly where it concerned the Army and Air Force. The only high priority they accorded MacArthur was for the Navy and the Marines in their mission of clearing the Japanese out of the islands they had captured. Plans for an attack on the mainland of Asia would have to wait.

Late in November 1943, Churchill and Roosevelt did finally meet with Chinese Generalissimo Chiang Kai-shek in Cairo to plan strategy against Japan, but they made it clear that Europe still had first priority. They then met with Stalin at Teheran to discuss future war operations. Stalin had been berating them about the delay in opening a second front in France. They told Stalin that plans were proceeding swiftly and that they hoped to invade occupied France by the spring of 1944. These conferences were important for all of us in the PWB newsroom as we prepared broadcasts to occupied Europe to tell them that the Americans would be coming soon.

Our transmitter had been officially named "United Nations Radio" and we made heavy propaganda use of an earlier Allied meeting in Moscow, in October, in which America, Britain, Russia, and

China had all agreed on the need for an international organization to prevent future wars. That was our first official knowledge that Roosevelt had moved on one of his most cherished projects, the creation of a world organization, to be called the United Nations. FDR had not forgotten the tour he had made in the twenties on behalf of Woodrow Wilson to drum up support for the League of Nations, and the failure of Wilson's plans. This time, Roosevelt meant to carry out Wilson's dream and bring Americans permanently onto the world stage.

General de Gaulle was excluded from the Allied conferences. He was not surprised but he was deeply angered. When I went to see him after the Moscow Conference, he told me: "The so-called Big Four have pledged to create an international organization. Well, I tell you now, and remember my words, there will be a Big Five at the head of it, and France will be one of them. France will regain her rightful place among the nations of the world or there will be no effective world organization. The world needs France and France will play its role in the world."

Then, on the day before Christmas, we were handed a communiqué that we had been waiting for anxiously. The Allied chiefs of government had named General Eisenhower Supreme Commander of all Allied forces for the invasion of Europe. We all had known for some time that Eisenhower would get the appointment but the communiqué told us that planning had advanced and that the time to strike at Hitler in Europe was no longer distant.

The French political and military leaders in Algiers were fuming. Not only had they been excluded from important Allied conferences, but they had not even been consulted or informed in advance about the appointment of Eisenhower or plans for invading their country. I went to see de Gaulle, expecting a tirade from him.

He was icy cold. When I entered his office, he did not get up from his desk to greet me politely. He just looked at me without expression and then nodded his head to indicate that I should be seated. He said, in his deep baritone voice, "These gentlemen seem to believe that they can invade France without the help of the French. Well, they are wrong. They cannot breach Hitler's defenses without the aid of the French people. French patriots control the raillines and communications of France. The Nazis have been unable to prevent the disruption of their internal security by the valorous fighters of the French Resistance. General Eisenhower will need them at the critical moment. France will not be occupied by the Americans. The French will liberate themselves with the Americans or, if necessary, against the Americans. One of your great patriots once said, 'Give me liberty or give me death.' We French, too, would rather die than be puppets or serve a foreign master."

I told de Gaulle that there were a great many Americans, in Algiers as well as at home, who would endorse his sentiments. We respected France and many of us loved France. We had not forgotten how France had come to our aid in our nation's most desperate hours. He certainly knew better than anyone that General Eisenhower admired him and his compatriots and was aware of the important aid that the Resistance could bring to him at the critical moment.

De Gaulle listened quietly. His hooded lids would close on his eyes from time to time, while his head, too small for his body, would sway a little from side to side, a habit of his that made him look like a camel about to suddenly bite its rider.

When he said nothing in reply to my statement, I cleared my throat and said, "General, I pray that you not take offense if I say that at headquarters there is a feeling that you seem less concerned about the fight against Hitler than your fights with Roosevelt and the Americans."

General de Gaulle looked at me for a long, painful moment. I thought that I had gone too far and was prepared to make earnest apology. But his first words surprised me. "Yes, that is true, and, from a French point of view, it is not illogical."

He arose from his chair and let me feel the full power of his size and strength. I started to rise but he motioned to me to stay seated as he paced his office and then came back to his desk. He opened wide his arms and said: "I am not concerned about the fight against Hitler, for Hitler is already doomed. The Russian army has broken his offensive and is driving him back along a broad front. The German has lost the initiative in the east. He has lost the war in the east. It will take time and much more bloodshed, but Hitler is doomed. His death will come more swiftly when the Americans hit him in an attack from the west. Hammered on both sides by the Russians and the Americans, he has no chance. So, why should Hitler be my concern?

"I will tell you my main concern. It is that the Russian bear will squeeze off eastern Europe and enthrall it in its embrace. And the Americans will liberate the other half and then buy it up. Where will Europe be, where will France be, if the eagle and the bear gobble it all up? That is my concern. I am fighting for the freedom and the sovereignty of France and, at this moment, the greatest threat to our freedom and independence comes not from the enemy but from our allies."

Back at my desk, still shaken from the experience, de Gaulle's words echoing in my mind, I typed up notes on the conversation. Then I sat silently reading the notes, wondering what to do with them. I think I made a very wise decision. I folded the papers, put them into my pocket, and later buried them deeply in my B-bag where they stayed until de Gaulle and Eisenhower were no longer leaders of their nations.

The year 1943 ended with an exciting communiqué from the Russian front. The Red Army had broken through German lines along a two-hundred-mile front and recaptured more than a thousand populated places. Early in the new year, on January 5, the Russians broke out of Russia and into Poland. German General Schmidt, commander of the 10th Motorized Division, committed suicide. Hitler, in an address to the German people, shouted, "Wherever the Allies land, they will receive the welcome they deserve." The next day we dropped one thousand tons of bombs on Berlin to celebrate the anniversary of the one hundredth Allied air raid on Germany.

All we were thinking about as 1944 rolled on was the date of D day, the day of invasion. We wore on the upper arm of our uniforms a patch with the letters AF, standing for Allied Forces. We all insisted that what it really stood for was Algiers Forever. Would we ever get out of Algiers, out from behind our desks and the war of words into the war itself?

CHAPTER 7

FOUR-STAR SERGEANT

The word spread rapidly through Algiers. Even the little Arab street peddlers, hawking peanuts and dates, heard what had happened and thought they knew what it meant. "Invasion, the invasion of France!" they shouted. It was June 4, 1944. There had not yet been the long-awaited opening of the second front. But a York plane, sent by Churchill to Algiers to pick up General de Gaulle and bring him to London, had landed at the airport. De Gaulle was certainly going to London to participate in the landings in France, and this was taken as a signal that the invasion was about to go.

The night before, the French Committee of National Liberation had been transformed by a vote of the Assembly into the Provisional Government of the French Republic. General de Gaulle, realizing the futility of arguing with Churchill and Roosevelt about the validity of a French government that had not been chosen by the French people, had simply decided to proceed on his own and create a provisional government.

The imminence of the Allied invasion of France made it imperative that de Gaulle represent the interests of the French people whether the Allies recognized his legitimacy or not. His liaison officer to the Allies in London, Claude Hettier de Boislambert, had sent him detailed reports on Roosevelt's intention to treat

France as an occupied country rather than a liberated Ally. FDR had already printed a special occupation scrip, paper money that looked like dollars but whose printed denominations were in French francs. The Americans intended to use this scrip in payment of all their purchases in France and then reimburse an officially elected French government for all the currency in circulation. It was a painfully insulting decision and de Gaulle intended to fight it with every means at his disposal.

De Gaulle could no longer hear Roosevelt's name without exploding in anger. FDR had sent him a memorandum outlining plans for the United Nations, informing de Gaulle that the Big Four—America, Britain, Russia, and China—would be the major powers, and offering France a "secretariat" in the organization. On the eve of what should have been a glorious day, the day of liberation and Allied amity, the French and the Americans were virtually at war with each other.

If the imminence of invasion was an open secret, the exact date and site of the landings were known only to a handful of men at the very top of the Allied command. Charles de Gaulle was not one of those. As with Operation Torch, the landings in North Africa, de Gaulle and the French had been excluded from the planning. Even worse, orders had been given by Churchill, under pressure from Roosevelt, that all communications between London and Algiers be sent "in the clear." That meant the French in London were not permitted to use their secret codes in communicating with de Gaulle in Algiers. The purpose of the order was to prevent any details of the invasion from leaking and being discovered by German spies. The French would not dare send any information on the invasion on an open channel. They understood that they were being obliged to use an open channel because they were not trusted to keep Allied secrets. It was profoundly wounding to de Gaulle, who would arrive in London in a raging temper, prepared to do battle with Churchill, Eisenhower, and anyone else who would try to keep him and his Free France forces from being in the very forefront of the landings in France.

Meanwhile, on that same day, June 4, while General Eisenhower was impatiently and nervously waiting for reports from his meteorologists on weather conditions in the Channel, a French duty officer, Captain Mamy, was monitoring radio communications from London to France at French headquarters in London. He tuned in on the program *Personal Messages,* broadcast by the BBC every night at eleven-thirty. It carried coded instructions to the Resistance inside France. "Darling, I kiss you three times," was a message to the maquis of the Ain Department, telling them that three planes would be flying over to drop arms to them. Mamy sat and smiled as he heard some of the messages. "The doctor buries his patients." "The crocodile is thirsty." "Baba is calling Coco." "The squirrel has a bushy tail."

The captain, leaning back in his chair, puffing on a coarse, rough-cut French Army Caporal cigarette, suddenly heard the words "It is hot in Suez." He almost lost his balance as he bolted upright and reached for a memo pad, checking his watch to note the exact time of the message. He would have to call General Koenig, the commander of French troops, for that was the signal to the Resistance for a general mobilization and the launching of a series of attacks in all of France in support of the Allied landing forces. As Mamy was reaching for his directory with Koenig's telephone number, he heard another critical message: "The dice are cast." That was a signal to the Resistance to lead a general uprising throughout the country. Mamy was puzzled and nervous. He had been told that the idea of a general uprising by the people of France, included in early plans, had finally been ruled out as too dangerous, for it would result in thousands, perhaps tens of thousands, of civilian casualties. Had the plan been reinstated? When? By whom? In fact, the messages were sent in error and not discovered until too late to abort.

In Algiers, I was wrapped in a blanket on the floor of our newsroom, trying to keep awake but also get some rest. I had had a long, difficult day but had also drawn my turn as overnight duty officer. We were on twenty-four-hour alert waiting for the flash that would tell us the invasion had started. In the hills above Algiers, in the suburb of Bouzaréa, and at Blida, atop the Atlas mountains, our monitoring machines were scanning the atmosphere and picking up radio broadcasts. They tuned in on the BBC messages. One of the operators called headquarters, as Mamy was doing in London. Then he called PWB and told me the news.

I had a number to call that would alert a personnel officer to call the top PWB people. If the invasion was confirmed, all our men would be called in immediately to go into high gear on broadcasts to France, with instructions, explanations, words of encouragement, a battery of plans prepared in advance for D day. I realized that the signals we were getting were instructions to the Resistance but not any official Allied word and nothing citing General Eisenhower himself. Nothing else could be taken as proof of the invasion. I paced up and down the newsroom, chain-smoking, waiting for the word.

It was all a tragic error. The invasion was not set for the fourth of June or even the fifth of June. The weather reports were not favorable, so Eisenhower delayed from day to day, knowing that he had to make a firm decision to go or not to go on June 6. If the weather were bad on June 6, it would have been necessary, because of the tides, to put the invasion off for another month. More than one hundred fifty thousand men, combat-packed, trained and honed to a fighting edge, were poised and ready. They could not be kept at an emotional peak for another month, nor would it have been possible to conceal their camps and jump-off positions from German spies. To delay a month was unthinkable. If Eisenhower did not give the signal on the sixth, the invasion might have had to be put off for another year, for weather conditions would have made it too risky.

Someone, it was never discovered who, had released the messages to the Resistance prematurely. It is impossible to know exactly how many men and women were killed and wounded in France from the morning of June 5 to the dawn of June 6 when the true signal should have been sent. The series of attacks by the Resistance did help to disorganize German communications on the eve of the landings. But the people who obeyed the order for an uprising were caught in a terrible trap. There was no invasion, therefore the Germans were not diverted and were ready to put down the insurrection with full force. There were a number of human errors committed in so vast and complex an operation, such as a teletype operator, practicing messages for D day, sending out news of the invasion by not knowing that the safety block on the machine had broken. Instead of practicing, the operator was unwittingly sending.

The next day found General de Gaulle in a fierce quarrel with Churchill and Eisenhower. Churchill was pressing de Gaulle to accept an invitation from Roosevelt to meet in Washington to discuss the issue of a future French government. De Gaulle refused out of hand. "The provisional government of France already exists, whether Roosevelt recognizes it or not."

Eisenhower, visibly uncomfortable, met de Gaulle in his field headquarters outside London and showed him the text of the proclamation he would make to the French and other occupied peoples of Europe. De Gaulle took the text and, before reading it, said to Eisenhower, "This is the text you are proposing to read?" and stressed the word *proposing* to indicate that it would first have to be approved by the head of the French Provisional Government. Eisenhower did not reply. He merely nodded his head. De Gaulle thereupon folded the paper and put it in his pocket without reading it. The atmosphere was icy as de Gaulle strode out of Eisenhower's tent.

Back in London, de Gaulle received the visit of Charles Peake, the British liaison officer to Free France. Peake showed him the list of proclamations that would be made the morning of D day. De Gaulle was stupefied and then livid with rage. The order of broadcasts was: the king of Norway; the queen of Holland; the grand duchess of Luxembourg; the prime minister of Belgium; the Supreme Commander, General Eisenhower; and then, in last position, after the American general, totally separated from all the other Europeans, General de Gaulle. De Gaulle paced up and down his office, clenching his fists. "First royalty, then a prime minister! And the tiny little duchy of Luxembourg before the president of the French Republic, provisional or not! Is this landing not taking place in France? Are Frenchmen and women not fighting and dying to help the Allies?"

De Gaulle angrily told Peake that he would not participate in such a broadcast schedule. Peake pleaded with him, saying that it was most important that the people of France hear from the leader of Free France. De Gaulle's only answer was "Indeed!" He finally told Peake that he would broadcast to the French, but not in the morning at the bottom of the list. He would make his own broadcast that evening, escaping the stigma of being last to speak, divorced from the other Europeans. Eisenhower agreed to let him do this.

We knew in Algiers that something had gone wrong in London, but being distant from invasion headquarters, we were careful to hold ourselves in check and not put out incorrect signals. When the official flash finally came through that the first commandos had already reached the Normandy beaches late in the night of June 5, and that the full force of the landings had been hurled against Hitler's Atlantic Wall at dawn on the sixth, we went into our prearranged broadcast schedule for southern France, Italy, Yugoslavia, and North Africa.

It seemed as though no one breathed for almost two days. The hold on the beachheads was precarious. Then the news became more encouraging. The Allies were widening the breach in the German lines, striking inland from the beachheads, while the navy kept ferrying across more men, ammunition, artillery, and tanks. The French Resistance heroically and successfully launched a series of sabotage attacks on German telephone and cable lines, and above all, on rail lines, to prevent the Nazis from bringing up reinforcements that might have thrown the Allies back into the sea.

One of the exploits of the lightly armed Resistance was to attack one of Germany's most powerful armored divisions, the Das Reich division, in southwestern France, and to harass it continually so that it was unable to carry out orders to rush north to hit the American beachheads. A Resistance fighter who participated in the running attacks on the Das Reich division was a future Nobel Prize author, André Malraux.

We had a new map up in our newsroom, a map of the western front, not as big as the eastern front but much busier. The Red Army of Russia was in the process of grinding up German legions from the Baltic to the Crimea. The issue was no longer in doubt. All of our attention was focused, naturally, on our own American, British, and Free French forces breaking out of the beachheads. Our first major objectives were the ports of Cherbourg and Le Havre that would enable the navies to pour in materiel for the liberation of France.

France had fallen to the Germans in June 1940. It had taken four years for the Allies to strike back and begin the liberation campaign. The Russians had borne, in Europe, alone for three bloody years, the full strength of the German assault. They were bitter about the long, lonely struggle. General de Gaulle also had long memories about America's hesitations before joining in "the war to save democracy" in 1917, three years after the French had lost their youth in the trenches.

World War I had marked America's emergence as a world power. World War II would see America become the world's strongest military, industrial, and economic power, its factories nourished by war orders and untouched by the war itself, while Europe and Asia were in the process of being destroyed. A profound jealousy and resentment permeated the European psyche. It is still strong today, for many of the leaders of Europe in the eighties are the young men and women of the forties who watched in desperation the devolution of their nations' fortunes.

Those of us who spoke Europe's languages and were sensitive to the feelings of Europeans could already perceive in the summer of 1944 the postwar problems that would erupt out of the emotions and dislocations of World War II. All through North Africa, from Casablanca on the Atlantic Coast to Egypt on the Suez Canal, there were undercurrents of unrest, new tides below the surface. I had made a number of reporting trips to Rabat, Morocco, where the sultan, the reigning sovereign, chafed under French "protection." One could see throughout the Moroccan capital posters listing the Four Freedoms proclaimed by the Allied powers: freedom of speech, freedom of the press, freedom of worship, and freedom from hunger. The French took it to mean freedom for them, not for the colonies of their empire. The indigenous peoples could not but yearn for the same freedoms. Freedom certainly was not to be won exclusively for the white, Western peoples.

We Americans had hit the shores of North Africa carrying with us our chocolate bars, chewing gum, and our promises of liberty. The people rushed to embrace all three of our offerings, generally in that order. Empty stomachs ached for chocolate. Children without toys were delighted with chewing gum. Finally, after the basic appetites were sated, people yearned for freedom, for self-determination, for their own identity, for the right to rule themselves. In World War II, the Western Europeans eliminated themselves as colonial powers.

These thoughts nagged at me, as I followed with intense concentration the battles my fellow Americans were fighting against the Germans in France. It was the most frustrating of times for me, watching at long last the destruction of the German armies, the approaching doom of Hitler, but watching from afar. I hammered away mercilessly at my friends Mike Bessie, Bill Tyler, Bill Doerflinger, asking to be assigned to any combat zone, to the Italian front where we were slogging our way up the boot, if they could not send me to the French front.

On July 4, in the course of a celebration of our national holiday at the American consulate, Mike Bessie signaled to me to come into the garden with him. He walked to a corner where we would be alone with no one near to overhear. "Friend, you can stop bugging me about a combat assignment. You are about to get your wish."

"Mike! That's great! When? Where?"

"Keep your voice down! Agreement has finally been reached on Operation Anvil, landings in southern France, all along the Riviera. I don't yet know when, but it'll be soon. I managed to get you assigned to the American Seventh Army. You'll be going in on the first wave. You'll get your orders soon. I'm leaving in a few days for Naples where convoys will be forming up. I'll see you there. Now, keep quiet about this." Mike grinned at me, squeezed my shoulder, said, "Ciao," and strolled away.

I stood there, my ever-present glass of pineapple juice in my hand, taking care of a fractious liver. At last I would get to France and into the real war. I could feel my stomach tighten. I could not help but wonder just how I would act in a firefight, facing enemy machine guns and mortars. I had heard more than enough stories from men who had stormed into Sicily or had hit the beach at Anzio under deadly German shelling by 88's. I was not afraid of death but of being wounded and crippled. I had a lively imagination and understood the terrifying truth of the old saying that a brave man dies only once, a coward a hundred times. I am not a brave man but I am not a coward, either. I had longed for action. I was going to get it. So be it! Turn off the imagination, David, old boy, and just do your duty. Feeling better, I finished my pineapple juice and decided that I had coddled my liver sufficiently. There must be some champagne left at the bar.

"See Naples and die." I grinned as I looked down upon the blue waters of Capri, as our ship made its way to the port of Naples. It had been a very long time since Naples had been able to live up to its old boast of beauty, as the ultimate site to end one's days. I might be on my way to die but it would certainly not be in Naples. And I was certain that it would not be on the French

Riviera, either. I knew from our intelligence reports that the Germans had had strong coastal defenses in southern France. But German forces in the east and the west were being hammered so hard by the Russians and the Americans that they had pulled much of their strength out of the south. We had complete naval and air superiority and would pound their defenses heavily before we hit the beaches. I was exhilarated by the prospect of being in the first wave and had felt like a released prisoner when I left my desk in the Maison Agricole. *Adieu, Alger la blanche.*

My backpack felt light and my M-1 rifle, carefully oiled, felt good in my hands. I could close my eyes and see the Camp Ritchie target range and my bullets close to the bull's-eye. Practice was over. I would be using it soon and I was confident that I knew how to use it. Whether I would be able to pull the trigger when I saw a human face in my sight was something I did not want to think about.

My instructions on how to find the PWB offices in Naples were precise. My Italian was rusty but good enough. I did not yet know that every urchin in Naples could speak a broken, dirty, army English and that, to my horror, every one of them knew that we were taking off to invade France. "Hey, Yank, cioccolata, cigarette, whatsa you ship? Zig-zig Frenchie ragazze!" My God, some security!

I had hitched a ride on a passing jeep. The driver looked at me curiously. On my arms were the new stripes of a sergeant, a promotion for the invasion. My rifle was slung over my shoulder and in my hand I was carrying a Hermes portable typewriter. He couldn't figure out what kind of a soldier I was. I wasn't even sure myself.

Mike Bessie was busy talking to a colonel when I entered his office. I eyed the colonel warily, preparing to salute, but he ignored me and went on talking to Mike, who waved at me to take a seat. I stowed my gear in a corner and sat down. They were going over a list of personnel and assignments for the PWB teams in Italy and schedules for southern France. They finished talking and taking notes and turned to me.

"Hey, paisan, good to see you." Mike then introduced me to the colonel who nodded and said, "My office is one floor up. I'll want to see you about a special assignment when you've finished with Bessie." He turned to Mike who interrupted him and said:

"No, please don't leave now. There's something I want you to hear and see." Mike looked mysterious and pleased with himself.

"David, I tried like hell to get you a commission for the invasion. Although you're Seventh Army, you'll be on detached service to General Jean de Lattre de Tassigny, the commander of the French First Army. I told headquarters how sensitive the French are to every real or imaginary slight. You just can't deal with General de Lattre as a sergeant. He will think we are cutting him down. Anyway, sensitive or not, there is no way a sergeant in any army can work comfortably with field-rank officers and generals."

Mike paused to let me ponder on his words. I could see no way out of the dilemma he had outlined.

His eyes gleamed as he continued. "Luckily we've got some good, smart friends at headquarters and you've got a fine reputation for getting along well with the French. Seventh Army knows it will need an American whom the French like, for there are certainly going to be frictions. So . . ." Mike paused, picked up a manila envelope on his desk, and, with the flourish of a magician, pulled a paper out and said, "Abracadabra, the solution!"

He handed me the paper and as I took it I saw the letterhead "Supreme Headquarters Allied Expeditionary Forces." I took it and noted, in the left margin, the words "Office of the Supreme Commander." Then, with unbelieving eyes, I read the text.

> TO ALL RANKS:
>
> The bearer of this letter, Sgt. David Franz Schoenbrun, serial number 32904876, is on special mission for this headquarters. The cooperation of all ranks is requested.
>
> Dwight D. Eisenhower
> *Supreme Commander*
> *Allied Expeditionary Forces*

I stood transfixed. I remembered the telegram pulling me out of Camp Ritchie, signed Eisenhower. But that was a telegram anyone could have sent. This letter actually had Eisenhower's signature on it. It was an incredible, open-end, no-date-limit, all-ranks order.

"Mike, this is a miracle. Many, many thanks. I'll never forget this."

"Don't worry, I'll never let you."

Mike then said: "Get a scissors, snip those stitches, and take off the sergeant's stripes. They're not needed."

The colonel turned to Mike.

"Hey, don't tell him to do that. He's going into a combat zone. It is a serious offense to remove insignia of rank. The military police will clobber him."

"No, they won't, colonel. Take a look at that paper David has."

I handed it over silently, curious as to what the reaction of the colonel would be. It would be a first test for the letter.

As he read it, his eyes grew wider and he began shaking his head.

"Great balls of fire! This is the damnedest thing I ever saw!"

The colonel handed it back and said, "Man, you are a four-star sergeant." He turned to Mike and added: "Everyone of us has to knuckle down to someone above us in the pecking order. This guy isn't going to be pecked by anyone below Eisenhower himself. Yep, he is a four-star sergeant."

We all broke into laughter. The colonel told me to get a waterproof envelope to hold the letter. "Guard it with your life. It may be worth your life. And now, sergeant, if you will be so kind, please accompany me to my office."

The colonel took a folder from his desk, handed it to me, and told me that my travel orders were in it. I was to proceed to Naples harbor and board a Liberty ship, the *John S. Cropper.* All instructions about the landings would be given me on board, and the army troop commander would issue ammunition on the eve of the invasion. I first had to go to the PWB motor pool and pick up a jeep that had been assigned for the campaign. Once on the beach, I would look for signs directing me to the Sixth Army Group Press Camp. The officer in charge would be General Tristram Tupper. I would report in to him first, then carry on with my assignments.

"Now, we have an important assignment for you. You will be shuttling back and forth between the U.S. Seventh Army and the French First Army. You will broadcast on army transmitters in French to the French, telling them of the exploits of the Americans, and in English to our troops telling them what the French have been doing. Fighting side by side, but in adjacent sectors, the men of both armies should know about what their allies are doing on their frontiers. It is good for morale and for communications. We are counting on you to help them to respect and to like each other and to fight as good buddies. So, you'll be in every combat sector, moving around constantly, getting to know the men and the officers."

The colonel held out his hand to me. "No need for saluting inside this office. You'll get further instructions from Mike Bessie before taking off. Good luck."

Mike Bessie looked up as I walked back into his office. "Got your army orders?" When I nodded yes, he continued, "Well, ours are simple. You cover the fighting campaign and send us news dispatches from the fronts every day. Our broadcasts will then tell the story of the Battle for France, citing the frontline reports from our own correspondents, along with excerpts from the broadcasts of the major networks and papers. CBS also has a program called *Correspondent's Roundup.* You are authorized to appear on that program whenever asked. One restriction only. You are official government personnel. You can only report on the fighting fronts. Not a word on politics or anything but combat. Okay?"

"Okay, Mike. Well, I guess that's it. I'm off now."

Mike arose from his desk, came around and gave me a bear hug. "*Merde, mon vieux.*"

I turned and left. As I was going through the door, I heard Mike's cheery voice. "See you in Paris, friend."

I went downstairs, made my way to the motor pool, picked up my barracks bags, and headed out of Naples to the harbor, to the *John S. Cropper,* and France.

Our convoy moved slowly through royal blue waters under a powder-blue sky. Cotton-ball clouds floated on high, like tiny sailboats, while a hot sun danced in a cluster of diamonds on the velvet sea. If we had not been heading for an invasion of a hostile shore, it would have been a perfect Mediterranean cruise.

The morale of the men was at a peak. The troop commander kept them busy all day and night as we headed toward France. Morning gymnastics were followed by tournaments that lasted through the day: boxing, wrestling, hand-wrestling had the men cheering and betting on each bout. Small groups played poker or shot craps for high stakes. Money meant little to men who knew they might not be around two days away. But no one would give any sign that he was thinking about the fight ahead.

My day at sea began early on August 13, at 6:00 A.M. That was the time for a BBC transmission to ships at sea, at dictation speed for ship's operators, giving the news of all the war fronts and the home fronts; battle reports; baseball, soccer, and cricket scores. I had volunteered to write a ship's newspaper, based on the BBC News, plus stories I would pick up from sailors and soldiers. They were mainly funny or scurrilous stories about their officers. The skipper had told me to write anything I pleased, no matter how scandalous, if it would entertain the men and keep their minds off the invasion until the last minute. In return, the captain permitted me to bunk in the "looney bin," the ship's padded cell for anyone who became violent or mad. It had happened often enough in the war. Happily there were no mental breakdowns on our cruise, so I could spend the two and a half days at sea in my own private "stateroom," although it only was a prison cell with thick blankets on its walls.

Best of all, I was allowed to eat at the sailor's table, instead of at the troop field kitchen. Sailors were the only men in the war who set a splendid table, with fresh instead of powdered eggs, and luscious Italian peaches and grapes instead of the syrupy cans of army rations. There was one ration hated by every soldier, a processed food called Spam, apparently made of plastic. After a month of Spam, no one, no matter how hungry, would touch it.

I wrote Dorothy long, funny letters about my army life, never once mentioning that I would be in combat. Before leaving Naples, I had written, in advance, six letters, including one dated August 16, a day after the invasion, and bribed a postal clerk to mail them for me every three days. When I was later caught in a fierce firefight in Montélimar, she was getting letters postmarked Naples. When the war ended, she learned for the first time that I had been in combat for a year, and, at one stretch, some fifty days in the line without a break.

At midnight, on the fourteenth of August, we were given our briefings for an assault at first light. We were a mixed lot on our ship: infantry attack troops; minesweepers; engineers; radar, radio, and signalmen. Our first wave would go in by function: riflemen, mortarmen, and minesweepers would go first, then communications, then more infantry and light tanks. I was scheduled to go in with the communications men. Navy cannons and the Air Force would cover us. They had already begun pounding the coastal defenses. Our invasion army would be landing on a wide front, from Cannes on the east to Cavalaire on the west. Special commandos would be hitting the island off the coast. My jeep would be loaded onto an LCV—landing craft, vehicles—and I would drive it from the landing craft onto the beach. I was warned that I might have to drive through a few feet of water, and given putty to waterproof the engine.

We all rushed to the rails at first light to see our target site. The *John S. Cropper* rolled easily on the gentle swell of the Mediterranean. Overhead, a cloudless, sapphire sky was streaked with pink as dawn advanced from Italy. From the land came the scent of grapes and honey and the rustle of a thousand wings as larks rose to greet the sun. A soldier from Tennessee, leaning over the rail next to me, said: "Man, is this ever a place for an invasion."

It was a perfect day, nothing like the awesome violence of the Normandy landings. The Germans had pulled back. Our bombers and naval shelling had blasted them out of their coastal positions. Rearguard suicide troops were firing from blockhouses and we would suffer some casualties, but in our sector there was virtually no opposition. We had been sent to the Gulf of Saint-Tropez, and our landing site was just outside the little, then almost unknown, fishing village of Saint-Tropez. If we had had the wit to carry out de Gaulle's prophecy of Americans buying up Western Europe, and if we had had any money, we could have bought beachfront property at Saint-Tropez for less than a dollar a square meter and would have become multimillionaires. In fact, one of our motor-pool sergeants did. He sold captured cars on the black market and bought land on the Riviera.

Off to starboard we could see the villas of Saint-Raphaël, rose clusters in the green hills. Beyond, to the east, was Fréjus. General Caesar called it Forum Julii when he sent in his landing parties two thousand years before General Eisenhower. Beyond view, to port, lay Marseilles. Greek settlers from Phocaea named it Massilia when they opened a trading post there six hundred years before Christ.

An officer's shout snapped us out of our gawking. "Get going, get going, goddamn it, you're not tourists." We saw men clambering down nets, and we rushed to the disembarkation rail. A sergeant was calling out the numbers of our units. I heard mine, and went over the rail, scuttling down as fast as I could to the landing craft. I saw my jeep and jumped into the driver's seat. Our boat filled rapidly and roared off. Ahead we could see men on the beach before us. A geyser of sand shot up. Shit, someone hit a mine. Now we could hear clacking noises, like typewriter keys. Rifle fire. Who the fuck said there were no Germans left? My knuckles were white as I choked the steering wheel. Spray hit my face and temporarily blinded me. Plop! A big splash. Our landing craft had dropped its flat iron prow.

"Go! Go! Go!"

The beach commander was bellowing at us.

A turn of the ignition key. The engine caught and roared. No time to think. Throw in the clutch. Hit the accelerator. The jeep lunged forward and a wave of water rose and caught me in the face. The windshield was down to avoid splintering if hit by a bullet. I blinked but kept my hands on the wheel. The jeep skidded as it hit the sand, and I went with the skid, then pulled it back straight. Through my watery eyes I saw parallel lines of white tape on sticks, leading from the beach to the road beyond. The engineers had cleared a passage through the mines. Right ahead, fast, until I saw a soldier waving a sign, "Slow Down." I was halfway up the beach, and eased my foot on the gas. The rifle fire was heavier but no bullets seemed to be coming our way. No one was falling. The beach traffic officers were smiling and waving us on.

Up an incline, shift into second gear, a lurch, and the jeep was off the beach and onto a coastal highway jammed with people. Men with blue, white, red brassards and the Cross of Lorraine were jumping up and down, brandishing rifles and shooting them into the air. That was the rifle fire I had heard. It was a local Resistance group welcoming the Allies. Men, women, children, hundreds of people, were dancing, drinking wine, cheering, crying. Some held up wine bottles and fruit, offering them to the soldiers.

As I waved a woman threw a bunch of grapes at me. With both hands still on the wheel, I could not catch it. It hit me hard on the side of the face. I reached up and felt a hot smear on my temple and eye. It was not grape juice. It was blood. The grapes had cut the corner of my eye. I started to laugh. After all the worry about hitting a hostile shore my only wound had come from a bunch of grapes.

I saw an ambulance and some medics parked on the road and drove over to them. "Hey, medic, I'm wounded. Patch me up." A soldier with a Red Cross patch came over, washed the wound and put a plaster on it. "Write my name down. Wounded in action. I want a Purple Heart," I shouted to him. He looked at me and asked, "How did you get that wound, soldier?" I replied, with a straight face: "Got hit in the face with a bunch of grapes as I came off the beach." The medic laughed and said: "Get the hell out of here, or you'll get a Purple Ass!"

I was near hysterical from joy and the breaking of tension. I had convinced myself that I was not afraid of the landing. I truly had not been conscious of any fear. But when it was over, so easily, so joyously, with dancing and wine-drinking, I almost came apart.

An arrow, with a sign "Press Camp," caught my eye and I made my way into a side road that became a country dirt road. There in a grove of trees was a tent. On a stake in the ground was the designation "Press Camp." I drove up, parked, and went in. A corporal checked my papers and my name. "I'm the advance party, all alone so far. The general and the reporters will be landing later, and we will find out where our quarters will be. Meanwhile, leave your jeep here, give me the key and the carburetor, and walk around town for a couple of hours. We should be organized this afternoon."

I walked back toward the road, and the village of Saint-Tropez. At last, at long last, I was in France, the France I had studied and dreamed about for so many years. It is one of the most beautiful countries in the world, with a richness of culture that has enraptured millions around the globe. It is a country and a people that incite the envy of their enemies and often the despair of their friends. The Germans, despite their rising graphs of production, look dreamily across the Rhine and say, "Happy as God in France." A book by a German, with that title, was translated by a Frenchman as *Dieu est-il français?*—Is God French? What marvelous conceit!

Spaniards, trying to scratch some sustenance out of their sandy, rocky soil, look across the Pyrenees at France and sigh with envy, "France is not a country, it is a garden." The British may look down their noses at the "savages in Calais," but give a Briton a passport and some pounds and he will fly off to Nice and Menton, British "colonies" in France. The British would say in the spirit of George Bernard Shaw, "France is a wonderful country. It's a shame to waste it on the French." As for us Americans, ever since General Pershing, our men have been singing, "How yuh gonna keep 'em down on the farm now that they've seen Paree?"

No song is more homespun American than "Home, Sweet Home." John Howard Payne wrote it in Paris. It was in Paris that James Farrell sired that most American boy, Studs Lonigan. James Fenimore Cooper wrote lovingly of *The Prairie* while sitting at a sidewalk café in Paris. Gertrude Stein wrote *The Making of Americans* in Paris. Hemingway and Dos Passos, John Steinbeck and Irwin Shaw, every generation of writers and artists from Leonardo da Vinci to Picasso, from every nation on earth, came to France to seek inspiration. Kafū Nagai's *Tales of France* is a modern Japanese classic. Kōjirō Serizawa entitled one of his books *I Want to Die in Paris.* Chinese scholars ranked two French philosophers among their highest orders, just below Confucius, Masters Lu and Man, or, in their French names, Jean-Jacques Rousseau and Montesquieu.

I walked through the woods, singing Maurice Chevalier's favorite song, "Valentine." Then, as a grasshopper jumped in front of me, I began reciting La Fontaine's "La Cigale et la Fourmi," laughing as I declaimed, purging all pent-up emotions. I emerged from the forest, joined the dancing throng as someone handed me a bottle of red wine. I lifted it to my lips and drank greedily. To hell with my liver. Anyway, every Frenchman has liver trouble. I'd be right at home in France. Not for long, I knew. The long road ahead to Berlin would be bloody. But the liberation of Saint-Tropez on a scented summer day was a time to drink and dance, particularly for a newly created four-star sergeant, unscathed except for a grape wound.

David Schoenbrun, as Paris correspondent for CBS, broadcasting from emergency studio in office on Champs-Elysées. The Fourth Republic of France had just fallen; General de Gaulle was recalled from retirement to prevent a collapse of French democracy. May 1958. (*Alexandre Brauer*)

Art and Ann Buchwald in Paris, taken during an outing with the Schoenbruns.

Dorothy Schoenbrun (left) and Ann Buchwald (right) on the beach, Deauville, summer 1956. (*Courtesy David Schoenbrun*)

Conversation with President Charles de Gaulle, Garden of the Elysée Palace. July 14, 1959. (*Courtesy David Schoenbrun*)

Interviewing American Secretary of State Dean Acheson during General Assembly meeting of the United Nations, in Paris. December 1950. (*David Seymour-Magnum*)

As CBS newsman interviewing, far right, General Francisco Franco, Pardo Palace, outside Madrid. November 1959. Franco's interpreter is center. (*Courtesy David Schoenbrun*)

Interviewing King Hassan of Morocco in the Throne Room of the royal palace in Rabat, Morocco. March 1960. (*Georges Markman*)

Interviewing chief of the AFL/CIO, George Meany, in Washington, for the *CBS Evening News* hosted by Walter Cronkite, spring 1962. (*Courtesy David Schoenbrun*)

Costume ball celebrating David Schoenbrun's birthday at the Tunisian Embassy, Washington. (Left) President Kennedy's press spokesman Pierre Salinger. (Right) The "Jeeter Lester" character out of Tobacco Road is actually the normally elegant and distinguished Ambassador of Tunisia, Habib Bourguiba, Jr., son of the President of Tunisia. March 15, 1963. (*Courtesy David Schoenbrun*)

CHAPTER 8

FIRST ON THE RHINE

D day at Normandy, the first great assault, had taken place on June 6, 1944. My D day, the follow-up invasion in the south, was on August 15. Troop carriers were unloading the combat units of the French First Army, most of them in the Gulf of Saint-Tropez on the western Riviera, while the American Seventh was coming in on the eastern Riviera coast, from Saint-Raphaël to Cannes. I strolled down to the beach and watched the French land with their weapons, some 15,000 men, 80 pieces of artillery and 30 tanks, a powerful combat division but not yet enough to tackle the objectives that the High Command had given to the French: Toulon, the naval base, where 25,000 Germans were heavily dug in with orders from Hitler to fight to the death; Marseilles, second city of France after Paris, a vast port of vital strategic importance.

General Omar Bradley, commanding the American troops in Normandy, had supported Eisenhower and Marshall in a long controversy with Churchill, who had wanted to cancel the southern landings. Churchill, ever concerned about postwar power politics, wanted to take the Balkans before the Soviets got there. Bradley wanted the port of Marseilles to be cleared as rapidly as possible. Marseilles, with access to the Rhone Valley, would permit the fastest transport of materiel to our troops when they reached eastern France and began the attack into Germany.

The planning staff for the southern landings had assigned the French the objective of taking Toulon by D+20 (September 4) and Marseilles by D+40 (September 24). It would be a tough fight, for Toulon alone was bristling with thirty forts and hundreds of blockhouses. Marseilles was a huge city and a vast port heavily defended by the Germans.

As soon as a French officer informed me that General Jean de Lattre de Tassigny had set up headquarters, I went to report in and explain my mission. The general was delighted. He wanted all the publicity he could get to restore the reputation of the French army. De Lattre was a kind of French MacArthur, a man of panache, his head held high, a swagger stick tucked into his armpit, his eyes shining with the passion of a crusading knight. He had drawn up a battle plan for a simultaneous assault on both Toulon and Marseilles, a daring plan that divided his forces instead of concentrating them on each objective by turn. De Lattre wanted to show the Americans the true fighting qualities of the French. Like most French officers and men, he was determined to wipe out the shame of the fall of France in 1940.

De Lattre took his battle plan to clear it with General Jacob Devers, commanding the Sixth Army Group, top man in the southern campaign, and General Alexander Patch, commanding the American Seventh, de Lattre's partner in the combined French-American operations. Both of them later told me that they had had some doubts as to its division of forces. They had orders, however, from Eisenhower to cooperate with the French and give them their heads even if some risks had to be taken. The Americans were determined to get along with the French in France.

On August 18, three days after our landings, I received a message in press camp that General de Lattre wanted to see me. I drove quickly to his HQ. He told me that he was going to launch his double attack on Toulon and Marseilles the next morning and suggested that I cover the Marseilles offensive, for that would be the most important attack in all France. He wanted to liberate Marseilles ahead of the high command schedule and become the first French general to take back the biggest city to be freed in the new Battle for France. He knew that Allied troops were driving for Paris and that General de Gaulle had ordered General Leclerc to be the first man into Paris with his famed 2nd Armored Division. General de Lattre was burning to take Marseilles and Toulon on or about the same time that Leclerc would enter Paris. If he could do that, he would have taken two major objectives against powerful enemy defenses in about a week, well ahead of Allied goals, an extraordinary feat of arms that would, he hoped, swiftly reestablish the reputation of what had some five years before been touted as the best army in the world.

Some two thousand men of the Resistance had joined forces with de Lattre's regular army. In addition they had brought him detailed maps of all the German fortifications and information regarding troop strength and defensive positions. De Lattre told me: "The Resistance has done a grand job, particularly in Marseilles where they are ready for a general insurrection coordinated with our attack." He went on, however, to express his misgivings about armed civilians, with their own command, separate from the main army. "The Resistance has contributed to the honor of France but the time has come to integrate it into our army. The day for clandestine operations has ended. No more irregular partisans. One army, one flag for France."

Orders to begin the assault on Toulon and Marseilles were given on August 20. One of de Lattre's officers came to see me in press camp. He was excited, telling me that General Hubert de Monsabert, leading the assault on Marseilles, had jumped off early and broken through the German perimeter defenses with ease. He boasted: "We are already mopping up German units in the city, with the help of the Resistance, the tough longshoremen of the port, and," he said, laughing uproariously, "even the Corsican mafia of Marseilles. All the gangsters are with us." He told me to hurry and be the first reporter into Marseilles. He was tipping me off before the official briefing at headquarters.

I ran to get my jeep and two highly competent American correspondents whom I had invited to share the jeep with me, Homer Bigart of the New York *Herald Tribune* and Robert Vermillion of *Newsweek*. They were as eager as I to be the first to report the liberation of the port city. We jumped into the jeep and set off at full speed from the heights where our camp was located down a series of hills to Marseilles, some twenty miles to the southwest.

We came over the crest of the last hill and saw a broad avenue descending down to the port. Down we went looking for the cheering, liberated populace. People walking along the road on their daily round caught sight of us, stared, and then began running away into their houses. Not a friendly, happy, liberated crowd. As we got to the bottom of the hill into the city proper we saw almost no one in the streets.

I had a map open on my lap, checking street names and directing the army driver toward the prefecture where we intended to interview the local authorities. As we turned into a narrow street, Bigart suddenly shouted "Tiger tank. Tiger tank." Since he stuttered wildly when excited it came out as "Tie-tie-tie-Gur-Gur-Gur." We did not have to understand him for by then we had all seen the ugly snout of a cannon on top of a Tiger tank snaking around the corner to which we were heading.

Our driver jammed on the brakes, did a turn on two wheels, almost tipping us all out of the jeep, and shot forward like a frightened rabbit, a fair enough description of the men in the jeep.

We were back in the avenue. I yelled at the driver to go straight ahead. Rechecking the map, I found the route to the prefecture and we made it without running into another German tank. By then we all knew that no one had liberated Marseilles and that we were the first into the port, not the kind of "scoop" we had been looking for. To our immense relief we saw a huge Tricolor flag of France flying from the prefecture. The Resistance had already launched its insurrection, that much was correct, and had seized a number of public buildings. We raced toward the fortresslike gates of the prefecture, shouting, "*Vive la France*" at full chorus, so that the defenders inside, who had probably never yet seen a jeep, would know that we were friends, not foe. As we approached the gates at full speed, they swung open before we would crash into them.

We were safe inside. The officer who had tipped us off back in camp was right about one thing. We surely had an exclusive and had beaten the opposition into Marseilles. Trouble was, we had also beaten the army into Marseilles. We would remain trapped inside the prefecture for thirty-six hours before the army did break through. We saw the assault, were briefed by the attacking officers, and made our way back to press camp to write our stories. Bigart said to me: "David, I just want to get my stories straight and on time. No more tips and no more exclusives, please."

I felt wonderful. I had gone through my baptism under fire, sent my first dispatch back to Mike Bessie in Naples, an exciting story. We would have to wait for the capture of Toulon before broadcasting. There was a powerful transmitter in the naval base that could reach Algiers. The even more powerful station in Algiers would record the broadcasts and then relay them back to France. I was in action at last. It had been a foolish action, but we had come through safely and it had taught me to check my sources more carefully before dashing off recklessly.

The Germans defended their positions courageously but they had no chance against the frenzied, sometimes suicidal attacks of the fired-up French forces. I watched in awe as the French threw themselves against the German blockhouses and forts. They blasted fort by fort, broke through gates, and ran right at machine guns. Toulon fell to them on August 27. The Germans suffered 5,000 casualties and the French took 20,000 prisoners in Toulon. They themselves lost 2,700 men killed and wounded in their incredibly brave hand-to-hand fighting.

On the same day, Marseilles was liberated by General de Monsabert in the same almost reckless attacks, and, on August 28, the victorious troops of the French First Army paraded through the streets of France's second city, celebrating a great victory in the war, compensating for their collapse in 1940.

General de Lattre had won his bet to capture Toulon and Marseilles ahead of schedule. The Americans flooded him with congratulatory telegrams. But he had lost his race with General Leclerc, who had entered Paris on August 25.

I was far from Toulon and Marseilles when they were parading. The U.S. Seventh Army had gone racing up the Rhone Valley toward Lyons, hoping to capture the city before the Germans, racing up themselves on the west bank of the Rhone, would pass north of Lyons and escape back to Germany. We were hoping to cut them off and catch them in a pincers between our Seventh Army, coming up from the south, and Patton's Third Army, speeding down from the north toward Orléans. Germany had some ten divisions and strong Panzer forces in southwest France. The Allies were trying to trap them between our armies.

The Germans, with highly competent commanders and disciplined troops, saw the trap. They assigned their most powerful armored units to slow our advance so that the bulk of their forces could make good their escape. An American unit that I was traveling with ran into one of the Panzer divisions outside Montélimar.

As my jeep advanced with the infantry, we came around a curve and were hit by heavy fire. Men were falling all around me. I jumped off the jeep, taking my M-1 from its rack on the dashboard and dived behind the cover of some rocks off the road. Our men began their return fire, while a captain called for aviation to strike the Germans ahead of us. German fire was heavy. I waited, as I had been taught, to spot muzzle flashes from the enemy line. I saw none but I began shooting straight ahead where we had been fired on. It was automatic and impersonal. I had no human face in my sight, just an idea of the place from which enemy fire was coming. The firefight lasted about an hour before the Germans pulled out and we could advance. They kept up that kind of a running attack all through the day.

We captured about fifty wounded Germans and counted about a hundred enemy dead. From prisoner interrogation, we learned that we had been fighting an elite German force, the 11th Panzer Division. It was my first personal meeting with Nazi soldiers. I wanted to shoot them down in a murderous hatred. It took a tremendous effort to curb my fury. I realized with shame how skin-deep my own humanity was.

Men and women from Grenoble and Lyons, commandos of the three principal Resistance groups in the south and east—Combat, Libération, and Franc-Tireur—were harassing German divisions. They cut cable and telephone lines, blew up bridges, and then attacked with gasoline bottles, "Molotov cocktails," the Tiger and Mark V tanks of the armored division. The Resistants stopped the German Panzers outside Lyons when the Germans had gotten within three miles of the headquarters of our 36th Texas Division.

We closed in on Lyons on August 23 and fought our way into France's third largest city, house by house. On September 2, the German XIXth Army ceased to exist as a fighting force. Torn and scattered elements fled Lyons. The third city of France was liberated in our southern advance. We chased them up to the Vosges Mountains where the dense forest stopped us.

I went out with a French unit on night patrol in the forest. It was a group of *goumiers,* fierce Moroccan fighters. The Moroccans were mountaineers and seemed unaffected by the cold rain and fog. I shivered and trembled as I followed them into the dank woods, not only from the cold but from stories I had heard about their reckless daring. Each goumier wore around his neck a leather pouch on a string. At the end of a battle, they would bend over dead enemies, slice off their ears and put them in their leather pouches. The number of dried ears a man would bring home would be a sign to his village of his prowess as a warrior. Sometimes, it was said, they would slice off the ears of the live prisoners. I never saw any evidence of this, and I believe it was untrue, but we did broadcast this to the Germans telling them of the Moroccans. Many German prisoners told us that their morale had been shaken by tales of the savage foe coming after them.

The Germans only had light forces in the mountains, but they had heavily mined and booby-trapped the woods. The major German defenses had been dug in and around Alsace in a curved line going from Basel, on the Swiss border, through Belfort, in the Vosges, and Colmar, in Alsace, around to Strasbourg, on the Rhine. It was called the Alsace pocket, and the mission of Sixth Army Group would be to clear it out. That mission was given to the French First Army, while the American Seventh moved further north to the Heurtgen Forest to join forces with General Patton's Third Army.

Few of the American correspondents went out with the French units. They were all naturally concerned with their own American troops and with sending back home stories of the prowess of the American divisions and tales of hometown heroes. We had a number of outstanding men and women in the press camp, including Eric Sevareid of CBS News; Mary Welsh of *Time* magazine, soon to become Mrs. Ernest Hemingway; and one of the best of correspondents, a tall, willowy blonde, Dudley Harmon of United Press.

One of the most remarkable of all the correspondents was a woman more than seventy years old, who shared my jeep one day, Mary Heaton Vorse, one of America's first and greatest labor reporters in the early years of the century. Mary was a militant crusader for workers' rights, a gay, witty, ribald character. Later in the war, I would team up with her equally ribald son, Joel O'Brien. Everyone fell in love with Mary and no one ever referred to her as a grand old lady. Mary Heaton Vorse was young in heart and spirit, and complained less about the cold and discomforts we were suffering than most of the men, particularly the tall, handsome but gloomy Eric Sevareid who never stopped grumbling about the wretched army mess and the bone-chilling cold of the Vosges.

Sevareid, however, had a lot of clout at headquarters and he became the press camp hero when he persuaded the army brass to put a plane at our disposal for a trip to Paris. We had covered the liberation of France's second and third cities and were all eager to get a chance to send home dispatches from one of the greatest cities of the world, the city of my dreams as a French student and then teacher. It had taken a cruel world war to bring me there.

As the airport bus took us into Paris, I had my nose flattened on the window and began to shout excitedly as the familiar streets and monuments of the photo studies became real at last. The bus dropped us off at the U.S. Embassy on the Place de la Concorde, surely the most majestic, beautiful square in the world. I walked quickly to the obelisk in the center of the square and stared up the Avenue des Champs-Elysées to the Arc de Triomphe high on the summit of the avenue, from which was draped the Tricolor of France, the biggest flag I have ever seen, yards long and wide. I thought my heart would burst. I headed for the U.S. Embassy to find out where the OWI offices were located. An information officer told me that they were scattered around Paris but my best bet would be to go to the Rue d'Aguesseau which was nearby.

I walked into the office, identified myself, and was directed to the executive offices down the hall. I opened a door and there they were: Mike Bessie and Bill Tyler, the Damon and Pythias of the OWI, the old faithful of Algiers. Mike jumped out of his chair and ran to embrace me. Bill, always more stately, a future ambassador of the United States, gave me a warm if more formal welcome. We chattered like magpies for an hour. Then I told Mike I was going over to the Hôtel Matignon, the seat of government, to check in with my French friends and bring myself up to date. He told me to meet him at six-thirty at the bar of the Ritz. "Hemingway will be there, and many old friends. We'll have a night out in Paris."

Many French friends from Algiers were at the Matignon and I spent the afternoon hearing the hair-raising story of the liberation of Paris. Friends explained that it was touch and go that the Germans would put Paris to the torch while the Allies and the Resistance were fighting each other in a struggle for power and control between Gaullists, communists, and American troops. I wondered how Paris ever was liberated, when the Allies were so busy fighting each other. It had been a close thing.

The communist resistance movement in Paris wanted to stage an uprising and take the city from the Germans before Allied troops could arrive. Paris, they argued, must liberate herself for the honor of France. The noncommunists, Gaullists, left-Catholics, and socialists suspected that the communists were cloaking their designs for a seizure of power in patriotic slogans. They knew that the Resistance was strong enough to harass the Germans as guerrillas but not nearly sufficiently armed to challenge the German Army.

Despite the evacuation of the bulk of their forces, the Germans still had armored columns in Paris with enough firepower to overwhelm any insurrection. The German commander in Paris was the dread conqueror of Sebastopol, General Dietrich von Choltitz, who had massacred Russians and left behind him a scorched earth. Von Choltitz was more than capable and likely to destroy Paris if the people rose up to challenge him.

The mayor of Paris, Pierre Taittinger, whose name was world-renowned through his family champagne, negotiated with von Choltitz, pleading with him not to destroy the treasures of Paris uselessly at the end of a lost war. Von Choltitz warned him that nothing would prevent the destruction of Paris if the underground came out to seize the capital. The German commander was ready to surrender to the regular army troops of General Eisenhower but refused to deal with the partisan irregulars and, above all, would not surrender to communists. The communists' insistence upon an insurrection endangered the very existence of Paris.

General de Gaulle had sent instructions to his representative in Paris, Alexander Parodi, to avoid a premature uprising at all costs. He knew it might result in the destruction of the capital but he also knew that it could be politically disastrous if the Resistance, led by the communists, should seize official buildings and liberate Paris before the French Army, under de Gaulle's command, could arrive.

De Gaulle had given the commander of the French 2nd Armored Division, General Leclerc, instructions to race into Paris as fast as he could. At the same time, de Gaulle had asked Eisenhower, as early as December 1943, in Algiers, to assign the 2nd Armored the honor of liberating the capital of France. It is essential, de Gaulle told Eisenhower, for the morale and honor of France, that the first troops into Paris be French.

Eisenhower, always sensitive to the importance of political and psychological factors in war, understood de Gaulle's plea for the French to liberate Paris. He agreed to give the mission to Leclerc and, in response to further pleas from de Gaulle, to hold the Leclerc division in reserve, keeping it out of combat in the Normandy landings and in the battles that followed the breakout from the beaches. Leclerc and his troops would enter Paris in high style, unmarked by combat, all colors flying to dazzle the people with their new French Army. Eisenhower did have misgivings about sending American and British soldiers into combat to fight and die for the liberation of France while France's best division was held in reserve. But he knew that the French were fighting hard in the south and that, after the liberation of Paris, Leclerc's armor would fight loyally and hard for him.

Eisenhower's decision did not sit well with his staff and his senior commanders. General Omar Bradley had no sentimental feelings for Paris and cared only about beating the Germans and invading Germany before winter conditions would make it more difficult. Paris had no tactical or strategic military value. It was, moreover, a tactical burden.

There were three million people in Paris living on near starvation rations under the Germans. A Swiss Red Cross report said that in mid-July Paris was on the verge of famine. Milk consumption before the war had averaged a million two hundred thousand liters a day. In July 1944, supplies had fallen to a hundred twenty thousand liters daily. There were more than twenty-five thousand undernourished babies in Paris. Only a quarter of the population received the daily ration of potatoes. There was not a drop of wine to be bought in Paris in July, outside German-frequented restaurants. Parisians received two eggs per month, ninety grams of cooking oil, and sixty grams of margarine. The only vegetable available was rutabaga, a prewar cattle feed. Three million starving people would have to be fed by the Allies after the liberation. This would be a severe drain on Allied supplies.

Eisenhower's staff gave him a twenty-four-page, top secret report, called Operation Post-Neptune, on the logistics involved in the liberation of Paris. It said that if the Germans chose to defend Paris it could turn into another Stalingrad, destroying the city and causing many civilian as well as military casualties. If, however, the Germans evacuated and surrendered Paris, the results would also be costly for the campaign. The Allies would be obligated to feed the hungry population. It would take hundreds of army trucks to carry supplies for three million Parisians. The report estimated that the cost of feeding liberated Paris would be the equivalent of maintaining eight combat divisions.

Eisenhower was alarmed by that last estimate. He was already in short supply of gasoline for his tanks. General Patton was in a rage, calling headquarters several times a day demanding gas and oil for his insatiable engines. He cared nothing for Paris or its people. All he thought about, correctly as an army commander, was breaking into Germany before winter. If Paris were liberated, he would not get the gas he needed and his tanks would be stalled.

Eisenhower was torn between military exigencies and political imperatives. General Bradley presented him with a combat plan for bypassing Paris on the north and the south, cutting it off, and then, when the Germans were surrounded and themselves starving, taking Paris without a fight or a casualty, at the opportune moment. The one thing that Bradley was worried about, however, was an uprising by the Resistance. If fighting broke out in Paris, the Allies would have to rush in. They could not, as the Russians did in Poland, stand by and let the Germans massacre the guerrillas before moving in.

While Eisenhower was pondering on the final decision, the French made it for him. The communists forced the other Resistance groups to follow them when they went ahead on their own to launch an insurrection in Paris. General Leclerc, against American orders, sent his 2nd Armored Division into Paris through the Porte d'Orléans just in time to save the Resistance from the folly of their uprising. By sunset August 25, Paris had been liberated. Sporadic fighting went on through the capital but von Choltitz surrendered to Leclerc's assault forces and Paris was saved from destruction.

Bradley's warnings and Patton's rages were proved to be correctly motivated. Just as the secret report had predicted, the liberation of Paris required seventy-five thousand tons of food and fifteen hundred tons of coal daily. The railroads had been sabotaged by the Resistance to halt German reinforcements and were not available to supply provisions for Paris. The tonnage was carried in army trucks by the famed Red Ball Express which moved supplies some five hundred miles from the port of Cherbourg to Paris, racing along almost bumper to bumper like an endless column of worker ants. The gas that could have taken Patton deep into Germany went into the trucks for Paris. We would be stalled on the Rhine for long months through a difficult winter, and would have to face an astonishing German counteroffensive.

Familiar as I was with internecine warfare among the Allies, I was startled by the stories of the race for Paris and the conflicting opinions on the validity of its premature liberation. There was little doubt in my own mind that the political and psychological need to free the nation's capital as fast as possible superseded all the military arguments, despite their validity. In any case, once the Resistance had launched an insurrection, Leclerc had no choice but to send his tanks into the city. And once Leclerc had entered Paris, the Allies had no alternative but to support him and help make the city and its people secure. Patton was right militarily but Eisenhower finally saw more clearly than Patton that a military sacrifice had to be made for a larger political goal.

I left my French friends, my head still filled with their dramatic accounts of the liberation of Paris. I walked down to the Seine and crossed on the bridge leading to the gardens of the Louvre. I stood behind the Arc du Carrousel and saw the extraordinary vista beyond, the sweep of the royal gardens of the Tuileries, then the obelisk of the Place de la Concorde, bisecting both the Arc du Carrousel and, in the distance, the Arc de Triomphe. And exactly in the middle of both arches was the setting sun, everything precisely in its place. If French politics were as orderly as French landscaping, the French would have one of the most stable governments on earth.

I turned and walked east, out of the Louvre buildings, and headed to the Marais and the Place des Vosges. I had promised Dorothy that I would visit her school as soon as I came to Paris. The Parsons art school had been closed down by the war but its building still stood in the Place des Vosges. It had been taken over by a school for barrel making. Young Frenchmen were learning the ancient craft of *tonnellerie*. Tired and thirsty, I headed for the corner of the Rue des Francs-Bourgeois and the Place des Vosges to a café called La Bourgogne, a promise of good Burgundy wine.

I walked in and was grabbed around the waist by a big, strong peasant with gnarled, calloused hands and the high flush of wine on his cheeks. "*Vive les Américains!*" he shouted, showing a mouth of gold teeth. He put me down and wrung my hand until it hurt, telling me he loved all Americans and he had *une bonne bouteille* for me. I sat down gratefully as he went to get his promised good bottle.

His name was Louis Beaugey and he would become one of my closest friends in France. He called himself Louis le Bourguignon. He had sold French wines in England and had learned to speak English fluently, with an accent as fruity as his Burgundy grapes. Louis had served as an interpreter with the Yankee and Rainbow Divisions of Pershing's army in the First World War, and had never forgotten those "brave American boys who came to help us drive out the Hun."

I told Louis that my wife Dorothy had gone to art school in the Place des Vosges and loved it. Louis nodded his head, smiled and said: "The Place de la Concorde is the most beautiful square in the world. But this," he said, sweeping his arm to the scene behind him, "this Place des Vosges is the most beautiful square in Paris."

I savored his words as I sipped his wine, thinking to myself that there is a poet inside every Frenchman. This simple Burgundian peasant had casually delivered an illuminating comment, distinguishing the two faces of Paris: the city of the world, the city of the French.

Mike Bessie was waiting for me later at the Ritz bar at a table presided over by the broad-shouldered, deep-chested Ernest "Papa" Hemingway. Despite his dominant personality, Papa was having difficulty controlling the conversation of a dynamic, highly talented group of friends. Robert Capa, *Life* photographer, reputedly the lover of some of Hollywood's most glamorous stars, as popular with men as with women, was evaluating critically some of the American generals he had covered in combat. He felt that Bradley was too cautious, Patton too reckless. At his side was his closest friend, ever since the Spanish Civil War, David Seymour, known as Chim, a gentle man, whose large, wide, bald head and smoked glasses made him look like a mad scientist. With Capa and Henri

Cartier-Bresson, the French camera artist, he would found America's most successful news-photo agency, Magnum.

Next to Chim was another wide-shouldered, barrel-chested man, Irwin Shaw, whom critics had already hailed as America's leading short-story writer. I had read and would never forget two of his best stories: "Girls in Their Summer Dresses," and "Sailor off the Bremen." Shaw would become one of America's most successful novelists, although his novels, aside from his first, *The Young Lions,* never received the same critical acclaim as his short stories. After the war, for many years, Irwin would become a part of our "crowd" in Paris.

Sitting opposite Irwin was Paddy Chayefsky, another talented writer, who would win fame and fortune after the war with films like *Marty* and *Network.* Paddy was not, as the name would seem to indicate, an Irishman. It was a nickname given to him by his fellow soldiers. One day Chayefsky, of Russian-Jewish origin, was assigned to early morning kitchen duties. He protested to the top sergeant that he could not take the duty because he had to attend morning mass. The sergeant, laughing uproariously at his outrageous excuse, took him off "kitchen police" and from then on called him Paddy, telling everyone that Chayefsky was a devout Irish Catholic. All of us would become friends for many wonderful years in Paris.

That first night we met in Paris was glorious. We were young, confident, grabbing life in our fists. From the Ritz we walked across the Seine to the Left Bank and devoured thick sandwiches at a brasserie on the Boul' Mich'. Then we went to a cellar club for wine and listened to a succession of chansonniers, who sang political and drinking songs. We all joined in on songs we knew and hummed those we didn't. The four-centuries-old stone walls of the cellar echoed with the music and the voices of a hundred men and women. After four years of German occupation, the heart of Paris was once again young and gay, and so were we. Rarely in life do dreams come true. They did for me that night in liberated Paris. Then came the chill reality of dawn and a return to the battlefield.

Reality brought me down to earth in the gloomy cold of the Vosges mountains the next day. My division in the French First Army was going to try to capture the fortress on a hill at Belfort. The Belfort Gap was a passage through the mountains that led to the Rhine. If we could knock out the cannons controlling the Gap, we could break through to the river and be on the frontier of Germany opposite the Black Forest. It was a daring plan. Those Belfort cannons were formidable and any column making its way through the Gap would be exposed to murderous shelling.

I wondered just why the attack had been planned, since it would do little good to break through to the Rhine at that point. The Black Forest on the other side of the river was impenetrable. There were no important strategic objectives in the area. It would be far more important to penetrate into Germany farther north, where flat land and many highways could bring us swiftly into the industrial Ruhr where we could knock out Germany's war factories and move on to the road to Berlin. However, the attack had been decided on and I had to report on it, with deep misgivings.

We jumped off before dawn, moving slowly in the total blackness. Strong patrols were ahead of our tank column. Infantry rode on the tanks or walked beside the armor. I sat on the third tank in line wondering just what I was doing there. If I was trying to prove to myself that I was unafraid, I had failed. I was cold-frightened. I thought I could see Germans behind every tree, although I knew it was too dark to see anything. I was briefly cheered by the thought that the Germans in the forest were probably more terrified than I was when they saw heavy French armor moving toward them.

Light began to filter through the trees and then a pale sun came up ahead of us. We were moving due east. The column halted and officers ran down the lines, giving instructions to the assault groups to fan out into the woods, away from the main road of the Gap. The mission of the infantry would be to climb up to and around the fort and attack from the rear and flanks, while our tank column would proceed straight ahead to challenge the cannons. My bones were chilled from the cold night air. But my blood turned icy at the thought that the tank I was sitting on would draw fire in a challenge to the cannons.

We moved ahead as the sun rose high above the forest. I was sitting behind the turret of the tank when suddenly I heard a whoosh and the tops of two trees just ahead of me disappeared in a shower of splinters that began falling on our tanks. It was not a cannon shell. It was a mortar, whose deep throaty grunt had become all too familiar to me. Mortars are deadly in a forest, for the shells break up on the trees into a hundred fragments of red-hot, jagged metal, propelled in an arc like spray from a fountain. There is no defense against a fountain of mortar fragments. You could defend against rifle fire by crouching behind rocks or trees. You could dig a deep foxhole to avoid artillery, except for a direct hit. But mortars did not come flat out at you. They fell from above. Helmets protected our heads but nothing protected our bodies from being ripped apart by the razor shards of a mortar shell.

I jumped off the tank and, in two leaps, reached the trees. I hoped that they would give me some protection. I could hear screams just behind me. Some of our men had been hit. Whoosh! Whoosh! Whoosh! The mortars kept up their death cough. I saw metal bouncing off the turret of the tank where I had been sitting. Then a series of booms. Our tanks were firing back and moving ahead. I moved with them, like an Indian, from tree to tree, holding my M-1 in my left hand, a grenade in my right, in case I ran into a German patrol. I was puzzled by the absence of any cannon fire. Had our men already taken the fort? It did not seem likely. It was too early. We would only learn later that the Germans had evacuated most of the fort, leaving few shells for the cannons. It was a rear-guard force that was raining mortar shells down on us.

I ran along the side of the road, zigzagging back and forth to the woods. Rifle fire and machine-gun bursts indicated fighting deep in the woods. Our men had made contact with an enemy defense force. Suddenly the mortars stopped. I ran alongside the tank, and when no more mortars could be heard, jumped up to its turret again. The road ahead was clear. We had broken through the Belfort Gap. By sunset our men had taken the fort.

We camped in the forest and, exhausted, began eating our rations, cold beef stew in a can and strips of jerky, dried beef which we all called monkey meat. I had a few American D-rations in my knapsack. They contained small packs of three Camel cigarettes and compressed, vitamin-rich chocolate bars. The bars were so thick and hard we could not cut them, not even with our bayonets. We would shave off chips of chocolate or, if we had a fire, would melt the concentrate in a tin. Ingenious French friends would take our tasteless, pasty American white bread loaves, pour melted chocolate over them, and call the concoction *gâteau harlequin.*

My hands were trembling as I started to shave my chocolate bar. I always had an attack of nerves after every battle. I fought through a great many battles and, in my career as a correspondent,

I have been in twelve wars and revolutions. Each battle was more terrifying than the last. Instead of becoming used to it, I kept waiting to be hit by the bullet that had my name on it. That it never came did not convince me that it would not be the very next explosion.

We had taken Belfort. Our commanders decided to push on at once to the Rhine. The next night we were there, on the west bank, staring across the river at Germany. There were celebrations and toasts, speech-making by the French who were proud to be the first Allied troops to reach the Rhine. I began to understand the reason for the attack. It served no important military purpose but, symbolically, it boosted French pride and morale to boast that they had beaten the Americans to the Rhine. Suddenly, one of the officers shouted: "Wait, there is an American with us."

They came running to me, pounding me on the back, congratulating me for being the first American soldier on the Rhine. They told me that I must tell the American people that I had achieved that distinction because I was with the valiant First Army of France. There was much laughter and drinking. I was tired but glad to be alive. I promised that I would report their achievement, and asked permission of the commanding officer to take off at sunrise for the press camp at Luxeuil where I could write my story of the Battle of the Belfort Gap. He laughed and said: "You can even leave tonight if you desire." I shook my head, yawned, and went off to curl up in a dry spot under the trees.

The next morning I drove to press camp and received a warm welcome. The commander had sent a courier back to report his triumphant victory. He had cited me for heroic action and awarded me a battle star. The only heroic thing I had done was not to run away. But plans were made for me to hold a press briefing to describe the action, and everyone congratulated me on being the first American on the Rhine. The mail clerk came over and gave me a fat letter from Dorothy. That was bigger than any award.

I tore the letter open with a broad grin on my face. The first words almost stopped my heart.

> My Darling,
>
> There is no easy way for me to tell you this. Two nights ago, your mother and father were driving home from a bridge game at a friend's house in Flushing. A car with a drunken driver

> came hurtling out of a side street and hit your parents' car. Your mother was thrown out. Dad was tossed against the steering wheel. He is in the hospital with cracked ribs but is getting better. Mother was in a coma for forty-eight hours. She just died. I was at her side, holding her hand. She did not suffer. She never regained consciousness.

I felt as though a mortar shell had finally hit me. I screamed and several correspondents came running over to me. Tears ran down my face. I couldn't talk. My throat was closed. I dropped the letter, ran up to my quarters, slammed the door, and gave myself up to an agonizing grief. I was overwhelmed not only by the loss but by the tragic absurdity of fate that had sent me through a deadly fight without a scratch while my gentle, sweet, beloved mother was being killed in a car accident in New York.

I finally came down and asked for a drink. Victor Bienstock, correspondent for ONA, came over to express his regrets. Carleton Kent, correspondent of the Chicago *Daily News,* and a poker buddy also came over. They all told me to apply at once for a "compassionate furlough," so that I could go home to see my Dad and put flowers on Mother's grave.

The next morning I drove over to headquarters company. I showed Dorothy's letter to the commanding officer and asked for a one-month leave.

He shook his head sadly. "Sorry, but I can't do that. If every man who had trouble at home asked for a leave we would have no one left."

I looked at him in amazement. "Trouble at home?" I did not have any trouble at home. I had asked for leave because of a tragedy. I was stunned at his lack of feeling or understanding.

Then he left me breathless with the most idiotic comment I had ever heard.

"Soldier, there's a war on."

CHAPTER 9

THE LAST TO KNOW

The weather in Belgium and northeastern France is almost always bad in late fall and winter. Constant rain and frequent snowfalls turn the fields into a soggy morass. When hundreds of thousands of troops and armor move across the mud, they churn it into gluey bogs that threaten to suck down men and machines. December 1944 was one of the worst periods of muck and fog in many years.

We were sitting around a table in the press camp bitching about the cold, the rotten food, Patton's raging tempers, knowing that he had run out of gas for his tanks and that we would be stuck there until spring. We were playing high-stakes poker, while in the alley behind us the motor-pool sergeants and the off-duty military police were engaged in a loud, quarrelsome craps game.

A major came into the room. "Briefing in five minutes. Something big is up."

We walked over to the briefing room. It was noon, December 16, 1944.

A colonel on Patton's staff was waiting, standing on an upturned crate so that everyone could see him and a map of the Ardennes sector of Belgium pinned on the wall behind him. He cleared his throat, picked up a pointer, and began.

"Just before dawn, under cover of darkness, thick fog, and intense cold, the enemy launched a powerful combined assault of infantry, tanks, and heavy artillery against thinly held American lines in the heavily wooded Ardennes. It was not an isolated assault. It is now clear that Marshal Gerd von Rundstedt has been preparing a major offensive along a broad front. Antwerp has been under heavy V-2 rocket barrages. We are holding the line and preparing a counterattack. The enemy has had some early success in penetrating some of our lines due to surprise and to lightly held positions in some places. I cannot be more precise at this moment for heavy fighting is going on and we are getting sketchy reports. There will be no questions."

We all went to the wall map, studied the terrain and the troop dispositions that had been posted the day before. Patton's Third Army was holding the southeastern sector of the Ardennes, nearest to the German border. The U.S. First and Ninth Armies were on the northern front, neighboring on the British forces under the command of Field Marshal Montgomery. "Monty" commanded all British and Commonwealth forces, while Omar Bradley commanded all American, French, and other Allied forces attached to the Americans. Eisenhower was in Supreme Command of all Allied forces.

As we looked at the map, we realized that Patton was alone in the southeastern sector and that the overall goal of the Germans, aiming at Antwerp and the Channel, ran through the northern sector, striking westward, so that the main action would probably be farthest from us. We were certain that Patton would want to hit due north to turn Rundstedt's flank and strike at his rear, and that this would bring us into action. But we would just have to wait until someone told us what was going on and where we could go to cover the story. We knew it would not be long because nothing could stop Patton from fighting and he wouldn't want to fight without having us there to record his triumphs. In about two hours, a briefing officer finally came to give us the word. Our guess had been correct. The main German thrust was westward in the northern sector. But we learned little else.

Our forces were that day falling back under the fury of the German surprise attack. Fog continued to ground our planes which could not come to help the embattled ground forces. The weather was a big break for the Germans. Their own air army, the Luftwaffe, had been all but driven from the skies and would not have been able to cover the offensive, but fog kept us from using our aerial advantage. Von Rundstedt's forces had penetrated into Belgium, creating a big bulge in the Allied lines. Inevitably, someone dubbed it the Battle of the Bulge.

We finally got some map guidance and piled into jeeps, carrying battle maps, with various command posts circled in red. As we pushed into the forest, past tank upon tank stalled in the mud, a heavy snow began to fall, making conditions treacherous for our light jeeps and impossible for the heavy tanks. Tankmen swore horrible oaths and invented new ones as their bare hands stuck to metal, stripping the skin off as they pulled away. Suddenly, out of the fog, we heard the blast horn of a command car. It was "Old Guts and Glory" Patton roaring along the line, exhorting his men to get the "goddamned machines moving." He shook his fists at the sky, cursing the "lily-livered Air Force," and promised to fight the Germans all alone if no one had the balls to come with him. He was beside himself with rage and the sheer joy of battle. The correspondents in my jeep were furious. We were caught in the fighting, unbriefed and lost in the woods.

The fight was going badly. Von Rundstedt's strategy was brilliant and his tactics seemed to come from some kind of X-ray vision into our lines. His troops found every weakness and exploited it skillfully. Somehow the Germans had reached down into their battered selves for one last supreme effort to break the Allied front. We came under fire at almost every bend in the road. Allied troops were falling back all along the line. Then, back at press camp, we learned of a large American force at Bastogne, in southeast Belgium, in Patton's sector, near the Luxembourg border, completely surrounded by the Germans. It was hopelessly outnumbered and outgunned, cut off from any help. The Germans called on General Tony McAuliffe to surrender his troops or be slaughtered. His curt reply, now part of American military history, was not elegant but it made its point. "Nuts," said McAuliffe.

We were in press camp writing gloomy dispatches after a frustrating, dangerous day of covering the battle when an officer came in with a new Patton story. Patton stories abounded, many of them true, some of them fanciful inventions. The most fanciful of the inventors was Patton himself. He used to love to tell stories, not only of his battle prowess but of his encounters and clashes with higher authority. Patton believed that most superior officers were fools if not cowards. He had a special hatred of Montgomery for his overcautious generalship. He considered Monty both a fool and a coward. He was enraged when General Omar Bradley had called him in on December 20 to tell him that the U.S. First and Ninth Armies were to be combined with the British forces in the north into one coordinated command to meet the German offensive and that all those forces would be put under Montgomery.

"You can't do that," Patton shouted at Bradley. "You can't put Americans in his goddamned fumbling hands. Give me the command, I'll break the back of the German assault," he demanded.

"Sorry, George," said Bradley in his mild, always friendly manner. "Those American troops are in the northern sector, next to the British. It's Monty's sector and he is the highest-ranking officer there. He is certainly not reckless and our boys will be in good hands."

"Not reckless? You can bet your ass he's not reckless. He won't do a goddamned thing until he has a five-to-one advantage, and von Rundstedt will end up in Antwerp while Monty's still lining up his artillery."

Bradley had had enough of Patton's defamation of a superior officer and a good ally. "George, you've had your say. Now knock it off. Monty is taking over. That's it. And that's a direct order."

Patton snapped to attention and threw Bradley a smart salute.

"Yes, General, sir, I confirm your order, sir. But one last word, sir. Give me the command, sir, and I will stop the Germans, sir, capture von Rundstedt, sir, and shove him up Monty's ass, sir!"

It was one of the great Patton stories. Of course, we did not know if there was a word of truth in it. No one had been present at the meeting other than Patton and Bradley. Two months later I saw Omar Bradley, our beloved "G. I. General," and asked him about the story. He gave me his shy, sweet smile and said, "Sure sounds like George, doesn't it?"

The fog lifted on Christmas Day and a weak sun broke through. Our planes took off at last and began strafing and bombing the German forces. We knew then that the tide of battle would turn against the enemy and that von Rundstedt's offensive would be stopped and beaten back. The Germans could not advance through the firepower of our fighters and bombers. But they did not cut and run. They fought on desperately against all hope with a courage and skill that we had to admire as much as we hated them. Our men, too, particularly the besieged "Bastards of Bastogne," fought on, taking heavy casualties, refusing to surrender, knowing victory would be ours. On January 16, the Germans finally broke and retreated after very heavy losses. The Battle of the Bulge was over. It was one of our costliest "victories" in World War II. The Allies lost seventy-seven thousand men.

While we had been engaged in the Battle of the Bulge, Soviet forces were advancing on the eastern front. On January 11, 1945, Soviet troops entered Warsaw. A controversy raged, and is still lively today among historians, about Soviet actions during this period.

The Red Army, which had the Germans on the run, had come to a halt at the Polish frontier just at the moment that Polish partisans of the Resistance had risen up out of the underground hoping to clear the way for the Soviets to come in and liberate Poland. The Soviets did not come. The Nazis crushed the Polish resistants, inflicting casualties so severe that it was a massacre. Only then did the Russians move to clear the Nazis out of Poland. Officially, the Soviets claimed that the London Poles had prematurely given the order for the uprising. The Poles charged that the Soviets had deliberately stopped to permit the Germans to massacre dangerous partisan fighters.

A summit meeting of the Allied chiefs of government had gone into session on February 4, 1945. Joseph Stalin, Winston Churchill, and Franklin Delano Roosevelt sat down at a conference table in the summer palace of former Czar Nicholas II near Yalta, in the Crimea. Just the day before, the U.S. Air Force had hit Berlin again with a devastating one-thousand-plane raid. Berlin was aflame, while the German armies on the western and eastern fronts were caught in the vise of a Soviet-American nutcracker. Germany was doomed. The first thing that Stalin called for at the Yalta Conference was a renewed pledge by Churchill and Roosevelt that they stood firm on the original Casablanca pledge of unconditional surrender. We would only hear about this on February 13, a day after the Yalta Conference had ended, when the White House announced some of the results of the conference.

Many of the Yalta accords were secret and would not be known until the conference documents were published in 1947. These accords provoked a furor which has never died down. In the summer of 1981, at a luncheon in an Alpine resort of Switzerland, the guests turned on me, the only American present, and asked accusingly: "Why did America turn over Poland to Russia? Why did you abandon all eastern Europe in the Yalta sellout?"

Sellout, betrayal, appeasement, these were charges hurled at Roosevelt and Churchill in the corridors and halls of Parliament, Congress, the press and radio. No international conference, not even the disgraceful surrender to Hitler's demands at Munich in 1938, had set off such instant, angry denunciations as the Yalta accords.

The controversy centered around a decision affecting Poland's eastern frontier. Some six million Poles living in a seventy-thousand-square-mile area would become Soviet citizens when Yalta transferred their province to Russia. In return for the loss of that territory on the east, Poland was granted thirty-nine thousand square miles of eastern Germany, smaller but much more valuable than the land they had lost because it contained industrial districts and fertile land in German Silesia. Poland also received a vital strip of Baltic Sea coast, including the ports of Danzig and Stettin.

In effect, Poland as a country was moved westward by the Yalta accords. Poland benefitted materially but was endangered politically, for the expulsion of Germans and resettlement of Poles in ancient German territory leaves open the possibility that at some future time, Germans could demand a return of their lost lands. This made Poland dependent on Russia for protection, and the Russian bear is a most dangerous "protector."

The Polish government-in-exile, in London, denounced the Yalta accords, calling them the "fifth partition of Poland." Many voices were raised in London and Paris reminding everyone that France and Britain had gone to war against Germany when Hitler's forces invaded Poland in 1939. Now that the Germans were about to be defeated and Poland liberated, the victorious Allies were cutting up Poland once again.

Despite some dissenting voices, both Democratic and Republican leaders in Congress voiced approval of the Yalta accords. And in London, Commons endorsed the territorial decisions on Poland by a vote of 390 to 25. Then the House of Commons voted unanimously, 413 to 0, to approve all of the Yalta decisions, including the controversial Polish issue.

It is particularly useful today, with Poland in constant crisis, to recall what the situation was in 1945 when the Western leaders met with Stalin at Yalta. The Red Army of Russia had borne the full weight of the mighty German offensive for three bloody years before the Allies had landed in Normandy. Soviet casualties far exceeded Allied losses. The Red Army had at first retreated but then had fought back and defeated the best, most powerful German armies. The Russians were in Poland and sweeping through eastern Europe. Militarily, Stalin controlled Poland and eastern Europe, and neither Roosevelt nor Churchill were in any position to tell him what to do there.

We did not "give" Poland and eastern Europe to Stalin. His armies had taken it, just as, later, we did not "give" China to the communists. Mao defeated Chiang and drove him off the mainland. It is easy today to ask, "Why did you give Poland to the Reds?" if one forgets the truth of what happened. Would anyone in his right mind seriously say that we should have or could have opposed Russia? Would Poland be any better off today if its borders had not been altered? This is not to say that the Poland settlement was just. It simply recognized the reality of Soviet power in Poland at a moment when Russia was still a vitally needed ally.

Those who criticize the Yalta agreements conveniently forget that Roosevelt was thinking ahead to the final phase of the war, the defeat of Japan. The Joint Chiefs had warned him that an invasion of the home islands of Japan could cost us more than two hundred thousand casualties. It was clearly in the best interests of the United States, which had not yet produced a successful atomic explosion, to persuade Stalin to join us in the final assault upon Japan. Stalin, knowing our fears and needs, was bound to ask a high price for his help.

When Stalin finally agreed secretly to enter the war against Japan within three months of the defeat of Germany, he was able to win acceptance of his Polish demands and, in addition, he was promised Japan's South Sakhalin and Kuril Islands. The Soviets occupy those islands today, have installed secret missile bases and guard them fanatically, which led in 1983 to their shooting down a South Korean commercial plane, a barbarous act which outraged the world. Roosevelt and Churchill also agreed to admit the Soviet provinces of the Ukraine and Belorussia as full members of the United Nations.

On March 1, FDR addressed a joint session of Congress to

report on the Yalta Conference. Some of its clauses were still secret. He called the Polish settlement a necessary compromise. He asserted that unconditional surrender applied to the Nazi leaders but did not mean "the enslavement of the German people." He told Congress that "we shall have to take the responsibility for world collaboration, or we shall have to bear the responsibility for another world conflict." He explained that the plan to create a new world organization, the United Nations, spelled "the end of the system of unilateral action and exclusive alliances and spheres of influence and balances of power and all the other expedients which have been tried for centuries and have failed." Roosevelt called Yalta "a turning point in our history and, therefore, in the history of the world."

At Yalta it was agreed that Germany would be put under four zones of Allied occupation: Russian, American, British, and French. It was also agreed that China and France would join Russia, America, and Britain as founding members of the United Nations. General de Gaulle had won his fight for top world rank for France. Winston Churchill had fought hard to win the inclusion of a French zone and a top position at the U.N. He wanted a strong France as a counterweight to the Soviet Union in Europe.

It was further provided that agreement among the "Big Five" would be necessary on those questions "regarding the use of force." Agreement by the Big Five meant that each could veto actions by refusing to agree. The veto was used often, from the very earliest days, by Russia, at a time when America could command a majority vote at the U.N. Constant criticism of Soviet vetoes by American political and diplomatic leaders gave the public the impression that the veto power was a sinister Soviet invention. In fact, it was Republican Senator Arthur Vandenberg who told Roosevelt that the Senate would never endorse entry into the U.N. unless American independence was assured by a veto power. The United States insisted upon the veto although it is Russia which has made the most frequent use of it.

The war was still being fought hard on all fronts during these political developments. On February 13, in one of the most destructive, violent acts in all human history, the Western Allies firebombed Dresden, killing one hundred thirty-five thousand people. The "conventional" bombs were as destructive of life as the atom bomb over Japan would be later that year. The atom bomb, however, has longer killing effect because of radiation disease, and opposition to the deployment of atomic weapons became a major political issue in Western Europe in the eighties, thirty-five years after Hiroshima and Nagasaki.

We were bogged down by bad weather in Europe and dug in to protect ourselves against the onslaughts of Generals Snow and Mud. We knew we would not break through into Germany before spring, so we just hunkered down, ate our revolting Spam and the meat-stew C-rations, the cold cheese and chocolate K-rations, and dreamed of home, of our wives, girl friends, and families. If war is hell, there are times when hell gets frozen over and men live like field mice in holes. Then war is a filthy, mind-dulling bore.

On April 10, we were informed that one of Patton's battalions had overrun a Nazi death camp. We had earlier heard reports from the eastern front that the Soviets had captured a camp at a place called Auschwitz. We could not believe the horror stories of living skeletons, and ovens in which thousands of Jews had been incinerated. The next day, General Patton went to see for himself what conditions were at a camp his men had liberated in a town called Buchenwald. We set out, on April 11, for Buchenwald.

I never had believed the phrase "the smell of death hung over the place" which I had read so often in novels. But I believed it and never have forgotten it since April 11, 1945. Minutes before our jeep had rounded a corner in a woods near Buchenwald we smelled death. It hung all over the place, dank, fetid, evil. As we approached a barbed-wire fence, we could see creatures that had once been human, in black and white striped rags, with skeletal faces and skulls out of which peered large eyes protruding out of bony ridges. They stared at us as we stared at them, neither quite believing what they were seeing.

We braked our jeep and walked slowly, nervously into the camp. Off to our right was a neat cross-stacked pile of firewood. As we drew closer we saw it was not firewood. It was a rack of dead bodies, thin as sticks, neatly stacked with German efficiency. Then, to our horror, we saw bare toes, in the middle of the stack, twitching. We screamed, "Someone's alive in that stack." A striped inmate, standing with us, shook his head and told us mournfully, in French, "No, they are all gone. That twitch is the rictus of death."

At that moment, General Patton came around the corner of

the barracks. His face was green, beads of sweat on his upper lip, his arms wrapped around his stomach as though he had severe cramps. We stared at him as he began to run toward the fence. Then he stopped, doubled over, and vomited, heaving in great gasps. We all turned away to give the general the privacy he needed in his moment of agony and grief. It was the first time I had seen any signs of warm, human compassion in Patton and I liked him better from that day on.

The mayor of Buchenwald was taken by our soldiers and forced to witness the evil of the camp. That night he went home and hanged himself. We never believed the Germans who told us that they did not know what was going on in the death camps. It was impossible not to know. The stench, the smoking furnaces, and the eyewitness testimony of those Germans who did business with the camp guards could leave no doubt. But they blinded themselves to the truth. When forced to face it, the mayor of Buchenwald could not live with the sight.

That day, for the first time in my life, I literally wished that millions and millions of Germans would hang themselves or be hanged by us. A fury that was madness gripped me. It can still flare up forty years later when I read the odious lies of men who are university professors and who write books denying the Holocaust. There are more than a million feet of horror film shot by our army cameras and by newsreel companies. I believe they should be shown once a year in every country on an international Holocaust Day. Every generation should know what hideous sins man can commit, and know that it, too, could be a victim. Unless all men and women begin to understand in their very being that we are all one and that there are no "others," humanity may be doomed.

April 12, in a company tent at Buchenwald lit by a kerosene lamp, stupefied by the scenes of horror, we sat in a huddle and listened to an American reporter from Chicago talking about Zionism, with passion, telling us that the establishment of a Jewish state in Palestine must follow inevitably upon the massacre of the Holocaust. His name was Meyer Levin, a major writer of our times. His book on Chicago, *The Old Bunch,* put him in a class with James Farrell. Millions read *Compulsion,* the story of the thrill-killers Leopold and Loeb. Meyer Levin would become best known for his moving stories of the founding and settling of Israel.

As Levin told us about Palestine that night in the shadows of the death camp, someone said he could not stand another minute of talk about death and problems and stood up to put on the radio. We heard the familiar voice of John Charles Daly, the CBS News broadcaster, in a most unusually slow and somber cadence. We could hear drums in the background. It took a minute or two to realize what we were hearing. It was a funeral procession. Daly's voice was half-choked and one could sense the muffled sobs in his throat. Franklin Delano Roosevelt was dead.

Men around me were standing in shock, some were weeping. I felt a terrible pain deep in my gut. I still grieved achingly for my beloved mother. Now I had lost a dear, close friend, almost a father, for, although I had only met Roosevelt once, the President had been the dominant personality in my life from youth to maturity. He had done many things that had disturbed me. I had even dared oppose his policy on de Gaulle and France. But I would never forget his voice on the radio, his warm and cheery "my friends," in the darkest hours of the Depression. He had been our leader in the war, as well as the architect of the New Deal, the champion of the forgotten man. And now he was gone. To listen to the description of his funeral near the gates of the Buchenwald death camp was too much to bear. I ran out of the tent and into the woods. It was one of the worst nights of my life. I walked until dawn, then returned to camp, fell on my cot, and lost myself in a long, deep sleep.

While the world was mourning the death of Roosevelt, the papers and radios were filled with horror stories of the Nazi death camps. At Buchenwald and Bergen-Belsen tens of thousands had died of starvation, disease, and execution. Prime Minister Winston Churchill addressed the House of Commons and warned that even worse horrors had been committed and would soon be revealed. He meant the gas ovens where millions had been asphyxiated and incinerated.

Two days after Churchill's address, Dachau was liberated and the stories of its ovens told to a horrified world. Churchill, Stalin, and President Harry Truman, in his first week in office, signed a "solemn warning," in Churchill's words, that there would be full and severe punishment meted out not only to the top Nazi leaders but to all those "who had carried out these foul deeds with their own hands." There would be no toleration of the military excuse

"I was only following orders." General Eisenhower called for a delegation from Congress and editors to come to Europe to see for themselves the evil of the death camps.

On April 25, the United Nations Charter Conference opened at San Francisco while on the same day Russian and American combat patrols met on the Elbe River south of Berlin. The vise had closed on the Germans. It was almost all over. On April 28, Italian partisans captured Mussolini and hanged him and his mistress Clara Petacci from a telephone pole. On May 1, reports from Berlin told us that Hitler, Eva Braun, Josef-Paul Goebbels and his family had all committed suicide in their bunker in Berlin.

On May 7, 1945, Germany surrendered unconditionally. The surrender took place in a ceremony at a schoolhouse in Reims, France. It was a small school, made of red brick, and we all called it the "Little Red Schoolhouse in Reims" in our dispatches. The surrender took place at 2:41 A.M. in the morning of May 7. Back home it was 8:41 P.M., May 6, Eastern War Time.

I sat in the classroom, exultant with joy, with a broad smile splitting my face as I watched Colonel General Gustav Jodl, Chief of Staff of the German Army, walk slowly to a row of desks, where Lieutenant General Walter Bedell Smith sat alongside General Ivan Susloparov of the Soviet Union and General François Sevez of France, looking like the board of trustees punishing a disgraced teacher.

We had all waited so long for this moment of ultimate triumph that the surrender ceremony itself seemed almost like an anticlimax. We were strangely dulled, stunned by the realization that it was all over in Europe, that Mussolini and Hitler were dead, the German General Staff humbled and humiliated by unconditional surrender. Later, driving back to Paris from Reims, the fields cloaked in darkness, the houses blacked out, shutters drawn, no celebration, not at three in the morning, all seemed unreal.

The sun was up when I parked my jeep in front of General Eisenhower's headquarters at the Hotel Scribe. As I walked into the lobby and headed toward the mess to get breakfast, someone called out my name. It was Mike Bessie, and he was looking grim. He put his arm through mine and we walked down to the breakfast room. Only when we were seated did Mike tell me what had happened.

Ed Kennedy, a fine reporter with the Associated Press, had

done the unforgivable, breaking our most sacred taboo. He had not respected the release date for the news to be published and had sent out his dispatch on the German surrender, scooping every reporter there, but, more importantly, making it public in the West before Moscow could release it to the Russian people. Moscow was in a rage, accusing the Allies of signing a separate peace with the Germans. German troops, which had stopped fighting on the western front, were still fighting, in a last gasp, on the Russian front. Stalin, ever the paranoid, suspected a massive double cross. Eisenhower was in a terrible temper, trying to explain what had happened to Stalin and threatening to arrest and court-martial Kennedy for violating censorship.

The AP, knowing that its man had broken the release date, had nonetheless put out his dispatch to all its worldwide clients. It was just as guilty as Ed Kennedy, and Eisenhower ordered an immediate ban on AP filing. Eisenhower sent a blistering signal to AP's Executive Director, Kent Cooper, a towering, legendary figure of American journalism. Ed Kennedy was stripped of all privileges when he admitted that he had been guilty of a deliberate violation of regulations and a grave breach of confidence. AP fired him.

Kent Cooper called Eisenhower to apologize, explaining that the AP news editor on duty had not known that Ed Kennedy had broken a release time. AP, the biggest press agency in the world, was too important to be cut off, so General Eisenhower lifted the ban on its filing. The correspondents were now furious with Eisenhower. Fifty-four SHAEF veteran war correspondents addressed a letter to the Supreme Commander protesting the lifting of the AP ban, stating that they had "suffered the most disgraceful, deliberate and unethical double cross in the history of journalism." Eisenhower replied that the guilty party was Ed Kennedy and that he had been suspended.

Mike Bessie told me that we had been broadcasting all morning, explaining to the people of Europe that the war had not yet officially ended and would not until the surrender had been ratified by all the Allies and all fighting had ceased. The aim of the broadcasts was to mollify the Russians. He wanted me to rush to the studio and explain, as an eyewitness, what had happened at the Little Red Schoolhouse, stressing the presence of a Soviet officer.

Meantime, news of the surrender in Reims had reached Paris

and people began to come out into the streets, carrying bottles of wine, singing and dancing. But it was not yet a true explosion of joy, for word had also spread that there was some kind of a quarrel and that Victory in Europe had not been officially proclaimed. The real explosion would come the next day, May 8, when the unconditional surrender was ratified in Berlin at 11:01 A.M. Central European Time, 6:01 A.M. Eastern War Time in Washington.

By noon May 8, Paris went wild. Millions of French civilians and thousands of troops converged on the traditional avenues of celebration, the Champs-Elysées, the République, the Bastille, the Opéra, and the Concorde. American jeeps, tanks, and trucks were crowded with girls carrying flowers and wine, looking like an anthill in full swarm over a cube of sugar. The birth rate in France, negative for some years, would shoot up some nine months after V-E Day. Accordions played the "Marseillaise" and an approximation of "The Star-Spangled Banner." Couples danced in the streets and on all the boulevards of Paris, while coupling was in full swing in the tree-shadowed alleyways of the Bois de Boulogne.

I had linked arms with two good friends, a young actor named Mickey Knox, a sort of John Garfield type, ruggedly handsome, and a wild Irishman, Joel O'Brien, son of Mary Heaton Vorse. The three of us staggered arm in arm down the Avenue de l'Opéra, stopping for hugs, kisses, and wine every yard of the way. We were smeared with lipstick and loopy with wine when we finally reached our destination, a bar about midway down the avenue, operated by two sensational young women, one Mickey's love and later his wife, the other, Joel's "girl." Mickey's love was named Georgette, Joel's Gilberte. I was, as always, odd man out. I am an old-fashioned sort of fellow. The vision of my beloved Dorothy, always in my mind, was enough to keep me free of any romantic adventures.

Georgette saw us entering and flashed her full-mouth smile, bright red lips, with a coquettish pout and gleaming white teeth, in contrast to her raven hair and dark brown eyes. She lifted her arms, waving a bar towel like a flag, signaling us to come behind the bar to join her. As her arms lifted, so did her full round breasts. Georgette was a lush beauty and we called her "The very ripe plum." Gilberte, whom Joel had named White Panther, was a perfect foil for Georgette's lush, dark beauty. Her hair was platinum, her eyes tilted upward at the corners, like a cat's eyes. They were the color of seawater flecked with sunlight. She was less lush than Georgette but no less curved, her breasts tilted up and away from her chest, her waist slim, her bottom round and tight, flowing into slim legs. The two of them together were a public danger. Cars would jump the curb on the Avenue de l'Opéra when Georgette and Gilberte would saunter down the broad boulevard.

The girls hugged and kissed us, and my joy at V-E Day was marred only by a most painful, all-day priapism. We ended up on top of the hill of Montmartre in the open-air cafés just under the Church of the Sacré Coeur. I watched the dawn rise over the rooftops of Paris, not wondering this time if I would survive the battles ahead. I had survived and was with friends who would remain friends for life, as though sharing victory in Paris was an indissoluble bond.

Our only worry at the time was the dread thought that General MacArthur would need more men in the Pacific and that we might be transferred to that theater. We had fought a long, tough war against the Nazis and wanted no more battle. Our chances looked good. We had many stripes and battle stars, were specialists in European languages, radio and movie documentaries. We would be needed in the early months of the occupation of Germany to explain the rules both to the Germans and the Allied soldiers and to report to the people back home what steps were being taken to punish the war criminals, what was being done to build a new, democratic Germany on the ashes and rubble of the Nazi ruins. Mickey was assigned to a Signal Corps unit to make short films on the occupation, while Joel and I, to our joy, were named as a roving two-man team, to drive through Germany and report on the occupation by radio.

In mid-July, I received a message from Paris informing me that President Harry Truman had landed at the airport in Antwerp, Belgium, where he was greeted by General Eisenhower. There he had changed planes for a flight to Berlin where he would participate in a "Big Three" conference, with Churchill and Stalin, in an old palace in the suburb of Potsdam. I was to proceed immediately to cover that Potsdam Conference and send through daily radio reports. Joel was to keep the jeep and continue on the occupation story until I rejoined him after the meeting.

I used my Eisenhower letter to get on a courier plane and arrived in Berlin on July 16, the day the conference was scheduled to begin. It didn't, for Stalin had not arrived. His failure to appear was not explained and so a flood of rumors rolled over press headquarters. Relations among the wartime Allies were strained. Soviet suspicion of all Allied moves and American dislike, even hatred of, communism had already poisoned the climate although the war was not yet over. Eisenhower, ever the peacemaker and conciliator, had said at a press conference in Paris that there was nothing to indicate that cooperation with the Russians was impossible. "Peace lies with all the peoples of the world, not just for the moment with some political leaders," he asserted.

I took advantage of Stalin's delay to tour Berlin. I drove through rubble and devastation so great that there were no streets left, nothing that corresponded to my map. I took compass bearings to head toward the suburb of Charlottenburg, the site of the beautiful Cassirer mansion that my mother had told me about so many times. I reached the site but there was no mansion there. Everything had been destroyed. I made my way back into Berlin, watching people slink in and out of spaces cleared in the rubble like ratholes. Men and women were indistinguishable, puppet figures in rags, with white faces ringed in black. I am a soft-hearted man but my heart did not go out to these miserable wretches, fellow humans though they might be. The stench of Buchenwald, the image of bodies stacked like cordwood were still with me. I felt no pity, until I saw the children, little shrunken dwarfs, with pinched faces, their bellies swollen with hunger. They were the true victims, the innocents of the world. I called them over and emptied my pockets.

Back at headquarters I heard some reporters talking excitedly about something called an atom bomb that had been successfully exploded at a place called Alamogordo, New Mexico. I paid no attention. Bombs never fascinated me, one of my blind spots. I should have paid attention, for that explosion would cast its evil shadow over the rest of my life, the lives of my children and grandchildren and all the peoples of the world. All I was interested in was the policy position of Truman and the American delegation to the conference. I found a friend at headquarters who filled me in.

The briefing was complete, as far as it could go in advance.

Truman, apprehensive at first about his first major inter-Allied conference, was buoyed up by news of the successful atomic explosion. In his duel with Stalin he would wield the magic sword, the new "ultimate" weapon, an American monopoly. He intended to press Stalin to carry out the promise of free elections in Poland. On the agenda was confirmation and final delineation of Allied occupation zones in Germany, including a plan for joint occupation of the city of Berlin. This would lead inevitably to a dangerous confrontation between the West and the Soviets, for the former German capital, Berlin, would be located inside the Soviet zone, with only a narrow corridor joining it to the West, an impossible situation.

Stalin arrived the next day, July 17, and the conference began. It went as scheduled and as foreseen. What was not foreseen was an event that took place far from the Potsdam Palace. In an astonishing reversal of political fortunes, Winston Churchill, the great wartime hero, the savior of England, was soundly defeated in a British general election. His fellow citizens regarded him as the great warrior but did not trust him to lead them into a complex new world. They turned instead to Socialist Clement Attlee, who became the peacetime prime minister of a victorious but exhausted England.

Another event outside the conference signaled a troubled future. In London, at the World Zionist Conference, the famed British chemist Chaim Weizmann called on the U.N. to recognize the establishment of a Jewish state as "one of the fruits of victory." When I asked Truman about it, he said it seemed like a good idea and would soon comment on it publicly. He had little else to say, the lid was on tightly on the conference itself. Truman finally did endorse the Jewish state, on August 16, calling for free settlement of Jews in Palestine, revealing that this had been the U.S. position at Potsdam, but that it had been opposed by the British.

I left Potsdam to rejoin Joel O'Brien at French occupation HQ in Baden-Baden. I would relive the Potsdam Conference thirty years later when producer David Susskind made a television special for the Hallmark *Hall of Fame* series on NBC, called "Return to Potsdam." It starred José Ferrer as Stalin and my old friend at OWI, John Houseman, as Churchill, with David Schoenbrun playing the role of David Schoenbrun, the American reporter at Potsdam. Not only did I play myself thirty years later, but I was the narrator of the film, explaining what was going on when it could not be done by action. The makeup man did a fabulous job on me but there is no way that anyone, except maybe Ronald Reagan, can look like himself thirty years earlier.

In Baden-Baden, I found Joel in a miserable little attic room, happy as a thrush, nesting with a cute little German bird. I routed them out of bed and went down to flash my magic Eisenhower letter at the billeting officer. We were in one of the most elegant, beautiful hotels in the world, untouched by the war, for it was well off the main strategic targets, the Brenner Park Hotel, in a grove of trees. It was a miniature Eden far, far from the war and its ruins. We lived it up for a week, playing gin rummy and drinking a local fruit brandy called *Himbeergeist,* a white, raspberry-flavored potent drink. Soldiers called it white lightning. Joel owed me one million four hundred thousand dollars on the rummy tally and grandly gave me an IOU for the entire amount. By then we were both hung over and miserable and decided we had better get out of Baden-Baden and get on with our radio reports before the military police were sent to find us.

We left early the next morning. I was driving our jeep when we stopped at the checkpoint between the French and American zones of occupation. I handed over our papers to a burly sergeant who looked at them and scowled. My heart was pounding when he said: "Your orders have run out. You're late in reporting back to headquarters." I started to make excuses about toothaches. But he waved aside my babblings and said, "Ah, shit, what's the difference. They dropped the atom bomb and the fuckin' war is over. Get your ass out of here."

I hit the accelerator with a heavy foot and the jeep jumped ahead. I began to cheer, thumping Joel on the back. "We made it, buddy, we got away with our papers running out. Now, all we have to do is square it at HQ." Joel, whose green face contrasted with his red hair, sick from white lightning and all-night sex, smiled weakly at me and said nothing. Suddenly he shot upright, his green face turning redder than his hair. "Stop the fucking jeep, stop the fucking jeep." I thought he was going to throw up so I hit the brakes and skidded to a halt.

"You all right, Joel?"

"All right? You ask me if I'm all right? Did you hear what that sergeant said?"

"Yes, he said it makes no difference about our papers, they

dropped the atom bomb . . . and THE WAR IS OVER! Jesus Christ, Joel," I shouted, it finally dawning on me what the sergeant had said, "Jesus Christ, the war is over! The war is over!"

We both jumped out of the jeep and grabbed each other and began dancing around the road, screaming, laughing, crying. Then Joel stopped, looked at me, and asked, "What the fuck is an atom bomb?"

I looked at him blankly. "Beats the shit out of me, lieutenant. Don't have a friggin' notion. Let's get back into the jeep. Screw headquarters. We'll go back to Paris, and with all our battle stars and service stripes we'll get out of this asshole army faster than that white lightning struck us back at the hotel. Let's go, let's go."

We jumped into the jeep and broke all records back to Paris. There we learned all about Hiroshima and Nagasaki, about the Japanese surrender, the ceremony on the battleship *Missouri,* the triumph of Douglas MacArthur. We, the senior correspondents of the U.S. Army and the Voice of America, had been playing rummy and been drunk for a week all through one of the most extraordinary events of history, all through the last days of the war. We were the very last to know what had happened. I felt it was the most dismal failure of my career as a correspondent. And I didn't give a damn.

I desperately wanted the war to end. But, from the first, I reacted violently to the story of the atom bomb in all its horror. If I had to miss a big story, that was one I would have selected to miss. Ever since, I have had a hatred for the bigger and bigger, more and more proliferated nuclear weapons.

We learned on our return to Paris that most of the world cheered the end of the war but a few, dissenting voices raised anxious fears of the new "terror weapon" and its potential threat to all life on earth. For the next forty years up to today, and certainly for decades still to come, the opening of the dread atomic Pandora's box has been the issue of worldwide angry debate and demonstrations. No one has yet found a way to put the lid back down on the box. Demons are loose in the world. Yet the atom bomb, acting as a deterrent on the powers, has kept an uneasy peace between America and Russia, the longest period of peace in centuries. It is not, however, a genuine peace, it is a balance of terror. I think I sensed this intuitively on that fateful day when I was the last reporter to learn that the war had ended.

CHAPTER 10

NEW WORLD, NEW LIFE

Back in Paris, I checked in with the personnel officer of Headquarters Company, the unit that carried my name on its roster but which had not seen me since I had boarded the *John S. Cropper* in Naples harbor for the invasion of southern France in August 1944, more than a year earlier. I had been on detached service to the U.S. Seventh Army, and on loan from that army to the French First, then to Patton's Third. My magic Eisenhower letter had saved me time and time again from bureaucratic examination of my papers and duties and granted total lack of supervision by anyone. I really had been a "four-star sergeant," as the colonel in Naples had predicted.

Up until the German surrender in May, I had been in the line, up front, almost without a break. The personnel officer checked my records, whistled in astonishment, and told me that I had about a year's pay coming to me. I had never reported in to headquarters to get my money. I had lived well enough at army camps, needed little cash, and what little I needed I had won at poker games.

I was told that I would be demobilized at a camp in Etampes about an hour's ride from Paris. Then I would call Dorothy and tell her I was free and talk about our future. I had already made up my mind that I wanted to stay on in Paris as a correspondent. I was fairly sure Dorothy would agree, for she had never stopped talking about her student days in Paris, a city she loved. She had lived in a small hotel in the Rue de Fleurus, right next to the home of Gertrude Stein, whom she met, along with Janet Flanner of *The New Yorker,* one of America's finest foreign correspondents and writers. I could sense that an exciting new life awaited us.

I knew that everyone's understandable rush to go home was my ace in the hole. Talented and experienced men, who could have filled up all the posts, were leaving. That was my big chance. I had heard Charles Collingwood and Eric Sevareid, the top CBS correspondents, talking about the great opportunities and big money waiting for them in America. Reconversion to private industry would bring a burst of prosperity, and companies that had not been able to make or advertise consumer products on any big scale were preparing a vast new expenditure on radio commercials. Radio had come into its own in the war, the whole country tuning in all day long for war news that radio brought them more quickly and more dramatically than the printed press. Charles and Eric knew that they would become highly paid stars and could not wait to get to 485 Madison Avenue and the CBS studios there.

Stardom was not my ambition. Not that I was modest. My own goal was set very high. Instead of my youthful dream of becoming a famed critic and essayist on French literature, I now wanted to become America's greatest expert on France, a leading foreign correspondent, explaining France and the French to Americans, America and Americans to the French, a worthy ambition and one within my reach. When I was in Etampes, at the end of August 1945, General Charles de Gaulle was in Washington, and, after all the conflicts and frictions with Roosevelt during the war, de Gaulle made a speech calling for a return to "old French-American friendship."

His appeal would be part of my goal and he would be the means to achieve it. I knew de Gaulle well, and would have access to him and his aides. He was surely the man to govern postwar France. All of my French comrades-in-arms in North Africa and in the Battle of France would be among the top leaders of France for the next twenty years and more. I would be more than just a correspondent to them. I was a fellow soldier who had fought along with them, side by side, for the liberation of France. My French was fluent and I had an encyclopedic knowledge of French affairs and French history, qualities certain to give me a competitive edge as correspondent in Paris.

In the war years I had known and worked with top men in the media. I knew that a number of them had been looking me over as a recruit for their publications or networks. As soon as I got out of Etampes, I would make the rounds and see what was available. I had no fear that I would not find what I wanted. The optimism of youth and a good measure of self-confidence strengthened my convictions.

It was sunset when I left Etampes as a civilian, with my pocket full of money, but it was sunrise on a new life for Mr. David Schoenbrun, citizen David Schoenbrun, no longer "soldier" or "hey you." I think I could have floated back to Paris on a high cloud if I had missed the bus.

I had no illusions about how easy my new life would be. In my five days at Etampes, awaiting discharge, I had had time to reflect on the new world in which I would be living, a new America, a totally different Europe, in fact an entire world in rapid movement and change. The power balance that had ruled the world and kept the peace, more or less, with only a few explosions in the nineteenth century, had exploded in the twentieth century. The world had torn itself apart in the First and Second World Wars and still lives in constant fear of an atomic World War III in the last decades of the twentieth century.

I was about to become an observer of this world as it approached the midcentury mark after a truly global war that had changed all the postulates of power. Germany, the workshop of Europe, and Japan, the workshop of Asia, were in ruins, their industrial capacities cut by more than half, with no prospect of recovery unless their conquerors would permit it and encourage it. The great empires of Britain and France, which had dominated Africa and Asia, and of Spain, which had conquered and settled South America, had all been diminished in power by wars that had bled them and reduced them to nation-states, without world power.

Towering over Europe and the world were two new giant powers, with little experience of world affairs, each convinced that it was the hope of the world. America and the Soviet Union were not only physical giants in territory and natural resources within their own borders, but each was convinced of its own righteousness and world mission. For America, democracy was not only a political system but a religion, as was its faith in free enterprise, just as for Russia, Marxism-Leninism was also a religion and the wave of the future. These two giants were on a collision course even while allied in the war against Hitler. Their alliance could not long survive, and when they split apart, the world would tremble.

One did not need to be a prophet to see clearly just how this new postwar world would change from any that mankind had ever known. Not only was Europe in ruins, France and Britain almost bankrupt, Japan humiliated and in shock, but China was on the brink of civil war and all the former colonies of the Western powers in Africa, Asia, and South America sensed that their opportunity for freedom and independence was at hand. World War II had destroyed the ancient imperia and set loose a liberating force that would rapidly bring a hundred new states into existence, most of them without the resources, educated population, and experience to make a success out of their freedom and independence. Chaos and anarchy threatened to be the nature of the postwar world, not a brave new world but an angry and confused one.

There were many signs of impending crises ahead, even as the war ended. On V-E Day, as we all danced in the streets of Paris, there were riots in Algeria, where hundreds were wounded and killed in demonstrations by the subject peoples calling for independence from France.

By the end of September, the war barely over, came reports from a city most Americans had never heard of and would eventually wish they never had heard of, Saigon, in Vietnam. The people, newly liberated from Japanese occupation, were fighting in the streets against British and French troops who had taken over when the Japanese had surrendered. These riots in Algeria and Vietnam were the death rattle of the French Empire, but the French, in the euphoria of their own newly regained freedom, were blind and deaf to the warnings. Everyone seemed unaware that the world was heading toward a series of global disasters. Right after the news from Saigon came word from Kunming, China, of armed clashes between Chiang Kai-shek's Nationalist forces and the Communists, led by Mao Tse-tung.

As I returned to Paris to begin seeking my post as a correspondent, I had little doubt that I would be in the middle of these eruptions in the afterquake of world war, for Paris was still the hub of a global empire and a Paris correspondent would be a world correspondent. I went back to my room at the OWI hotel in the Rue d'Astorg. My friends told me that I could keep it and keep my job as a civilian broadcaster for the Voice until I found my new position as a correspondent. The very first thing I did was to book a call to New York to tell Dorothy that I was out of the army and hoped that she would come to join me as soon as possible in Paris.

My hopes were well based. Dorothy was overjoyed to hear that I had been demobilized and was looking for a job as Paris correspondent. It matched her own desires and plans. She said: "I can work in Paris, design magazines, do fashion illustration, or something much more important. I can work with you on making a baby. And I intend that we work very, very hard at it."

I explained to Dot that Europe was still, in principle, a theater of war operations. No peace had been signed, no armistice, just unconditional surrender, unique in history. No one could get passage to Paris or obtain a billet without army authorization and an official accreditation at General Eisenhower's headquarters. Dorothy would have to become a foreign correspondent. She told me at once that that would be no problem. She had done a lot of work for *Harper's Bazaar* and *Vogue,* and was very well known at *Women's Wear Daily* and Fairchild Publications. They would be only too happy to get her sketches on the first postwar fashion shows in Paris. Dorothy told me she would get started on the procedure and keep me informed.

The next morning I set about making the rounds of those who had been looking me over during the war. I telephoned to say hello and announce my army discharge to some of the top journalists of the profession. More accurately, I should say craft, for journalism is not a true profession. It has no fixed set of rules or laws or body of knowledge. Journalists are not licensed and need pass no examinations as doctors, lawyers, architects, engineers must do. The best journalists develop their own professional standards. It cannot be otherwise, for to attempt to institutionalize and regulate journalism would lead inevitably to dangerous restrictions on freedom of the press. I have often wished that journalists would somehow develop their own informal code of ethics for there are many irresponsible people who practice journalism, but no way has yet been found consistent with freedom.

My first appointment was lunch at the Ritz with Charles Wertenbaker, chief of correspondents of Time-Life. I was hesitant to join Time-Life, for I felt I was already too old, at thirty, to start at the bottom of the ladder of a complex organization. I feared I would be lost in the vast Time machine, although the temptations of Time-Life prestige, high salaries, and generous benefits made it most attractive.

I spoke frankly to Wertenbaker who understood my fears about working for Time-Life. Wert, as his friends called him, wished me luck and said that if I changed my mind I should give him another call.

Next on the list was another major figure in journalism, Relman "Pat" Morin, of the Associated Press. Pat warned me that a press agency job was a "perpetual rat race." He said, "Our men must be accurate, that goes without saying, but, above all else, they must be first most of the time." Pat warned me that some good men were slated for the top jobs in Paris and that I would have to be patient. But I was in a hurry, not the least patient. My real dream was to become Paris correspondent of CBS News and I knew that I had a real chance with both Collingwood and Sevareid going home. Murrow had shown interest in me in our wartime meetings, so I decided to fly to London and check him out.

Ed received me in his Hallam Street office, a modest suite in an apartment house near the BBC studios.

Murrow asked me whether I was going back to teaching. I told him that I would first have to take my doctorate and that I did not have the time to spare, although I would miss teaching, my first love. Ed looked at me in a manner he had, his head lowered, his dark eyes peering up and out of heavy black eyebrows, his rich baritone under control but bright with colors and shades of emotion. "Well, one day I could give you the biggest classroom in the world."

"Harvard?" I quipped.

"No," said Murrow, "CBS News." He said, "We are going to make CBS the greatest news network in the world. We are going to inform and educate the people of America. They have lived almost all our history in isolation and know little or nothing of the world we live in. But now America is the world's greatest power, with enormous responsibilities and opportunities to advance the cause of democracy. It can no longer afford to be ignorant of the world. That's why I see CBS as a giant national classroom. I've been recruiting men with university backgrounds. Howard Smith was a Rhodes Scholar at Oxford. So was Collingwood. That's the kind of man I want." Murrow paused and laughed. "You know, you can't teach a pear-shaped tone or a pretty face to think. But you can teach a brain to broadcast."

I was awed by Murrow and tense with excitement. I took a deep breath and asked the big question. "What are my chances, Ed?"

Murrow, a kindly man, knowing how nervous and eager I was, became serious. "David, I don't want to raise false hopes, but your chances are good. We are going to have to review our staff requirements now that the war is over. Executives back home will also be reviewing the role of news in overall programming. Budgets are involved and also perceptions of the role and scope of news. All this will take some time. In a year or so, maybe sooner, I'll be going home. Howard Smith will replace me as chief correspondent. We have a man in Paris now, a New York broadcaster, Douglas Edwards, getting some foreign experience. He won't be staying, for he is needed back home. I don't know who will replace him or when. I advise you not to wait for us. Take a job that will give you a chance to build a reputation. Keep in touch with Howard and me. One day, out of the blue, you may get a signal from me asking you to come aboard. No guarantees on that. But a good chance. Good luck."

I flew back to Paris feeling ten feet tall. I was sure that I would make it to CBS one day. Meanwhile, I would have to find a job that would permit me to send back clippings to Murrow to show him I was ready and able to become one of his "teachers" at CBS. First, I had to continue checking out those who had been kind enough to indicate an interest in me. I had just about made up my mind what job I would take, one already offered firmly.

I called a man who had been in the campaign with me, a professional reporter, Victor Bienstock. In the fall of 1945, Vic Bienstock was the correspondent of a small but well regarded news agency called ONA, the Overseas News Agency. It was run by Jews, deeply concerned about the future of the Jewish people in the wake of the Holocaust, but not exclusively Jewish oriented. It was a liberal, democratic group of men and women dedicated to peace, social justice, and exposure of the evil forces in the world that endangered those goals. It was not well known to the public but it had a good list of client papers, including *The New York Times.* It could not offer major, mass exposure but it was a good platform and my work would come to the attention of important editors and a serious public.

Bienstock, many months earlier, had made me a firm offer of a job as soon as I was demobilized. It was an excellent opportunity, for ONA had no Paris office. I would be the bureau chief and call all the shots. It would not be easy, for I would have many difficult and important responsibilities. ONA put out a daily file of news and columns from a number of world capitals and by some famous writers. I would have to send back my own dispatches for the news file, and also try to sell the service to the Paris papers.

Vic and I had a coffee at the Hotel Scribe as he explained all this to me. The pay was pitiful: seventy-five dollars a week, in francs, plus twenty-five dollars a week deposited in a savings account in New York, and a raise to fifty dollars a week in New York the following year. I could have bargained for more, but I had a year's back pay and Dorothy had earned and saved a lot. It was important to get started as fast as possible. If successful, I could renegotiate. Also, I had received a letter from Abe Schechter, the news director of the Mutual Broadcasting System, asking me to be his Paris stringer at twenty-five dollars a broadcast, guaranteeing at least one, possibly two, broadcasts a week. I was okay and eager to get on with it.

I had been given good advice by Victor Bienstock, himself a highly motivated, moral man. Older, more experienced than I, Vic told me of the perils of honest journalism. Someone will always make indiscreet remarks and then shout that he was misquoted or quoted out of context when the interview bounces back on him. Keep full notes on what anyone says, Vic advised. He then talked at length about balanced reporting and objectivity, so little understood even by editors, let alone by officials or the public. "Balanced reporting does not mean that all things are equal and that wrong matches right. A good reporter must present all sides of a question.

That's balance. But it does not mean that all sides are equal. There is a right and wrong. You have the duty to report all elements but not to suggest that they balance out. You have the right, after a comprehensive study, to reach a conclusion. Those who evade this are 'on-the-one-hand-on-the-other' neuters. They are eunuchs. Find out who is right and what is right and make it clear. The best way is to write your story so that the reader can reach the conclusion without you pointing it out. Sometimes, however, you've got to say: 'This is the way it is.' "

I had a lot to learn and I listened to him carefully. I learned, and I pass this along to young reporters today, that there are good guys as well as bad guys in government and other fields of human enterprise. There are those who do not respect the Bill of Rights, who hate the press, but there are always others who understand what Thomas Jefferson said, after he had been pilloried by a vicious press: "Without a free press, there is no free government. Without freedom of speech for bad ideas, there is no freedom of speech for good ideas." In the years of reporting in Paris, I met some of the finest, most decent, and brilliant men in the U.S. Embassy and other embassies, and in many governments. I also came upon a number of villains. The thing to do is to look for and cultivate the good guys and defy the bad guys.

Vic Bienstock gave me a thick bundle of francs, for which I signed a receipt, an advance on office funds. He told me to find an office suite, scout out the prices of furniture, and make up a budget for rent, salaries, and office expenses. Ida Landau, co-owner of ONA with her husband, Jake, would come to Paris in a few days and handle financing and more funds. I was lucky and found a two-room suite on the fourth floor of the New York *Herald Tribune* building, then located at 21 Rue de Berri, a street that began at the Champs-Elysées.

My very first client was one of the major afternoon papers, *Paris-Presse,* co-owned and published by two splendid people, Eve Curie and Philippe Barrès, famed names in France. Eve was the daughter of Pierre and Marie Curie, discoverers of radium, Nobel Prize winners. Her book about her mother, Marie Curie, had been a worldwide best-seller, and she had written another excellent book about her wartime experiences as a foreign correspondent, *Journey Among Warriors.* Philippe Barrès, tall, slimly elegant, and handsome, was a writer-editor, the son of one of France's pre-war writers, Maurice Barrès.

I had first met Eve after the landings in southern France, at General de Lattre's headquarters in Aix-les-Bains. She was one of the great beauties of Europe, thick raven hair, dark eyes, white skin, high-breasted and graceful. She was also as bright and intelligent as she was beautiful. The fact that she liked the ONA service and bought it gave me a big jump.

I went to the conservative morning paper *Le Figaro,* with a big circulation, and they bought a six month's trial service. So did *Libération,* a paper that had emerged from the underground Resistance and was run by an extraordinary, dashing, and controversial figure, Emmanuel d'Astier de la Vigerie, from one of France's oldest aristocratic families. D'Astier, a hero of the Resistance against the Germans, was closely allied with the Communist Party. I believed that he was simply an adventurer and anarchist, enjoying the consternation he caused among members of his family and rightist friends. A very talented young editor at *Franc-Tireur,* another Resistance-born paper, Charles Ronsac, liked my work and the ONA file. He became the top man at Opéra Mundi, one of the biggest news agencies in France and Europe. In a short time, I had signed up enough client papers to put ONA operations in the black. It was time, then, to begin to devote more time to writing my own dispatches.

I had, of course, not neglected my reporting duties, sending through three or four pieces a week on postwar France. I had proceeded cautiously, feeling my way, trying to write solid but not spectacular stories. I spent several hours a day making the rounds of government and political party offices, introducing myself, lining up sources, seeing old army friends, until my files had a long, excellent list of informed men and women, with their office and home phone numbers. I was ready now to do something unusual, to make a big splash and put my name and the ONA logo on the front pages and everyone's tongue. I brooded about how to do it, until I hit upon the right device.

General de Gaulle and his followers of the Free France movement, and the leaders of the Resistance movements, had decided not to resurrect the Third Republic, whose parliamentarians, in 1940, had voted full powers to Marshal Pétain, as the once great

French Army was being crushed by the Nazi legions. Pétain had set up a fascist state. The Third Republic had died, having legally put itself out of existence. It was decided, therefore, that a new Fourth Republic, with a modern constitution, should be created. This issue could only finally be decided democratically by the French people. A referendum on the issue was scheduled for October 21. Simultaneously with this referendum, elections to a Constituent Assembly would permit the people to select the legislators to draft the new constitution, were it to be approved—a question not in doubt.

I thought that I ought to get the most important political personalities to tell me what their party positions and predictions were on these questions. I chose three men to be interviewed all on the same day, so that I could do a kind of reportorial "hat trick," scoring three goals in one game. That would certainly make a big noise in Paris.

The three men, to all of whom I had good access, were Georges Bidault, leader of the Christian Democratic Party, called the Mouvement Républicain Populaire, a mildly liberal centrist group; Léon Blum, venerable statesman-philosopher, prewar prime minister, and leader of the Socialist Party; and the roly-poly, wily, witty spokesman and number-two man of the Communist Party, Jacques Duclos. Blum was a revered figure in the world. Bidault and Duclos, the Catholic and the communist, had emerged from the Resistance as heroic figures. Bidault was also claiming that his party was the party of General de Gaulle, since, at that time, the general stood above all parties, refusing to organize a party of his own. If I could get them, I would have the three most authoritative spokesmen of the new France. Overnight ONA and David Schoenbrun would be known throughout Paris.

I got them.

It was the big kickoff of my new life. Not only did I send the interviews to my clients, I gave it as a free bonus to a new client who signed up for my service, the Paris edition of the conservative London *Daily Mail,* a big score for a liberal American service.

Georges Bidault told me that France would need a new constitution to meet the new conditions in the postwar world. They would not resurrect the Third Republic, which had collapsed of its own instability as much as under the German assault. The new Fourth Republic must find a way to keep governments in office long enough for long-range planning and to win the confidence of the French people and the respect of the world. The French Empire must be taken back from the Germans and the Japanese and made strong again in unity between the colonies and the motherland. He showed no sign whatever of understanding that the days of empire were over and that an attempt to preserve it would in little more than a decade destroy the Fourth Republic. I felt this strongly but it was not my job to argue with him. I would let my readers know of this possibility after they had read the interview.

Léon Blum was a tired old man who, to my disappointment, mouthed old social-democratic slogans about peace and justice and equality, all valid and noble thoughts, but no practical program for achieving those goals. I could see no great strides for socialism in postwar France under his worn-out leadership.

Duclos fascinated and frightened me. The communist was clearly the brightest, most vigorous, most confident of the three political leaders. He was witty, cynical, and arrogant as he promised to cooperate with the Gaullists and social democrats but boasted that the Communist Party was the largest, strongest party in France and one day would come to power at the polls, "not on the barricades." Then he added with a laugh: "And when we do, the government will never fall again."

I accomplished my purpose. The three interviews, with the ONA logo and my byline, were on the front pages. It was a sensation, and from then on I never had to explain who I was when I telephoned anyone. New York's well-known labor lawyer Theodore Kheel once told me that a good definition of power was the ability to get someone important to come to the phone himself when you called. If that is true, then I became a power in Paris.

By then, I had obtained a room in the correspondents' hotel, the Scribe. Eisenhower had flown home where he had been nominated in Washington to become the new Chief of Staff of the U.S. Army, replacing General George Marshall. Marshall was on a mission to China, hoping to reconcile the Nationalists and the Communists and avert a Chinese civil war. Eisenhower would fly to China to confer with him. But in Paris, the Hotel Scribe was still known as "Eisenhower's headquarters for the press," and that is where most correspondents lived and congregated, still receiving regular briefings from army and diplomatic officials.

A small act of kindness on my part in the lobby of the Scribe, on the night of October 21, 1945, would have a great influence on my career. That was the day that the French voted on the constitutional referendum and the candidates for election to a Constituent Assembly.

A blackboard had been set up in the lobby at the entrance to the big briefing room. An official kept writing totals on the referendum, next to a long list of party names. In addition to the major parties, there were a dozen or more small or splinter factions in French elections, hoping to elect a deputy or two, particularly under the system of proportional representation, which allocated seats by percentage of votes, and favored small parties. It is a very democratic but bad system, for it leads to excessive pluralism and unmanageable legislatures.

Standing in front of the blackboard, with a doleful expression, was a young American in a correspondent's uniform. Paris was still technically a war zone and most men wore uniforms. This man looked as though he was going to break into tears as he tried to fathom the mystery of the French party list. It included such "parties" as *La défense de l'automobiliste, Les royalistes socialistes,* whose emblem was a red fleur-de-lys. The numbers kept changing on all the parties. I was on top of the story, for French friends who were political experts had explained it to me all day long, and I had covered the story for more than a month.

I walked over to the correspondent in shock and said quietly, "Hi! How's it going?" He looked at me like a drowning man and groaned: "Christ, this is a mess. I can't make heads or tails of it. I've been on a trip, and just arrived. Do you know what this is all about?" I grinned, tapped him on the shoulder, and said: "Come on down to the bar and buy me a glass of wine and I'll fill you in." He looked as though I had thrown him a life belt and his sad face lighted up with a broad grin.

He was Douglas Edwards, the CBS correspondent, a wonderful man, with a beautiful voice and good heart. We would become close friends, inseparable in Paris, and later colleagues at CBS. I could not have picked a better man to help. Doug absorbed my political briefing rapidly, taking quick, detailed notes. In about an hour, he was up to date on the story and told me to hold the line at the bar, he was going to do a broadcast and be right back.

I was running up tremendous phone bills calling Dorothy every night to get reports on how she was coming along on her official accreditation and travel plans. An editor of *Women's Wear Daily* had influence in a new magazine called *Scope,* and arranged for Dorothy to be accredited as its Paris correspondent. She had to be cleared by State Department and various armed forces intelligence services, as well as by the FBI. Investigations were proceeding and she hoped to sail on a troop carrier, the *Vulcania,* in about a month. Meanwhile, we would keep in touch by phone.

The expensive phone calls did pay off later, however. It is vital for a correspondent to have the best possible communications at his or her disposal. That means knowing the overseas operators and telephone supervisors. I made it my business to visit the PTT, the Post, Telephone, and Telegraph offices in Paris, and met key personnel. From time to time, I would drop off flacons of perfume for the women and cartons of American cigarettes for the men. Operators can not only put a reporter through in five minutes instead of five hours but they do occasional listening-in on lines to make sure the circuits are good, so they are often well informed. It is also necessary for correspondents to have excellent relations with airline ground personnel, air hostesses, and pilots. I have sent many an urgent piece of news film by hand from places in Africa and Asia or from countries with severe censorship, thanks to good friends in the airlines.

Doug Edwards called me one day in the fall of 1945 to tell me that the Air Force had invited him on a tour of our bases in Greece and Turkey. He asked if I would fill in for him on CBS for about two weeks.

I was delighted. It had been a long time since I had done any CBS broadcasts. I was doing reports for Mutual but had protected my CBS chances by using the name of David Brown on MBS. Abe Schechter, at MBS, knew that David Brown was David Schoenbrun, and it did not bother him.

During Doug's absence, I did three broadcasts weekly for CBS and two for MBS. Fortunately, they were scheduled at different hours on different days, so that David Brown never had to compete with David Schoenbrun. I sweated that period out with some anxiety. CBS liked my reports and, once or twice, the CBS news director, Paul White, came on the circuit to say hello, with a small word of praise. We both remembered the old days at the CBS monitoring station and the *PM* articles for which White had scolded me for not bringing to him. I felt that I was carrying out Murrow's instructions to be patient, take what comes, and try to do a good job to impress CBS for a possible future posting.

Meanwhile, I was learning the procedure. Abe Schechter of Mutual Broadcasting sent me a long message one day saying that he was planning a big, first postwar Christmas program to wish season's greetings to the children of America and he wanted me to get General de Gaulle to record a message of good cheer from the French. I knew de Gaulle well enough to be certain he would do nothing of the kind, so I shot off a cable to Schechter telling him that General de Gaulle never gave interviews to the media and never sent personal messages of any kind. Schechter, furious, sent me back a rocket that said, "WANT DEGAULLES REFUSAL NOT YOURS ASK HIM."

Schechter was well within his rights, of course. It was a lesson I had to learn. It did not matter what I thought de Gaulle would do, it was my duty to ask and hope for the best. I had no choice but to call de Gaulle's spokesman for the press, Gaston Palewski, and read Schechter's cable to him, apologizing so that Palewski should not think I was some kind of fool asking for what I should have known to be impossible. As expected, Palewski laughed on the phone and told me to forget it. De Gaulle would not do it. I now had de Gaulle's official refusal for Schechter.

Finally there came the telegram I was waiting for: "SAILING VULCANIA ARRIVING LE HAVRE NOVEMBER TWENTIETH LOVE DOROTHY."

My heart jumped as I saw her coming down the gangplank. She was pale and had lost pounds on the awful voyage. But Dorothy is curvy and even with the lost weight she looked, in her new uniform, like a too-plump airline hostess. Of course, to me she was the vision of an angel. I shouted, ran to her as she ran to me. We collided with a thud that almost knocked both of us into the Channel. Then friends who had driven me to Le Havre got their share of hugs. They had heard so much about Dorothy and she had sent us so many huge boxes of cookies every week that all the correspondents knew her long before that happy day.

We had a merry ride back to Paris, stopping at a roadside inn for a most delicious onion pie and several bottles of Beaujolais.

Dorothy sang for us the latest hit tune: "Kiss me once and kiss me twice and kiss me once again, it's been a long, long time."

At the Scribe we ran into a small problem. Wives were not permitted in the war zone. We argued that Dorothy had her own official accreditation. The concierge, a bureaucrat who knew the rules and who also knew how to extort tips, pointed out that Dorothy had the right to her own room, as a correspondent, but had no right to be in my room as a wife. I thought a moment, until a solution emerged. Several of the correspondents were, in the language of those days, "shacked up" with girl friends. So I told the concierge that Dorothy Scher—she used her professional name, her maiden name, on the accreditation papers—was not really my wife. She was my "shack job." As I said it, I folded a big banknote, preparatory to passing it on in a handshake, if he gave the right answer. He did. "*Ah, une petite amie? Très jolie. Félicitations.*" He snapped his fingers, sent a bellboy to get Dot's bags, and ordered him to take them to my room.

Dorothy grinned at me. "I always suspected you were shacking up and now you've proved it."

We headed for our room.

It had been a long, long time.

CHAPTER 11

TIME BOMBS TICKING

Two days later, Dorothy and I came down to join the press crowd, which greeted us with ribald, heavy-handed remarks. I grinned, ignored their remarks, and began introducing Dorothy. She was warmly greeted by Toni Howard, correspondent for *Newsweek* and a spectacular young woman. Toni had ink-black hair and wore matching black sunglasses, day and night, contrasting to her fireman-red coat. Somehow this irritated Papa Hemingway who growled when Toni strode in, "There's the girl whose hair is prematurely black." Hemingway was a generous, often kindly man but he had a sardonic streak in him and one never knew when he would lash out.

There were so many talented and colorful men and women in liberated Paris. Paris in the forties and fifties would become the political and cultural capital of the Western world, homesite of NATO, the North Atlantic Treaty Organization; of the Marshall Plan; of UNESCO in its finest days, with Britain's brilliant biologist Julian Huxley, brother of novelist Aldous Huxley, at its head. It was also the Paris of the New Look in fashions, the Nouvelle Vague in the cinema, Paris of the initiators of style in every domain.

It was the Paris of restaurants and cafés that became seminar centers when philosophers met and held court at night. The guru of the new cult of existentialism, Jean-Paul Sartre, presided over his nightly table at the Flore, assisted by his disciple, Simone de Beauvoir, while a handsome, tormented young writer named Camus would duel verbally with him while crowds of worshipers strained, at neighboring tables, to listen to their discourse.

Just across a narrow street from the Flore, fronting on the corner of the Boulevard Saint-Germain and the Rue de Rennes, was the Café des Deux Magots, another rendezvous for writers, artists, directors, movie stars, journalists, Turkish peddlers of candied fruits, Arab peddlers of shredded kif or rolled marijuana cigarettes, buxom blonde Swedish girls on tour looking for adventure, and bearded Sorbonne University students looking for buxom, blonde Swedish girls. The Café des Deux Magots was a nightly sideshow, a carnival.

On the Right Bank another, more lavish and spectacular show was played nightly at Maxim's, the famed restaurant-institution on the Rue Royale, just a few steps off the majestic Place de la Concorde. At Maxim's were assembled the "beautiful people" of the world. Aristotle Onassis and his good friend, the diva Maria Callas, were always seated at the King's Table, stretching along the wall to the left of the entrance of the Grande Salle to the corner where two walls met. The corner seat was the only seat in the Salle that permitted a survey of the entire room, with no one at one's back, hence La Table du Roi.

Henry Ford would dine with the American ambassador and an assortment of counts, duchesses, and former Russian, Spanish, Yugoslav princes and kings. Americans adore royalty. The fashion world was well represented with Balenciaga, the designer's designer whom all the couturiers admired, and with the new sensation of Paris, the creator of the New Look, who in 1947 made women look like women again, a shy young man named Christian Dior. At another table was another newcomer who had just risen from the ranks of drapers and cutters and opened his own salon. Pierre Balmain smiled as he looked over the room and saw many of his famous *clientes* wearing his flattering Jolie Madame dresses and gowns. Balmain did not strive to be an innovative, avant-garde designer but he was the best dressmaker in Paris.

At cafés along the Champs-Elysées, Le Colisée, Fouquet's, a number of American writers, photographers, and reporters would meet to drink and talk for hours. Papa Hemingway, a grizzly bear, would occasionally leave his lair at the Hotel Ritz to join friends at Fouquet's: James Farrell, John Steinbeck, and Irwin Shaw. In the late fifties, James Jones would bring his own brand of talent and machismo to the tables. It was astonishing to note how many great American writers looked and talked like prizefighters and football players, and were thoroughly obsessed with sex.

Some of the world's greatest photographers were part of "our crowd." Robert Capa, darkly handsome, Hungarian, who carried a passport he had made himself that said: "The Royal Hungarian Government has no proof that Robert Capa is not a Hungarian subject," was a joy to be with. Capa was one of the bravest of war correspondents. On D day, he landed on Omaha Beach, in a hail of German bullets, *before* the first troops, so that he could get a good picture of them breaching Hitler's Atlantic Wall.

Before getting down to work, after our two-day honeymoon, Dorothy wanted to see her own beloved Paris and visit the haunts of her student days. We went first to the Parc Montsouris, and The Cité Universitaire, the dormitory buildings of foreign students in the thirties. Dot had had a room in the Maison des Etats-Unis, the American dorm. From the Cité, we took buses to the Place des Vosges, where her school had been located. We walked around the lovely square and then went for a glass of wine to the café Ma Bourgogne, on the corner, opposite the historic Hôtel de Richelieu. I had planned a surprise for Dorothy, by calling my friend the café owner, Louis Beaugey, Louis the Burgundian, to tell him that Dorothy had arrived.

Like everyone else, Louis and his wife, "Maman" Beaugey, knew all about Dorothy. When we walked in, Louis saw us at once, came bounding out from behind the bar, flashing his big gold-tooth smile, and grabbed Dorothy in his smothering bear embrace, shouting, "*Maman, Maman, viens vite, c'est Dorothée!*" Maman Beaugey came running out, a parrot perched on her shoulder, her German shepherd, Blacky, leaping at her side, and a big fat pullet clucking furiously, upside down in Maman's right hand. Maman kept shouting, "*Dorothée!*"

At the welcome-home feast, Louis told us his favorite Burgundian story about the longevity of his people. He had a sign that ran over the mirror behind his bar that proclaimed: "*Pour vivre centenaire, 'faut boire du Sancerre.*" No one believed that one could live to be a hundred by drinking Sancerre wine, but Louis stoutly insisted it was true. He told the story of the prewar American Ambassador William Bullitt, who took a train to Burgundy for a wine festival and sat next to a wizened ancient who talked constantly and seemed bright for his years. When asked to explain his old age, he boasted that he drank three bottles of Burgundy every day of his life, morning, noon, and night. Asked if he were married, the oldster cackled, "Yes, indeed, and I've got two mistresses, also. Pleasure my women every day." Bullitt, astonished, said: "You make love to three women a day and drink three bottles of Burgundy daily! My God, man, how old are you?" The old man cackled again and screeched: "Thirty-four!" We all laughed until we cried.

Most of the time there was more reason to cry than to laugh. The world was dangerous and belligerent. Moscow accused London and Washington of breaking the Potsdam agreements. London, Paris, and Washington accused Moscow of breaking the Yalta agreements, and demanded immediate free elections in Poland. Hindus and Moslems rioted in Bombay against the British and against each other. Jews staged a general strike against the British in Palestine. On Red Army Day in Moscow, Foreign Minister Molotov warned the United States that "We will have atomic energy and many other things," a clear warning that Moscow was working on the bomb. Congressman Kenneth McKellar of Tennessee charged that Britain was distributing Lend-Lease arms to the Arabs and called it "a death sentence on Jewry." Major-General Patrick Hurley accused State Department officers of "sabotaging" American policy in China, the forerunner of a witch-hunt which would destroy America's corps of China experts and frighten some of the best young graduates away from government service.

The Frenchmen and women who had banded together from far left to far right to fight the Nazi occupation of their country were already fighting among themselves for power in the new Republic which had not yet even been formed. As in the times of Julius Caesar, all Gaul was still divided into three parts. In the October 21st elections, the communists won five million votes; the Catholic MRP, carrying de Gaulle's banner, won four million seven hundred eighty thousand; and the socialists four million five hundred sixty-one thousand, and each was suspicious of the others. All were mistrustful of de Gaulle and he held them all in contempt.

As 1945 drew to a close, the socialists challenged de Gaulle by suddenly putting forward an amendment to cut the military budget by twenty percent because of "the scandalous waste and disorder in the defense establishment." De Gaulle announced that he would resign as prime minister if the amendment were not defeated. He won the day. But a month later, on January 20, 1946, General de Gaulle, disgusted with politics and a constitution that left the executive weaker than the Parliament, unable to govern efficiently, resigned. He told me he did not expect to return.

France was in a mess. Reconstruction of war damage had barely gotten underway. There were sporadic uprisings against French colonial rule in Algiers and in Vietnam. The communists were calling strikes in France, and everyone knew they had large caches of arms accumulated during the Resistance which they had managed not to turn over to the army after the war. France was a political time bomb waiting to explode. So was the French Empire. So was the British Empire. So was the hostility between Russia and America.

Anti-British riots left 14 dead and 173 wounded in Cairo on February 21, 1946. Riots broke out anew in Bombay on February 22. On February 24 Drew Pearson asserted that Russian troops were set to invade Turkey. And Walter Winchell told his national audience that same day that "World War III is on." French friends in the press and government began calling me to ask me who Winchell was. Did he speak with authority? I reassured them that he was only a sensationalist gossip columnist and that he did not know what he was talking about. But within two and three weeks, Winchell began to look like a prophet.

On March 5, 1946, speaking at Fulton, Missouri, as the guest of Harry Truman, the old warrior Winston Churchill let off a blast against the Soviet Union and called for a virtual U.S.-British military alliance against the Russians. Russia tightened its grip over eastern Europe and Churchill asserted that an "iron curtain" had "descended across the continent of Europe." The phrase would catch on and give the Russian-haters the slogan they had been seeking. Stalin reacted furiously to Churchill's Iron Curtain speech and charged that it was "a call to war with the Soviet Union." The term "Cold War" had not yet been put into circulation by Walter Lippmann, and the Cold War itself would not chill the world for about another year, but the freeze was setting in.

In that same period, during the Ides of March, 1946, the French and the Vietnamese were speeding toward a head-on collision that would bring about one of the longest, most destructive tragedies of this tragic, bloody century. In Saigon an anachronistic figure was sowing the seeds of the future tragedy. His name was Admiral Georges Thierry d'Argenlieu, appointed by General de Gaulle to be France's high commissioner for Indochina.

Indochina was composed of three countries, Vietnam, Cambodia, and Laos, each with its own history, its own royal dynasties, theoretically autonomous and self-governing but each, in fact, a colonial possession of France, ruled by the French. D'Argenlieu had been one of de Gaulle's earliest *Compagnons,* in the Free French days. He had come out of the monastery into which he had retreated after World War I. A Carmelite monk, whose name in the order was Père Louis de la Trinité, he was a warrior-priest, a throwback to the medieval crusaders of Cluny. Before resigning, General de Gaulle had given him instructions to reestablish French sovereignty over the colonies after the Japanese surrender. I had met d'Argenlieu before he left for Saigon, talked with him, and was appalled by his plans to crush any insurrection, any independence movement "with full force."

The new socialist government in Britain, realizing that World War II had changed the old order, was preparing to grant independence to India. Clement Attlee, the man who had replaced Churchill as prime minister, had already talked of "self-government" for India, a big step toward independence. The war had shaken giant China out of a long sleep and submission to foreign rule. China was free and would be a major power in Asia. Why could the French not understand, not see the handwriting on the wall? How could Indochina, between free China and free India, remain a vassal of a weakened and diminished France? D'Argenlieu and de Gaulle brushed aside these arguments as anticolonial American naïveté. They were not aware that they themselves were ignorant of the new world. They lived in the past and would thus turn the future into a nightmare for many millions.

A Vietnamese leader of an underground guerrilla movement that had worked in close cooperation with American agents sent to Vietnam by General MacArthur emerged from the underground after the Japanese surrender. His name was Ho Chi Minh. The guerrillas who emerged with him formed a "People's National Liberation Committee." It met and "elected" Ho president of a "free Vietnam." There were no French troops in Hanoi, in the north of Vietnam, to put him down at that point. Admiral d'Argenlieu and General Leclerc were in Saigon reclaiming the southern provinces for France. The puppet emperor of Vietnam, Bao Dai, astonished his French masters by asking Ho Chi Minh to form a new imperial Cabinet. The "emperor" then sent a telegram to de Gaulle warning him not to try to reestablish French administration. "It will no longer be obeyed. Each village will be a nest of resistance. Your officials . . . will be unable to breathe."

Bao Dai then went further. He abdicated his throne, became a citizen and "Supreme Advisor to the Liberation Committee." Ho promptly proclaimed a new "Democratic Republic of Viet Nam," whose constitution began with these words: "We hold these truths to be self-evident. That all men are created equal . . . ," opening lines of the American Declaration of Independence, a clear and clever bid for American sympathy for his anticolonial revolution.

Despite d'Argenlieu's threat of putting the "insurrection" down by force, the French did not yet have enough force amassed in Indochina to win back its colonies in the spring of 1946. Playing for time, the French signed a "Treaty of Association" with the Democratic Republic of Vietnam, "as a free state, with its own government, parliament, army, and finances." In return, Vietnam promised to join a new "Indochinese Federation and French Union," a kind of French commonwealth of nations. It would be created by a new French constitution which did not exist at that time but was being drafted. On March 6, 1946, Ho Chi Minh was recognized by the French, with their fingers crossed behind their backs, as president of the Republic of Vietnam. He was invited to come to France, to a conference at Fontainebleau, outside Paris, to work out the terms of the new federation and union.

As a reporter at the Fontainebleau Conference, talking with Ho Chi Minh and the men around him, I wondered if my French friends were deaf or suicidal. I talked to them at length about the folly of their policy. They paid no attention. They were driven by the need to reestablish France as a great world power. They believed they could easily defeat the lightly armed peasants of Indochina. They wanted to wipe out the memory of their collapse in 1940. Nothing else mattered.

Americans were paying little attention to Vietnam. For days on end, I was the only American reporter in Fontainebleau talking to the Vietnamese. Another Asian event, far from Indochina, in Southwest Asia, on the Persian Gulf, and on the Soviet border, was far more interesting to Americans. It was the apparent Soviet attempt to take over the oil-rich country of Iran. On March 12, 1946, the State Department asked Moscow to explain why Soviet troops were on the move in Iran. On the eighteenth, Kurds revolted and demanded freedom from Iran. The Russians said they were only trying to maintain order in Iran and responding to calls for aid from local leaders in Azerbaijan province on their frontier. Those "local leaders" were communists supported by and paid by the Soviets.

We enjoyed an atomic monopoly at the time. In the war, Stalin had seen our apparently limitless resources. At the United Nations, America could count on a majority of votes on almost all issues. There were only some fifty-four members at that time, and the majority belonged to the democracies of Western Europe, the British Commonwealth, and U.S. "client states" in South America. Today, the U.N. majority is a strongly Third World and communist bloc, and the United States is often in the minority. Most Americans in the 1980s have forgotten or never known the period of American dominance of world affairs in the forties and most of the fifties.

It has become a cliché to talk of "Soviet expansionism," and how the Soviets have "pushed us around" in the world. Forgotten is the period of American expansion as a world power with world influence. American influence is always regarded as benign. Often enough it was. We have been the most generous people in the world, but not always generous, not always wise, not always defending freedom. When it came to "pushing around," we did our share and we did not let the Soviets get away with unchallenged expansion. That is a myth.

Harry Truman met the Soviet challenge in Iran and made them withdraw. He met the Soviet blockade of Berlin and made them abandon it. We defeated a Soviet attempt to win the Italian elections for the Communist Party. The Soviet Union has not advanced an inch into Europe since 1945. They are now where they were then because we contained them. They did invade Afghanistan in 1980, on their own border, far from our strength. But they have had to send one hundred thousand Soviet troops to control a backward, almost unarmed people and have suffered thousands of casualties, and they only control the cities by day. The Afghans control their country by night. The Russians are not ten feet tall. They are not supermen.

American myths in world affairs are largely based upon internal political rivalries. The Republicans charged the Democrats with "giving China to the Reds," as though China were ours to give in the first place. Democrats, stung by charges of being "soft on communism," waged a useless, cruel war in Vietnam, blaming the Chinese for being behind Ho Chi Minh, ignoring the long, historic hatred of the Vietnamese for the Chinese. We have played the power game, as others have, and are still playing it today. That does not, by any means, put us on the same level as the Soviets. They repress their own people as well as their neighbors. The Soviet Union is a tyranny. We are still, despite our imperfections and failures, a democracy, the major hope of freedom.

This was clear in 1946, much clearer than it is today, for the world has become infinitely more complex and power more and more diffused. The diffusion of power, the emergence on the world scene of new states, resentful of, hostile to, the major powers, had already begun in 1946 in Iran, Egypt, Syria, Lebanon, Palestine, China, Indochina, and many other lands around the globe. New leaders arose, condemning both the United States and Russia. In Yugoslavia, Josip Broz, known by his wartime name, Marshal Tito, introduced the unfamiliar phenomenon of a communist hostile to the Soviet Union, a "nationalist communist." He defied Moscow and Washington both.

When Tito broke openly with Stalin, America's leading Soviet specialist, Charles Bohlen, counselor of the State Department, told us reporters that "Tito will not last six weeks." Americans have always overrated Russian strength and underrated opposition to Moscow, especially by communists. Tito warned Americans and Russians not to overfly his territory. In August 1946, Yugoslav fighter planes fired on a U.S. transport plane and forced it down. They also forced down a Hungarian plane. Then Tito released seven American and two Hungarian fliers, warning everyone to respect the sovereignty of his state. Small nations were showing a readiness to stand up to great powers.

A number of small nations came to Paris in the summer of

1946 for a peace conference. They were the former satellites of Nazi Germany, considered to have been victims of Germany more than enemies of the West. They were liberated and free, seeking a new life, but living fearfully under the continued occupation of the Red Army of Russia. Czechoslovakia, Poland, Hungary, Yugoslavia, Rumania, Bulgaria, and Austria were represented at that conference in the French Senate building known as the Luxembourg Palace.

It was there that I met Jan Masaryk, Tito, Envers Hoxha of Albania, and other leaders of Eastern Europe. Of them all, the only one finally to emerge as a truly free nation was Austria. Its brilliant foreign minister and later socialist chancellor, Bruno Kreisky, earned the gratitude of the Austrian people when he went to Moscow and persuaded the Russians, with the help of American pressures, to withdraw the Red Army from his country. It was my special pleasure to interview him at the beautiful Schönbrunn Palace, in the suburbs of Vienna, the village from which my father's father had emigrated to America, taking the name Schoenbrun, its spelling Americanized, as his own.

Kreisky told me that his small nation in the heart of Europe, between East and West, could only survive as a neutral. "If we join either a Russian or an American power bloc we will be crushed." Masaryk, facing the same problem, said he, too, would like to see a neutral Czechoslovakia but feared it would be impossible. "We are caught geographically between Germany and Russia. The Soviets will never forget their terrible casualties in the war against Hitler. Anyone on their border who is not friendly with them will be considered an enemy. I fear for our survival. We were liberated by the Russians and many of my people admire them. I can't join with the U.S., much as I would like to, without alienating many Czechs and alarming the big Red Bear." Almost every Eastern European diplomat said the same thing. They all sensed a Soviet-American power struggle for Europe and did not know where to go. Austria went neutral but Czechoslovakia, Poland, Rumania, Bulgaria, Hungary ended up as Soviet satellites. Tito of Yugoslavia and Hoxha of Albania were communists but broke with Russia. Tito and his troops were too strong for Stalin to bluff or attack. The small mountain fortress of Albania was too remote and not worth the trouble for Stalin to attack.

World affairs kept intruding upon the conference. One day delegates were buzzing about the extraordinary proposal for international control of atomic energy outlined by Presidential advisor Bernard Baruch at a meeting of the U.N. Atomic Energy Commission. European leaders simply could not understand how America, with such a mighty advantage as the atom bomb and a big head start on atomic energy, could offer to put it all under international control. Masaryk told me it was the most generous and possibly the most foolish offer he could imagine. We need not have worried. The Russians, often more foolish than the Americans, turned the offer down. On June 24, *Pravda* announced rejection of the Baruch atom plan.

On July 22, a Jewish underground organization called the Irgun, led by a man named Menachem Begin, blew up the King David Hotel, a British police and military headquarters in Jerusalem. The British authorities denounced Begin and the Irgun as "terrorists." So did President Truman, warning, on July 24, that terrorism might retard a solution to the Palestine problem. To the surprise and anger of the Jews in Palestine, the American Jewish Committee in New York and the Zionist Emergency Council also denounced the bombing.

Begin was furious. He had telephoned the British authorities in advance, informing them of the bombing and asking them to evacuate the hotel to avoid bloodshed and death. Later that year, when I went to Jerusalem, Jews would tell me: "We are Freedom Fighters, not terrorists. What terrorists do you know who call in advance to warn of a bombing? Arab terrorists do not do that. And we are fighting the British police and the army, not leaving bombs in crowded marketplaces to kill innocent women and children shopping. That's what the Arabs do. They are cowards and do not fight the occupying forces. We are doing that and will continue to, no matter who denounces us."

The Jews in Palestine were also furious about news of continued anti-Semitism in Poland. A dispatch from Kielce, Poland, reported a pogrom. Thirty-six Jews were beaten to death by a mob, thirty-six Jews, the pitiable remnant of three million killed by the Nazis in Poland, with the help of fascist Poles, who, like the Russians, had carried out pogroms against Jews before Hitler. More than three decades later, during the courageous struggle of Solidarity in Poland, and the sufferings of the Polish people under martial law, there were more anti-Jewish demonstrations and the arrests of two of the Solidarity union's leaders who were of Jewish origin. The government would blame the Jews once again for Poland's troubles, although neither Lech Walesa, the leader, nor ninety-nine percent of the dissident workers were anything but the most devout Roman Catholics, certainly not Jewish. Lech Walesa denounced the government's anti-Semitism.

General George C. Marshall was still in China in the summer of 1946, trying, with little hope left, to arrange a permanent truce in the fighting between Nationalist and Communist forces. By September he would give it up as hopeless. The Russians, to our surprise, were not supporting Mao and his Communists. In fact, they had taken steps that would help Chiang and the Nationalists. Nevertheless, there were voices raised back home blaming the Russians and charging that communists had infiltrated the State Department and were sabotaging our efforts to help Chiang. They would not admit that Chiang and his people were inefficient, incompetent, and, above all, corrupt. A book, *Thunder out of China,* by Theodore H. White, told the truth about Chiang and predicted a Communist victory in China.

Meanwhile, French and Vietnamese delegates at Fontainebleau were making no progress, for it was becoming apparent that the French concept of a federation and a French union of states was merely a fig leaf to cover up the reality of French Empire under another name. It was clear to the Vietnamese that only the old imperial relationship was in store for them and they walked out of the Fontainebleau Conference. Only Ho Chi Minh remained behind to salvage something from the wreckage of the talks, as the others headed home.

Ho went to see Jean Sainteny, who had been with him in Hanoi, and pleaded for some face-saving gesture. Sainteny, in his memoirs some years later, quoted Ho as saying to him and to the minister of Overseas France, Marius Moutet: "Do not leave me like this. Give me some weapon against the extremists. You will not regret it." Ho was offered nothing. He prepared, in deep sadness, to leave France, knowing that his people, particularly the hot-headed young nationalists, would force him to make war upon the French. He did not doubt that he could win such a war but at a terrible price.

That is what Ho Chi Minh told me on September 11, 1946, when he came to dinner in my house in Saint-Cloud. I had invited two American reporters, good friends, to join me: Arthur Gaeth of the Mutual Broadcasting System and Alexander Kendrick of the Philadelphia *Inquirer,* later my colleague at CBS. The interview lasted four hours, as he analyzed in detail all the issues of the conflict, and then forecast the future course of the war, how it would be fought and how it would be won.

Ho came into my house dressed in the plain, high-collared tunic popularized at the time by Chiang Kai-shek and Stalin. He wore no decorations or insignia. A small, thin Oriental, Ho had large, burning eyes that dominated a narrow face, made even narrower by a long wispy beard that descended from the point of his chin. Ho could speak some English but he was more fluent in French and used that language throughout the evening. He kissed Dorothy's hand, in the continental European manner, and bowed low before my father and stepmother who were visiting us.

The interview did not begin promisingly. Ho was evasive and spoke cryptically. When I asked about his background, where he had been raised, he pulled at his chin-beard and said: "Who knows who a man is? Does the man himself really know? What is important is to know where he is going." I took the cue and asked him where he was going, whether he would create a communist state in Vietnam. Once again he played the inscrutable Oriental. "Communism takes different forms in different countries, as does capitalism and democracy. Communists would normally nationalize all the banks. Well, we hardly have any banks at all in Vietnam. We must first create wealth before we can share it."

I pressed the point, asking him to confirm the fact that he himself was a communist, and a graduate of the Moscow school of revolution. He laughed at the question. "I learned about revolution not in Moscow but right here in Paris, capital of Liberty, Equality, and Fraternity." I did not know why he had agreed to come to spend the evening with us just to make quips and small talk but I simply kept asking questions, knowing that sooner or later he would come to the point. I had already learned that the Vietnamese preferred to make their points by circular routes. Vietnamese friends in Paris had often warned me that Vietnamese would say yes out of politeness but not mean it. One had to proceed circuitously to find out what they were thinking. Ho took me well around the circle before I learned what was on his mind. Here, from notes I wrote that night, is a transcript of what he said.

"Your country can play a vital role for peace in Southeast Asia. America is loved by our people. The memory of Roosevelt is still strong. You never had an empire, never exploited the Asian peoples. The example you set in liberating the Philippines was an inspiration to all of us. Do not be blinded now by this issue of communism."

I protested that the communist issue was important to Americans, that we did not think communism compatible with freedom and would hesitate before straining our relations with the French, with whom we shared common ideals, by giving support to a revolutionary government about which we knew so little.

Ho stroked his chin-whiskers, nodded his understanding but went on to say: "My people hunger for independence and will have it. If men you call communists are the only men to fight for independence, then Vietnam will be communist. But independence is the motivating force, not communism. The communists are a small minority in our country now. The strongest political element is nationalist. We are all in agreement, communists, Catholics, peasants, workers. If we must, we will fight together for our aims."

I picked up his lead and asked whether he thought he would have to fight.

This was his reply: "Yes, we will have to fight. The French have signed a treaty and they wave flags for me, but it is a masquerade. We do not have the true attributes of independence: our own customs control, our own diplomatic representatives abroad, our own currency. Our country is truncated. They have set up puppet, separatist regimes in the south. Yes, I fear that in the end we will be forced to fight."

Since Ho Chi Minh was still in France, still theoretically and juridically a treaty partner of France, his open statement that he would fight the French was astonishing. Neither Ho, nor his aide-de-camp who accompanied him, had said anything about the interview being off-the-record or for background. They had put no restrictions upon me. I asked Ho when he would be leaving Paris. He understood the import of my question. "In a few days. But I have already warned the French about the gravity of the situation. They will not be surprised to read this interview."

"But, President Ho, what you have said is extraordinary. How can you hope to be able to wage war against the French? You have no army, no modern weapons. Why, such a war would seem hopeless for you!"

"No, it would not be hopeless. It would be hard, desperate, but we could win. We have a weapon every bit as powerful as the most modern cannon: nationalism! Do not underestimate its power. You Americans above all ought to remember that a ragged band of barefooted farmers defeated the pride of Europe's best-armed professionals."

"But that was in 1776," I countered. "The weapons of war and the organization for a modern war have advanced so that I would seriously doubt that a ragged band of farmers could do the same again. There were no planes then, no napalm bombs, no radio communications."

"They can be procured if they must be," said Ho, waving my arguments aside. "And you are forgetting some recent examples of what ragged bands can do against modern troops. Have you already forgotten the heroism of the Yugoslav partisans against the Germans? The spirit of man is more powerful than his own machines. And we have other weapons that are most effective against machines. We have swamps that are better than antitank guns. We have thick jungles that planes cannot fly through and where the trees are a shield against firebombs. We have mountains and caves where one man can hold off a hundred, and we have millions of straw huts that are ready-made Trojan horses in the rear of any invading army."

"Then it will be a guerrilla war?" I asked. "A war of harassment and attrition?"

"It will be a war between an elephant and a tiger," Ho replied. "If the tiger ever stands still, the elephant will crush him with his mighty tusks. But the tiger does not stand still. He lurks in the jungle by day and emerges by night. He will leap upon the back of the elephant, tearing huge chunks from his hide, and then the tiger will leap back into the dark jungle. And slowly the elephant will bleed to death. That will be the war of Indochina."

Ho spoke those words on September 11, 1946. On December 19, the tiger struck and the battle of Vietnam began. I could not know it then, but I would go there, I would watch the elephant of France bleed slowly to death as Ho had predicted. I would see Ho again, in Hanoi. And, to my everlasting sorrow, I would see my own beloved United States step into the same jungle traps as the elephant of France, making the same mistakes, with the same results.

A most interesting statement by Ho came at the very end. "I would very much like to go to Washington to see President Truman. I am sure that I could explain to him what is happening and that we could have good relations with the Americans. General MacArthur praised us highly. We fought side by side against the Japanese. But your embassy will not grant me a visa. Perhaps you might look into this?"

I went to the embassy the next morning to report Ho's words and was told bluntly to mind my own business, to remember that I was a reporter, not a diplomat, and had no right to "put in a plea for a red revolutionary." I replied tartly that I was not putting in a "plea," that I was doing my duty as a reporter, reporting Ho's words. I added that Ho was not just a "red revolutionary" but the president of the Republic of Vietnam, officially recognized by the French and an honored guest in their country. I slammed the door on my way out. That was not a wise thing for me to do, however stupid the embassy official had been. They would strike back at me later.

I rode home, somewhat depressed, and found Dorothy waiting, her cheeks flushed, her eyes shining. She was radiant. She rushed to me, hugged me, and shouted: "David, David, the rabbit died!"

My mind still on Ho, I could not fathom what she was shouting about, until, suddenly, my brain functioned. "You're pregnant!" I shouted.

"So, Sherlock Holmes, you solved the mystery?" She laughed and danced around the room. "Sit down," I begged, taking her arm and pushing her to a chair. "You must rest, take it easy."

Dorothy pinched my nose. "Idiot! I am about a week pregnant. And I'm not supposed to rest. I'm supposed to keep busy and take long walks and watch my weight. That's all."

Dorothy had been busy working in Paris. Her friend Helen Gordon, a fashion editor in New York, had married Pierre Lazareff, one of France's leading prewar editors, who was reconstructing the collaborationist paper *Paris-Soir* into a new daily, *France-Soir,* which would become, under his leadership, the largest circulation national daily. Helen was planning a new women's magazine, *Elle,* and Dorothy had been helping sketch dummy pages and designs. She intended to keep on until late in the pregnancy, if all went well. I agreed, of course, to accept any decision she would make on condition that she promised to consult her doctor first. And then we sat down and began making a list of names. I told Dorothy there would be no problem about the name and I was sure she would agree, for she had loved my darling mother and been with her when she died.

"Lucy," I said, "Lucy would be just right for the baby."

"Funny name for a boy," Dorothy replied.

I laughed. "Oh, of course, it could be a boy. But it won't be, it'll be a girl."

"Stop saying 'it' and get used to saying 'our baby,' " Dorothy snapped at me. I apologized at once and then we both laughed about our quarreling over a week-old squibble that probably wasn't bigger than a comma. We got into my car and drove to the Avenue de l'Opéra, to Brentano's bookshop, and bought every book on pregnancy and the care and raising of babies, in both French and English. Then we went to the Café de la Paix, where I ordered a bottle of champagne and toasted Dorothy: "To my own true love and your last glass of anything alcoholic for nine months." She sipped her wine and said, "More than nine months, darling, I intend to nurse the baby, so from now on, milk it is."

Dorothy went on to do some scouting out of baby things in Paris. I went to my office and found a letter from Ed Murrow, marked "Personal." I had not heard from anyone at CBS for some time. Doug Edwards had gone home to begin his career as anchorman of the CBS News 8:00 A.M. World News Roundup, and to begin experimental broadcasts on a new medium, called television. To my disappointment, he had been replaced by a man named Don Pryor. He was cold and unfriendly when I called on him, and my career as CBS stringer had come to an end. Pryor seemed to regard me as some kind of threat. He was insecure and wanted no part of me. So I eagerly tore open Murrow's letter.

He began with a few kind words about some of my dispatches, and broadcasts for Mutual, but said nothing about CBS. Instead, to my surprise, he went on to say that he was deeply disturbed by reports of violence in Palestine and fighting between Jews and the British. Murrow admired the British. More than anyone, he knew what a debt we all owed the British, who had withstood the Nazi blitz, and held out alone when all other Western countries had fallen to the German war machine and Stalin had a nonaggression treaty with Hitler. Ed loved the British. But he had strong empathy for the Jewish people, knew all about the horrors of the Holocaust and believed the Jews had a right to live in peace in their own land, worshiping their own God, as they saw fit. He wanted to know more about what was happening in Palestine and what, if anything, he could do to help. He asked if I had any plans to go there, and if I did, would I send him detailed written reports, for which, of course, he would pay a fee.

I would learn later that Murrow, from time to time, would go outside regular CBS News channels for information. It was not that he did not trust his own correspondents. They were the best. But he looked for confirmation and also wanted reporters to be able to work without the pressures and tensions of writing or broadcasting to the public, always measuring their words, being sure of fairness and balance. He wanted me to dig deeply down into the situation and then write to him with a completely open mind and heart, with complete frankness.

I pored over maps of Palestine, assailed the Paris offices of the Jewish Agency, and HIAS, the Hebrew Immigrant Aid Society, to learn all I could about Palestine and build up a source book of names, addresses, and phone numbers before taking off. I had met a number of Palestinian Jews who had come to Paris seeking help from the Rothschilds and even from General de Gaulle, who, in 1945, was enthusiastically Semitophilic.

The French admired the Jews and saw in them a natural ally against the Arabs, who were showing signs of rebellion in French North Africa. There was a strong alliance between France and Israel, after the Jewish state was created, on the common ground of defense against Arab radicalism. They provided Israel with more arms and planes than the United States did. Later, circumstances would change and de Gaulle and France would turn against the Israelis and indulge a bit in the ancient game of Jew-baiting. But not in October 1946, when I flew off to Jerusalem to look up a man I had met earlier at the Jewish Agency office in Paris, David Ben-Gurion.

As my plane circled over Tel Aviv and I saw the narrow but

verdant crescent to the north, the desert and the hills stretching out to the south and east, a verse from Genesis came into my mind: "Thy name shall not be called any more Jacob, but Israel shall be thy name . . . And the land which I gave Abraham and Isaac, to thee I will give it, and to thy seed after thee I will give the land." Tears came to my eyes and my throat constricted as I saw as clearly as though they were before me the stacked corpses of Buchenwald, the ashes of Dachau, the gas chambers of Auschwitz.

I checked into a small hotel on the Mediterranean coast. It was raining, to my disappointment. I had always envisaged Palestine as a land of sunshine. But it gave me an opportunity to go over my research notes. There were about a half million Jews in a rather small part of the vast and ancient region called Palestine. Many of them, called sabras, after a native cactus fruit, prickly on the outside, soft and sweet within, had been born in Palestine; many others were European Jews, early refugees from Russian and Polish pogroms and Nazi terror, or the survivors of the death camps. They spoke a Babel of tongues, practiced different forms of their religion, but were united by a fierce determination to create a Jewish state in the ancient homeland of the Jews.

The most significant fact about Palestine is that the word is only a geographical not a political designation. Since the Roman destruction of the kingdom of Israel, there had never been a native state of Palestine, governed by the people of Palestine. Palestinians have lived, through the centuries, under foreign rulers. The Jews were fighting for the rebirth of their state but were not displacing any existing Palestinian state. This question, and the issue of displacement of Palestinian Arabs when the Jewish state finally was created in 1948, became and has remained one of the most bitterly contested and explosive issues of our times, up to and including today.

One of the most tragic errors of history was committed by one of history's great men. In the early 1920s, after the collapse of the Ottoman Empire, a defeated ally of Germany in World War I, a senior official in the British Colonial Office, Winston Churchill, decided to carve out a piece of empire in old Palestine. He took a crayon and circled a bit of territory. He proclaimed it to be the new sovereign state of Transjordan, and selected an emir of a minor tribal dynasty, the Hashemites, to be the king of Transjordan. The land bordered on Syria and then extended south down the east bank of the Jordan River toward the Red Sea and eastward to the edge of the Saudi desert. It had few natural resources. Among its people were nomadic Bedouin tribes, but the great majority was composed of Palestinian Arabs, long stateless, but offered the chance to become Transjordanians, under an alien dynasty, but still a land and state of their own.

Of all the ifs of history there is none more poignant, more tragic than the thought: if only Churchill had called the new state, the state of Palestine, instead of Transjordan. It was in truth a Palestinian state, not a Hashemite kingdom. Had Churchill had the foresight to call it Palestine, there would today be no PLO, no displaced Palestinians who lived so many years in squalid camps for the homeless and stateless. There would probably still be an Israeli problem because of Arab anti-Semitism, despite their claims to be Semites and therefore incapable of anti-Semitism. That is like saying that Catholics and Protestants cannot make war upon each other because they are both Christians. Tell that to the Irish! The problem of Israel would be less dangerous, less explosive without the fires and hatreds of the Palestinian issue. I sent a background note to Murrow about this.

Friends came to see me at the hotel and discussed the historical question with me. One told me that David Ben-Gurion had gone to see General Eisenhower near the end of the war to seek his support for a Jewish state, in accordance with the Balfour Declaration, a promise made by the British in World War I to Jewish scientist Chaim Weizmann for his wartime services. Eisenhower had talked about the almost certain conflicts with the Arabs and had suggested that perhaps the Jews could found their state somewhere in the vast expanses of Africa, in Uganda, perhaps. Ben-Gurion was said to have laughed aside the proposal, saying: "General, if you want to give me someone else's country, please make it Switzerland." As Ike laughed at his quip, Ben-Gurion had added: "No, sir, nowhere else but in our own ancient homeland, which is no one else's country now, or ever has been."

I went to see Ben-Gurion. It was not easy to find him. He changed residences often and was surrounded by several cordons of guards. But we finally met and I told him of my mission. He knew Murrow, had seen him in London, admired him greatly, and was aware that he had a powerful influence and a national audience. He was delighted to hear of Murrow's concern and interest, for he was sure that Murrow was a true friend. Later, as prime minister, he would honor Murrow with Israel's Watch-Tower award.*

"Tell Mr. Murrow that I have no bitterness toward his British friends. Many Jews fought in the British army against Hitler. We do not like to fight now against our former allies. But the British mandate from the defunct League of Nations [the League had officially expired on April 18, 1946] is no longer meaningful. The British will have to turn it back to the United Nations. The United States is the most influential member of the U.N. You can help us get a Jewish state in Palestine. And one for the Arabs, too. There is enough land for two states and we will learn to live together as Jews and Arabs have in fact lived together here in Palestine for centuries."

Ben-Gurion advised me to go to the universities, the factories, and the kibbutzim, to speak to young Jews as well as old, to native sabras and European immigrants. "They will tell you of their dreams and their determination to make them reality at any cost. Some are Jews who fought and survived in the ghetto of Warsaw and as partisans in the Polish woods. We have witnessed the Holocaust and our slogan is 'Never again.'

"The world will see that Jews are farmers and fighters and the same as other people. Here there is no such thing as Jewish professions, there is only human work to be done. Here we mean to be like everyone else, to do everything, with no quotas or restrictions, yes, like everyone else."

Ben-Gurion ran his hand through his thick white tufts and laughed: "Well, perhaps not exactly like everyone else. Maybe just a little bit better." His afterthought was typical of what I came over the years to recognize as a special and necessary kind of Israeli arrogance. People who have been persecuted, tortured, held in contempt for millennia, fighting against enormous odds, cannot help but be a little arrogant. It is an element in survival.

A British friend, who had been on Eisenhower's staff with me in Algiers, most sympathetic to my mission, who idolized Murrow

* Murrow won some one hundred awards, plaques, statuettes, which he threw into his office closet. The only award he kept on his desk was Israel's Watch-Tower award.

as the "Voice of London" during the worst of the blitz, lent me a jeep and I proceeded to follow Ben-Gurion's advice. I began with long talks with the "kibbutzniks." The kibbutz, a communal settlement, was, in those early pre-Israel days in Palestine, the heart and soul of the Jewish dream. All were collective agricultural communities, social democratic in ideology, and many were intensely socialistic. In many settlements, all the money earned by the kibbutz and all the properties belonged to the kibbutz as a collective and not to the members individually. Mothers nursed babies interchangeably, their own and those of others. It was a utopian society, truly a dream that would not last long. I would learn on many subsequent trips how the kibbutz changed as Israel grew. But that first experience was both inspiring and somewhat frightening.

I decided to return to reality when someone told me of a young soldier, Yigal Allon, who had created a paramilitary movement, much in the style of partisans, called the Palmach, which was preparing to play a role in the creation of Israel. I was determined to join a Palmach band on patrol. They were scouting out British forts and arsenals, carrying out raids for guns, protecting isolated Jewish farms under constant attack by Arab marauders and frequent searches by British army units. It was extremely difficult to make contact with a clandestine organization, but I was known and trusted and one day a man came to me in Kibbutz Yavne and told me to pick up, get my jeep, and come with him.

We made our way to a wooded region near Lake Galilee. We parked the jeep under some trees and made our way on foot through a swampy area and a dense cluster of greenery, where I made out the forms of a number of men belly down in the shrubbery. My guide pressed my shoulder, signaling me to get down, too. We crawled toward the others. They wore khaki shirts, shorts, and open sandals and did not seem to be armed. It was simply a patrol, innocent looking if any British unit came upon them. One of them was peering upward through powerful army binoculars. Finally he brought the glasses down and signaled the others to move out.

They made their way to an open grove and began setting up braziers, cups, tins of tea, crackers, and cigarettes. One started a fire and put a pot of water on it. It looked like a group of friends on a picnic in the woods. The one with the glasses hanging from his neck appeared to be the leader. His name was Moshe. It had been Maurice when he had been a lieutenant in the British Army, pronounced, in the British fashion, "Morris." He whispered as he described the scene. "The hill has about a thirty-degree grade, a bit steep, but we can manage swiftly under cover of darkness. They have two cannons, front and back of the fort, but the whole fort is ringed by machine-gun emplacements, about five meters apart. It's a hell of a tough position. But I only saw two gun teams this time, just yesterday. They feel secure. Only lunatics, they think, would dare assault them. Discipline is lax and sloppy. I am sure we can take them. And there are a lot of guns, grenades, and ammo in their storehouse."

I listened as they talked in English, for my benefit. At times they went into Hebrew, knowing that my own Hebrew was biblical and distant in my education. But I had heard enough to have been appalled by their suicidal plan to attack a powerful fort. I said nothing, waiting to see if I would be asked. Finally, I was. Moshe turned to me and said: "So, you have been a soldier and, I am told, were for a time with the French Resistance. What do you think?"

"I think you are all mad as hatters. There is no way that you can take that fort, going up a steep hill in the jaws of cannon and machine guns, even under the cover of darkness. Your losses will be heavy. It is a desperate project."

Moshe looked at me with a big smile on his face, not the least offended by my blunt evaluation. "So, my friend, we are mad? Yes, probably we are. Heavy losses? Certainly, we risk that. You are very correct to call it a 'desperate project.' Yes, we are desperate. We need those arms and shall have them." He stopped talking to me and turned to the others. A rapid conversation in Hebrew ensued. Then Moshe turned back to me.

"Please listen to what we have to say. We appreciate your coming here and we do not quarrel with your evaluation. But you must not tell us what we can or cannot do. Let us tell you what we must do. We must attack this fort. We will go up this hill. Some of us, perhaps many of us, will fall wounded, perhaps dead. But enough will make their way to the top and we will win.

"Go back home, go see Ed Murrow. Give him this message from the Palmach, from the Jews of Palestine: 'We will do what has to be done to create the state of Israel. Many of us will fall.

Many more will live to fight on. However long it takes, ours is the generation that will see the rebirth of Zion. We want your help. But we can do it ourselves if we have to.' "

I stood up, took his hands in mine, then opened my arms for an embrace and the ritual parting word, "Shalom." I told Moshe and his comrades, "The message of the Palmach will be made known to Americans. I will be back and hope to see you in Jerusalem."

Three days later, I would learn in Tel Aviv, waiting for my plane back to Paris, that Jewish terrorists had attacked a fort near Lake Galilee. Six of the terrorists had been killed, five wounded and captured. British forces had suffered twelve casualties and had had to evacuate the fort. By the time reinforcements had been brought up, the remaining terrorists had fled, taking guns and ammunition with them.

I wondered which of them had died and been arrested, which had finally won out. I left Tel Aviv both saddened by the losses and proud of their courage and success. All this I wrote to Murrow.

I returned to our house in Saint-Cloud to find Dorothy in perfect health. I wanted to celebrate my return and invite friends for a New Year's Eve party. We did not like holiday crowds and noise and were always uncomfortable around drunks, particularly if they were our friends. When drunk, they would become other people, sometimes funny and cute, often as not ugly and violent. As we were greeting our guests for cocktails around six at night, we were listening to a Voice of America broadcast, when suddenly the announcer said, "Stand by for a special message from the President of the United States."

Harry Truman came on, with his Midwestern twang and crisp delivery, in a surprise announcement. We had not had any legal end of World War II. There had been no peace treaty, of course, for we had insisted that the enemy surrender unconditionally, and all the wartime statutes and regulations were still in force. Truman decided that New Year's Eve, 1946, was the right moment to end the state of war and begin a real new year of peacetime law.

"With God's help, this nation and our Allies, through sacrifice and devotion, courage and perseverance, wrung final and unconditional surrender from our enemies . . . Although a state of war still exists, it is at this time possible to declare, and I find it in the public interest to declare, that hostilities have terminated." The

President went on: "Under the law, a number of war and emergency statutes cease to be effective upon the issuance of this proclamation . . . This is entirely in keeping with the policies which I have consistently followed, in an effort to bring our economy and our government back to a peacetime basis as quickly as possible."

We all cheered and raised our glasses in a toast to the first year of "peace" since 1939. We knew that it was not a very peaceful world. Fighting between the French and Vietnamese, predicted by Ho Chi Minh, had broken out in Hanoi on December 19. On that same day clashes were reported between Greek Royal Army troops and communist guerrillas. The Russians had finally that week pulled their last troops out of Iran but they were still massed there on the border. Nationalist and Communist forces were fighting again in China. The Haganah, the Jewish Independence Army, was attacking British outposts. French patrols were searching for arms caches in the warren of alleys in the Casbah of Algiers. Every time bomb in the world was ticking away, signaling a coming explosion, as we toasted the advent of peace on New Year's Eve, 1946.

As CBS Chief Washington Correspondent, in one of a number of conversations with President John F. Kennedy, Oval Office, White House, 1962. (*Courtesy David Schoenbrun*)

Interviewing former President Dwight D. Eisenhower on U.S. trade policy, on Eisenhower's Gettysburg farm, spring 1962. President Kennedy granted an interview and appeared on the same program, a most unusual joint appearance by America's then oldest and youngest presidents. (*Courtesy David Schoenbrun*)

Speaking with North Vietnamese Premier Pham Van Dong, in the gardens of the Presidential Palace in Hanoi, at the height of the Vietnam War, Sept. 2, 1967. This is a rare photo of President Ho Chi Minh's closest associate. The official interview was published worldwide. (*Courtesy David Schoenbrun*)

Champs-Elysées Paris kiosk advertising *Le Figaro*'s feature article by David Schoenbrun on America after Kennedy, 1964. (*Courtesy David Schoenbrun*)

As master of ceremonies at Washington, D.C., dinner honoring then Vice-President Lyndon Johnson, 1963. (*Courtesy David Schoenbrun*)

In rare interview granted by CIA Director Allen Dulles, Washington, 1961. (*Courtesy David Schoenbrun*)

Interviewing Françoise Sagan on set of the movie, *Bonjour Tristesse,* Paris, 1960. (*Courtesy David Schoenbrun*)

Interview at Maxim's with Irwin Shaw and Marlon Brando, 1957, during shooting of *The Young Lions.*

On the set of the film *Gigot* starring Jackie Gleason in Paris's Boulogne Sound Studio. May 1961.

With Françoise Sagan, Ingrid Bergman, and Yves Montand, on the set of *Bonjour Tristesse,* preparing a news report on the film. (*Courtesy David Schoenbrun*)

CHAPTER 12

THE YEAR IT ALL HAPPENED

New Year's Eve celebrations were being "televised" for the first time. The new medium, television, was born just before midnight, December 31, 1946. Pictures were being transmitted in eleven metropolitan areas of the United States. Sets were expensive, ranging up to three thousand dollars, and only 9,758 had been sold. RCA president David Sarnoff made the startling prediction that there would be 100,000 sets in use by the end of 1947. He also predicted that 1947 would be the first year of "peaceful prosperity" since the war.

Radio was, however, still supreme as a news medium. It had come into its own during the war years, as the fastest means of communication, leaving the slow printing presses hours behind.* Radio commentators had become household deities, national oracles. Elmer Davis, his dry, Hoosier voice low-key and cool, his mind precise, had won millions of listeners. Raymond Gram Swing, Lowell Thomas, Gabriel Heatter all had more listeners than the most famous columnists had readers.

But news was not the prime-time program. Amos and Andy filled the living rooms of the nation weeknights, and headed the

* Neither radio nor television is an adequate substitute for the print medium. Their advertising structure and the dominance of entertainment programs leave radio and television insufficient time to be much more than headline newscasts. Their strength is speed and movement not completeness.

industry's "barometer," a ratings system called the Hooper. After Amos and Andy came Bob Hope, who would go on to become a kind of perpetual motion time machine. On the popular "soap operas" Our Gal Sunday posed the question: Can a girl from the little mining town of Silver Creek, Colorado, find happiness as the wife of one of England's richest, handsomest peers, Lord Henry Brinthrop? A *Newsweek* poll to select the "most popular living person" was won by Bing Crosby, followed by Frank Sinatra, Pope Pius XII, Eleanor Roosevelt, General Eisenhower, Bob Hope, and Joseph Stalin!

The Junior Chamber of Commerce selected the "Outstanding Young Men of the Year." On the list were two little-known Harvard men: Arthur Schlesinger, Jr., and John F. Kennedy.

At Miss Porter's School for young ladies, a girl named Jacqueline Bouvier nervously awaited word of admission to Vassar. Her marks were good, she had style and breeding, and her classmates said she was sure to succeed in life.

Somerset Maugham's *The Razor's Edge* was number one on the best-seller list. Ben Hogan won the extraordinary first prize of ten thousand dollars at the Los Angeles Golf Tournament. Al Capone died of syphilis in a federal prison. And the top pop tune was "Bongo, bongo, bongo, I don't want to leave the Congo, no-no-no-no-no-nooooo!"

One of America's most experienced diplomats, Averell Harriman, had his doubts about "peaceful prosperity" and no doubts at all about the Soviet danger. He saw Stalin as a ruthless tyrant with boundless ambitions. He warned President Harry Truman that the destruction of Hitler and Nazism did not mean the end of the totalitarian threat.

Truman himself had few illusions about the Soviets and Stalin. He had met Stalin at Potsdam and saw him as a cunning, scheming, sinister force. Truman looked like a sure loser in the Presidential elections scheduled for 1948. New York's Governor Thomas E. Dewey, always wreathed in a broad smile, was just marking time, waiting to be elected President.

The Republicans, after fourteen years of being trampled by Roosevelt, were on the upswing. In the midterm congressional elections of November 1946, the Republicans had won majorities in both the House and the Senate, for the first time since Hoover. In the Eightieth Congress, there were 51 Republicans and 45 Democrats in the Senate. Many of the so-called Democrats were Southern conservatives, some of them extreme right-wingers who would often vote with the Republicans, giving them a much stronger control than the paper majority. The Republicans were even more powerful in the House, with 245 members against 118 Democrats. Powerful isolationist, conservative voices dominated that Congress: Robert Taft of Ohio in the Senate; Charles Halleck of Indiana, the new majority leader of the House; and Speaker Joe Martin.

The conservative majorities wanted to return to prewar policies, a withdrawal of American forces from the world, across-the-board income tax cuts of twenty percent, and very heavy cuts in government spending. They shouted in protest, on January 10, 1947, when President Truman, in his budget message, proposed the huge spending total of $37.5 billion dollars. The Republicans charged that he would pile up big deficits and ruin the value of the dollar. Thirty-five years later, in 1983, Republican Ronald Reagan would run up a two-hundred-billion-dollar deficit, the largest in our history.

Truman pleaded for an emergency billion dollars to prevent starvation, disease, and unrest in occupied Germany and Japan. The opposition told him that the Germans and Japs had brought their misery on themselves by starting the war. Only strong recommendations from the Republicans' hero, General MacArthur, and Truman's warnings of communism festering in areas of famine and distress, carried the day for aid to our former enemies.

Reading American national news every day in the Paris *Herald, The Times* of London, and the French press, we wondered whether anyone back home was aware of the grave crisis threatening democratic interests in Europe and Asia. Republican demands for cuts in government spending even extended to the armed forces in those days. They proposed an overall six-billion-dollar cut in Truman's budget, including almost two billion dollars of cuts for the Army and Navy.

General Marshall returned from China to warn that full-scale civil war would break out between the Nationalists and the Communists and that Chiang, whom we were backing against the Communists, would need more help. The Republicans, who would later accuse the Democrats of "giving China to the Reds," were not interested in big foreign-aid programs or foreign entanglements. Marshall was appointed secretary of state. Truman admired Marshall and told intimates that Marshall ought to be President.

In Eastern Europe, the Red Army of Russia was dug in for what looked like annexation, not occupation. Elections were held, and noncommunist parties did surprisingly well, particularly in Hungary, but the Russian Bear towered broodingly everywhere. Only one country in Eastern Europe had had a democratic government, Czechoslovakia, the only country where there seemed some hope of reconciliation between East and West. The Czech government, headed by a revered old statesman of Europe, President Eduard Beneš, talked about "finding its own road to socialism," meaning freedom from domination by the Soviet Union but not hostile to the Soviets.

Czech Foreign Minister Jan Masaryk had come to Paris in the fall of 1946 to represent his country at the peace conference with the former satellites of Nazi Germany. I had interviewed him at the Luxembourg Palace conference site and we had gone for long walks and talks through the beautiful Luxembourg Gardens of Paris.

Masaryk came to dine at my house in Saint-Cloud where he told us stories of his earlier life in the United States. He had worked in Chicago for the Crane Company, a major manufacturer of plumbing and bathroom fixtures. "I made toilets," he said, "really very good training for a foreign minister."

At that time, early in 1947, I was still Paris correspondent for a small news syndicate called the Overseas News Agency, ONA, and doing freelance broadcasting for the Mutual Broadcasting System and CBS News. My editors, interested in what was happening in Eastern Europe, felt that I could learn a lot in Czechoslovakia with Masaryk's help and then go on to explore other countries behind Russia's Iron Curtain. They asked me to leave for Prague and try to find out what was happening.

Dorothy insisted upon accompanying me. We had been separated so long by war that she was determined to travel with me on a peaceful assignment. When I protested that she was pregnant, she laughed and said: "So what, they have babies in Prague, don't they?"

We arrived in Prague in a blizzard at midnight. We had to carry our bags through the storm, across a park to our hotel, luckily not far from the station. Our room was a tomb, the washbasin a block of ice. We undressed hastily and plunged under the deliciously warm, old-fashioned eiderdown covers and fell into a deep sleep.

Suddenly, it seemed only minutes later, but was in fact seven in the morning, there came a pounding on the door and a voice shouting, "Telegramme!" A yellow sheet was slipped under the door. Dorothy stuck her head out of the covers, saw it and said: "David, David, there's a telegram!"

I groaned. "It's freezing out there, and I'm still sleepy. It'll keep."

A blast of icy air hit me. Dorothy had thrown back the covers and was racing across the frozen floor. She came racing back to bed even more swiftly. She pulled up the eiderdown and then put two blocks of ice-cold feet on my derrière. I screamed and tried to wrestle her away. She laughed as she tore open the telegram and pushed me back to my side of the bed. Then, to my horror, she screamed: "Daaaviddd!"

I shot upright. "God, what is it?"

Dorothy, radiant, said in a clear, strong voice: "Listen to this: 'If you're interested in being CBS News Paris correspondent, please call me collect soonest. Edward R. Murrow, Vice-President, CBS News.' "

Suddenly the room was warm. I jumped out of bed and began dancing around. I was wild with joy. Ed Murrow was a man I admired enormously. CBS News was the finest news organization in radio, as good a news staff as any in journalism. Admirers called it *The New York Times* of the air. To be Paris correspondent of CBS News had long been my dream.

I ran down to the lobby to call Murrow and accept his offer, agreeing to work out salary, starting date, and other details later. At one point, I said: "Ed, it's such a great post. I don't know why CBS is paying me. I ought to pay to be your Paris correspondent." Murrow laughed. "Don't worry, Buster, you'll pay plenty. We intend for you to earn your keep."

I still had to finish my assignment for ONA before returning to Paris to join CBS. Our very first thought was to walk around Prague and get the feel of the city, to talk to shopkeepers, to try to sense how people were living in the shadow of the Russian Bear.

Dorothy and I walked through the snow to the center of action, Wenceslas Square, and then down the Na Prikope. On the frosty air came a delicious odor that led us directly to a kind of iron hut on the pavement. Big, fat sausages were boiling in a huge pot. The vendor looked at us and asked, "Horke parky?" We nodded yes, guessing that was the name of the sausage. It was the granddaddy of all hot dogs, fat, succulent, delicious. He speared one, put it on a plate, slapped down a slice of thick black bread and a smear of mustard. I held out my hand with Czech coins and bills. He laughed and picked out the price.

"Americans?" he asked in a thick, Germanic accent. When we said we were, he asked, "Do you know my cousin in Cleveland, Anton Smirz?" We told him that we were New Yorkers and that New York was far from Cleveland, and that we did not know his cousin. Laughing and munching, we continued our walk. Wherever we stopped, for a beer, for an apple, someone had a cousin in Cleveland, Pittsburgh, Chicago, Dayton. A week later, Jan Masaryk took us out to meet ailing old President Beneš, in his estate outside Prague. The first thing the grand old man of Europe asked us was, "Do you know my cousin in America? His name is Harold Stassen." At last we knew someone's cousin.

Beneš thanked me for coming to visit his country and said he was pleased and honored. I protested: "I am the one who is honored, sir. I am just a young reporter, a nobody . . ." Beneš interrupted me and said: "We have an old Czech saying, young man. 'Don't make yourself so small, you're not so big.' " I had been neatly put in my place but most gently. Dorothy and I were thrilled to see Beneš but depressed to note his frailty and his depressing words about the situation in Czechoslovakia and Eastern Europe. He told me, in confidence, for he dared not say so publicly: "Democracy is doomed. We must follow instructions from Moscow. We will not long be able to maintain our sovereignty or our own road to socialism."

Masaryk told us the same thing. "The world is being divided into two camps, East and West. The power struggle between Moscow and Washington will dominate the rest of this century in world affairs." We were both embarrassed when he added, "I do not have long to enjoy life, perhaps to live. I have bad pains in my shoulder. Worse, I have become sexually impotent, either for physical or psychological reasons."

I could not use those interviews then and am publishing them now for the first time. Masaryk is long since dead, murdered, I am convinced, by the communist secret police. They said he had "fallen" out of the window of his apartment. I was certain he had been thrown out, after the communist coup d'etat in 1948. Defenestration is a classic, traditional Czech form of assassination.

Our Prague visit was not a joyful second honeymoon. We were

depressed and miserable at the thought that this country, created by Woodrow Wilson and Masaryk's father, Tomas Masaryk, one of the few democracies in Eastern Europe, was living its last days, as were Eduard Beneš and Jan Masaryk.

We returned to Paris in a somber mood the first day, but cheered up when we crossed the Rhine and entered France and thought of the wonderful new life that awaited me as the Paris correspondent of CBS News.

Murrow proved right about one thing. I would earn my keep. 1947 was a terrible year of global crises and I would rarely get a moment to catch my breath.

The Middle East was a powder keg just waiting for a spark. Arab delegates to the London Conference on Palestine, on February 8, 1947, flatly rejected a British proposal to create two states, Arab and Jewish, and to admit one hundred thousand Jewish immigrants every two years. Two days later, the Jewish Agency and the Jewish National Council formally refused to cooperate with the British government against terrorists. On February 24, Britain's foreign secretary, Ernest Bevin, announced that Britain had failed to settle the Palestinian problem and would have to turn it over to the United Nations.

Later in February, Secretary Bevin informed the State Department that Britain, virtually bankrupted by the war, its forces stretched thin, would withdraw all troops and end all military and economic aid to Greece and Turkey by March 31. Greece was on the brink of civil war. Turkey was anxiously watching Soviet troops across its border. Both were hungry and defenseless, depending upon a Western power for help. Britain's withdrawal would pose a new problem for the United States, the need to pick up the responsibilities in the world once borne by the British Empire. It could not have happened at a worse time for Harry Truman, an unpopular, minority President, with an isolationist majority in the Congress.

Blow followed blow upon the old order of the world. Prime Minister Clement Attlee announced on February 20 that Britain would transfer all power to the Indians by June 1948. Nehru approved the British policy of swift evolution to independence and invited the Moslem League of India to cooperate in forming a new government. Mohammed Ali Jinnah, head of the Moslem League, declared that he would only cooperate if Nehru agreed to the formation of an independent Moslem state. It looked as though India would celebrate independence in a civil war between Hindus and Moslems.

Many years later, in the mid-fifties, when Nehru was prime minister of a free India, I attended a cocktail reception at the Indian Embassy in Paris and overheard an extraordinary conversation between Nehru and America's Secretary of State John Foster Dulles. It was at a time, at the height of the Soviet-American power rivalry, when Dulles was seeking to counter the Soviets by building blocs of alliances around the world. He was exasperated with Nehru's neutralism and his leadership in forming a group of "nonaligned" neutralist nations in the world.

"Neutralism," Dulles fumed, "is foolish and sinful. You can't be neutral in the struggle with atheistic communism trying to dominate the world. Those who are not with us are against us."

Nehru, dressed in a long white tunic, holding in his hand a long-stemmed rose, smiled gently, sniffed the perfume of the rose, and replied: "No, Mr. Dulles, neutralism is not foolish, it is wise. And you know perfectly well that democratic India is not against you. We are, under present circumstances, only following the excellent advice that your George Washington once gave the American people. America was young and weak and could not afford to become entangled in the power rivalries of Europe. India, today, is very large but we are also weak, we lack arms and we cannot yet feed our people. We have much to do to build and strengthen India and we cannot get entangled in your rivalry with Russia. That is not sinful, it is common sense, as President Washington knew in his time."

In London, the deputies of the foreign ministers once again met without success, unable even to agree on procedure for framing a German treaty. The French government again rejected an appeal from Ho Chi Minh for a cessation of hostilities in Vietnam. Sixteen British soldiers were killed when the Jewish underground blew up an officers' club in Jerusalem. In China, Chou En-Lai asserted that the Chinese would work out their destiny without interference from the Americans or the Russians. It was a clear indication, which the State Department chose to ignore, that the Chinese communists were not satellites or puppets of the Soviets. We would pay a terrible price for consistently misreading the Chinese and for insisting, against considerable evidence, that all communists were Moscow agents. Meanwhile, America and Russia were bucking heads like angry rams. It seemed as though the whole world was blowing apart at the approach of the Ides of March, 1947.

President Truman understood the significance of the global upheavals following upon the collapse of the British Empire and the liberating force of World War II. He knew that the Soviet Union and a worldwide communist network would seek to fill the global vacuum left by the collapse of the Western European powers.

On March 7, Truman called his Cabinet into session to inform the members that, in his view, "The United States is confronted by a challenge as great as any in its history." He saw the British notes on Greece and Turkey as the signal of the end of the Pax Britannica, an essential element of the European and world balance of power. Truman felt the time had now come for America to pick up the mantle of the British. Truman told his Cabinet that he intended to take action to meet this challenge.

The first step that Truman took on March 10 was to ask Congressional leaders to authorize loans of $250 million for Greece and $150 million for Turkey to help strengthen the two countries against an internal communist subversion or Soviet pressure from outside.

At 1:00 P.M., President Truman entered the House and proceeded briskly to the rostrum. Without delay, he stated his purpose. "The gravity of the situation which confronts the world today necessitates my appearance before a joint session of the Congress. The foreign policy and the national security of this country are involved."

The Truman speech, laying down what would come to be called the Truman Doctrine, was one of the most far-reaching decisions in all American history. It reversed the policy laid down by George Washington in his farewell address, warning Americans to beware of foreign entanglements. It ended the tradition of isolationism. Almost overnight, Harry Truman would take America out of isolationism into internationalism and global interventionism.

The core of the Truman Doctrine was contained in three terse paragraphs:

> I believe that it must be the policy of the United States to support free peoples who are resisting attempted subjugation by armed minorities or by outside pressures.
>
> I believe that we must assist free peoples to work out their destiny in their own way.
>
> I believe that our help should be primarily through economic

and financial aid, which is essential to economic stability and orderly political processes.

The wording of Truman's message was carefully chosen to leave him many options. The words meant much more than they said. On the surface, it seemed that he was merely proposing some economic aid to struggling peoples. But his "doctrine" did not limit him in any way. In effect, it set the frontiers of American freedom anywhere and everywhere in the world where freedom was threatened. It was an open-end, global commitment. And the key word, in the third paragraph, was the word "primarily." Critics of the Truman Doctrine, on the Republican right wing and the Democratic left wing, understood that this meant that American aid need not be limited to economic and financial aid. Economic aid would be only *primary* aid. Secondarily, critics charged, would come military aid. They were right.

Economic aid is always the first commitment. Then it rapidly becomes necessary to protect the investment by bolstering the recipient state with arms, then with military advisors, then with American troops. That would be the evolution of the Truman Doctrine for decades ahead. But at the time, the critics were very much in the minority. It seemed to most Americans that America was and should be the champion of freedom. Few understood that the phrase "free peoples" was not specific and was open to many interpretations. "Free" can be a synonym for independent but not necessarily for democratic.

Soon enough the word "free" would be degraded to mean anticommunist, and Americans would be defending repressive, fascist regimes simply because they were, or appeared to be, threatened by communist forces. In the 1980s, America would impose sanctions against the Polish and Soviet governments, guilty of repressing the Polish people, but would not take sanctions against repressive governments in South Africa, Guatemala, El Salvador, and Argentina. Our foreign policy since 1947 has been significantly influenced by the terms and philosophy of the Truman Doctrine, far beyond anything that Truman himself imagined. Its main thrust has not been the defense of freedom but the power rivalry with Russia. This has been true under Republican as well as Democratic Party Presidents, up to and including Ronald Reagan.

Truman received much-needed support from a leading Republican. Senator Arthur Vandenberg called a news conference to announce his endorsement of the Truman proposal. Vandenberg told reporters: "The independence of Greece and Turkey must be preserved, not only for their own sakes, but also in defense of peace and security for all of us."

Vandenberg, at least, understood the far-reaching implications of the Truman Doctrine, stressing not just economic aid but peace and security. He went on to say: "We are at odds with communism on many fronts." He knew that the sure way he could sell a foreign-aid program to Americans was to wrap it in an anticommunist cloak and to insist that it was in the interests of American security.

The senior Republican in the country, sometimes called Mr. Republican, Senator Robert Taft, disagreed sharply with Truman and with Vandenberg. He, too, knew there was much more involved than an innocuous and modest aid program. He put it bluntly: "I do not want war with Russia." Taft was a genuine, traditional Republican isolationist, not like the war hawks who would follow him in later years.

At the Council of Foreign Ministers in Moscow, the Russians screamed their fury, charging that Truman was destroying the U.N., exposing the world to the risk of war and the advent of a new American imperialism to replace the bankrupt British Empire. Truman and Vandenberg, realizing they had made a mistake, hastened to repair it. Truman sent Warren Austin to the U.N. to propose a series of U.N. involvements in his plan. Senator Vandenberg amended a bill he was submitting on Truman's proposals to provide for consultation with the U.N. on American foreign-aid projects.

Truman's proposals were finally accepted by the Senate, and from March 1947 on, there has been no turning back, no turning away from America's entanglements in world affairs. In this sense, it might be said that March 12, 1947, the date of Truman's address to Congress, was the third most important date in American history. The first was July 4, 1776. The second came in 1860 when Abraham Lincoln affirmed that the Republic was indivisible. March 12, 1947, marked the emergence of the United States as a permanently committed world power.

Secretary of State George Marshall, on a brief visit to Paris, explained some of the aspects of Truman's policy that were below the surface. He told me that Greece and Turkey were threatened and that there were powerful Communist Party forces undermining

Italy and France. In a time of economic crisis, they could subvert democracy in both countries. Marshall explained that the destruction of Germany, the greatest industrial power of Europe, had seriously weakened Europe's marketplace and the availability of products and goods. Germany, he explained, would have to be helped to restore its productive apparatus. Herbert Hoover had just completed a study of European problems at Truman's request and had recommended urgent action to "end American charity in Germany and restore the nation's ability to produce and take care of itself."

General Marshall also revealed that he had received alarming reports from the State, Commerce, and Treasury departments, all stressing the danger of the lack of dollars in the world to pay for import of American goods. Europe and Asia were in ruins and unable to produce enough to earn dollars with which to buy American products. This, said the secretary, could result in a severe loss of trade and lead to another depression in the United States and in the world. Something had to be done quickly to avert these grave threats to democratic capitalism. Otherwise, widespread misery would lead to the triumph of communism. By the time Marshall had finished his explanations, I was thoroughly alarmed by his no doubt accurate but apocalyptic world view. I could not quote him, but he did authorize full use of all the facts and arguments in his briefing. I feared his analysis was leading to war with Russia. I would only discover later that I had been listening to the reasoning behind another dramatic new American foreign policy in that watershed year, 1947.

Meanwhile, I had my hands full trying to keep on top of French events in every sphere. Each day would bring a new political crisis or a new creation, in economics, fashions, cinema, literature, philosophy. Paris was in ferment in 1947.

On March 20, the socialist prime minister of France, Paul Ramadier, threatened to resign when the Communist Party refused to vote credits for the war in Indochina. The communists backed down, but later supported a strike at the Renault auto plant. Ramadier then threw them out of his Cabinet. For the first time since the war, the Resistance alliance of the democratic and communist parties of France had broken up, just as the wartime allies, Russia and the West, were breaking up.

There was more to life in Paris than world crises. Dorothy took me to the fashion shows and told me about a sensational new couturier, Christian Dior, who was the talk of Paris and the fashion world. He had designed a beautiful line of very feminine clothes, a welcome relief from the wartime uniform styles. Dior had decreed, "No more shoulder pads." He offered rounded shoulders, gave support to the bustline, nipped in the waist, sculpted hips, flaired full skirts down to ankle length. Fashion reporters dubbed his line the New Look. It would be the big fashion story of the year and would establish Dior as the leading designer of Paris. Dorothy also took me to meet other talented couturiers: Balenciaga, Jacques Fath, Pierre Balmain, and a friend from prewar days, one of the few prewar designers to stay on top in the postwar period, the creative, colorful Elsa Schiaparelli, Schiap to all her friends. She loved Dorothy, who had come to sketch in her salon as a student, and we would see her often.

At night, at the Flore, Jean-Paul Sartre would be joined by actor Jean-Louis Barrault who came to the café with friends. His latest film, *Les Enfants du Paradis,* had been hailed by critics in America as well as Paris as a modern masterpiece. French moviemakers were set to launch a new revolution of *cinéma vérité,* rivaling the new Italian directors and actors. Paris would become the capital of *la nouvelle vague,* the New Wave in movies and practically everything else. This delighted the French and compensated for their loss of power in the world. They would rather lose military leadership than cultural leadership of the world.

French creativity and innovation were not confined to fashions, the cinema, art, and literature. One of the most creative men in France and in the world was hard at work, with a brilliant team of engineers, economists, and political scientists, working on a plan to reconstruct war-torn France. His name was Jean Monnet. I had first met him in North Africa where he was one of the commissioners of the French Committee of National Liberation.

Monnet had traveled the world, selling cognac and then helping solve world problems. He had been an assistant secretary-general of the League of Nations. He had conceived the plan for the free port of Danzig. He had reorganized the Soviet Union's internal distribution system and had gone to China to reorganize its railways and set up new banking systems. He had advised Churchill on war production and then gone to Washington to help Roosevelt organize our own productive capacity for war. He was the quintessential planner of the world, and he had come home to France to solve his own country's postwar problems.

Monnet had set up working headquarters, for what would come to be called the Monnet Plan for Reconstruction, in a cloisterlike building opposite an old church on the Rue Martignac. His assistants included some of the best brains in France: chemical engineer Etienne Hirsch; economist Pierre Uri, a graduate of the Sorbonne, the London School of Economics, and Princeton's Institute for Advanced Study; political scientist Felix Gaillard, a future prime minister of France; economist Robert Marjolin who would become one of the principal economists of Europe. These dedicated young men worked with devotion around the clock. They were like Roosevelt's young brain-trust team in the early days of the New Deal, but so religiously devoted to Monnet and his plan that they were called the monks of Martignac Abbey.

Monnet's plan provided for a five-year period of modernization of the French economy based upon reconstruction of the basic industries: cement, steel, tractors, fertilizers, transport, and energy. Monnet set target dates and goals for each basic industry, organized special committees composed of government officials, economists, industrialists, and trade union leaders. Monnet was not himself a specialist in anything. He had never even gone to college. But he was a man of extraordinary vision and wisdom, discipline with imagination, and he had the ability to inspire other men to turn his dreams into the blueprint of reality. He would enchant me as he would mesmerize all who came into his orbit. He would have personal "acolytes" in every major capital: American Ambassador David Bruce in Paris; McGeorge Bundy, Kennedy's National Security advisor in Washington; men of similar power in London, Rome, and Bonn. President Eisenhower, John Foster Dulles, Winston Churchill, Konrad Adenauer, all would look to Monnet for advice over the years.

The only country in which Monnet was not fully honored was his own, France. Monnet was an internationalist, Charles de Gaulle a passionate nationalist. De Gaulle had approved Monnet's five-year plan for France, but clashed with him when Monnet later began talking about European unity and integration of national efforts. What Monnet was doing in the winter and spring of 1947 would prove invaluable not only to France but to the United States, when Secretary Marshall put forward his foreign policy initiative which became known as the Marshall Plan.

The Marshall Plan was an enlightened act of foreign policy. Winston Churchill called it "the most unsordid act in history." Churchill had a taste for putting positive statements negatively. He was fond of saying that democracy is the worst system of government—except for all others. The Marshall Plan could only have come out of a democratic form of government. No autocracy, no dictatorship could have proposed so "unsordid" an act as that which grew out of a commencement speech by George Marshall, one of the greatest of Americans, at Harvard University on June 5, 1947.

June 5, 1947, was, for me, a memorable day but not because of Secretary Marshall's speech. It was a day of professional and personal challenge. The chief European correspondent of CBS, Howard K. Smith, had taken a week's vacation and I had been asked to do his Sunday news program, a fifteen-minute analytical report on politics in Europe. It was the most highly praised report in radio in those days. Substituting for Howard Smith was like being asked to pinch-hit for Babe Ruth. On June 5, I was poring over my notes of the week and preparing to write the analysis to deliver two days later. At that point, the most exciting event in my life occurred. Dorothy came to me with a big smile and whispered into my ear, "Darling, my water just broke. Our baby is coming."

I shot out of my chair, took her arm, led her to my car, and took off for the American hospital in Neuilly, the suburb of Paris. Smith's show, Marshall's speech, everything else flew out of my mind. I could think of nothing but the coming birth of our child. I sat in Dorothy's room all day, holding her hand, kissing her and assuring her that everything would be fine. She was not the least disturbed. I was the nervous wreck, the cliché model of the anxious father-to-be.

The doctor chased me out at sunset, telling me that the baby would not be coming until the next day. I went home, remembering with a chill that I had not written a word for the broadcast and was not in the mood. A lifetime of discipline came to my rescue and I sat down at my typewriter and began pounding away. The script was finally finished at midnight. I could reread and edit it the next day. I fell into bed exhausted.

By noon, June 6, Dorothy's labor began. It lasted for almost twelve painful hours for both of us. Just before midnight, Lucy was born. I was a proud father of a beautiful little girl, and a broadcaster on the way to a fine career. Congratulations poured in from New York, on the two "babies," my little girl, and my first fifteen-minute analysis piece. And my country had been launched by George Marshall on one of the most enlightened and successful foreign policies in our history. Marshall's speech would change the history of Europe.

The secretary had begun his address by sketching, in colorful, dramatic terms the agony of Europe, lying bruised and weak in the ruins of war. For humanitarian reasons, and also for the security of the United States, he said, we could not stand by as spectators or live on as an island of luxury in the impoverished world. The words were already familiar to me. But I was exhilarated when I came to the key paragraphs which Churchill would praise.

"It is already evident that before the United States government can proceed much further in its efforts to alleviate the situation and help start the European world on its way to recovery, there must be some agreement among the countries of Europe as to the requirements of the situation and the part those countries themselves will take in order to give proper effect to whatever action might be undertaken by this government.

"It would be neither fitting nor efficacious for this government to undertake to draw up unilaterally a program designed to place Europe on its feet economically. This is the business of Europeans. The initiative I think must come from Europe."

In its simplest terms, Marshall's address proposed that Uncle Sam would help those prepared to help themselves. This was exactly the right approach. The European nations had destroyed themselves by making war upon each other three times in a single lifetime, the Franco-Prussian War of 1870 and then the two world wars of this century. They would have to learn to work together, to cooperate, to build not only prosperity but a permanent peace. We could not do that for them, but we could bring them together, be the essential catalyst. We could generate what would become a self-generating machine. This was not only generous, it was farsighted, enlightened. It was not charity or a dole. It respected human dignity and national independence. Western European states would not become satellites or dependencies of the United States, but respected partners.

French Foreign Minister Georges Bidault understood this at

once. So did Jean Monnet. Bidault told me that Monnet's five-year plan for French reconstruction was the bedrock on which Marshall's proposal could build. France knew what its requirements were and already had a plan of its own. Monnet understood more than Bidault did. He said that it was not enough to have a French plan. That was not all that was needed, not what Marshall had said. Monnet's dream, building in his mind for years, all through the war, was to integrate the industries of Europe. That was the only way to avoid future wars and to create a genuine prosperity. He reminded me that on March 6 three small countries, Belgium, the Netherlands, and Luxembourg, had agreed to form a full economic and monetary union of their states. It was called Benelux, and Monnet said that reporters had overlooked the significance of that union of states. "It is as important as the original union of your thirteen former colonies. Or, it will be when France and Germany join in to such a union. That is the core of the Marshall proposal."

Great Britain's foreign secretary, Ernest Bevin, former leader of the stevedores of London's docks, a tough, feisty Laborite, jumped at the Marshall proposal. A blinding, paralyzing blizzard had hit England again on March 5, completing the grave damages to its industry that the January snows had first inflicted. Britain was bankrupt and desperate. Marshall had thrown out a lifeline. Bevin picked up his phone and telephoned Bidault in Paris. He suggested that they jointly convoke a meeting of all interested European countries to discuss the Marshall proposals. He also announced to the press that Britain would act at once to answer Marshall's challenge to come up with its own self-help plan.

Bidault agreed with Bevin but he insisted that first there be preliminary talks with the Soviet Union. Unlike Britain, France faced a powerful communist opposition which controlled its biggest trade union. No French government could afford to make a major policy move without demonstrating careful consideration of the workers' interests. It would not be possible for Bidault to proceed without at least inviting and consulting with the Soviets on a major European issue. Bevin, a fierce anticommunist, agreed with reluctance. He knew Bidault could not do otherwise. But he was determined not to let the Soviets and their communist allies veto Marshall's proposals.

After an initial hesitation, the Soviets announced that they would come to Paris for preliminary explorations with the French and the British. The date for their tripartite conference was set for June 27.

It was hot in the palace of the Quai d'Orsay where Molotov, whom we had dubbed Old Stone-Bottom, for his ability to sit rigidly still and say "Niet" all day long, was meeting with Bidault and Bevin. At the end of the first day, briefing officers held background meetings with reporters. They told us that Molotov had raised every conceivable objection to the American proposals. Britain's Bevin deliberately baited Molotov, while Bidault nervously tried to find some middle way between the dour Russian and the belligerent Briton.

Day after day, we would be told that Molotov had denounced the Marshall proposals as an American imperial scheme to penetrate and control the European economies. He charged that the capitalists would use the plan to prevent the rise of socialism in Europe, to maintain reactionary, colonial regimes in power. He accused Marshall of forming up an anticommunist crusade and quoted at length from speeches made in Congress at the time of the Truman Doctrine speech to prove his point.

On July 2, Hervé Alphand, director of the Economic Affairs Department of the French Foreign Office, called to tip me off that the conference would break up that day with a final Soviet negative. He was a bit nervous about the communist reaction in France but was elated. Hervé, a sophisticated linguist and wit, who knew and loved America, told me that he had told his foreign minister: "Congress will not vote a penny for the Marshall Plan if the Russians join in. Our only hope is that they refuse." Alphand, who would become ambassador to America and hold every major post in the French diplomatic service, a kind of Averell Harriman without money, was precisely right in his judgment.

I had visited every nook of the Foreign Office and knew that there was a private elevator leading down from the conference room to the side entrance, off the Quai d'Orsay. Roger Vaurs, a youngster in Alphand's service, then a press spokesman, later the most successful and loved chief of the French Information Service in the United States, was another good friend who would help me out when he could. He informed me that, before meeting the waiting press, Bevin and Bidault would come down the side elevator. I made my way to the side entrance and waited for the elevator to descend. It took about an hour and then I saw it come down with Bevin, Bidault, and Molotov. I hung back in the shadows until they had taken leave of Molotov, who strode out, his expressionless face as unreadable as ever. Then I stepped forward.

I came to Bidault, who knew me well, and asked: "What's the result, sir?"

His face twitched and he chewed his lips as he replied: "It's all over. Europe is splitting apart."

Ernest Bevin was ruddy-faced and smiling. He clapped Bidault on the back and said: "Come now, nothing is over. It is all just beginning. Now we are going to proceed and rebuild a new Europe."

They were both right. Europe did split apart, East against West, and never have the twain met. There have been brief periods of détente but never genuine cooperation. Cold War was about to break out, almost as deadly as any hot war. Bidault knew that. But Bevin was right, too. Europe was on the verge of a renascence in an entirely new system of international exchanges that would change its history and make it impossible for France and Germany ever again to make war or want to make war on each other. I would report this on CBS News, on its excellent 8:00 A.M. World News Round-up, anchored by Douglas Edwards, and on Ed Murrow's evening news program.

The day after Molotov had walked out of the Marshall Plan preliminary talks, Bevin and Bidault sent out invitations to twenty-two European nations to come to Paris on July 12 to discuss a collective response to Marshall's proposals. The Russians had made one of their most serious blunders. Molotov did not understand that a "Da" could have been more deadly to American plans than his "Niet." Congress would not have voted substantial funds for a European pool in which Russia had been a member. Even if it had, the Soviets could have frustrated and sabotaged every move toward European economic cooperation. They could have killed the Marshall Plan by joining it, as Alphand had foreseen. Instead, they opened the door for the Americans and their allies by walking out.

One of the first telegrams to Bidault came from Jan Masaryk expressing his pleasure and acceptance of the invitation to a Marshall Plan conference. But, the very next day, Masaryk received a call from Molotov telling him that the Soviet Union would regard his attendance at the conference as a hostile act. Instead, Molotov invited Masaryk to Moscow, where he offered him a five-year trade pact as a substitute for American aid. Masaryk had no choice but to accept. He knew it meant the end of any hope for Czechoslovakia to become a bridge between East and West. His country was a prisoner of the Soviets and the days of its free Republic were numbered.

Sixteen countries did finally come to Paris for the conference and agreed to a procedure for submitting reconstruction plans and the mechanics of receiving aid. By the end of 1947, Harry Truman would ask the Congress for the unprecedented sum of seventeen billion dollars to finance the reconstruction of Europe over a four-year period. It was the biggest grant of aid, the largest single peacetime appropriations bill ever to be passed in American history up to that time. When I saw Truman later that year in Washington, and asked him about the relationship between the Truman Doctrine and the Marshall Plan, he grinned and said: "They fit like two halves of a walnut." He then laughed and said: "Some nut. They'll find it hard to crack." There was no doubt whom he meant by "they."

I flew back to New York for a special report on the conference. My trip was my first back home since the war. I was dazzled by the splendor, the wealth, and power of New York. A walk down Fifth Avenue was a fantasy trip through Arabian Nights splendor. After war-torn Europe, the United States was awesome. The CBS correspondent in Berlin, Bill Downs, seeing Fifth Avenue, whistled and said, "What a place to loot!"

In Washington I stood before the statue of Lincoln and felt the same reverence and inspiration as when I had seen Michelangelo's "Moses" in Rome. Washington was so beautiful, America so powerful and generous, that I felt a surge of joy and pride. Truman, it seemed to me, had surprised everyone and was filling Roosevelt's shoes. He was not the midget from Missouri caricatured in a critical press. He was a giant. I wondered at the alchemy of the American system that could transmute a small-town politician, a member of a corrupt political gang, into a world statesman.

On that trip back home, I made my first broadcast, on the European crisis, in the new, experimental system known as television. CBS was doing a nightly news show, anchored by my friend

Douglas Edwards. And the producer of the program was my cousin Henry Cassirer, who had made his debut into journalism, as I had, in our series for *PM*.

Our eyes, as almost always, were focused on Europe, but Asia was explosive and dangerous, too. In Korea, American correspondents were denied permission to visit the Soviet Zone of occupation. U.S.-Soviet negotiations were deadlocked there on every issue. The superpowers were on a collision course in Korea.

In India, the once-proud British Empire troops pulled down their flags and marched out, with the bands playing "The World Is Upside-Down." The British granted freedom and independence to India, but, at the same time, announced its partition into two states, one Hindu, the other Moslem, India and Pakistan. A Hindu mob halted a train and killed eleven Moslem passengers in retaliation for two Hindus killed by Moslems. The day the flag of India was hoisted to the flagstaff of the United Nations, the same day that Pakistan became an independent state, August 15, 1947, the death toll from Hindu-Moslem riots in Lahore came to 268. A month later, Nehru was called in by Viscount Mountbatten to confer on the discovery of mass graves in the Punjab, where one hundred thousand Moslems and Sikhs had been massacred.

In China full-scale civil war was raging between Chiang Kai-shek's Nationalists and Mao Tse-tung's Communists. The Communists had cut rail communications to Peking.

In Indonesia, Dutch armed forces invaded eastern Java. The Netherlands delegate told the U.N. that his government was only "taking police measures of a strictly limited character." Hundreds, then thousands, would die.

North Africa, too, was flaming. In Morocco, Algeria, Egypt, and Palestine, all along the North African coast of the Mediterranean, riots, bombings, and sabotage were exploding into daily death lists. The Moroccan Independence Party, Istiqlal, demanded the end of the French Protectorate. Algerian nationalists demonstrated for self-government. The British had just ended their sixty-four-year military occupation of Cairo but Egyptians were demanding that they pull all troops out of their country. Palestine was aflame. Jewish Irgun guerrillas bombed the Haifa district police headquarters, killing ten British and Arab policemen and civilians. The Arab Higher Committee declared that Palestinian Arabs would never accept partition, warning that any attempt at creating a Jewish state would drench the Holy Land in blood.

Refusing to be intimidated by the Arab threats, both the United States and the Soviet Union, in a rare instance of agreement, announced, in mid-October, that they endorsed plans for partitioning Palestine into an Arab and a Jewish state. At the United Nations, on November 29, 1947, the General Assembly voted 33 to 13 to partition Palestine. There was not the slightest doubt that just as soon as British troops pulled out of Palestine a war between the Arabs and the Jews would break out. What no one could know was that the Jewish-Arab conflict in Palestine would result in four wars and be one of the most explosive issues of our time, right up to the present, more than thirty-five years of killing and hatred, with no end in sight.

Europe, too, had its flash points. There was civil war in Greece and fighting on the borders of Greece, Albania, and Yugoslavia. There were riots and strikes in Italy. France finally underwent the challenge it had so long feared. Communist leader Thorez picked up his telephone and the CGT called a series of strikes that crippled the country. Socialist Minister of the Interior Jules Moch called out the army as well as the police and France teetered on the brink of civil war, until the forces of order won out and the workers, beaten and angry, went sullenly back to work.

The parliamentary leader of the French Communist Party, Jacques Duclos, attended a secret meeting in Poland, where international communists formed a new organization they called the COMINFORM. It was a re-creation of the prewar communist international called the COMINTERN. It was Moscow's answer to the Marshall Plan. Communist spokesmen made no secret of their intention to wreck Truman's and Marshall's plans to unite and rebuild Europe as allies of the United States. The Cold War had plunged into subzero temperature.

The United States looked like the only peaceful, prosperous nation in the world. But it was not without its problems. Foreseeing a long struggle with Russia, Truman had decided to bring all the armed forces under one command. He proposed and Congress approved the creation of a new Department of Defense, which would include the old Departments of War and Navy, as well as the Air Force. James Forrestal was appointed first secretary of defense and he called for a greatly increased military budget. At the same time, President Truman created a new agency, the Central Intelligence Agency, CIA, and named Allen Dulles, former European chief of the wartime OSS, as its first director general. His brother, John Foster Dulles, was just waiting for the 1948 election victory of Governor Dewey to be named secretary of state, a position he had prepared himself for from his youth with a single-minded ambition and drive. General Eisenhower told a "Draft Ike" committee that he would not accept a nomination to be President of the United States. Instead, he would later accept appointment as president of Columbia University.

A number of State Department employees, who had been dismissed in June for "security reasons," were refused a hearing on formal charges. They were also refused the opportunity to resign without prejudice. Their careers and lives were wrecked without charges or evidence or trial. It was the beginning of a massive witch-hunt, violating the most cherished American principles of democracy, conducted by HUAC, the House Un-American Activities Committee. At first it was a comic scene. Later it was perceived to be a grave threat to American democracy.

HUAC received worldwide publicity when it called some of America's greatest movie stars to a hearing, which the press called the trial of the "Hollywood Ten." Tough-guy star Humphrey Bogart, coming out of the hearing, twitched his lips in his famous style and growled, "They clobbered us." Beautiful Paulette Goddard, angry and fearless, told one committee member, "If you ask me once more whether I am a commie, I'll hit you on the head with my diamond bracelet." Perhaps the most thoughtful comment of all was made by the president of the Screen Actors' Guild, Ronald Reagan. He said: "I hope that we never are prompted by fear of communism into compromising any of our democratic principles."

Millions of New Yorkers got a taste of what had happened in Britain when Mother Nature put the cap on the year with a year-end blizzard that dumped twenty-six inches of snow on the city in sixteen hours, the worst storm in New York's history. The year that had begun with a blizzard that had brought down the shaky structure of the British Empire, ended by paralyzing the world's greatest city. It froze U.N. delegates from around the world, meeting at a site ironically called Lake Success. The entire world was either frozen or in flames as the fateful year 1947 finally came to an end.

CHAPTER 13

BLOOD, SWEAT, AND LAUGHS

A dinner party at Eve Curie's was always a very Parisian evening. Eve's apartment was on the fifth floor of a building above the Vert Galant restaurant, just opposite the Palais de Justice. It was on the Ile de la Cité, in the middle of the Seine, where two thousand years ago Julius Caesar conquered a tribe called the Parisii. Paris was born on that island in the Seine. Eve's apartment had a terrace that looked out over the river with a superb view of the old Latin Quarter, the Panthéon, where great men of France are entombed, and Sorbonne University, one of the oldest in the world. To dine there with the daughter of two of the greatest scientists of the twentieth century, a woman of dazzling beauty and intelligence, was one of the highlights of being a correspondent in Paris.

The dinner party at Eve Curie's, one of the many marvelous evenings in the Paris of the forties and fifties, when that City of Light was the political, diplomatic, economic, military, and fashion center of the Western world, was one of the consolation prizes of the tense life we otherwise led. Among her guests that night were a number of bright, witty, cultured men and women:

Couve de Murville, a Foreign Office official, with the rank of Inspecteur des Finances, the highest and most prestigious rank of the French civil service. Tall, elegant, every inch an Englishman in appearance and manner, he is a passionately patriotic Frenchman who has held top jobs in his country's service. Couve, as his friends call him, would go on to be ambassador to the United States, foreign minister, and, under de Gaulle, prime minister of France. Today, he is a deputy to the National Assembly from the Seventh arrondissement of Paris, an influential voice in Parliament.

Guillaume Guindey, another top civil servant, graduate of a *grande école.* Guindey would become one of the most important economists in the burgeoning community of Europe. Beautifully dressed, immaculate, handsome, he had apparently read everything and knew everything. Talking with Guindey was as valuable as, and much easier than, reading an encyclopedia.

Harry Labouisse, a ruggedly handsome lawyer from New Orleans, economic counselor to the American ambassador. Harry would head up the Marshall Plan team for France and go on to become the United Nations director for the Palestinian refugee program, and then one of the highest officials of the U.N., as director of ECOSOC, the Economic and Social Council. He would also become the husband of Eve Curie.

Finally, the guest who fascinated everyone at that table, who, without effort, dominated all the brilliant, articulate men and women at the dinner: Eleanor Roosevelt.

At one point during dinner, one of the French guests was deploring the deterioration of public manners in Paris. There had been a big change since Heinrich Heine had once written that he loved to walk down the Champs-Elysées and deliberately bump into someone, just to hear the exquisite language of a French apology. Today, someone said, you'd get bumped back. And the language would not be exquisite. You would probably be called several species of a sausage, a unique French insult.

Mrs. Roosevelt shook her head and said: "That has not been my experience. Everyone has been kind to me, helpful, even warm and friendly." She stopped and thought a moment, then added: "I suppose it is because of Franklin."

There was a moment of silence as everyone looked at her tenderly. Then, Couve de Murville, a perfect diplomat, took Mrs. Roosevelt's hand and raised it to his lips. "No, dear lady, it is because of you." We all broke into applause, and Eleanor beamed at us, delighted with the compliment.

We began to talk of President Roosevelt, each telling some war story. Eleanor Roosevelt added some funny stories of her own about Roosevelt and Churchill, when Churchill was their guest at the White House. "He was very fond of brandy and walking at night naked in the White House, not a good idea given his bulging pear-shaped figure." She spoke admiringly of Churchill, while making it clear that she and Franklin had had sharp quarrels with him, particularly on imperial policy.

Then Eve Curie told us of having been invited by Prime Minister Churchill to a banquet on the lawn at Chequers, the P.M.'s magnificent country estate. The dinner took place on the evening of the surrender of the Nazi generals. Churchill was alive with happiness, almost drunk with victory and a number of beakers of brandy.

Eve turned to him and said: "Prime Minister, now that it is over, the terrible war ended, can you tell us what was your blackest moment of the war?"

Churchill thrust out his chin, in his most pugnacious bulldog pose, his eyes twinkling, as he replied: "Frankly, my dear, I enjoyed every minute of it." Then he roared with laughter and pounded his thigh.

Dorothy looked at her watch and gasped. "It's a quarter to ten."

Eve laughed and said, "Dorothy, you won't turn into a pumpkin until midnight."

Dorothy grinned at her ruefully. "Eve, this is the most wonderful dinner party and I love everyone here and would like to stay until dawn. But I am still nursing the baby and it's her feeding time. I really must go. Thank you for an unforgettable evening."

We left in a hurry, telling Eve at the door that she must come to dine with us soon.

I crossed the Pont Saint-Michel, as we saw Notre Dame shining in the spotlights looking like the superstructure of a giant ship sailing up the Seine. I turned into the quai and sped up the Left Bank, keeping within the speed limit for fear of suicidal French drivers who would shoot out of side streets without warning. Suddenly I heard a siren and saw a policeman on a motorcycle in my rear mirror. He pulled ahead of me and motioned me to pull over.

He thrust his black-helmeted head into the open window of the car, put out his hand, and said crisply, "*Vos papiers, monsieur.*"

"But, officer, what's wrong? I was driving carefully."

"Yes, you were. But your rear light is out."

"Officer, please listen. I'll pay any fine, do anything, but please do not delay me with paperwork. My wife has to get home to nurse our baby. Please, just follow me, and we can handle the details as soon as I bring my wife home."

The policeman grinned at me, and looked over at Dorothy who had her arms folded under her breasts, cradling them.

"No, monsieur, I will not follow you. You follow me! The baby must get its milk!"

He jumped into the saddle, with the agility of a cowboy, put on his headlight, set his siren to screaming, and burned rubber as his motorcyle leaped forward. I followed him at about eighty-five miles an hour, trying to stay with him, while Dorothy slunk in her seat in terror but laughed at the same time.

In what seemed just a few minutes we pulled up in front of our apartment. Dorothy rushed out and headed for the elevators. I got out to thank our gallant escort. He smiled and said: "Get that rear light fixed first thing in the morning. You won't always have such a good excuse."

The wit and "intellectualism" of even the most ordinary Frenchman, a policeman, a cabdriver, is found at every level of society. The so-called little people of France are most stimulating, if frequently exasperating. Of them all, the most voluble and anarchistic is the Parisian cabdriver. One conversation in a cab, some thirty years ago, is one of my freshest, most inspiring memories of the French spirit.

It was midnight in Paris and I had just finished a newscast on yet another French Cabinet crisis. I hailed a cab in front of the Café de la Paix, went speeding down the Avenue de l'Opéra to the Left Bank of the Seine, heading for my apartment on the Avenue Bosquet, overlooking the river. Suddenly the cab began slowing down near the Pont Alexandre III. I saw a red light ahead and expected the driver to slow to a stop. Instead he just slowed down and then burst through the red light, speeding along the Quai d'Orsay. He repeated the performance at the Pont de l'Alma just before turning into my address on the Avenue Bosquet.

As I paid him the fare, I asked why he had driven through two red lights.

He looked at me in astonishment at my foolish question. "Why, what's wrong with that?" Then he cut me off as I began to answer him.

"Just listen to me before you complain. So, I went through a red light. Did you ever stop to consider what a red light is?"

"Certainly," I replied. "It's a stop signal and means that you must stop to avoid colliding with traffic rolling in the opposite direction."

"Half right but incomplete, monsieur. It is only an *automatic* stop signal. It does not mean that there really is cross traffic. Did you see any cross traffic in our trip? Of course not! I slowed down at each red light, looked carefully to the right and to the left. Not another car was on the streets at this hour. Well, then! What would you have me do? Should I stop like a dumb animal because an automatic, brainless, blind machine turns red every forty seconds? No, monsieur, I am a man not a machine. I have eyes and a brain and judgment, given me by God. It would be a sin against nature to surrender my humanity to the dictates of a dumb machine. I would be ashamed of myself if I let those blinking lamps do my thinking for me. Good night, monsieur!"

I am no longer sure if this is a bad or good trait. The intellectual originality and eccentricity of the French is a corrupting influence. It has wrecked their politics, even their industry. They do not always work well collectively. They are free, individualistic spirits. That gives them extraordinary creative abilities, and makes the very air of Paris a tonic of inspiration and creativity. After a quarter of a century of living in Paris, I find my old Anglo-Saxon standards somewhat shaken. I still think it is wrong to drive through a stop signal, except possibly very late at night, after having carefully checked to make sure there is no cross traffic. After all, I am a man, not a machine.

When people tell me, as they often do, how difficult, contentious, and rude the French are, I always grin and paraphrase Eleanor Roosevelt. "Not to me. I suppose it's because of Dorothy." In fact, there *are* rude people in Paris. And in New York, and everywhere else. But we have enjoyed the friendship and many courtesies of some of the finest people we have ever known in the more than thirty-five years that we have lived in and visited Paris. There have been bad times, of course. But, in the spirit of Winston Churchill, we can truly say, "We enjoyed every minute of it."

The world we covered was a violent world. We worked hard, often under difficult and dangerous conditions. CBS correspondent George Polk's body would be found floating in a bay in Greece, his hands tied behind his back with wire. He had gone into the hills in the middle of the civil war to try to make contact with the communist rebels. We would never discover who killed him, the communists or the royalist troops. Many of my closest friends would die, men who had survived the landings in Normandy and the most terrible battles of World War II, Chim at Suez, Bob Capa outside Hanoi.

Many men would have their careers wrecked by Senator McCarthy and other witch-hunters, without any evidence against them, without being able to face or answer their accusers. I, myself, was saved by the courage of a splendid official who risked his own career to rescue mine and that of a dozen other men never charged with anything, but blackballed by vicious, stupid officials. We would work ten, twelve hours a day, and in a crisis, around the clock. We paid our dues to a tragic world. But we also were well rewarded and lived a magnificent life of gaiety and laughter in the midst of the blood and sweat.

I was involved in all the hot-and-cold running wars and political crises from the communist coup in Prague through the birth of Israel, the Berlin blockade, the war of Indochina, the Presidential elections of 1948 and 1952, the creation of NATO, the outbreak of war in Korea. I knew and interviewed the principal actors in these events. The old world order had been destroyed but a new world order was not, and still has not been, found.

As 1948 dawned, the communist minister of the interior in Prague started placing reliable Party members in key posts in the police. Packages containing incendiary bombs were sent to Jan Masaryk and other democratic ministers. The police "revealed" alleged plots against the national security and "discovered" acts of espionage, all, of course, attributed to Western agents. Everyone knew that the Communist Party was creating a situation where it could claim the need to "protect the nation" against its external enemies, a convenient cloak for their plan to strike for power.

Weapons were distributed by the communists to former militia men and communist workers. Communist Prime Minister Klement Gottwald threatened the Social Democratic Party, telling its leaders, "If you do not march with us, you will be liquidated the same as the others." Democratic Czechs, fearful for their lives, fled to Paris. Masaryk had given several of them my name and phone number. They told me what was happening and urged me to expose the plot, with the hope that the West could help save democracy in Czechoslovakia. But there was nothing the Western powers could do without invading Czechoslovakia and starting World War III. We have faced the dilemma of coping with Soviet power in Eastern Europe constantly, from the Czech crisis in 1948, through successive crises and revolts in Czechoslovakia, Hungary, and Poland, into the eighties.

On February 21, twelve noncommunist members of the Prague government resigned in protest against the communist purge of the police and threats against the government. Only one democrat remained in the government, my old friend, Jan Masaryk. Czech refugees told me in Paris that President Beneš had pleaded with Masaryk to remain and to be a witness to what was happening.

On February 25, 1948, the communist premier, Gottwald, presented a new list of Cabinet members to the president. Twelve communists replaced the twelve noncommunists who had resigned. President Beneš yielded and accepted the new communist-controlled Cabinet. Gottwald rushed over to Wenceslas Square, where a cheering crowd of workers greeted his announcement that the communists had taken over the government. It was a bloodless coup but a coup nevertheless. Two weeks later, the new government put forward a new constitution, a replica of the Soviet constitution. The next day, March 10, 1948, Jan Masaryk jumped or was thrown to his death from his office window. I have never doubted that he was murdered. Based on my knowledge gathered in my reporting trip to Czechoslovakia the year before, I did many CBS news broadcasts all through the Czech crisis.

Ed Murrow, reacting swiftly to the Prague coup, called London and Paris and asked Howard K. Smith and me to join him and other CBS correspondents in Berlin. Dispatches from Berlin reported a mass exodus of refugees from Czechoslovakia. First reports suggested that the communists were conducting a purge of "reactionary elements," and that Czech democrats were fleeing for their lives. Murrow had strong personal feelings about the tragic events in Czechoslovakia, whose democracy had been destroyed twice in a decade. Murrow had been in Munich in 1938, had begun his broadcasting career there as he watched in dismay the surrender of the British and French leaders, Chamberlain and Daladier, to Hitler's demands on the Sudetenland.

In Berlin, at a huge assembly point for the refugees, I began my interviews for the documentary program that Murrow was preparing. I discovered almost immediately that most of the refugees were not Czech democrats fleeing to freedom. They were German-speaking residents of the Sudetenland, many of them pro-Nazis, who had staged the demonstrations that had given Hitler his excuse for taking over Czechoslovakia. They had not been "purged" by the communists but certainly were expecting to be, as former supporters of the Nazis. They had helped subvert Czech democracy and were afraid of reprisals.

After two days of intensive interviewing, Murrow called us in to hear what we had all learned and to listen to recordings of our interviews with refugees who spoke English. He listened intently, thanked us all, said, "That's a wrap. We have all we need. You can go back to your capitals. I'll be hearing from each of you on your regular beat." As I was walking out the door of his suite, I heard him call out, "David, would you please stay behind a minute?"

Murrow looked at me for a long moment, then got up and began to pace the room. "You really were worked up in those interviews. You seemed to hold the people you were talking to in contempt. It will be hard to use those recordings in a story about the plight of the poor refugees. You didn't think they were poor victims of the communists, did you?"

"No, Ed, I did not. Many of them are stinking Nazis who stole land from the Czechs, took over factories, persecuted democrats and Jews. I cannot sympathize with them now. Sure, they are homeless and frightened. But so were their victims ten years ago. They are getting a taste of their own medicine and I would see them in hell."

Ed grinned at me. "You sure do lay it on the line. And I think you are right about some of them. David, don't take offense, but I can't use your interviews, they are too emotional and hostile. We are doing a story about the victims of the communist coup, and it is not the moment to bring up the Nazi coup ten years ago."

Ed then clapped me on the shoulder and said, "Okay, Buster,

don't worry about it. Now get the hell back to Paris. I promise never to send you into Germany again."

He kept his promise, even when, later that year, another dramatic event would make Berlin the center of a titanic clash between the Russians and the West, which threatened almost daily to break out into war. But, before that happened, another historic event would capture the attention of the world and remain a constant threat to peace from then on until today.

The British withdrew the last of their occupation forces from Palestine on May 13, 1948. The next day, May 14, David Ben-Gurion proclaimed the creation of the state of Israel, bringing back to life, after almost two thousand years, a Jewish state in Palestine. Ben-Gurion was immediately named the first prime minister of that state, while Dr. Chaim Weizmann was named president of the Republic.

Harry Truman, rejecting the negative advice of Under Secretary of State Dean Acheson, offered recognition of the Jewish state. The very next day, the armies of the Arab League, Egypt, Jordan, Iraq, Syria, and Lebanon, invaded Palestine and vowed to destroy Israel. The Israelis, poorly armed, were outnumbered more than ten to one. Many observers believed they would be crushed and massacred. The world would learn, however, that Jews could fight when they were alerted to what was happening to them. Never again would they be herded in confusion and impotence into death camps. "Never again" became their slogan, their vow.

I telephoned Murrow and reminded him that I had gone to Palestine for him in 1946. The story was important to me, I had good sources there. The rebirth of a Jewish state in Palestine was one of the historic events of our times. Murrow agreed to clear the assignment for me. He wanted me to concentrate on the fighting, and not conflict with the political reports of the regular correspondents in Tel Aviv and Jerusalem.

I flew into Tel Aviv on a small charter plane from Rhodes. There I contacted friends who brought me up to date. The new Jewish Defense Forces, emerging from the clandestine Haganah, the Palmach, and the guerrilla fighters of the Irgun and other groups, had captured the Arab city of Jaffa, just outside Tel Aviv on April 25, even before the proclamation of the state of Israel. I had arrived on May 19, and the day before, Israeli troops had captured the port of Acre in the north. The Egyptians had invaded Gaza but had been stopped as they tried to push on to Tel Aviv. There was fierce fighting in Jerusalem.

The Arab Legion of Transjordan, trained and commanded by a professional British officer, who called himself Glubb Pasha, was closing in on the Old City, the walled Arab quarter. Inside those walls was one of Judaism's most sacred shrines, the remnants of the wall of the Second Temple which the Romans had destroyed. Israelis called it the West Wall. It was better known around the world as the Wailing Wall, or, more elegantly, the Wall of Lamentations.

"It will be a fierce struggle against great odds, but we will win," my Israeli friends told me. "It is really quite simple to understand. We are fighting for our very lives, for our right to exist, to live as free men. We seek only a small territory, already approved by the U.N. The Arabs are fighting out of hatred, anti-Semitism. They have a hundred, a thousand times more land than we. But our motivation is positive and stronger than theirs. Why should Arab men die only to prevent us from living? Our nationalism is greater than their anti-Semitism."

As my friends spoke, I could hear Ho Chi Minh's words echoing in my ears. "We have a secret weapon, nationalism." Nationalism, a need to be free, the end of persecution and colonization; these were, indeed, more powerful motivations than greed and hatred. Later, the Israelis themselves would encounter a new nationalism, the demand for statehood by Palestinian Arabs. But that issue did not arise in 1948. There was no PLO, no Yasser Arafat in 1948. The Arabs had been offered a Palestinian state in the partition proposal of the U.N. But the Arabs were not interested in creating a Palestinian state in 1948. All they wanted was to destroy the new Jewish state.

I made my way back to the Galilee, but the Palmach band I had traveled with there two years earlier had been reorganized and was fighting elsewhere. I went out daily with the new Israeli army troops and was impressed by their knowledge of arms and tactics, by their bravery and ability to work efficiently together with no outward signs of military discipline or procedures. Officers often did not wear any insignia of rank. Even when they did, privates would call majors, even generals, by their first names. There was no saluting, no spit and polish.

The Israeli troops impressed me as members of a family, tightly knit, respecting each other. In their life-or-death struggle there was no place for standard protocol. When I left, after some ten days of watching them in action and talking to their leaders in Jerusalem, I knew that they would throw back the Arab armies and that Israel would live. Obviously, I had no idea, and I doubt that anyone had, just what kind of a life the state of Israel would have to live and how complicated and controversial it would become over the decades.

On my return to Paris, I was delighted to learn that W. Averell Harriman, America's most senior diplomat, had resigned from his post as secretary of commerce in the Truman Cabinet to accept appointment as administrator of the Marshall Plan. Harriman had come to Paris to set up his headquarters at the corner of the Rue de Rivoli and the Rue Saint-Florentin, opposite the Tuileries Gardens. The building had once housed the French Foreign Minister Talleyrand, one of the architects of the peace that emerged from the Congress of Vienna, after the defeat of Napoleon.

Paris is living history, its streets a public museum. I could just visualize the long, lean, athletic figure of Averell Harriman, presiding over the House of Talleyrand, seeking peace in an always troubled Europe. Harriman would bring to Paris the most efficient, dedicated team of economists, financiers, industrialists, political scientists ever gathered together in one capital at one time. The Marshall Plan would become the most successful, enlightened American foreign policy program in our history.

The United States had a twenty- to thirty-billion-dollar trade surplus in the world. We could sell everything we made. Everything marked "Made in America" would be snatched up and our factories had huge back-orders awaiting production and shipment. Inevitably, this produced an American hubris, an exaggerated pride in our superiority. We did not stop to think that all the best factories in the world had been destroyed in the war and that we, alone among the industrial powers, had never been invaded or bombed. Our products were not just the best in the world, they were, in many fields, the only products available. We were the only game on the globe and everyone had to play our way.

With a generosity that was blind to reality, we set about rebuilding the workshops of Germany, Japan, and many other highly skilled industrial nations. It was the right thing to do, the safest way to make sure that democratic capitalism would withstand the communist challenge. What was foolish, shortsighted, and excessively prideful was our failure to renew our own obsolescent industrial plant. I went to Lorraine, in eastern France, and reported on the Marshall Plan creation of the world's biggest, newest rolling-strip mill. Our steel industry had nothing like it. General MacArthur, our proconsul in Japan, was funding the building of similar modern plants, as our teams in Germany were also doing. But we neglected to invest in the modernization of American industry inside the U.S.A.

We had had such success that we became convinced that we were the natural leaders of world industry. We forgot that some of our greatest machines had been invented by Europeans. Even that most American of industries, atomic energy, was mainly a European creation. Europeans had conceived it, we had only engineered it, at a time when they were living in rubble. With the rubble cleared away, with Marshall Plan money to seed their reconstruction, Europeans and the Japanese would soon enough begin to rival, then to surpass us. They were not better producers. Our managers just failed to reinvest in new plants, and Detroit stubbornly refused to believe that Americans would agree to ride in smaller cars with higher mileage.

American capital thought the "bottom line" was profits, and neglected investment. We would not calibrate our machines or print our sales brochures in metric measures, which the entire non-English-speaking world used. And labor, as shortsighted as capital, thought the bottom line was wage increases and social benefits instead of competitive pricing. Nobody beat us. We beat ourselves. Once we understand this and correct our errors, we can again become the most successful society in the world.

One of the contributing factors to our economic and financial crises in later years was the ever-increasing allocation of funds to the military. It began in the Cold War, when military aid followed upon economic aid, in a global expansion of American activities, enthusiastically endorsed by both the Democratic and Republican parties. It reached new, astronomical peaks of spending and deficits under Lyndon Johnson and Richard Nixon during the Vietnam War. And then came a quantum jump under Ronald Reagan. Without a war to drain our resources, Reagan proposed, and the Congress rushed to approve, the biggest military budgets in history, a program to spend more than a trillion dollars in four to five years. One trillion dollars plus for the military alone in the eighties is ten times greater than Harry Truman's budget for all government programs in the forties. The few voices raised in criticism were drowned out by the full volume of approval voiced across the nation, not only in the White House and the Congress, but endorsed by an overwhelming majority of Americans. The arms race had speeded up, out of control.

It all began back in December 1947, when Secretary George Marshall came through London and was invited by Britain's Secretary Ernest Bevin to a quiet tête-à-tête dinner in Bevin's flat in Carlton Terrace. Bevin proposed a military counterpart to the Marshall Plan. He told Marshall that Europe needed a "powerful shield" against a Red Army attack. Behind that shield, the Marshall Plan would permit Europe to rebuild its industry and economy and save democracy from internal communist subversion. Without that protective shield, Europe would not be able to concentrate on its reconstruction.

Marshall told Bevin that he thought his proposal was sound, but to proceed with caution while he checked out opinion back in Washington. Word began to spread, and about a year later, at a cocktail party in Harriman's apartment in Paris, I heard him say softly and casually, too casually: "David, we have a lot of World War II arms and ammo still stored here in Europe, rusting away. What do you think the press reaction would be if we proposed turning it over to our allies?" I grinned at him and replied: "We will simply report the facts and some of us will speculate that it points to plans for a big military buildup in Europe. Congress will love it, you know better than I." It would take another year before this military counterpart to the Marshall Plan would lead to one of the most dramatic departures from traditional American policy: a peacetime military alliance and a commitment to go to war if any of our allies came under attack.

In June 1948, the United States took two steps that pointed to the increasing possibility of armed conflict. On June 11, the Senate approved a program for military aid to "free nations." The day before, Congress voted to install a two-year peacetime draft. Everyone knew that although the United States was not at war, we were not at peace, either. A "peacetime draft" was a misnomer for the troubled world we were living in.

And then, suddenly, we were on the very brink of war.

After months of constant quarreling between the West and Russia in the Four-Power Kommandantura which administered Berlin, the Soviets, in a warlike move, lowered the boom on the West. They erected barriers all around Berlin. Berlin was located inside the Soviet zone, the biggest mistake made by Truman and Eisenhower when they accepted that anomaly. The Soviets blockaded Berlin on June 24, cutting it off from all road communications to the Western zones. General Mark Clark called for an armored train to break through the Soviet barriers. Had his proposal been carried out, the United States and the Soviet Union would have been at war. Many thought at the time, still do, that we should have gone to war. We still had an atomic monopoly. But cooler, wiser heads came up with a better answer than atomic incineration.

The simple, effective answer was an airlift. With speed and efficiency, the American military organized a fleet of cargo planes, protected by swift, armed fighter planes, to fly from our zone in West Germany to Berlin over the Soviet barricades. Under the ill-conceived Four-Power agreement that had set up the administration of Berlin, we had insisted on one farsighted arrangement, a "corridor" assigned to the Western powers, permitting overflights of the Soviet Zone. The Soviets could not put up any barriers in the sky. If they wanted to close down that corridor they would have to send up Soviet fighters to challenge the American fighters. And back in 1948, we were the unchallengeable air power of the world. There was no way short of precipitating a war that the Soviets could stop our airlift. Their aim was to choke off Berlin but not to go to war with the United States. The Berlin airlift was the most intelligent and peaceful answer to the blockade of Berlin.

Every day, our fleet would load up and fly over the Soviet barriers, carrying tons of food, medical supplies, industrial machines and parts, everything needed to keep Berlin functioning. The Russians were furious but stymied. Every now and then, we crept close to the brink of war when the Russians would send up fighters to make a pass at our cargo planes. But our fighters would close in and the Soviets would veer off. It was a bluff, a calculated war of nerves, hoping that antiwar sentiment in Europe and the United States would force Truman to call off the airlift. They underestimated Truman and the American people. Only a few extremists wanted war but the Americans were not about to surrender to a

Soviet power-grab and a violation of all agreements negotiated when the Nazis capitulated.

The war of nerves continued for many months. It was extremely dangerous, for any hot-headed young Russian or American pilot could have triggered off a shooting war. But we held firm and finally it was the Soviets who caved in and surrendered. They lifted the blockade of Berlin. It was a humiliating defeat for them and a triumph for us. It gave the lie again to those who argued that the Russians pushed us around, while we did nothing. The Russians certainly tried to push us around but we met every push and shoved back.

Ed Murrow flew to Berlin during the blockade. He hated sitting behind his anchor desk in New York, broadcasting news that other men had reported. Murrow was one of the first and the very best of America's foreign correspondents, and like an old firehorse, he would gallop to the scene whenever the flames shot high.

En route home from Berlin, he stopped off to spend a day with me in Paris. He called in advance to tell me he was coming in and said he would want to know how the Western allies were reacting to the airlift. Were they supporting us? Were they standing firm? He felt that if the French, a key ally, were not behind us, it might lead to a disruption, even a cancellation, of the Marshall Plan. He said he would want all of the information and analysis. Robert Trout was substituting for Murrow as anchorman on his evening news in New York. But Murrow was doing a five-minute analysis piece from the field.

I picked Murrow up at the airport and drove him to the Hotel de Crillon, where I had reserved a suite for him with big windows overlooking the Place de la Concorde. On the table of the salon, I had put a few bottles of Jack Daniels and Glenlivet, single-malt Scotch. These were unfindable in Paris except at the U.S. Embassy commissary. The press attaché's office was only too happy to be of help to Ed Murrow, the most influential voice in America.

We got to his suite at about 4:00 P.M., about two hours before Murrow was due at the studios of Press Wireless to broadcast his piece to New York, at noon N.Y. time.

We broadcast by shortwave radio in those days. This was a constant problem before the cable was laid down. Many years later, Dorothy and I were watching the Johnny Carson show when comedian Robert Klein came on and we were delighted to hear him deliver a new routine that had Carson in stitches. It was based on my CBS broadcasts from Paris in the late forties and early fifties.

"David Schoenbrun used to frighten and frustrate me," said Klein to Carson. "Remember those broadcasts? 'A crisis has erupted in Paris today. Glub-glub-whistle-wheeze, glou-glou. It is really very dangerous, whoosh, waash, gleep, gurgle, and then de Gaulle proceeded to whiz, wheep, glump, glunk, and Washington is shaken.' Then, clear as a bell, he would say, 'Now back to CBS News, in New York.' I would have to rush to work and spend the day chewing my lips, wondering what had happened." We rocked with laughter as Klein concluded his routine, jamming his fingers into his mouth to imitate my voice distorted by shortwave.

That night in Paris, when Murrow was due to report what he had seen in Berlin, he surprised me. He took two shots of the Glenlivet and made no move to leave for the studio. It was getting within an hour of broadcast time.

I had briefed him thoroughly on the French and Western European reaction to the airlift, expecting that he would then write his script. He had another drink and we finally got to the studio about a half hour before air time. Murrow then stopped off at the Cintra bar near the studio. I told him that I would "warm up the circuit for him," warning him that there was a quarter of an hour to air. I left for the studio.

Murrow walked into the studio about three minutes before air time, cool and relaxed, every hair in place, his Savile Row suit fitting his lean frame perfectly. Never did I admire a man more than Murrow when, without a script, he sat down calmly, put on his headset, and told New York he was ready. I heard Bob Trout say, "And now, for his special report from Paris, here is Edward R. Murrow. Ed?"

Murrow began: "Last night you heard me from Berlin, tonight from Paris, tomorrow from London. If I can travel from capital to capital and report what is happening it is because CBS News has the best informed reporters in every capital and they can brief me on what is happening."

I listened in admiration and gratitude. What a great guy Murrow is, I thought, always boosting his "colleagues," giving us all a big plug. No one else did that.

Then I heard him say: "No one knows Paris as well as my colleague David Schoenbrun. He has been covering events here all during the airlift. David?"

I gulped. He had not given me the slightest hint that I was to be on the program with him. I had no script and my head was not completely clear. But I had to respond. I hesitated and then began telling him on the air what I had told him in the earlier briefing at the hotel. I expected that he would cut in with questions. But the devil just sat there and grinned at me, not making a move. I just had to keep talking. Ed had a stopwatch in his hand and kept checking it. He then gave me a one-minute-to-get-off-the-air signal. Somehow I finished and returned it to Ed, who merely said, "Thank you, David. Now back to Robert Trout in New York."

Ed got up and walked out of the studio. I sat there trembling from the fast curve he had thrown at me. I knew where I would find Ed. He was sitting in the Cintra in a heavy wooden armchair carved out of a wine barrel, at a table which was a wine barrel. I sat down opposite him, bitterly angry. He looked at me and said, "You need a drink, Buster." He signaled the waiter, ordered a port for me. There was a Scotch in front of him. When my wine came, Murrow lifted his glass and toasted me: "Buster, you have just won your wings."

"Ed, why did you do it? It was a rotten trick. I thought we were friends."

"We are friends, David. But I had to do it. I hired you because I thought you were one of the best. You've done fine pieces for us, well written, insightful. But carefully prepared. Radio news is mostly live. Anything can happen when you're on the air. Remember when Charley Daly was describing the arrival of the first transatlantic dirigible and it blew up as it was landing? Daly was magnificent. He first groaned in shock and grief and said, 'Aaahh, the humanity!' Then he went on to describe the awful scene. I had to find out how you handled yourself when the unexpected hit you. I just found out. There was no other way I could have tested you."

I took a deep swallow of my port. "Ed, you are the greatest, toughest son of a bitch I've ever known. It's good to be on your team." I would be grateful to Murrow when, some years later, I had something very unexpected happen to me on a live, national network broadcast. It was in Detroit, Labor Day 1952. Presidential candidate General Eisenhower was reading a speech from a TelePrompTer when the machine broke down and Ike stopped talking and backed away. I had to jump in and talk until Eisenhower was ready to resume.

After the Murrow surprise, I returned to work with new self-confidence, although still just a bit shaken from the experience. The news continued to be bad, in France and everywhere. French Cabinets were rising and falling like the tides. The average government in the Fourth Republic lasted about three and a half months before being defeated in Parliament. French politics were chaotic and anarchic. I wondered how long the Republic itself could last. General de Gaulle had returned to active politics, leading a movement called the *Rassemblement du peuple français,* meaning, roughly, the Rally of the French People. It was a movement, not a political party, for de Gaulle felt he was above parties. His dilemma was hopeless.

In a democracy, one must function through political parties. Only dictators were "above party" and de Gaulle refused either to play democratic politics or to be a dictator. His "movement" did enter elections and emerged as the number one vote-getter in France. But de Gaulle would not try to form a government with less than at least fifty-five percent of the votes. He wanted to rule, but to rule democratically, which was like trying to square the circle in multiparty France. De Gaulle, disgusted, would again fold his tent and wait in the shadows for the Republic to disintegrate. He told me one day, "The Fourth Republic governs poorly but defends itself well." He had just about given up all hope and retreated to his country estate on the eastern reaches of France in the village of Colombey-les-Deux-Eglises, named for its two churches. He thought, mistakenly, that he would never be called back.

Meanwhile, excitement was stirring as the American election campaign got underway. Governor Dewey, certain of victory, took care not to say anything that might provoke anybody. All he had to do, he felt, was to avoid a big mistake, and the election would be his. That proved to be his big mistake. He took the American people for granted. Harry Truman, a feisty fighter, went on an old-fashioned whistle-stop tour of the nation by train. Cheering crowds greeted him at every stop, people shouting, "Give 'em hell,

Harry!" Reporters were not impressed, for the crowds were fairly small, and all the public opinion polls showed Dewey far ahead.

The United Nations held its session in Paris just before the elections. On the American delegation was the man everyone called "the future secretary of state," John Foster Dulles. I made it my business to call on him regularly and to interview him on every subject, for his thoughts would soon become official U.S. policy. Then I had a grand idea. Dulles would be in Paris on Election Day. Why not hold a big party for him and the U.S. delegation and interview the future secretary as soon as Truman conceded defeat? I called News Director Ted Church who thought it was terrific and okayed a generous supplemental budget to pay for the party, which would be held in the rooms of the Palais de Chaillot, opposite the Eiffel Tower, late at night after the U.N. session had ended. I called Press Wireless to get a transatlantic circuit connected to the Palais de Chaillot, so that we could hear the returns on the Voice of America and then put Dulles on the network when Truman conceded.

A caterer had loaded a buffet table with row upon row of delicacies, fine wines, and liquors. Dulles liked just a little Scotch, with a lot of ice and water. He had a curious habit of stirring the ice in his Scotch with his index finger, then taking it out and licking it before he lifted his glass for a sip. I had noticed that his brother Allan, head of the CIA, had a strange and disconcerting habit of his own, which would break my concentration during an interview. Allan always had a smoking pipe in his hands, and his lips would move in a sucking gesture, but the pipe would remain an inch from his lips, and he would suck on air instead of on the pipe.

The Dulles brothers would become the two most powerful men in America and the world. They were brilliant but would make ghastly mistakes that almost plunged us into war, with John Foster's "brinkmanship" and Allan's "masterminding" of the Bay of Pigs fiasco. When someone praised John Foster for his lawyer's quick mind and ability to extricate us from tight spots, my colleague at CBS, Alexander Kendrick, growled: "Yes, Dulles gets us out of every tight spot he put us into in the first place."

John Foster Dulles was serene that night of November 2, 1948, waiting to be interviewed as the future secretary of state. Then his smile wore thin as the incredible results came rolling in. Truman running neck and neck with Dewey! Truman running ahead in New York and New Jersey. New York! Governor Dewey's home state! Illinois, Truman edging ahead. Finally, as everyone listened in disbelief, Tom Dewey came on the air and conceded. Harry Truman had won!

I picked up my microphone, called New York. The editor heard me and switched me to Bob Trout, who announced: "David Schoenbrun is standing by with John Foster Dulles in Paris. David, come in please." I quickly sketched the scene, then motioned to Dulles to come to the microphone, and said to him: "Well, Mr. Dulles, what can you tell us about your plans now?"

Dulles, whisky glass in hand, took a sip, grinned at me, and replied: "I suppose that hereafter you can refer to me as the former future secretary of state." The whole room broke out into laughter and applause. Dulles was a good loser. I had never really liked him very much, for he was inclined to be a bit sanctimonious and self-righteous. But that night, he was witty, humble, and a damn fine sport. It was one of those moments of wit and laughter in the midst of tension, moments that release tension and defuse angers when most needed.

One such instance of the perfect retort occurred at a cocktail reception at the French Foreign Ministry in the ornate and historic salons of the Quai d'Orsay. An American Embassy attaché, one of the witch-hunters of the day, walked over to a French diplomat with whom I was chatting. He said testily: "I just heard you are going to give our American sculptor Jo Davidson the Légion d'honneur, is that correct?" The Frenchman said that it had not yet been announced but was correct. The American protested sharply. "Don't you know that he is a fellow-traveling commie?" The Frenchman smiled sweetly and replied: "Oh, yes, but it is not for that distinction that we are honoring him." I roared with delight, for Jo was a good friend of mine, and the witch-hunter had been put neatly into his place. He glared at me, and I knew that another black mark would go down against my name in his book. I never did learn when to keep my mouth shut.

I called Jo that night to tell him, and his guffaw almost blew the receiver out of my hand. Jo Davidson was a Falstaffian character, burly, with a heart as big as his stomach. His face was covered with a bushy, black beard. He used to tease my daughter, Lucy, by begging for a kiss, just to hear her say, with a child's perfect logic, "But Uncle Jo, there is no room on your face." Jo thanked me for my call and then asked me to come by with Dorothy at teatime the next day. "I'll have a wonderful surprise for you."

We entered his studio, with its many pedestals, on each of which was a bust of a famous man or woman. Two women were standing with him, and one was running her hands over one of the busts. Jo saw us, waved a greeting, and as we came over, he said: "Dorothy and David, I want you to meet the most remarkable human being who has ever graced this world—Helen Keller."

One of the women took the other's hand and began rapid tappings on her palm. It was Helen's companion and translator into the perpetual darkness and stillness of Helen Keller's blind, deaf existence. It was not Anne Sullivan, the original miracle worker who had first released Helen Keller from her black prison, but one of her successors. Helen turned in our direction, for she could sense vibrations. She smiled and I have never seen such a magnificent radiation of intelligence and goodness on any face.

She had learned to speak, but since she could not hear herself and modulate her voice, it came out distorted, like the voice of someone who had suffered a stroke. "I am pleased to meet you," she said and then added with a broad smile, "I listen to you every morning on CBS." Her companion said: "Helen loves the news reports and I translate the program for her into our touch language." Helen then turned to Jo and said: "The bust is wonderful, Jo, it feels just like me."

We sat down to take our tea and to "talk." Dorothy asked what was the thing Helen would most like to see if she had sight. She replied, "A sunset. I have heard about sunsets but I do not know what colors are. I would like to see a flaming sunset."

Just before we left, the companion said: "Helen wonders if you would mind if she were to run her fingers across your faces. That is the way she 'sees' people." Helen then ran her fingers over my face. They moved softly, like butterflies, over my forehead, cheeks, the entire face. Then Helen said: "Strong. You are strong." Dorothy leaned forward and the companion guided Helen's hands to her face. Helen smiled and ended up by pinching Dorothy's full cheeks. "Good. You are a good person," said Helen Keller.

We thanked Jo, went home and got Helen Keller's autobiography from our bookshelves, and spent the rest of the day rereading the most inspiring story of the human spirit that has ever been told. It is the rare beings, the great ones, the creative ones, that compensate just a bit for the cruelty and madness of the human condition.

CHAPTER 14

THE MIDCENTURY MARK

January 1, 1949—a date that calls for a reckoning, a summing up of where the world is, how it got there, and where it is going. 1949 was the last year of the first half of the twentieth century, the end of a fifty-year cycle of violence, revolution, and an explosion of science and technology on a global scale greater than any half-century in human history. Men and women in the industrial nations of the West were living better and longer than kings and queens of the past. Millions more were not living much better than the cave people at the dawn of human history. Nations were producing more but distributing it badly. Hope for peace remained a distant, future dream, as the world began splitting apart simultaneously with the splitting of the atom.

The United States was the mightiest, richest, most generous nation on earth. We consumed the greater part of the earth's resources but we fed the world from the cornucopia of our fertile fields. We cared for our poor and lent generously to many peoples of the world. We sought to carry out the aims of our Founding Fathers by promoting the general welfare of our citizens and democracy in the world. We had reached a high peak of power and success, yet we were fearful, knowing that the Soviet Union and international communism threatened our success. So many events erupted at the midcentury mark, sometimes at one and the same moment, that it would be very difficult to follow a strictly chronological narrative and absorb all the swirling tides at once. To understand each of these events clearly, it is necessary to sort them out and watch them develop, one by one. The picture becomes clear when each element can be observed by itself and related to the others.

One of the most important and long-lasting developments of the midcentury was the movement toward U.S.-European and intra-European unity. It laid down the bases of the alliances which are still the cornerstone of European and American foreign policy and security today, more than three decades later.

It was my good fortune to be reporting positive and historic moves to peace and unity in Europe in the early postwar years. Winston Churchill had been the first leader to call for a united Europe as early as 1943. He had been persuaded by Jean Monnet of France that the balance-of-power game had to be ended and Europe united in the West to meet the challenge of the Soviets from the East, and to end forever the futile, bloody, fratricidal wars among England, France, and Germany.

In May 1948, Churchill had convoked a Congress of Europe in The Hague, which resulted in the creation of a European Movement. For Churchill, Europe was a civilization, a culture, and a common cause. For Jean Monnet it was all that but more. If Europe were to be truly united, it would have to be, in Monnet's view, in a common institution, a supranational institution, above the jealous, chauvinistic national governments.

Europe advanced toward that goal through 1948–49 and reached it on May 9, 1950. I was one of a hundred reporters who were convoked that day to the historic Salon de l'Horloge at the French Ministry of Foreign Affairs. There, Foreign Minister Robert Schuman put forward his plan for a Coal and Steel Community, a supranational institution created by its member nations, France, Germany, Belgium, Holland, and Luxembourg, who had agreed to put their mineral resources into a common pool, sacrificing their national authority to a high authority of the Community.

As I took notes, my elbow was jostled by an usher, who put his fingers to his lips to command silence and signaled me to get up and follow him. Puzzled and a bit nettled about being pulled out of the news conference, I nonetheless followed him. The veteran ushers at the Foreign Ministry knew what they were doing, and it had to be important. He took me down a side hall, opened a door, and led me into the office of Foreign Minister Schuman.

Sitting behind Schuman's desk was Jean Monnet, flanked by his two principal aides at the office of the Plan for Reconstruction which Monnet headed: Pierre Uri, the brilliant political scientist and economist, his thin, foxlike face alight with a bright smile; and Etienne Hirsch, a chemical engineer, with his square, freckled, confidence-inspiring face also smiling broadly. Monnet was wearing his inscrutable Mandarin visage.

"Well," asked Monnet, "what do you think?"

I grinned at him and said: "Congratulations on your new brainchild."

Monnet frowned. "It is the Schuman Plan. Keep that in mind and do not joke about it. I want you to understand it fully. It will change the history of Europe and advance peace a giant step. Come to my office at the commissariat this afternoon, if you can, so we can have a long talk about this."

Before I went to Monnet's office, I called on some friends in the Ministry and found out that the author of the Schuman Plan was indeed Monnet, as I had guessed. He had submitted the idea first to Prime Minister Georges Bidault, who had been too busy to study it, so Monnet had moved it on to Schuman, who was inspired by it. It was a strange accident of history that Robert Schuman had been born and raised in Lorraine, which had been annexed by Germany in the France-Prussian War. He had gone through law school under the Germans, as a German citizen, but had become a French citizen after the Versailles Treaty had returned Lorraine to France after the First World War. Twenty-eight years later, this German lawyer had become the foreign minister of France. At the same time, the chancellor of Germany was Konrad Adenauer, born and raised in the Rhineland, just across the river from Schuman's birthplace. In his youth, Adenauer had been an advocate of French-German union, appalled by the constant wars between the two neighbors.

Monnet knew that both Schuman and Adenauer yearned for a practical plan to bring about union; not rhetoric, not dreams, but a blueprint of union. Monnet was just the man to draft one, for he was a poet who composed his odes in plans, a dreamer but a most pragmatic one. Monnet used to tell me over and over again:

"David, man must live under law and in institutions to control the beast within him. No ideal, no matter how dazzling its vision, is worth anything without a practical plan to make it reality."

That afternoon, he stood before a map of Europe and told me about his practical dream.

"Look at Europe physically. What is it? Here, on the right bank of the Rhine, are rich beds of hard coking coal. There, on the left bank of the river, are equally rich fields of mineral ores. Between them is water, the swift river Rhine, a prime source of energy. Coke, iron ore, and power, what does that add up to? Steel! This region is the greatest source of steel production in the world. But the Rhine is not being used for common energy. It has been designated a border between rival nationalisms. It has run red with the blood of Germans and Frenchmen, lusting for each other's treasures. Now we will put an end to this murderous folly. Now we do not talk of Germany or France, or national production, but of a new community of common interests, pooling all resources for the common good. Never again will Germany and France war upon each other. They no longer have a reason to, and we will integrate their economies and industries to the point where they cannot unscramble them. No more war!"

Monnet's eyes were shining, his cheeks flushed, his Mandarin mask dropped, the poet revealed. He shook himself, coughed dryly, and walked over to a wall cabinet. "A spot of Monnet brandy, David? Good for the heart, you know. Makes it pump."

It was a splendid moment in my life. Like Monnet, I am an idealist. Like Monnet, I had learned that the grandest of ideas means nothing without a plan, a method, a practical procedure. The dream of government by consent of the governed, the ideals of the Declaration of Independence would never have been realized without the Constitution. The first ten amendments and the institutions and laws that grew out of them contain, in constant challenge, rival human interests. I never saw this very clearly until Monnet taught me his wisdom.

I left his office that day, a perfect day in May in Paris, the pink and white chestnut trees just beginning to flower. I hoped that perhaps the second half of the twentieth century would see an end to wars and usher in an era of world peace.

Even as Monnet was talking about economic unity advancing

the cause of peace, a big push toward a military buildup was underway that would seriously impede economic reconstruction, for military moves, necessary as they may often be, drain off monies, materials, and talented men from the civilian sector. That was, at the midcentury, the major dilemma of the Europeans and the Americans, just as it still is in 1984 and will be for many decades still ahead.

I had been on the alert for signs of a major military move by the United States. It seemed to me to be inherent in Truman's containment policy and the Truman Doctrine. We could not depend on the atom bomb alone to match Soviet armed strength in Europe. Europeans would not want their lands to be defended by atomic radiation that would endanger them as well as the Russians. Europe, by itself, slowly emerging from the destruction of war, could not raise armies to match the Red Army of Russia.

The economic and industrial reconstruction of the Marshall Plan and economic unity would help European democracies resist internal communist subversion, but Europe would remain a tempting target for Soviet assault and conquest. Something had to be done, it seemed evident, to build a strong alliance as a deterrent to a Soviet attack, particularly since the most knowledgeable European scientists knew that the Russians were working all-out to build their own atomic bomb. The leading atomic scientists of the West told Washington that the Soviets would have their bomb within four to five years after the end of the war. Therefore Europe had to have conventional strength so that it need not depend upon the atomic bomb alone. Above all it needed a strong American screen around it. War-bled Europe could not do it alone.

President Truman sent invitations to twelve nations to participate in a defensive association: the United States, Canada, the United Kingdom, France, Italy, Portugal, Iceland, the three Benelux states, Denmark, and Norway. They all met in Washington on April 4, 1949, in a truly historic conference to sign the first peacetime military alliance that the United States had ever consented to join.

It was called the North Atlantic Treaty. Article 5 of the NATO Treaty provided that an attack on any one of the signatories would be considered an attack against all of them. This represented a total rupture of traditional American policy adhered to ever since the birth of our nation. The article stipulated that each of the parties would take "such action as it deems necessary, including the use of armed force, to restore and maintain the security of the North Atlantic area." This was an escape clause made necessary by the American Constitution which provides that only Congress may declare war. The Senate would never agree to any automatic commitment for the United States to go to war. However, the stipulation that an attack on one was an attack on all was a powerful political and moral commitment to war and the treaty came under severe opposition in the Senate.

The opposition came from the left and the right. Henry Wallace, former Vice-President, leader of the Progressive Party, asserted that the Atlantic pact gave the U.S. Army "military bases up to the very borders of the Soviet Union." Wallace recalled that the Russians had been attacked by foreign armies five times in the past twenty-five years. NATO, said Wallace, looks just as aggressive to Russia as a Soviet alliance with military bases in Mexico and Canada would look to the United States.

On the right, Robert Taft of Ohio, the diehard, conservative isolationist, echoed Wallace by charging that the Atlantic pact "will promote war rather than peace," and that it was "wholly contrary to the obligations we assumed in the United Nations Charter." Taft said he would vote for the pact if its aim was to promote cooperation and peaceful trade but no "legal or moral obligations to provide arms."

The senators listened politely to Wallace and Taft but were not swayed by their warnings of war or burdensome commitments. They were far more impressed by testimony from our two most prestigious generals, Marshall and Eisenhower, in favor of an Atlantic alliance, and by the forceful, brilliantly presented arguments of Dean Acheson. The vote to ratify the treaty was 82 to 13, on July 21, 1949. The most telling argument in the debate was Acheson's assurance that if the Russians saw an American army in place, alongside our allies, they would know that they could not attack any country without finding themselves at war with the United States. This, he argued, would deter the Soviets.

The area of Europe that concerned us most was, of course, Germany, in the very heart of Europe, where Soviet and Western troops faced each other. Truman, Marshall, Eisenhower, and Acheson all agreed that one day Germany, too, would have to become free, independent, and an ally in NATO. It would be difficult to overcome the historic fears of the French and the reluctance of many Americans to accept the notion of a rearmed Germany and a reborn German General Staff. Devices would eventually have to be invented to overcome those legitimate anxieties. The first thing to be done would be to create a democratic Germany, and to end the occupation status of the Allied armies.

Washington and its allies had sponsored the formation of a German government for their western zones in Germany. On May 8, 1949, the Parliamentary Council in Bonn promulgated a basic law prescribing a federal system of government for a Federal Republic of West Germany. On May 18, Washington appointed John J. McCloy, an international banker, to become the first civilian U.S. High Commissioner for Germany. Military control was ended. The midcentury, with the Marshall Plan, the Atlantic alliance, European unity, and the progressive democratization of Germany and Japan, was that rarest moment when American ideals and national interests coincided and were supported by a broad bipartisan consensus.

The political consensus could not indefinitely survive the many pressures of party rivalries, economic and financial pressures, and public anxiety about global commitments. These all came together to make Americans reexamine their role as world policemen after the Vietnam War. Our freely expressed doubts and wavering commitments would warn our allies around the world that it might be dangerous to become too dependent upon American protection.

In today's world, Americans are genuinely alarmed by the dangers of conflict with both friends and foes that grow out of our worldwide networks of more than three hundred military bases. Economists and financial analysts are even more alarmed at the current estimated cost of those bases: some two hundred billion dollars a year.

Many allies are beginning to think like General Gallois about the reliability of the American atomic umbrella. They wonder whether it ever would be used in their defense and whether such a defense, if used, might not be worse than the threat it is designed to meet. Today the alliances that were created so successfully at the midcentury mark, to meet the nature of the challenges of the 1950s, are being necessarily reexamined, for it seems likely that they no longer meet the challenges of the eighties.

But at the midcentury mark order and cohesion were emerging from the chaos of Europe. At the same time Asia was exploding over a wide area: in Korea, the easternmost peninsula of the continent, down through giant China, Indochina, and across to the westernmost peninsula of Asia, where an ancient nation, the land of the Jewish people, was being resurrected in the new state of Israel. These Asian explosions, which started erupting as soon as World War II had ended, would reach new paroxysms of violence and change by the midcentury mark and would continue to shake the world up to and including today's world.

During World War II the Jews of Palestine, then under a British mandate granted by the League of Nations after the First World War, fought bravely and loyally on the side of the British against the common enemy, Hitler. I recall the day in Algiers in 1943 when a British lieutenant, Morris Perlman, told other staff officers at Eisenhower's headquarters: "Gentlemen, we Jews shall fight to the end for the victory of King George over the bloody Nazis. We shall overcome Hitler. Then we shall fight to the end for the creation of the state of Israel and we shall drive the bloody British out of Palestine and overcome King George."

The Jews of Palestine did just that. In May 1948, the last of the British pulled out and the state of Israel was born. At the very moment that Monnet, Acheson, and European statesmen were moving toward unity, the Middle East was erupting in warring nationalisms. The Arabs, waiting for the British to withdraw and get out of their way, launched a massive five-nation assault upon the newborn state of Israel: Egyptians, Jordanians, Syrians, Iraqis, and Lebanese attacked on all sides.

The Jewish defense forces, formed in the underground and honed to fighting trim in their guerrilla war against the British mandate troops, fought valiantly against overwhelming odds and drove the Arabs back on all fronts. As the Arabs fell back, their friends in the United Nations, who had at first cheered their early advances, began clamoring for a cease-fire to save them from their rout. Finally, as the midcentury year began, on January 6, 1949, Israel and Egypt accepted a U.N. proposal for a cease-fire in the Negev, the scrub desert bordering on the Sinai peninsula.

The next day General Marshall resigned as secretary of state and was replaced by his under secretary, Dean Acheson. That was not good news for Israel. Acheson had strongly opposed Truman's recognition of the new state.* That recognition had been granted in principle, but the necessary steps to a legal recognition and full diplomatic relations had not yet been taken. Knowing that Acheson and almost all the State Department permanent civil servants were pro-Arab and anti-Israel, to say nothing about a good deal of anti-Semitism throughout the department, American Jews were pressing Truman to complete the process.

In January 1949, moving swiftly to forestall any sabotage by the State Department, the Israelis held a national election to choose a Parliament and government as a true expression of the will of the people. It was the first election of a Jewish government in Jewish history, an occasion for rejoicing in a new democracy for Jews in their own state. Impressed, Harry Truman rejected Acheson's opposition and granted Israel formal, de jure recognition by the United States, on January 31, 1949. After almost two thousand years of exile and persecution, the Jews had found a home that the U.N. would recognize, granting Israel full membership and the theoretical protection of the U.N. Charter. Washington was surprised and Israel delighted when Russia also recognized the new state. The Jews of Israel would, however, have to spend the rest of the twentieth century defending themselves against hostile neighbors, for the U.N. Charter proved to be merely symbolic and not a real guarantee against aggression.

Two days after Truman's recognition, the Jews had driven the Arab Legion of Jordan out of the new city sector of Jerusalem and back into the ancient walled city. The government of Israel promptly annexed the new sector and declared it to be an integral part of the state. I received a call from Georges Bidault, the foreign minister of France, and leader of the Catholic party, the MRP. We were good friends. I had interviewed him often and talked of his brave role as head of the Council of the Resistance in the underground war against the Nazi occupiers of France. He was seething with anger when I entered his grandiose office on the Quai d'Orsay, shouting as I came through the door: "What have you people done? You cannot defy the United Nations! Jerusalem is not a Jewish city!"

* In his memoirs, entitled *Present at the Creation,* Acheson asserted that he tried hard to talk Truman out of recognizing Israel, and boasts of his wisdom in so trying.

I was startled by the words "you people." Bidault assumed that since I was Jewish, I automatically supported and was somehow responsible for the actions of the Jewish state of Israel. He certainly meant no insult, no offense. We were not only friends but Bidault was a diplomat, a historian, a gentleman. His accusatory words taught me a lesson that I would never forget, and that no Jew should ever ignore. The creation of the state of Israel forged a link between that state and all Jews everywhere in the world, whether the Jews liked it or not, whether it was fair and accurate or not. Many Jews, in France, England, the United States, do support Israel wholeheartedly, but many others do not accept responsibility for the actions of Israel or want their fate to be linked to the fate of the Israelis. However, the Christian and Moslem world, indeed the entire world, looks upon Jews as people of two loyalties, to their own nation and to Israel, perhaps also of divided loyalties.

This is manifestly unjust and highly inaccurate. It is an accusation that is not made against Americans of Polish origin who sympathize with their fellow Poles in Poland. They are not called communists because they support communist Poles. America, by 1960, finally elected a Catholic President, abandoning the myth that all Catholics are subservient to the Pope and the Vatican State. Many Jews in the West do support Israel and so do many Christians. Others are critical of Israel.

The Arab propaganda charge that the American media is owned and controlled by Jews is simply a lie. Jews do not own and control the press of America, although Jews do own two of the best papers in America. Even those papers, *The New York Times* and *The Washington Post,* are not propaganda organs of Israel. They do support, as do almost all papers and the American government itself, Israel's right to live in independence, behind recognized and secure frontiers, free of harassment by her neighbors. However, many prominent Jews are not uncritical defenders of the policies of Israel. I. F. Stone, a leading liberal columnist for years, a Jew, has been one of the most outspoken critics of Israel's policies and actions. So have Anthony Lewis of *The New York Times* and Professor Noam Chomsky of M.I.T. The severest critics of Israel are the Israelis themselves, for there is freedom of speech in Israel, as there is not in many of the countries that decry Israel.

The French foreign minister's anger at the partial annexation of Jerusalem was based upon a United Nations resolution calling for Jerusalem to be an international city. As a Catholic, Bidault felt strong historical and emotional ties to Jerusalem and the Christian shrines. I tried to point out to him that the Israelis would surely respect the sanctity of all shrines and keep them open and available to all pilgrims. I also pointed out that one of the holiest sites of Judaism, the remnant of the wall of the Second Temple, known as the Wailing Wall, was under occupation by the Arab Legion of Jordan, which was digging in in Old Jerusalem.

Bidault said he would oppose an Arab annexation as vigorously as a Jewish annexation of Jerusalem. I told him that I understood his position and would, of course, make it clear in my broadcasts. I walked out of his office wondering just how far the Israelis might go to re-create ancient Israel and how far the world would go to prevent them.

All through 1948 and 1949, the United Nations had watched the flow of battle between the Arabs and the Jews. Under the U.N. Charter, the Arabs were clearly aggressors against a state whose creation had been overwhelmingly voted by the U.N. members. No actions were taken against the Arab aggressors, no sanctions voted. Only when it became apparent that the Jews were winning the war did the U.N. move to halt it. There were demands made on all participants to send delegates to the island of Rhodes where the U.N. proposed to hold a peace conference.

The Arabs agreed, led by Egypt. Israel was only too anxious to end the bloody fighting, for it had few resources, few friends, and a population so small, barely six hundred thousand people, that every loss of life and limb was a major loss. The talks began in January and continued through the spring of 1949. They were unable to reach a peace agreement, for the Arabs resolutely refused to recognize the right of Israel to exist as a state in the Middle East. The talks finally ended in a truce. There was no agreement then and still none today on the boundaries of Israel. The truce lines simply recorded the reality of the tides of battle. The contending armies remained stationed where they were when the fighting stopped and therein lies a most significant and almost forgotten issue: What happened to the land that the U.N. had originally proposed as the site of a Palestinian state?

The U.N. partition plan of November 1947 had provided for the creation of two states in Palestine when the British withdrew, a Jewish state and an Arab state of Palestine. The Palestinians today accuse Israel of rendering them homeless and stateless. What happened to their state? Very simply, it did not come into existence because the Arab nations had no interest in creating a Palestinian state. The kingdom of Jordan annexed the West Bank, which had been won by its Arab Legion. Egypt annexed the Gaza Strip, which it had conquered in the war. Jordan took over the old walled city of Jerusalem and Israel held on to the modern sector of Jerusalem. No Yasser Arafat arose to denounce Jordan and Egypt and to claim the West Bank and the Gaza Strip. There was no PLO. Homeless and stateless Palestinians were herded into wretched refugee camps to live for decades in squalor, misery, and hatred.

Who herded them into camps? It was their Arab brothers, who had all the space, oil, and monies needed to take them out of the camps and offer them and their children a decent life. Homeless and stateless Jewish refugees, suffering persecution in Arab, communist, fascist, and other lands inhospitable to Jews, came flooding into Israel. Poor little Israel, without space, the entire width of the nation some eight miles from the Mediterranean Sea to the West Bank, without oil, without resources, took in its brother refugees and gave them jobs and a new life in freedom. American, British, and French Jews gave their money to Israel to help the struggling poor state absorb the refugees. Why did not the Arabs do the same for their "brothers"?

I visited the refugee camps and spoke to U.N. administrators and leaders of the Palestinian inmates. The Palestinians ranted against Israel for having driven them out of their homes and destroyed their villages. They refused to acknowledge that this had happened when the Arab armies had attacked Israel. I pointed out that the Voice of Cairo, the most powerful transmitter in the region, had told them to leave the land of Israel and get out of the way of the invading armies, promising that they would return after the Jews had been defeated and take all the land for themselves. Tens of thousands had heeded that call from Cairo and had fled Israel, not been driven out.

Some of their villages were damaged or destroyed in battle. Undoubtedly some of them were also driven out. No one will ever know how many were made homeless by the Israelis or how many had fled to await a victorious return. It is in any case a futile argument used only to keep hatred alive. What mattered is that hundreds of thousands of Arabs did decide to stay in Israel and others did not. What mattered is that Israel became a sovereign state, and like every sovereign state in the world had the right to decide for itself residence and citizenship qualifications. What mattered, and still matters, although always disputed, is that the U.N. agreed to partition Palestine into a Jewish and an Arab state and that only the Jewish state came into existence because Jordan and Egypt annexed the land designated for a Palestinian state.

Jordan and Egypt held the West Bank and the Gaza Strip from June 1949 until June 1967, when another war broke out and the Israelis drove them out. For eighteen long years, Arafat's "brothers" could have created a Palestinian state in the West Bank and Gaza Strip. Only after Israel conquered the West Bank and the Gaza Strip did Arafat arise to demand a state. Later in the chronology, it will be fitting to discuss the new situation today. The past is not a justification for present policy. However, the traumas of the past weigh heavily upon the emotions of the present. And history is its own justification. In the midcentury world, the Jews created their state while the Arabs refused to create the one promised to the Palestinians. That record, at least, should be recognized.

No sooner than peace, or at least an armistice, ended war in the southwestern extremity of the Asia continent, a violent war broke out in the extreme northeastern peninsula of Asia, in a place few Americans had ever heard of: Korea.

On June 24, 1950, the army of North Korea, armed and primed by the Soviet Union, invaded South Korea. The U.N. Security Council, acting on an American motion, charged North Korea with violating the charter by breaching the peace.

On June 30, President Truman authorized use of U.S. ground troops and air missions against North Korea, and, on that same day, already alerted and prepared, the first American ground troops landed in South Korea ready for combat. We were at war in Korea, although war had not been constitutionally declared. Truman would evade his constitutional responsibilities by declaring the combat in Korea to be a "police action," not a war. So we were not only in war but in a constitutional crisis, which would continue for many years, from Korea to Vietnam, Cambodia, and Laos, to say nothing of other military actions ordered by other Presidents without the consent of the Congress.

Truman, however, did not act without the consent of the United Nations. Secretary of State Dean Acheson was gardening at his weekend retreat, on Saturday, June 24, when he was called by his duty officer who informed him of the North Korean invasion of South Korea. His very first thought was to telephone Trygve Lie, the secretary-general of the United Nations, to convene an emergency session of the Security Council.

It met on Monday, June 26. The Security Council voted 9 to 0 to condemn the North Korean aggression, and later, on the morning of the twenty-seventh, passed a second, stronger resolution, authorizing member nations "to render such assistance to the Republic of Korea as may be necessary to repel the armed attack . . ." All this took place before American troops landed in Korea on the thirtieth.

Russia made a monumental error. The Soviets, championing China's right to join the U.N., were boycotting the Security Council because of American vetoes against communist China's membership. Thus, the Soviet representative was absent from the key council meeting which gave Truman the green light he wanted to fight in Korea. Had the Soviet delegate been present he could have vetoed the resolution.

The rapid American reactions to the North Korean aggression caught everyone, particularly the Russians, by surprise. Few Americans had ever heard of Korea. My French friends, in Paris, kept calling me to ask just where and what Korea was and whether the United States was responsible for South Korea. The last was more than a fair question, and the simple answer was: No, in no way at all. This puzzled the French, who wondered why we were jumping into action in a far-off land for which we had no responsibility and apparently no strategic interests. It puzzled just about everyone, including the bewildered citizens of the United States.

They all had good reason to be confused. The United States had not declared Korea to be of strategic interest to American security. Nor did Truman send our troops into combat for security reasons. As so often in our history, and the history of other countries, we went to war for internal political considerations, not for national security.

Extreme right-wing Republicans, whom Dean Acheson contemptuously called "the primitives," had been systematically attacking Truman, the State Department, and the Democratic Party for having "given" China to the communists. Senator William Jenner denounced General George Marshall as "a front man for traitors," part of a "criminal crowd of traitors and Communist appeasers." Even a Democrat, a young Congressman, John F. Kennedy, talking of China, charged its loss to "our diplomats and our President." The McCarthys, the Tafts, the Wileys, Jenners, and other Republicans would have made political capital if Truman had not moved against another communist takeover of an Asian country, Korea. The Republicans, always ready to accuse the Democrats of losing countries to the communists, were nonetheless themselves opposed to any American involvement in Korea.

The Democrats were far from innocent of foolish policies and even more foolish pronouncements on those policies. The most foolish of all was made by the brilliant but vain and arrogant Secretary of State Dean Acheson. What he did and said are worth remembering, but not to fix blame more than thirty years later on an intelligent man and devoted civil servant. It is rather a necessary reminder to American citizens that even the most brilliant and best informed leaders of government are, after all, fallible men, and, no matter how brilliant or knowledgeable, are not always wise and prudent.

Over the years, in lectures and broadcasts, particularly during the Vietnam War, people would arise to challenge my criticism of Washington policies, to tell me that the President and secretary of state and Joint Chiefs of Staff were all honorable and able men, who had more information at their disposal than I had, so how dare I challenge their policies and judgments? The answer, very simply, is that often enough they are unwise or badly motivated. Citizens should listen to critics as well as officials and try to make up their own minds. Without abandoning faith in the system of democratic government, we might well be a bit more skeptical about the men who run the system. After all, that is the essence of democracy. Our leaders are our servants not our rulers.

Acheson's colossal error occurred in January 1950 in extemporaneous remarks made to reporters at Washington's National Press Club. Acheson outlined America's security perimeter, from the "Aleutians to Japan, to the Ryukyus to the Philippine Islands." Acheson was not stupid, uninformed, or careless. His omission of Korea from our defense perimeter was clear and deliberate. The Administration simply did not consider South Korea an essential strategic element in America's line of defense.

Ever since the surrender of Japan, the Russians had noted America's lack of strategic interest in Korea, but were afraid of MacArthur and what he might do if they were to move in. After Acheson's talk, the Soviets believed that, at last, they had received the green light. They gave orders to Marshal Kim to strike. To the end of his days, Acheson hotly denied that he had led the Russians to believe Korea was theirs for the taking. He insisted that he had not *specifically* ruled Korea out of our defense perimeter. That is true. He did not *say* that Korea was *excluded.* He did, however, leave it out. Is that not an exclusion? Acheson's omission misled the Soviets and they misread it. Tens of thousands were killed and international relations poisoned for decades because of grave miscalculations by American and Soviet leaders.

As all these explosive events were erupting around the world, pouring the fiery lava of nationalist rivalries and hatreds everywhere, a young television producer, Don Hewitt of CBS, who would decades later become America's premier news producer, with the number one program *Sixty Minutes,* was puzzling one night over the many quick and bewildering twists and turns of world news. As the midcentury mark was reached, Hewitt was producing the evening TV news show. Each night, when he went home, he felt he did not really understand the crazy quilt of worldwide news he had just offered his viewers. Hewitt thought something should be done to bring some kind of overall understanding, some deeper analysis, of the breaking spot news. With that thought, he would raise television to a new and higher level.

Hewitt went to see CBS News Director T. Wells Church. He suggested to Ted Church that he bring all the foreign correspondents home at the end of the year to join forces with Eric Sevareid, our Washington correspondent, and Ed Murrow, our senior newsman. "December 31 is the midcentury mark," said Hewitt. "It's a good peg for stepping back from the spot news and taking a longer, deeper look at where we and the world are as we enter the second half of the twentieth century."

After a great deal of discussion and budget controversies, the top brass agreed to the Hewitt suggestion. CBS would put on a program to be called "Mid-Century—Years of Crisis," to be broadcast on New Year's Day, January 1, 1950. Called to New York urgently were: Howard K. Smith from London, David Schoenbrun from Paris, Bill Downs from Berlin, Winston Burdette from Rome,

Bill Costello from Tokyo. We were to join Larry Lesueur, our United Nations correspondent; Eric Sevareid, chief Washington newsman; and Ed Murrow, the anchorman.

It was a first-rate group of reporters. In those days, CBS News was not just number one, it was in a class by itself. Its competitors finally caught up with it and there is now a close race among the networks, but for a few brief years the Murrow team was nonpareil. There was CBS and then the others. It was a magic moment early in the history of television, and it was my good luck to be one of the pioneers at a time when Murrow towered over all broadcasters; and, because of his prestige and integrity, we correspondents called the turn on what was to be covered and broadcast. Our day did not last more than a decade before the producers, managers, bookkeepers, and lawyers took over, but while it lasted it was dazzling.

We rapidly reached agreement on the format of the roundtable program. Murrow would talk about the "great pivots" on which history had turned in the past fifty years and then ask Sevareid, for America; Smith, for Europe; and Costello, for Asia, to sketch out the "big footprints of history in their areas."

Sevareid, in a brilliant summary of a half-century of American life, began by saying that the first year of the century, 1900, "ended the age of the great barbecue," and that 1950, the midcentury mark, "begins the great age of anxiety."

Smith asserted that the story of Europe these fifty years can be quickly told. "Europe declined." He went on in an essay as precise and insightful as Eric's. They were both at the peak of their form then.

Costello, drier but no less perceptive, talked of Asia awakening from a long sleep, rubbing from its eyes "the crusted traditions of centuries." He said that the Russo-Japanese War of 1905 had exploded "the nineteenth-century myth of white supremacy." He said it "set fire to the tinderbox of native nationalism," and that the midcentury would find Asians struggling to win personal liberties while trying to advance economic security. Strangely, he did not speak at all, during the entire program, nor did anyone else, of the most extraordinary event that had occurred so shortly before: the victory of the Chinese Communists over Chiang and the Nationalists. We talked about it daily on regular programs but it apparently did not fit into the sweep of a midcentury show. In retrospect it was a serious error of omission.

At the end, Murrow gave us each thirty seconds to say anything we felt like saying. I offered the thought that we Americans are not content just to have allies. "We want to be loved, by pals, buddies, with a Presidential system just like ours and perhaps a dash of ketchup on their hamburgers. We wear our hearts on our sleeves and are easily hurt. Maybe the trouble is that our pocketbooks are as open as our hearts and we are secretly afraid that we're loved only for our money. I wish we'd grow a thicker skin in the next fifty years." So far, we haven't.

The program was the first worldwide report and analysis by very articulate men. Television had come of age as a serious news medium and was on its way to becoming a major influence in American life. Some think it is too influential and is not just an observer but a participant, even a shaper of American life.

Some CBS officials were themselves alarmed by the sudden surge of television. Ted Church, a radio man, mistrusted TV, said that pictures distracted from the story and turned newsmen into actors. He predicted that cameramen and producers would move in to determine news coverage. He loved radio for its simplicity and immediacy which permitted no distractions from the story. He knew that nothing would stop the march of television and that radio as a major news medium was destined to be overwhelmed by TV. But he held out against TV as long as he could, and, by so doing, made the career of a young reporter named Walter Cronkite.

CBS management, knowing how Church felt, realizing that television was a different medium, requiring its own direction, hired a TV News Director, an amiable gentleman, Sig Mickelson. Sig, then junior to Ted, went to him and asked him to make available his big radio "stars," Ed Murrow, Eric Sevareid, and Charles Collingwood, to anchor TV news shows. Ted, jealous of "his boys," turned Sig down. And the radio correspondents did not press for television. Mickelson put out the word that he wanted to audition journalists for work at CBS TV News. Among those who applied was Walter Cronkite, a veteran United Press war correspondent, who had hit the beaches at Normandy, and then had filed news reports from UP's Moscow bureau. At least another hundred applications poured in.

They need not have bothered. Sig had liked Cronkite's experience with a major news agency and then he sat transfixed as he watched Cronkite's audition film. Cronkite's rich, baritone voice, powerful delivery, yet somehow unsensational, even avuncular air of decency and integrity won Sig over at first sight and hearing. Cronkite would be his man.

A new star rose over Washington and New York, and Cronkite was off to a most remarkable career, eventually becoming, according to the polls, "the most trusted man in America." With it all, Walter, a genuinely nice person, remained modest, never let the fame go to his head. Late in his career, well established as number one in TV news, Walter was making about a half million dollars a year. He was asked what he thought about ABC News offering Barbara Walters a million dollars a year, and would he now demand as much from CBS?

Walter growled: "Hell no, we are all paid too much money already." Not even Walter could imagine that the man who would follow him on his retirement, Dan Rather, would be paid more than two million dollars a year. That kind of money cannot but have an impact upon a man's objectivity, independence, and courage.

Dan Rather, Tom Brokaw of NBC, and Peter Jennings of ABC are all professionals, skilled, integrious reporters. By their talents and personalities they have been elevated out of reporting into the half-world of newsmen-stars. The president of ABC News, Roone Arledge, said on *Sixty Minutes* in September 1983, that all three really ought to be doing what they do so well and what is so needed: reporting the news, not editing and reading it. But the system projected them into anchormen roles at huge rewards. There seems to be no other way to do this. It is a dilemma and an embarrassment to everyone, particularly the intelligent, sensitive men who are trapped in a golden spotlight.

I returned to my Paris post after our "Years of Crisis" program, exhilarated by its success, by critical acclaim, yet disturbed by the thought that we had only half done what we had set out to do. We had given television news greater depth and seriousness, and offered our viewers a better understanding of the complex world in which we were all plunged at the midcentury mark. But one program, once a year, was clearly not enough. Not even a succession of thoughtful documentaries in the course of a year could create an enlightened, informed citizenry. And TV alone could not do it. I felt that there needed to be an upgrading of the daily press, more attention to understanding and meaning rather than dramatic headlines. Books could do the job better than any other medium, but books, except for the most popular, did not reach enough citizens in a country of more than two hundred million people.

Since then, the hot-and-cold running wars of the first half of our century have not slowed down. If anything, they have multiplied. There have been more than a hundred and fifty internation wars and intranation revolutions and uprisings since the end of World War II. There is no end in sight to violence as the twentieth century melts away in heat and fury. In addition, the complexities and mysteries of economics and of atomic weaponry have become so arcane that not even the scholars and specialists really understand them.

If there is any answer to the puzzle of communications in a complex and technological world, it probably must come at the root level of our culture: our schools. We need better schools, better equipped, with better pay to attract and keep the best teachers. But that is not a high priority in our nation today. It was also a low priority at the midcentury mark and we paid the price of a sharp decline in the levels of our culture.

We were too engrossed with the tremendous problems the West faced at the turn of the midcentury to worry about our schools: the economic and industrial reconstruction and rehabilitation of the European democracies, and the simultaneous creation of a military alliance to protect those renascent, weak democracies from the threat of a heavily armed and hostile Soviet Union and the sabotage of large communist parties inside the democracies.

When we defeated the Nazis and the imperial Japanese in 1945, we rushed to bring home our men and to enter a brave new world in the last half of the twentieth century. We were in for a rude awakening.

CHAPTER 15

EISENHOWER: "MAN OF PEACE"

Barely six years after his great victory over the Nazis, a victory of the combined Western nations and the Soviet Union, General Eisenhower was back in Paris to establish a new Supreme Command of the Western powers. This time he would head a new alliance against his former Soviet comrades-in-arms. The Red Army had never been demobilized and was seen at the midcentury mark as a new threat to the democracies.

General Eisenhower's headquarters was temporarily installed in an office suite in the Publicis building, on the top rise of the Champs-Elysées, facing on the Arc de Triomphe. Publicis, one of the largest advertising agencies in Europe, had been founded by Marcel Bleustein-Blanchet, one of the prewar pioneers in radio. When he joined de Gaulle's Free French forces he had taken a *nom de guerre,* Blanchet. After the war, he kept his wartime name and attached it to his birth name.

Bleustein-Blanchet's admiration of America and his gratitude for all that Americans had done for France have made him one of the best friends we have abroad. He provided excellent facilities for Eisenhower's advance representative, General Al Gruenther, whom the media had dubbed "the brains of the Army." Gruenther had everything well in hand when Eisenhower arrived in Paris.

As I walked into his office, Ike flashed his wide smile, his face seeming to light up like a Thanksgiving pumpkin. It warmed the room on a bleak, wintry Paris day.

"Well, here we are again." Eisenhower laughed. "Would you have believed it?"

"No, sir, not really. It never occurred to me that you would come back."

"Never occurred to me, either. I'd have taken bets against it."

"What happened, sir?"

"Well, now, we are just talking? No interview!"

"Yes, sir."

"We've had a disaster in Korea. MacArthur made a serious miscalculation. He did not believe the Chinese would come in, all the way in. They did. We are going to push them back, but it's a tough fight and casualties are heavy."

Eisenhower paused, then went on.

"All through the fighting in Korea and in Indochina this past year, we have been worrying about the need to build a strong military force for NATO. They say history never repeats itself, but, by gosh, I seemed to be hearing echoes of our wartime debates over priorities for the Atlantic or the Pacific theaters. General Marshall and I had to keep pressing Roosevelt not to yield to MacArthur's demands in the forties. Mac is now in bad straits in Korea, but we can't let Korea, which is not a vital strategic front, prevent us from building the force needed for the most important theater of all, Europe. I had told President Truman and General Marshall that I felt there simply was no alternative to the rearmament and defense of Western Europe. Sonuvagun, if they don't say 'Okay, go ahead and do it.' "

"General, what should I be looking for in the organizing months ahead?"

"Well, we are going to have a tightly integrated command structure, as we did in the war. Cooperation is not enough. We need a unified command. Why, right now, every army has a different rifle and an English shell won't fit a French howitzer. Hell, all the screws in Europe have different threads. There is duplication and waste. We've got a lot to do to build a strong, efficient NATO defense force. But we're going to do it. I have come back because I am convinced that if we are strong no one will dare attack us. I am not here to make war. I have come back to keep the peace."

If almost anyone else had made that statement, I would have been hard-pressed not to laugh. It was so nearly Orwellian—War is Peace—and seemed to come directly from the copywriters of Madison Avenue. I had seen billboards in front of American army bases proclaiming, "Peace is our business," a plastic slogan demeaning peace by reducing it to a commercial enterprise. But when Eisenhower said it, it rang true, because he rang true. His hatred of war was one of his best qualities.

Ike's statement about peace was clearly the end of our conversation. As I was getting up to go, I turned to him and said: "General, no one can explain your purpose of arming for peace better than you can yourself. I can include it in my reports, and I will, but only you can make it real. Why not do a radio or television interview about it?"

"No, David, no interviews. It's too early for me to be sounding off. Besides, you know what I think about radio. And TV is much worse."

I knew very well what he thought. Over the years I had had occasion to talk to him about the power of radio. I would remind him at times of Roosevelt's successes in his fireside talks and how he had won approval of the American people for his programs. Once I had explained how General de Gaulle had become the most loved and loyally followed leader of France while in exile in England and North Africa, all through the power of his radio addresses. De Gaulle had been an obscure brigadier general when he went to London to create Free France. He was virtually unknown in France. But when he led his Free French troops back into France for the liberation four years later, he was the best known and admired leader of the people, all achieved by radio.

I had chosen the wrong example, true though it was. Eisenhower disliked and was uneasy about de Gaulle's grandiosity, his pomp and ego, his manipulation of masses of people. "Don't you see how frightening this is?" Eisenhower asked me. "A clever demagogue, a Huey Long, a Hitler, can control radio for evil ends."

"But, General, you know CBS. You are a good friend of Bill Paley. You know that Frank Stanton and Ed Murrow are men of the highest integrity."

"Well, I don't like or trust radio or TV. I don't like the idea of something where you have to depend on the integrity of the men who run it and not the basic integrity of the institution. It can get into the wrong hands."

"But that can happen to the press, too. A paper can get into evil or foolish hands."

"Schoenbrun, don't compare the press to radio. They are not comparable. There are thousands of newspapers. No one man, no ten men or more can control the press. But radio and TV! There are only three or four major networks and they can be controlled. Furthermore, they speak with a loud voice. Newspapers are silent, they have less impact. What is the circulation of *The New York Times?* A half million? How many people listen to news on CBS? Fifteen, twenty million? No, no, they are different and dangerous."

I knew well that this was a sincerely held belief but that behind it was also Eisenhower's well-founded suspicion that he did not come across well on radio and the fact that he was terrified of the TV cameras. Ike had a habit of rambling and sometimes produced almost incomprehensible sentences, his grammar and syntax horribly distorted. His clumsiness served to buttress his criticism of the nature of the electronic medium.

I grinned and told him I would raise the question again another day. Neither he nor I could have possibly guessed how true and important that would prove to be, with extraordinary consequences on our careers and lives.

The French cleared ground for Eisenhower's headquarters at Rocquencourt, some twelve miles west of Paris. They gave the Supreme Commander a magnificent estate for his personal residence at nearby Marly-la-Coquette. There was another world-famous personality as his neighbor there, Maurice Chevalier. I spent one delightful day lunching with Eisenhower and then interviewing Chevalier for my weekday program *Your Man in Paris.* He was so charming and witty and told so many marvelous anecdotes that I was able to edit the tapes into five segments and ran the Chevalier interview from Monday through Friday on the national network.

Chevalier talked at length of his life and loves and the many beautiful women he had known. His most tender memories were of his co-star at the Folies-Bergères, Mistinguette of the "million-dollar legs." At one point I said that he had known and loved so many women that I wondered what he thought of the aphorism "at night all cats are gray."

Chevalier laughed his throaty, liquid chuckle, pushed out his lower lip à la Maurice, and said: "Ah, zat ees—how you say?—bool, a lot of bool! Women are not gray cats. Each is beautiful in her own way, even ugly women. No one is the same, in zee dark or zee light. Zey are wondairful, and I loved zem all, one by one." He chuckled again, his eyes sparkling, and suddenly he put on a lewd grimace: "And sometimes two by two."

General Eisenhower was less amusing that day. He was furious about inter-Allied wrangling and jealousies and the stubborn refusal to give up their own weapons and tools and adopt standard NATO materiel. Then, always fair-minded, Ike flashed his warm grin, rubbed his chin, and added: "Of course, we all want them to standardize on our equipment and buy all new materiel from us, so we're not all that innocent."

I spent at least two days a week at Eisenhower's headquarters, SHAPE. I did not see him often but I saw a lot of his genial press chief, General Charles "Buck" Lanham, and his right-arm, General Al Gruenther, and many others. Then I would work closely with him when Ed Murrow arrived early in 1952 to do a documentary on SHAPE. It was one of the rare television programs that Eisenhower agreed to do, mainly because of his high regard for Ed Murrow.

Murrow, always sensitive to the prerogatives of his correspondents, gave me the major part of reporting for the documentary. But he himself, as the star of the program and the man for whom Eisenhower had agreed to do the program, did the interview with the Supreme Commander. I was able, standing behind and to the side of the cameras, to watch and hear the interview. It was a disaster and would require painstaking editing to get something usable out of it. Ike was awful. He refused to look at the camera lens. He mumbled, was incoherent, clumsy, out of his element. He looked and sounded wretched.

When it was all over, Murrow simply told him the truth and suggested that he get help. Murrow told him that whether he liked television or not, it was on the way to becoming the most important means of communication of our age and would surely become the dominant medium. Refusing to use television was as out of touch with our times as de Gaulle's refusal to use a telephone. That made Ike bridle. He did not want to be compared to de Gaulle or to be told that he was a nineteenth-century anachronism refusing to live in the twentieth. However, he thanked Murrow for his frankness and promised to do something about TV.

About a week later, Eisenhower called me in and asked whether, confidentially, I would coach him a little on how to use the television cameras. Murrow had warned me that I might get such a call. He knew I was fearful that I would be crossing a professional line, getting too close to a news source in a nonnews capacity. But he gave me his endorsement and told me he had recommended that Eisenhower get help.

I came out to SHAPE alone. We would use Army Signal Corps cameramen, to restrict the civilian participation, instead of using my CBS News team. It would not do to use French technicians, not subject to army discipline, and likely to tell all their friends in Paris about Ike taking TV lessons. Army technicians, under orders from a five-star general, would clam up.

The sessions went badly. Ike practiced at the end of the day, when he was tired and inclined to be grumpy. He was angry when I told him that there was a problem with his baldness. "I know I'm bald," he snapped. "What do you want me to do, put on a wig?"

"No, sir, but you can counter the baldness by keeping your head up and at a slight angle from the camera. That way, the camera gets some of your side hair. When you look down, it elongates your head, makes it more oval, like an egg."

"So I have an egg head, do I? What else don't you like?"

I was certainly not doing him or myself any good with exchanges like that. He would end up hating me and would not be any better in the medium. I knew he would blow up but I had to tell him that he needed powder and a little makeup because his naked pate was reflecting the lights.

"Why don't you just get an actor? That's what you really want, isn't it? Get me a double to do my interviews for me."

In those early days, we did not have video cameras. We worked with movie cameras, using film. I would have to wait a day or two for the labs to print and develop the film, then I would run it for Eisenhower and show him how he looked. He did not like what he saw and knew that he would have to work at the techniques I was instructing him in, and permit some makeup. When he did that, he saw at once the great improvement in his picture. But he still did not like what he had to do to achieve it. And his reading ability did not improve. We tried letting him talk extemporaneously, with just a few notes as guidelines, and sometimes it worked well. At other times, his thoughts would wander and his rhetoric would ramble, then entangle itself in a snarl of words that could not be undone.

Finally, my own nerves frayed, tired of being scolded by Eisenhower, I snapped back at him. "You'll never read properly. Why don't you memorize your lines?"

"Why in hell should I do that? That takes time and I have more important things to do."

"What's more important than running for the Presidency?" I shot at him.

Eisenhower turned purple and shouted at me in a voice of thunder. "Who told you I was running for President? What the devil are you talking about?"

"Sir, there is an unnumbered, unmarked door, down the fourth corridor. Behind it sits a man named Kevin McCann. He is writing a book called *The Man from Abilene.* Why would he be doing that if you were not going to reply affirmatively to all those Eisenhower for President groups clamoring for you back home?"

Ike began to chuckle as the red faded from his cheeks. "Now, just how did you get to see McCann and jump to this conclusion?"

"Well, I had an appointment with General Pierre Gallois. As I left his office I noticed a blank door. Everyone on your staff has a door with a name and a number on it. I was curious, so I pushed the door open. There was a gray-haired, bulky civilian hunched over a typewriter. I introduced myself and we began to chat. He told me he was the president of a small university in Ohio and that you had given him permission to write a biography."

"Yes, that's right. He's an old friend and I'm just helping him out. That does not make me a candidate for the Presidency."

"Well, if you deny it, I won't report it, although I could report it along with your denial. I have no doubt that you will run and I hope you will. I think you'll make a great President."

"Thanks, but let's just forget it, okay?"

"Okay. But if you don't improve your work on TV, you'll never get elected."

Ike laughed and said: "Get out of here before I start throwing things at you."

The question of his Presidential ambitions had been a top news story in Paris in January of that year, 1952. Republican Senator Henry Cabot Lodge, Jr., had come to see the general in the name of an Eisenhower for President committee. Lodge announced after his meeting that the general would accept the Republican nomination if offered to him. At a news conference the next day, Eisenhower confirmed, for the first time, that he did have a "Republican voting record." He went on to say that American citizens certainly had the right to organize and call upon men to lead them, but, he insisted, "Under no circumstances will I ask for relief from this assignment in order to seek nomination to political office, and I shall not participate in the preconvention activities of others who have an intention with respect to me." He was asking to be drafted, hoping to stay out of the rough and tumble primaries.

Eisenhower did leave the door open just a crack for Cabot Lodge. At the end of his statement he added the thought that "if I had no choice," he might feel required to answer a "call to duty that would transcend my present responsibility." Cabot Lodge took this to be a signal to go ahead and create circumstances that would oblige Eisenhower to run. That could be brought about by entering his name in primaries. If he won enough primaries, that could be considered a call to duty.

The first primary, traditionally, is New Hampshire, a small state with few delegates to the convention but, often enough, psychologically potent, serving as a springboard for a successful campaign. The primary there was held on March 11. The Eisenhower committee leaders, Lodge and New Hampshire's governor, Sherman Adams, entered his name and mounted a campaign for him. The first "I Like Ike" buttons and banners appeared. Ike won the primary, defeating the favored candidate, Mr. Republican, Senator Robert Taft, by some 45,000 votes to 35,000, not a big turnout but a convincing victory. He then received more than 100,000 write-in votes in Minnesota, a powerful showing for a man who was not an avowed candidate. Eisenhower then won New Jersey, Pennsylvania, and most of the delegates in New York. He decided that this chain of primaries was putting him into the political spotlight, conflicting with his duties as Supreme Commander. He cabled Truman a request to be relieved of his command. Truman granted Eisenhower's request and named Matthew Ridgway to transfer from the Supreme Command in Asia to the Supreme Command in Europe, a sure indication that Western rearmament and defense still had priority over Korea and Asia.

A letter arrived from News Director Ted Church bringing with it a turning point in my career. He informed me that I would have a principal assignment in the election campaign. He had conferred with Murrow and agreed to name me as the CBS News correspondent attached to General Eisenhower.

Eisenhower had decided to launch his campaign from his hometown in Abilene, Kansas. Bill Paley, a wartime colonel on Eisenhower's staff in London, asked Sig Mickelson about televising the speech, and Mickelson had answered that he had asked ATT about costs and been told that it would run more than five thousand dollars. Ordinarily that would have been enough to send Paley away. But he felt a special obligation to his wartime chief and he approved a special budget for it. More than that, he sensed that this would be a giant step forward for television.

Ed Murrow was in Abilene for his own evening radio news program. He disliked television news and refused to do anything but documentaries. I was the man on the spot. And, as it turned out, very much on the spot.

Technicians had laid their cables in a barnlike structure just off the local ball park. A rostrum had been set up for Eisenhower at one end of the grounds. I went to it to check out the microphones and the public address system. Some fifteen to twenty thousand people from farms all around Abilene had begun to pour in early. Then it began to pour. Storm clouds burst open and a drenching rain fell just as Eisenhower's car drove up to the rostrum.

Eisenhower got out of the car and mounted the steps to the rostrum. The wind caught the few hairs on the general's head that he had tried to brush over his baldness, and his hair was literally standing on end. His spectacles were blinded by rain. I asked him to follow me down off the rostrum and led him to the barn where we were keeping our cameras dry. Inside the barn, I suggested that we had just enough light for him to make the address to the national audience waiting for him.

"No, damnation, I'm not going to hide away here while twenty thousand good people are out in the rain waiting to see me!"

Eisenhower strode out of the barn, made his way back to the rostrum. We hurriedly dragged cameras out. He obviously didn't care whether we got our cameras into position or not. He began to address the crowd. The papers of his speech, each inside a celluloid cover, were whipped back and forth by the wind. Occasional thunderclaps would drown his voice. It was ghastly. Doggedly, Eisenhower fought on. He managed to make the points he had wanted to deliver: This election, he asserted, was about liberty versus socialism; he wanted the Senate to share the elaboration of foreign policy with the President; he called for an armistice in Korea, for cutting government spending and unnecessary federal agencies, and for the "rooting out" of subversive elements. He wanted to remove government controls in order to fight inflation and to turn civil rights responsibilities over to the states.

I listened to him with surprise and dismay. I had never talked with him about anything other than military or foreign policy and had not heard his views on other issues. This was a deeply conservative speech, very different from the views held by the Eastern Republican "progressives" who had chosen him to fight against the conservative Senator Taft. That day in Abilene, Eisenhower sounded more like Taft than Taft did.

I wondered whether this represented his true views or was a tactic to win the conservatives over to his side. Taft's staff was already claiming some 580 delegates out of the 604 needed for the nomination. Whatever the reason, Eisenhower gave the most conservative speech heard since Herbert Hoover, and the ideas he put forward would not be heard again until Ronald Reagan some thirty years later. Eisenhower had the Eastern "liberal" Republicans in his pocket. Taft could be in trouble if Eisenhower began wooing away the conservatives.

I returned to the hotel a bit nervous about what Murrow would ask me. No one knew exactly where Eisenhower stood on taxation, civil rights, inflation, the size and function of government. We would all get a chance to question him closely at a news conference scheduled for the next day.

Murrow, his head down, looked up at me from under his dark brows and said: "There's a small problem about that news conference, David. And it's on your shoulders."

Wet and chilled, I felt even colder as I noted Murrow's somber look. He went on to explain that Jim Hagerty, Eisenhower's press chief, a top-notch *New York Times* reporter and a most amiable fellow, had told Murrow that TV would be barred from the conference. "Your lights and cameras turn the event into a kind of circus," Hagerty had said, adding that Reston of the *Times* and other top Washington press men had demanded that TV be kept out.

I told Murrow that it was hard to believe that a man like Reston, the finest reporter in the country, would try to exercise a form of censorship through a blackout of TV. I thought it more likely, knowing Ike, that he was the one who had told Hagerty to bar television.

Murrow said it did not much matter who had forced the decision. It had been made, and the men who ran the networks had decided that they would not put up with it. He told me that he had just had a conference call with the three network chieftains of America: Bill Paley of CBS, David Sarnoff of NBC, and Leonard Goldenson of ABC. Paley had told Murrow: "We want a live camera, broadcasting to the network pool, all three networks transmitting the pictures across the nation, and we want it right on Schoenbrun as he walks into the Abilene theater. Schoenbrun has been named all-networks pool correspondent. Backing him up will be Frank Bourgholzer of NBC. David is to march right in, and if there is a police or security barrier, he is to force his way through it, with the camera on him. If they stop him and order him out, he is to defy the order. I don't want Schoenbrun to walk out of that theater. If they won't let him in, they will have to carry him out, with our cameras showing the entire nation that the American people are being prevented from watching the Eisenhower news conference. The voters will know whom to blame and it won't be Reston of the *Times,* or the news services."

Paley was an Eisenhower man as a voting citizen, but he was above all else a television network chief, and he was not going to let anyone, Eisenhower or anyone else, bar TV from a public news event. NBC and ABC completely concurred.

"So, there you have it, Buster, you're our boy. Upward and onward to the barricades," Murrow said, not quite laughing. He knew what a terrible spot I would be in on my first national assignment. It was a moment of testing, not only of me but of television itself. It had not yet become the power it would be and it was literally fighting for its life, for equal access to the news. Our slogan became "Wherever a pencil goes, our cameras go." Television, despite its enormous power, has not yet fully won that right. TV is barred from Congress, except on special occasions and in specially controlled situations, as it is, generally, barred from courtrooms. In Abilene we were fighting for our most fundamental right to be at a news conference of a Presidential candidate.

I walked into the theater, where guards were checking the credentials of correspondents. Bourgholzer, my "backup," was prudently very much in back of me. A cameraman toted a camera on his shoulder, while a soundman held cables that seemed to me to be writhing snakes. I walked right up to and past the guards, holding my breath. They did not make a move. I just kept on walking. Inside, up an aisle leading to the orchestra seats, another guard waited. He blocked my way but pointed me to steps leading to the balcony. I would not be permitted to sit with the other reporters. Back of the bus for us. But we were in.

I sat down and let my breath out. Bourgholzer sat next to me and reached over kindly to shake my hand. Most of the reporters were seated. I saw the tall, lean frame of Murrow, up front, looking back toward me and giving me the V for victory sign. I felt a lot better, not knowing that an almost total disaster was waiting to blast me.

Everyone was chatting, waiting for someone to come out on stage to start the conference. I looked around to find my television monitor that would show me the picture we were sending out, and for my earphones that would carry the sound from the stage. I almost fainted when I saw nothing at all. The technicians, in all the excitement about getting our camera in, had forgotten to give me the sight and sound without which I would be broadcasting blind and deaf. I looked at Bourgholzer who raised his arms and shrugged, knowing I was doomed but that there was nothing he could do about it, except to run down and look for technicians who might still have time to install the equipment we had to have. Frank was only too happy to run out of the balcony to find the technicians. He did not desert me. He wanted to help, but it was my problem.

Before anyone could come to help, Jim Hagerty stepped out of the wings. I was trembling, on the brink of a mind-boggling decision. If the stage mike was not feeding into our network, no one in the nation would know what Hagerty was saying. If I sat there like a dummy, I would fail miserably. If I spoke, I would risk talking over Hagerty, and then possibly over Eisenhower himself.

Hagerty began, apologizing for the delay, saying Ike would be right out. I could hear him clearly in the theater but had no idea if anyone could hear him on the network. I began explaining what Hagerty was saying, using a technique I had used at de Gaulle news conferences, when I would do a running translation of de Gaulle, holding his voice under, mine over, in English. But this, of course, was no translation. If the television audience could hear Hagerty they would wonder why I was explaining what he was saying. So first I had to explain that I was blind and deaf on the circuit.

I only learned later that the top CBS brass was gathered in the office of Vice-President Hubbell Robinson and that I was driving them crazy. Ted Church was groaning and screaming futilely at the television set: "David, shut up! Please shut up!" Someone jumped up and bellowed: "Fire him, fire that son of a bitch."

Hagerty finished and General Eisenhower walked out on the stage. Reporters stood up respectfully. Some Eisenhower staffers began applauding. During that brief lull, I said: "I hope you are hearing this. I do not dare to try to do a running explanation on the general, as I did on Hagerty. I will now be completely silent. If you cannot hear, I will summarize after Eisenhower has finished. Now, here is General Eisenhower." My timing was perfect. No sooner had I introduced him than General Eisenhower, as though on cue, began talking. I sank back in my seat, exhausted and shaking. Bourgholzer, back in his seat, squeezed my shoulder sympathetically, and passed me a note. "They're getting it all, the circuits are perfect."

Frank and I took out our notebooks, began jotting down summaries of Eisenhower's opening remarks, then of the question and answer period. Someone came up and passed us a note telling us to wrap it up quickly when Eisenhower left the stage and to return it to the networks as soon as we could. I do not remember a word that was said.

I staggered out of the theater feeling I was doomed and went back to my miserable little closet "Sleeperette" on the train. About an hour later, Murrow opened the door and told me to come out and have a drink in the bar car. "It was touch and go, David. At the beginning, they could have murdered you. But you showed good judgment when Ike started. And I don't blame you at all for the mess with Hagerty. It was the fault of the technicians. No one is angry with you in New York. They know what happened. It's going to be a long campaign, and there'll be plenty of chances for you ahead. This will soon be forgotten. What is important is that we have won a great victory. No one will ever try to bar us again."

Murrow was wrong. Someone did try to bar us again, Senator Taft, and, I am convinced, it cost him the nomination. And it gave me a chance to redeem myself for Abilene.

Eisenhower had almost lost the election before his campaign had even started and I had almost lost my job. Eisenhower had not realized, as he eventually would, that television was his only hope to win a nomination that Taft and the party regulars had all but tied down. Eisenhower was a national hero but not a Republican stalwart. For the men who ran the party machinery, he was an outsider. He owed them nothing, and if he could beat Taft, he would be the complete master of the party without ever having been a party man. For the men on the right, true believers and ideologues, men who would rather be "right" than President, Eisenhower was an invention of the Eastern, big-city sophisticates tainted with liberalism and deviationism. They were solidly behind Taft.

The only way that Eisenhower could break the grip of the regular and party leadership on the convention would be to force open the doors and bring in the American people who cared little about party lines and revered him as their conquering hero. Only television could bring all the people into the convention hall. Eisenhower would only be able to wrest control from the regulars and Taft by a groundswell of voter pressure, and only television could help him do that.

Eisenhower had set up his campaign headquarters in Denver at the famed Brown Palace Hotel. From there we would make our way by whistle-stop on the train to Chicago. During one of our stops, I heard that the Taft people had decided to bar television from some of the proceedings, particularly the important meetings of the credentials committee which would pass on the validity of delegates. That was a crucial committee for the nomination. Stacked with Taft men, it was certain to validate Taft supporters on every credentials conflict among several factions. This was particularly true in Texas and a number of Southern states where the Republican Party was all but nonexistent. A few machine men would handpick the delegates, without primaries or other expressions of popular will. They would pick Taft delegates, giving him the margin he needed for victory on the first ballot, freezing out Eisenhower.

I went to the cafeteria car and saw Jim Hagerty having coffee and going over his notes. I sat down and told him that his man was in deep trouble, that Taft was banning TV in key committees. Hagerty looked startled. He at once saw the danger. I told him I had an idea that could blast the doors open. Eisenhower could address a small crowd at the next stop and tell them that he had been in Europe and had seen the death of liberty when an Iron Curtain came clanging down in the heart of the continent. He could then say: "Now I have come home to see an Iron Curtain being put in place in Chicago, at the Republican Convention. There is a ban on television at the convention. You the American people are being blacked out. They don't want you to see them picking a candidate by party rule instead of by the will of the people."

I thought that Hagerty would kiss me he was so delighted. At that moment, Eisenhower came in for a cup of coffee and Hagerty jumped up to greet him and to lead him to our table. He told him what had happened and what I had suggested. Eisenhower gave me a sharp look. "At it again, are you?" Irritated, weary of being scolded, I got up and said, "General, do what you want. I've been trying to help you and all you do is lash out at me. I've had it." And I stalked out of the car.

A few minutes later, Hagerty came looking for me. "Listen, David, calm down. The boss is very grateful to you. I think he finally knows that you're right. You've just been pressing him too hard about TV. He likes your idea and we are going to stop the train at the next town and he'll make the Iron Curtain speech. It's great."

I was elated. I walked down the corridor to the sleeper of Don Whitehead, the Associated Press correspondent. I knew that my editors in New York, unsure of themselves in the new medium, were reluctant to put out a big exclusive story. They always wanted confirmation from the written press or the wire services. Many times in Paris I would break a big story only to hear the editor say, "But it's not on the AP, it's not in *The New York Times.*" I would snap back, "That's why you're paying me to be your Paris correspondent. If all you want is the AP, or the *Times,* hire an announcer and let him read their file on the air."

My job was to beat NBC and ABC. So I didn't mind sharing with the AP. I told Whitehead what Ike was going to say. He would have a clear beat on his main rival, UP. When the train stopped, Don and I jumped off with the other reporters, but when they went to the rear platform where Eisenhower would speak, Don and I sidled off to the station, grabbed telephones and dictated the news break to our editors. We sauntered back to the train where our confreres were returning from the Eisenhower talk to the citizens. Don and I looked at each other with puzzlement when we heard the reporters saying what a bore it had been and they could not understand why the train had stopped for about twenty people lounging around the station.

We ran to the bar and saw Hagerty with his head in his hands. Jim looked up and said: "He forgot to say it."

We groaned. "Jim, the wires are sending that story to every newsroom in the nation. CBS put a bulletin on the air. He has got to make the Iron Curtain speech. We said he made it."

"Yeah, I know. I spoke to the general. He told me to stop the train again at the next village. He'll make it there."

At the next stop, Don and I went out with the others to listen. Ike rambled on for a few minutes, talking about liberty against socialism. He then said: "And I have come home to find an Iron Curtain in our own country. Thank you all very much. Good-bye." He walked back onto the train, leaving some fifty mystified people wondering where the Iron Curtain was in America. Reporters charged at Hagerty. "Jim, what the devil is he talking about?" Hagerty sighed and told them that Ike was referring to the ban on television in Chicago. They looked at him blankly, said "Oh?" and walked away. Don and I laughed until we cried. Our stories had at least been partially confirmed. Above all, our dispatches had reached tens of millions of Americans. It turned out to be a lifesaver for Eisenhower. Letters, phone calls, telegrams began coming in to Chicago demanding an open convention. The American people wanted to be in, not banned. They were angry with Taft for trying to rig the convention.

The party regulars did not understand the power of television. It was still new and growing. Radio still had the larger audience in the summer of 1952. But it lacked television's punch, its power to dramatize events. Despite the complaints that were coming in, the Taft people voted 60 to 40 to bar television cameras from the credentials committee. Don Hewitt sent me a camera team which I installed in front of the door of the committee room. I looked directly into the eye of the camera and said, "You have all heard of the smoke-filled room where party bosses pick the men to be your leaders without consulting you. Well, it's right here, right behind me."

The camera moved in tight on the closed door and stayed on it while I went on. "Behind that door, Republican Party regulars are meeting to decide on the credentials of the delegates who will pick the nominee for the Presidency. We thought you had a right to be there and see and hear the proceedings. They did not think so. They put us out and locked the door. But by so doing, they put you out and locked the door on you."

Every word I said was true but I confess it was a bit demagogic, not just straight reporting. When I thought about it later I became alarmed, for I realized that we were not just covering the political process, we had become a part of the political process. I wondered just how far this would go and what effect it would have on American politics and American society. Other serious men were feeling the same qualms as I. Reston was thoroughly alarmed. So was the man the Democrats would choose at their convention, Adlai Stevenson. So, too, was Eisenhower.

Eisenhower knew what television was doing for him. He needed it. But he did not like it or trust it. What it had done for him it could do against him or for someone who was a less dedicated man of peace and freedom. Trouble was, and is, that no one has come up with any solution to the problem of television's penetration of and influence on the political process. For the next thirty years, as television grew more and more potent and intrusive, it would rival the weather as a subject everyone talked about but could do nothing to control.

More and more protests flooded in to Chicago. Eisenhower spoke on television to call for an open convention. Taft came on to defend himself against charges of rigging. Eisenhower's somewhat shy, country-boy clumsiness, coupled with his wide, warm grin, enchanted the viewers. Taft came across ice-cold, stiff, like a frozen image in a Grant Wood painting. Delegates pledged to Taft were getting messages from people back home complaining about what Taft was doing to Eisenhower. One by one they began moving over to the Eisenhower camp. The convention was slipping out of Taft's hands.

Something strange was happening in the CBS broadcasting booth high over the convention floor. A young man, in his early thirties, with a flat Kansas prairie accent, who pronounced words like "going" as though they were spelled "goeen," was calling the story, shot by shot, straight, clear, factually. It was Walter Cronkite, who had won the assignment as anchorman of the convention when Mickelson, the TV News Director, had been turned down in his request for Murrow, Collingwood, or Sevareid.

Cronkite was a veteran UP wire-service reporter, who had learned to be first and fastest with the facts. No punditing, no larger meaning of it all, no concern about why, only about who, what, when, where, and how. He was Middle America, middle-of-the-road, middlebrow. He was fascinated by what he was watching and he projected that fascination to his listeners in words they could understand. He knew everything that was going on, knew all the delegations, and by his knowledge managed to project an air of authority and truth. He was an overnight sensation, a national figure on his way to becoming the best known and most trusted man in the land. He would hit some bumps along the road and go into skids but he would end up as the giant of television.

Sig Mickelson knew he had a winner and that TV was on its way to greater things when the radio stars who had snubbed him and Cronkite for a year and more, and who had refused television assignments, began coming around to the broadcasting booth to ask humbly whether they could be of any help.

The right-wingers, extremists, and cavemen of the Republican Party, whom the public associated with Taft, although he was not truly one of them, did not help his cause. General MacArthur managed to deliver a keynote address that was both hysterical and boring. There were so many references to God that it sounded like an appeal to a personal friend. Halfway through his address, delegates were moving around the floor, visiting friends, talking politics. Then, Satan himself, Joe McCarthy, came on, with his blue beard, wet lips, saturnine countenance, in a slavering tirade against "slimy traitors" in the "Red Dean's State Department." If MacArthur was boring, McCarthy was terrifying. By contrast, Eisenhower, with his appeals for national unity and peace, came through as Mr. Clean, a decent patriot, a man to be trusted. Television caught and enhanced those images.

Almost every hour of each day Eisenhower's strength grew. Delegates, under pressure from their home districts, began switching from Taft to Eisenhower. By the time balloting began the Eisenhower people knew they had won. On the first ballot it was: Eisenhower 595, Taft 500. Before a second ballot could be cast, delegation chairmen were jumping up, calling on the chair to let them change their votes. Taft's floor manager, Senator Bricker, surrendered and moved to make it unanimous. The all-conquering hero had won again.

After the celebration, Eisenhower's managers asked him whom he wanted as a running mate. Eisenhower was surprised. He did not know that the Presidential nominee could pick his own Vice-President. Eisenhower had a lot to learn about the American political system. He reacted as he always did in the army. He turned the problem over to his staff. He would do that in the White House, too. He was not an activist President.

His advisors chose a freshman senator, Richard Nixon of California. The choice was obvious. Eisenhower had been put forward by the Eastern wing of the party. He needed a running mate from the West. Eisenhower was an internationalist. He needed a superpatriotic nationalist. Nixon was on good terms with the party scourge, Joe McCarthy. Together they had fought Alger Hiss and Dean Acheson. McCarthy could not attack his antisubversive buddy, Nixon. Nixon was a hard worker and a tough campaigner. Eisenhower stood above the fray. It was a dream ticket. The only trouble with it was that Eisenhower, in private, told friends he did not much like Nixon. He found him "shifty" and said he would not look a man in the eyes. He did not at all like his or McCarthy's tactics and methods. But Tom Dewey assured Eisenhower that Nixon would be a loyal, valuable worker and would follow orders. That was good enough for the general.

Eisenhower left Chicago to take a brief rest before the campaign. I stayed on to cover the Democratic Party convention. It was an anticlimax for me. I was assigned to the stage, an important position where I had a desk and telephones to Cronkite in the broadcasting booth. My job was to keep him on top of the program, to know what events and which personalities would be coming to the rostrum. I learned a lot about conventions and politics but it was less exciting than being assigned to the man who would become the nominee. I did get to meet Stevenson at a cocktail party in the home of a Chicago socialite, Rosemary Bull.* I was charmed by him as everyone was, including Eisenhower himself, who told me how much he admired Stevenson.

Although Stevenson's views, his wit and learning, were much more to my taste than Eisenhower's limited range, I felt early on that Eisenhower would and should win. I supported Eisenhower but not because of my association with him or access to him. I simply felt that the times and the issues through which we were living required a national hero and a Republican. Stevenson would not have been able to unite the people or end the war in Korea or face down Joe McCarthy and the Republican extreme right. Under him the country would split apart and Congress would be at the throat of the President. Only Eisenhower could bring us peace abroad and at home with honor and consensus.

Eisenhower's political brain trust believed that peace would be the main issue of the campaign, followed closely by conservative economic and fiscal policies. His managers brought Madison Avenue into his camp and gave the advertising giant BBD and O the assignment to "package" their candidate, the first packaging job of American electoral history. They set about selling Ike as they sold shaving cream and cereals. They produced a thirty-minute film, with a minimum of talk, all carefully set-up action shots of the hero, the cheering crowds, adoring Mamie, the American flag. Then they sent out marketing surveys to special mailing lists, asking people which of several campaign techniques they preferred, what image they wanted of Ike. The results were clear: the war hero who was a man of peace.

The advertising wizards sat down with those results and came

* I also met a pert, bright young delegate from Eau Claire, Wisconsin, Eppie Lederer, who would become a good friend for the next thirty years. She is better known by her pen name, Ann Landers.

up with a campaign slogan: "Eisenhower, the man who will bring us peace." They then brought it to Eisenhower for his approval. To their dismay, he refused. He told them that he would make no such promise. This was Ike at his very best. The Merlins of Madison Avenue were not stumped. They went back to their drawing boards and came up with a simpler, better slogan, one that Eisenhower could honestly approve: "Eisenhower, Man of Peace." They were off and running. Republicans can always raise big sums of money for their candidates and they raised a huge amount to pay for a flood of one-minute political commercials for their man of peace, more than a million dollars, a vast budget thirty years ago.*

There never was the slightest doubt who would win the election: an American hero, born in Texas, reared in Kansas, with a homey name like Ike and a plain, good woman named Mamie at his side. Ike and Mamie, the all-American couple, Mr. and Mrs. America. Stevenson, sophisticated, divorced, quick to quip, sometimes with bad timing and taste, was never in it. In October, Eisenhower promised that if elected he would go to Korea. Stevenson cracked back: "If elected, I will go to the White House." They laughed in New York and Hollywood but nowhere in between.

I felt badly for Stevenson. He was a good man, better than that, he was a splendid man, with every quality to be President, except one. He lacked a common touch. Americans might admire him but they did not want him for President, certainly not in the troubled midfifties and certainly not in a choice between him and Eisenhower.

Back in New York, I was pleased to receive a luncheon invitation from CBS President Frank Stanton, who congratulated me on my first national assignment. At cocktails before lunch, the chairman himself, Bill Paley, came in to say a kind word. He felt that I had done much to advance the cause of television. I was riding high, feeling proud. Just the right moment for a bad fall.

Murrow brought me the bad news, very bad. Omar Bradley, chairman of the Joint Chiefs, had called confidentially to tell him that a Pentagon security officer had refused to issue me an accredita-

* In the midterm elections of 1982, the Republicans had a treasury of $146 million against $38 million for the Democrats.

tion card to army bases on the grounds that I was a security risk. Bradley had tried to overrule him, telling him that he knew me well and that I was a fine, loyal citizen. But such was the climate of witch-hunting in 1952 that a four-star general, chairman of the Chiefs, could not overrule a lower-ranking security officer. Murrow told me that I would have to clear myself.

"Clear myself of what, Ed? How does a man go about proving he is innocent? Aren't they supposed to prove me guilty? What is the evidence? Who is my accuser? What are the specific accusations?"

Murrow only looked gloomier. He did not know how to handle this.

My entire career was in danger. Without an accreditation I could not cover Supreme Headquarters. There would be a stain on me. CBS would have to fire me. No one else would hire me. I stood on the brink of the abyss. Ed told me that if I could not find any other way out, I should go to Eisenhower and he would personally clear me. But he was the court of last resort. And he might not want to endanger the Presidency by getting personally involved in a security case. I felt like a character in a Kafka novel, guilty of nothing but about to be executed.

I called Morris Ernst, the New York lawyer, president of the Civil Liberties Union. Morris, a good friend, picked up the phone and called Lou Nichols, deputy to J. Edgar Hoover, number two man at the FBI. Morris told me that Nichols would see me to discuss my "problem."

In Washington, Nichols, sympathetic and kindly, told me what had happened and said frankly that it was an injustice. He explained that the Pentagon, preparing to issue cards to a group of correspondents, had called for their FBI files. "We sent the files over. The Army cleared you, the Navy cleared you, but the Air Force security officer turned you down."

"Why, what was wrong? How could he say no when the others plus Bradley had cleared me?"

Nichols shrugged. "It has to be unanimous. One man can blackball you."

Nichols went on. "David, I think highly of you, and we at the FBI do not believe you are anything but a loyal citizen. But we don't rule on military security. I'll do one thing for you. I'll let you see the file. After you've read it, come to me and we'll talk about the next step."

He led me into a reading room and a clerk brought me a fat file from the FBI dossiers. I was one of the very few men whom the FBI permitted to see his own file. It was the greatest shock of my life. It was full of hate mail, anonymous letters, absurd reports, unsubstantiated charges, garbage. The American Embassy red-hunter in Paris had carefully clipped out of the communist press every article with my name on it. He just as carefully did not clip out articles in the anticommunist press. I had worked for a news agency, selling its file to everyone, as the AP did. But they had managed to make it look as though I had been working for the communists.

I found letters calling me a secret member of the Irgun underground, smuggling guns into Israel, and other letters calling me a secret French agent collaborating with the Arabs. I found reports going back to 1942 when the FBI had cleared me to work for the Voice of America, reports saying that most of the visitors to my apartment did not wear hats and that I spent every night in a Latin-American nightclub frequented by South American agents. It was absurd, odious, rubbish. But the Air Force security officer, brushing aside my many earlier clearances, my assignment to Camp Ritchie military intelligence school, my work on Eisenhower's staff in Algiers, had decided that I was a security risk.

I went back to Nichols.

"Well, I've read it. It's drivel. Tell me, does the FBI just keep all this junk in a file and then send it out unevaluated and without comment?"

"I'm afraid so. I'm trying to get the system changed but that's what it is."

"Is there anything to be done about this?"

"Yes, David, there is. I suggest you go home and spend some time writing about yourself. Describe all the wonderful things you have done for your country. Include anticommunist articles and broadcasts you have written. Give a list of the most distinguished Americans with whom you have worked and whom you have helped, men who would vouch for you. Thus, when anyone asks for your file, your own best face will be shining right on top of the file to counter all the garbage."

"My God, I have to get down on my knees and beg them to believe I am a loyal citizen?"

"Yes, that's about it."

I flew home almost in tears and then did break down and cry with anger when I told Dorothy about the humiliating experience and what they had asked me to do. She was furious and wanted me to tell them to go to the devil. She asked me to ignore Murrow's advice and to take this case directly to Eisenhower. "You have proven yourself to Ike over and over again. And to Doug Dillon and David Bruce and Ave Harriman. Now is the time for them to rally around you."

I told her that I would think about it. This was too important to act impulsively. I felt I had to write myself up for the file. I could not let that filth go out by itself. Dorothy agreed to that.

I spent an agonizing three days composing an ode to myself, red with anger and shame as I typed the report. I sent it on to Nichols with a note of thanks for his cooperation. He had done all he could for me.

Suddenly, I was saved from disaster. Ted Clifton called and asked me to come and see Bradley. He had my accreditation card in hand. He would explain why in his office. I knew it had nothing to do with my visit to Nichols or my report, which I had just mailed. I flew to Washington on a pink cloud. I was so high, I almost didn't need the plane to carry me. No last-minute rescue in the Perils of Pauline could match this sudden release of my card.

Bradley told me that there were at least a dozen to fifteen cases like mine. They had ended up on the desk of the secretary of defense, General George Marshall. He, or a staff member to whom he could delegate authority, could overrule the Pentagon security men. Marshall had investigated the cases and found the men accused totally innocent of any wrongdoing. However, he hesitated to sign the accreditation cards himself. He was not afraid of McCarthy, although he had already come under attack from the mad slasher. He did not, however, want the office of the secretary of defense, a key Cabinet post, to be damaged in a security fight. So he checked the lists of his principal aides to find a man who could risk the battle. He decided upon a distinguished Southerner, former editor of the Louisville *Courier-Journal,* Clayton Fritchie.

Marshall called in Fritchie and laid it out for him. Fritchie grinned at the secretary and asked: "Am I to be your sacrificial lamb? The most easily expendable man to throw into McCarthy's gullet?"

"No," said Marshall, "not quite that. Clay, you are the best man to stand up to a fight over this. You can be hurt, your reputation smeared, I won't hide that. But you are in the strongest position of any man in the department. You are young, strong, intelligent, and able. I think you've got the best chance to do this. But I am not asking you to volunteer. I will not think less of you if you turn this down. It is your free choice. But, remember the careers and lives of a number of good men depend on your willingness to sign their cards."

Fritchie burst out laughing. "General, that is some free choice you're giving me! Well, let's get it over with, sir. I'll take the cards." Fritchie sat down and signed the cards that would give me and others a reprieve from a dread sentence. It was a brave and shining thing that he did. Obviously, I never made this public. To tell the story would have been to help smear myself. There is always someone to say, "Where there's smoke, there's fire. Something wrong with those fellows."

Today, it doesn't matter anymore. I have had a rewarding career and a good reputation and can no longer be hurt. McCarthy and Hoover are dead. There are still character assassins lurking about, and apprentice McCarthys. But they can no longer touch me. I tell the story now to pay tribute to a courageous, generous man, Clayton Fritchie, and to give my fellow Americans an idea of the terror that reigned in the 1950s when Americans abandoned some of our most cherished traditions of freedom and decency. I do not think that anything on the scale of Joe McCarthy can occur again, but one of the best ways to assure it will not, is to expose what it did, not only to its victims but to the good name and the very soul of American democracy. And I do not forget that I was lucky, had powerful friends. Hundreds of other men were destroyed.

Angered by my Kafka-like experience, I rejected out of hand Ted Church's suggestion that I accept assignment as White House correspondent for the Eisenhower Presidency. I told Church that I had been too close to Eisenhower to function freely and objectively as the White House reporter. I also told him that I was disgusted with the gutless politicians and leaders of our society who cowered before McCarthy and all the witch-hunters and book-burners. I was eager to get back to Paris where I could function at my peak. In Paris, I was bureau chief, as well as correspondent. I ran my own ship. I was Mr. CBS there: Murrow, Church, Stanton, and Paley, all in one.

I threw myself back into my work and the social whirl of Paris. After weeks of waiting, I finally received an invitation to spend an afternoon at the studio of Georges Braque. I sat in a corner, sipping wine, watching the master grind and mix his colors, then build up his palette and begin with precision to paint a still life of fruits, flowers, and a guitar. He worked slowly, stopping often to stare at the canvas, chewing the end of his brush, then carefully applying paint. He worked for about three hours, then broke off and began cleaning his brushes, knives, and spatulas. He had covered only a very small portion of the canvas and I could not make out any design or pattern.

Braque was a handsome old man. He wore a blue Dutch boy's cap over his white hair, a blue smock, and burnt orange slacks. On his feet he wore Basque rope sandals. His blue eyes contrasted with the apricot tone of his face. He took me on a tour of his house. We climbed a spiral staircase leading up from his ground-floor studio. On the wall were niches spaced about three feet apart, following the spiral of the stairs, and in each one was a small bronze figure. The bronze was covered with verdigris and I asked Braque how old the figures were. He smiled and told me they were quite new. He had finished them within the past year. I asked the master how they had acquired the verdigris. Braque told me that when he finished a figure he would bury it in his garden after having "made pipi on it." Braque laughed as he said, "Pipi is a fine acid and by using it I never run out of raw material."

The world of Pentagon security officers and FBI files gradually began to fade away back in my beloved Paris among the talented men and women I so admired. Art and Ann Buchwald would call and invite us to dinner with Humphrey Bogart and Betty Bacall. We would invite the Buchwalds to dine with Isaac Stern and Pierre Mendès-France. One night we went to the Salle Pleyel to hear Stern play and then visited him in his dressing room. David Oistrakh was there, hugging Isaac, and congratulating him on his magnificent performance. We would all then go to Dominique's where Isaac, who had sweated off ten pounds during the concert, would put it back on by devouring mounds of blini and caviar.

There were many visitors from America. James Thurber came to dinner, brought to us by Janet Flanner. Thurber was almost completely blind. But when we guided his fingers to a blank space on the title page of a book, he rapidly sketched a rabbit, a frightened man, and a crouching, predatory female. Lucy, my eight-year-old daughter, climbed on his lap, and Thurber began a conversation with her, starting with the question: "Have you seen any good trains lately?" He enchanted her with his stories.

Bill Paley sent me a letter telling me that Edgar Bergen was coming to Paris with a good friend and CBS advertiser, a man named Justin Dart, head of Rexall Drugs.* He is today president of a conglomerate, Dart Industries, the man who persuaded Reagan to run for governor of California, one of his biggest backers for the Presidency and member of the "kitchen Cabinet."

Bergen had a new puppet with him, Podine Paddleford, a Southern Belle girl friend of Charlie, his most famous creation. Bergen asked me if I could get a famous Paris couturier to make a wardrobe for Podine. I called Annie Buchwald and she arranged for Pierre Balmain to design dresses for the new puppet. Bergen had also brought to Paris his little daughter, a beautiful, sweet little angel whose name seemed to be Candy. Years later, when she grew up to be a movie star, I discovered her name was Candice. I spent a lot of time catering to Bergen and Dart but never got even a note of thanks from Paley.

I had the same experience with Jack Benny and his wife, Mary Livingstone. Benny affirmed his screen reputation as a tight-fisted miser by never once reaching for a check, by failing to tip his driver or send Dorothy flowers. Mary drove me crazy by asking me to buy a perfume that Babe Paley wore. But she did not know the name of the fragrance. I had to name a dozen before she finally reacted to Vent Vert of Balmain, saying that was it. She wanted quarts of it at once for they were leaving the next day. But it was

* I introduced him to Marcel Bleustein-Blanchet, who admired the American drugstore and planned to install one in his Publicis building. Dart sent him some Rexall blueprints. Marcel's staff put a French twist on it and the now immensely popular Le Drugstore was born.

the fourteenth of July, France's Independence Day, and every shop was closed. Mary looked piercingly at me and said, "Bill Paley told us that you could do anything in Paris. So get me my perfume." Dorothy told me to tell her to get lost and suggested I resign from CBS, which no longer respected its correspondents and used us to service its program stars who treated us as lackeys.

I was, however, amused by the challenge and so happy that I had not been fired under a cloud that I did not mind making a special effort. I finally reached Balmain, who was spending the weekend with his horses on a stud farm in Normandy. When I told him it was urgent to do this to please Jack Benny, Balmain asked, "Who is Jack Benny?" I managed to convince him and he called his watchman, who opened the perfume closets and gave me the Vent Vert for Mary. She did not thank me any more than did Bill Paley.

Thurber came back for dinner another night. Dorothy had just read one of his short stories, in French, in *Elle* magazine. She told him it was excellent in French. Thurber smiled and said: "I am not surprised. Many of my things lose something in the original." Paris was a joy. However, the important story was in Asia—the French-Indochina War—and I was eager to go there.

I did a reaction story about Europeans cheering Eisenhower for keeping his campaign promise and flying to Korea to get peace talks moving seriously. I kept pressing Ted Church to give me a budget to go to Vietnam. I felt peace negotiations in Korea would force the French to follow suit. Unfortunately for them they were losing the war and peace negotiations would simply confirm their defeat and force them to withdraw and turn the country over to its people. The French decided, however, on one last attempt to win at least a face-saving victory. They set up a fortified camp at a site called Dien Bien Phu, athwart the crossroads between Vietnam and Laos. Tired of chasing the elusive guerrillas of Ho Chi Minh through jungles and mountains, they were challenging Ho to a pitched battle, defying the Viets to attack the camp.

It took a long time but I finally received my orders to fly to Vietnam in March 1954. A final, historic battle was underway there.

I had followed the chain of events in Indochina ever since the French-Indochinese War had broken out in November-December 1947. The United States did not support the French then and we were highly critical of their imperialist motives. We remained true to our anticolonial tradition until January 1950. In that month, China and the Soviet Union officially recognized Ho Chi Minh as the leader of a genuine native independence movement. One month later, Secretary of State Dean Acheson announced that the Soviet and Chinese recognition of Ho and his recognition of them "revealed Ho Chi Minh in his true colors," that is, as a servant of international communism and not a true nationalist fighting for independence. Later that spring, Acheson accorded recognition to the French puppet regime of Emperor Bao Dai and offered to provide "aid to restore security and develop genuine nationalism" in Vietnam.

The aid, at first, was a mere trickle but it rose soon enough to flood tide when the North Koreans invaded South Korea. We were then ourselves plunged into an Asian war against communists and were ready to listen to French pleas for aid in their anticommunist war in Indochina. From $98 million, our aid jumped to $125 million, then $350 million, and finally reached a total of $3.73 billion. I had something to do with the American offer of $350 million, one of the strangest transactions of our history.

I have never before revealed what happened, for reasons that will become obvious as the story unrolls. Some of the principal characters are now dead. Those still alive are out of power. The Fourth Republic of France itself died in 1958 to be replaced by de Gaulle's Fifth Republic. Its statute of limitations under the law has expired and men who feared that they would be brought before the High Court of Justice are now safe. I can tell the story now.

The story begins with a telephone call from a close friend, Jacques Duhamel, one of France's most able, devoted civil servants. At the time, he was *chef de cabinet,* chief administrative officer, to Edgar Faure, the minister of finance. I knew something strange was up when he told me to meet him in the public gardens behind the Ministry, opposite the Louvre, and not in his office. Jacques greeted me with a grin and said: "This is a cloak-and-dagger operation, very hush-hush."

He said that the French treasury had been drained by the costs of the war in Indochina, with impending high costs for Western rearmament. "Unless we get very considerable American aid, we will have to pull out of Indochina. That will have an immediate and dangerous impact on your war in Korea and on all Asia. It will be a victory for the communists. We need some three hundred to four hundred million dollars urgently."

"Well, Jacques, do you want me to do a broadcast about this crisis?"

"*Mon Dieu, NON!* Not a word, not a whisper. This is top secret, old boy. I am just telling you what the situation is. The prime minister, Joseph Laniel, will tell you about our dilemma and what we want you to do. He is waiting at his office in the Hôtel Matignon right now. I cannot tell you more. Please go to see him at once."

I drove across the Seine to the prime minister's office wondering what he could possibly ask me to do. This was a problem for him or Foreign Minister Georges Bidault and the American ambassador, Douglas Dillon. Not for a reporter.

The cloak-and-dagger aspect grew more lurid when Prime Minister Laniel greeted me silently, got up from behind his desk, and signaled me to follow him into the private gardens behind his office. Nobody wanted to talk to me in an office. It struck me that even the prime minister of France suspected or knew that his office was "bugged."

Deep in the garden, Laniel turned to me and asked: "Did Duhamel tell you about our pressing needs?" When I nodded yes, Laniel continued: "We know that you are a good friend of France, that you fought in our army for our liberation and that we can count on you in a crisis. I have also been informed by Foreign Minister Bidault that you were on General Eisenhower's staff and that you have good relations and access to him now that he is President." My head was automatically bobbing up and down affirming his statements, but it felt like a balloon that was about to fly off my shoulders and then I would wake up and find it was all a dream.

But it was no dream, it became a waking nightmare when Laniel said: "Well, we want you, in the utmost secrecy, to inform President Eisenhower of our plight. No one must know about this but the President. Eyes only! Ultra secret!"

I was profoundly shocked, too shocked even to be angered. This was the theater of the absurd. They could send their own message to Eisenhower. Or inform their excellent ambassador in Washington. Or, more properly, inform our excellent ambassador in Paris, Douglas Dillon. Why in the name of sanity ask an American reporter?

I told this quite bluntly to Premier Laniel. He shifted his big bulky body uncomfortably, bit his lips, sighed deeply, looked up as though imploring Heaven, and said: "I think you must go to see Georges Bidault and ask him. You are good friends with Bidault, he told me. He trusts you. This is his idea. Go to him. He is waiting for you."

I left the Matignon gardens, drove over to the Quai d'Orsay, feeling like a character in an implausible paperback thriller. Meetings in gardens, men telling me that the premier is waiting for me, the foreign minister is waiting for me. And they want some three to four hundred million dollars!

Pierre-Louis Falaisze, Bidault's *chef de cabinet,* received me and told me Bidault would see me in a moment. We sat there silently, staring nowhere, avoiding each other's eyes. We were friendly, had lunched and dined together, but we could have been marble busts in the ornate office. A buzzer sounded and Pierre-Louis jumped a foot off his chair. He arose, opened sliding doors, stuck his head in, then turned and motioned me to enter Bidault's office.

Bidault, beautifully tailored as always, small, slim, elegant, was pacing up and down in front of the Marie de Médicis fireplace. He came and offered me his two hands in a manual embrace instead of a formal handshake.

"*Cher ami,* we need your help. I need your help. We must have that money but we cannot ask for it. You must pass the word."

"Why can you not simply inform Doug Dillon? Why me? Why this extraordinary secrecy?"

"All right, I'll tell you why. Washington is a sieve. Any important telegram that Dillon sends to the State Department appears in print the next day in the column of Joseph Alsop."

"That's all? You're afraid of a leak? What's the difference, so it leaks, but you'll get your money if Eisenhower agrees."

"No, David, there is something else. We do not want to ask for this money. If it is refused it will cause a great crisis and damage French-American relations."

"Please, Monsieur Bidault, I have been a diplomatic correspondent too long to believe that anything like that can happen. Chances are you'll get the money. If not, some face-saving way will be found to explain it. You are holding something back. What is the real reason for this extraordinary procedure? I can do nothing unless you tell me the whole truth."

Bidault, his face reddening, began pacing again.

He stopped, having reached a decision, and turned back to me. "Very well, I will trust you. But you must not reveal this to anyone. If I officially ask for this money and your President grants it, as I do believe he will, I will then be accused here in France of once again selling French blood for American money. One day when this terrible affair in Indochina ends, and it will end badly, I will be called before the High Court and accused, as I fear, of selling French blood, of being a French lackey to the Americans. It will not be fair, not just, but it will happen. I cannot risk it. I cannot ask Washington for this money that we so desperately need."

My mouth gaped open. "My God, Monsieur Bidault, are you suggesting that Washington *volunteer* to give you four hundred million dollars without you even asking for it?"

His face was shamed as he said: "Yes, I am afraid that is precisely the case. We want you to write a personal letter to explain this to your old chief, Eisenhower. Nobody else must know."

"Mr. Foreign Minister, I deeply regret that I cannot carry out your request. It is a serious breach of diplomatic protocol, as you know better than anyone. I cannot go behind the back of Douglas Dillon. He is Eisenhower's ambassador. I am a foreign correspondent. I am not, and legally am not permitted to be, an agent of the French government unless I register as such. I must tell you frankly that, from the start, as you know, I have been sharply opposed to your war in Indochina. I cannot contribute to the continuation of that war, a war that you yourself have just told me will end badly. I mean no offense, but this all strikes me as a move of desperation bordering on madness. I will not be a party to it."

Bidault heard me out without expression, almost as though he knew in advance exactly what I was going to say.

"Yes, yes, all that is true. But listen to me. I do not expect you to be an agent of our government. I respect your opposition to the war. I am not asking you to recommend anything to Eisenhower. You say you are only a reporter. Fine, splendid. That is how I want you to act, as a reporter. Simply report to Eisenhower everything we have told you today. He will make the decision. Your conscience can be at ease. You are not contributing to our war. You are only a messenger, a mail drop, as we used to say in the Resistance. And you are our good friend. You cannot refuse."

I looked at Bidault for a long moment, thinking of a way to help him that would be ethical and proper.

"Yes, I do believe in the need for French-American friendship. And I do not want to refuse you. I will do as you ask. I will write to Eisenhower. But on one condition. If you do not accept the condition, I will walk out of here and we will forget this conversation. The condition is this: I will tell the whole story first to Ambassador Dillon. It will then be his decision to tell me what he wants to do. I will only insist that he hear me out in the strictest confidence and inform him of your fear of leaks in Washington. That is what I am prepared to do. Dillon must approve. I will do nothing behind his back. My first loyalty is to my own country."

Bidault sighed, then reached out and took my hands. "So be it. I thank you. I am sure I will hear Dillon's decision."

I left the Quai d'Orsay and drove across the Pont de la Concorde to the American Embassy on the Right Bank, opposite the Quai d'Orsay. There, Dillon's secretary informed me that he was in Dijon at a celebration of the Tastevin *confrérie.* The Dillon family owned one of the most famed vineyards of France, Haut Brion, one of the finest grands crûs of Bordeaux. Dijon is the capital of Burgundy, the friendly enemy of Bordeaux. I knew that Dillon must be having a grand time in a brief escape from the constant crises that swirled around his embassy. I shuddered at what he would say when I called him back to Paris.

Dillon was furious. "What do you mean I must return to Paris at once but that you can't tell me why? Have you lost your mind? Are you sober? What the devil is going on?"

"Doug, I am sane and sober. If this were not of the utmost importance, would I risk my career by calling you? Do you know what Ed Murrow would do to me if this were a hoax or a minor matter? I'd never work again. You know me well and you know my contacts with the French. I am not fooling. This is important."

In a much calmer voice, Dillon told me that he would leave for Paris at once. He asked for my home phone number and told me he would call on arrival and that I would then come to see him at the residence, then on the Avenue d'Iéna facing on the Palais de Chaillot and the Tour Eiffel across the Seine.

As I walked into his study and told him my story, Dillon exploded. "Damn, damn, damn, the French have panicked. This is insane, unheard of. I won't have a private citizen writing a message of this importance from the prime minister and foreign minister to the President of the United States. You are a reporter and this is top secret. We can't go around Foster Dulles, over his head, directly to the President. Damn, damn, they ought to be whipped."

I was surprised at the fury of the usually cool, controlled diplomat and banker that Dillon was. I just sat there and let the waves of his anger roll by me. I was not going to say a word, not make a suggestion of any kind. He was going to have to make the decision, not I. I was an innocent bystander hit by a French truck. Dillon would have to be the ambulance driver and paramedic. Me, I was unconscious, out of it all. I was not about to take the most microscopic responsibility for this affair.

"I'm going to sleep on this. David, thank you for coming to me. I didn't mean to snap at you. You are only the bearer of unpleasant tidings. It's the French I'm furious with. You have done the right thing and I am grateful to you. Come to the embassy at 9:00 A.M., please, and I will have reached a decision."

I drove home, had a stiff drink, and tossed all night. Dorothy wanted to know what was wrong. I never had had a secret from her. I told her I would tell her when it was all over. I only assured her that I was not in any personal difficulty.

The next morning, Dillon told me that I should write the letter to Eisenhower at his desk. He would read it, seal it with the embassy seal, and write "Eyes Only for the President" on the envelope, then send it in the pouch that day. "Now, David, you forget the whole thing. You know nothing about any of this and you will not know what happened if and until the President acts upon it."

I was wise enough not to argue, not to ask for any kind of news break. I wanted to efface my role completely. I also knew that Dillon was grateful and that the President would be, too. One day, if I really needed a favor or help, this could count. I was, in any case, glad to be out of this mess unharmed.

"Bidault told me he expected to hear from you about this."

"Oh, he will, he will, you can be sure."

I got up and left after he had read and approved my letter. Dillon thanked me again for what I had done.

I smiled and said: "What are you talking about? I don't remember doing anything."

He grinned back. "Good man."

About a week later, browsing through the AP file in the office of their bureau chief, Preston Grover, one of the finest correspondents in the highly skilled Paris press corps, my eye caught an item that reported the arrival of a State Department envoy, Douglas MacArthur II, nephew of the contentious general. The news item stated that he would be talking with French officials about the combined French and American struggle against international communism in Asia.

I went to my CBS office three floors down in the 21 Rue de Berri *Herald Tribune* building and called Jacques Duhamel. I asked him if MacArthur's mission had any reference to our talk in the gardens. He told me it did and it looked as though everything would work out as desired. I debated sending a dispatch to Murrow, decided against it. This was one story I did not want to be first with. I would wait for an official announcement. It came the next day. Considering the heavy responsibilities of France in Asia and the high cost of fighting there, the United States government had offered aid to the extent of some three hundred and fifty million dollars. Bidault and Laniel had gotten what they wanted, the money, as an offer, without their asking for it.

I felt it was a waste of money, and a more tragic waste of French blood in a war they should pull out of. I felt badly that I had had anything to do with it. But I could not see, given the circumstances, what else I could have done. There are those who will certainly say that I should have refused the very minute the prime minister had told me what he wanted, and surely after Bidault's confession. I am vulnerable to criticism for having violated a professional standard, performing not as a reporter but as a diplomatic intermediary. I will not quarrel with such critics. I can only tell them that they cannot understand how I felt or why I did what I did. They were not in my shoes and did not share my long wartime comradeship with the French, my life of French studies, my passionate belief in the closest ties between France and the United States.

Soon after, I flew to Vietnam. In March of 1954, I watched the last acts of the Indochinese tragedy being played out. I spent only a few days in Saigon, just long enough for someone to ransack my room at the Hotel Majestic, pulling out all drawers, turning my clothes inside out, searching, apparently, for incriminating documents. The secret service of the South Vietnamese or the French must have known about my meetings with Ho in Paris and thought that I was planning to contact him. Two nights later I was having a drink on the terrace with CBS cameraman Wade Bingham, when a drunken sailor lurched toward me, muttering belligerently. I waved him away but he kept coming forward. Suddenly, Bingham, who had gotten up and walked behind the sailor, so that we could come at him front and back if he tried to fight, shouted, "Look out, Dave, he's got a knife." I reacted quickly, as I had been taught in hand-to-hand combat at Ritchie years before. I picked up the iron cocktail table and used it as a battering ram, pushing it into the sailor. Then, in another excellent self-defense move, I turned tail and ran like a rabbit into the hotel lobby, shouting, "Call the police!"

The drunken sailor turned surprisingly sober, got up and ran before the military police could come. It seemed to me that someone did not want me reporting from Saigon. I flew up to Hanoi, which was completely under army control. Many of the officers there were war buddies from North Africa and the liberation campaign in France. I was safer there in the heart of the combat zone than I was in Saigon.

The commanding general of the northern front was a six-feet five-inch giant who looked like a running guard for the Dallas Cowboys, René Cogny. He greeted me warmly and gave me a full briefing on the action. When I suggested that it was all in vain, and that the peace negotiations in Korea and the scheduled conference on Indochina in Geneva would bring an end to the war, he agreed. But he added: "We are hoping to inflict a defeat on the Viets at Dien Bien Phu and then pull out in good order."

I went over the map of the fortified bastion with him and asked what defenses he had against artillery from the crest of hills around Dien Bien Phu, which was down in a bowl and could be blasted to bits. Cogny frowned and said that they did not believe the Viets had much artillery or could bring it down over mountain trails from China. Therein he and the entire French command were grievously in error. The Vietnamese, helped by hundreds of Chinese coolies, with artillery shells lashed to their backs and howitzers and mortars trundled on double bicycles, could and did bring heavy artillery to the hills overlooking Dien Bien Phu. They had already begun bombardments when I reached Hanoi.

No correspondents were permitted into Dien Bien Phu but I talked an old friend from Algeria into letting me fly in on a medical evacuation plane, on my promise to remain just long enough to get the wounded on and then fly right back to Hanoi. Our plane circled the hills and I saw the puffs of smoke from the artillery and then mounds of earth defying the laws of gravity and gushing like a dirty brown fountain up into the air. Antiaircraft bursts shook our plane and I was relieved when the pilot dipped down swiftly and made a landing over a rutted strip that bounced our plane and threatened to tip us over.

Litters of badly wounded men were stretched out under canvas, waiting to be picked up. The men in the camp were smeared with dirt, wearing bloody bandages. Exploding shells whistled in. Later Bernard Fall would call it, in his book, "Hell in a very small place." There were about ten thousand men in the fortified camps and one woman, Geneviève de Galard, a nurse, whom they called "the angel of Dien Bien Phu." One could see at a glance that they were all doomed and that they knew it. I flew back in the med-evac plane among groaning and screaming wounded, my heart heavy at the senseless tragedy. Brave men were dying in a hopeless battle in the last hours of a cruel and stupid war.

I flew from Hanoi back to Saigon and saw the prime minister of South Vietnam, Nguyen Buu Loc. I had befriended him when he was lonely and snubbed in Paris as the ambassador of South Vietnam. He was a cousin of Emperor Bao Dai. I had also met in Paris another cousin, one of the most brilliant, finest men I have ever known, Nguyen Buu Hoi. Hoi was a member of the royal family but above all a distinguished scientist, an oncologist and pharmacologist, specializing in diseases that afflicted the poor and miserable in tropical and jungle countries. Hoi was a genius, on his way to a Nobel Prize as head of the Curie Laboratory in Paris when suddenly his heart burst and he died walking to his office. We had become close, and through him I had met many leaders of the Vietnamese colony in Paris and had come to respect them as extraordinarily creative people.

It was a tragedy that the French had given the communists a chance to wear the mantle of fighters for national independence against a colonial, white, Western power. Given a chance in freedom, the Vietnamese could have become a most successful people in Asia. They never got that chance, and after suffering for years under foreign rule suffered more when the communists finally took over the country.

Prime Minister Buu Loc told me that his observers in Geneva were reporting that the French would sign a peace treaty and withdraw from Indochina. He was both elated and distressed. Like all Vietnamese he wanted the French out, but he did not know whether his government, in the southern half of the country, could rally the people against the communists who controlled the northern half and could easily defeat South Vietnam in a civil war. He hoped that a Geneva peace treaty would divide his country in half, as in Korea, and keep the communists in the north. He was planning to fly to Geneva to make a plea to the Americans to hold the line against the communists and suggested that I fly with him. We agreed to talk again the following week.

I flew back to Hanoi for the death watch on Dien Bien Phu. I was in General Cogny's command blockhouse when the end came. Cogny was on a radio circuit with the commander of the bastion, Colonel de Castries. Castries told him that all his strongpoints had been overrun and that the Viets would soon be blasting into his last redoubt. "Well, then, good luck, old boy," said Cogny. "Yes, well, so long, General," Castries replied as we heard shouting and crashing noises. "Yes, so long, old boy," sighed General Cogny, and then there was silence.

It was May 7, 1954, a date that will live in Asian history. It was the first time that a band of peasants, lightly armed, had fought for seven years against one of the best Western armies and won. Japan had earlier shown that Asian soldiers could face the best troops of the West and defeat them, but Japan was an industrial power. Vietnam was an agricultural nation, small, underdeveloped, very much like the thirteen states and the minutemen who had fought and beaten the finest troops in the world of that time. The Vietnamese could look upon Ho Chi Minh and his commander, General Vo Nguyen Giap, as the Washington and Jefferson of Vietnamese independence.

Americans could not conceive of a communist Washington, and, indeed, Ho was not a Washington or a Jefferson, in our terms. He was, however, exactly that to many Vietnamese, the national leader of the fight against a colonial master. Ironically, the date, May 7, was the anniversary of the surrender of the Nazi generals in 1945. It would be a sad V-E Day anniversary in Paris. Just as Ho had predicted at dinner in 1946, eight years earlier, the tiger of Vietnam had clawed the elephant which had finally fallen, bled white in a trap of its own making.

I flew back to Saigon and discovered that the censors would not allow a word to be filed about the fall of Dien Bien Phu. I promptly sent the following message to Ted Church at CBS News headquarters in New York: "Unless you authorize me to proceed immediately to Geneva I resign. Fed up with this war. Nothing left to report anyway." Church read my telegram, called in his news editor, and told him to put out a bulletin: "CBS News has learned on reliable authority that Dien Bien Phu has fallen. The French-Indochinese War is all but over. The struggle now will be fought at the diplomatic conference in Geneva." Church then sent me a telegram of congratulations, clearing me to leave at once for Geneva. He took my telegram, had it framed, and put it on his office wall. I suspect that he was equally pleased at his own quick understanding of my message as he was of the means I had found to get through the censors.

I went to Prime Minister Buu Loc and he immediately booked two seats on the next morning's flights from Saigon to Paris to Geneva.

On arrival in Geneva, I went to see the under secretary of state, General Walter Bedell Smith, Eisenhower's wartime deputy, to whom I had sent my intelligence reports during the Battle for France. John Foster Dulles, whom President Eisenhower had appointed secretary of state, had come to Geneva as an "observer." He refused to participate officially in a conference alongside the representative of communist China. He left as soon as he could.

I told Bedell Smith what I had seen, told him that there was no hope of the French maintaining control. The only way to stop the communists would be to negotiate a partition of Vietnam into South and North, with the threat of massive intervention if the communists did not agree. It would be a poor solution and would not hold for long but it was the best that could be done.

Prime Minister Buu Loc told General Smith that this was his view, adding that the South, by itself, could not hold out. There would have to be a coalition of allies to defend it. Dulles was calling for a Southeast Asia Treaty Organization, SEATO, an Asian equivalent of NATO. He would get it later, as part of his worldwide game of building blocs, but it would be meaningless, with no Supreme Commander, no troops committed, no teeth, just a paper tiger, and all Asia knew it. Dulles fooled only himself and the Republican hawks, trying to prove that they were more anticommunist than the Democrats. Foreign policy was often the illegitimate child of domestic politics.

In Paris, the government of Joseph Laniel was defeated and the National Assembly turned to Pierre Mendès-France, the one political leader who had denounced the Indochinese War from the start. Mendès startled everyone in Geneva as well as Paris by proposing a thirty-day contract to end the war or resign as premier. The conferees went to work and finally produced a series of accords at the very last minute of the thirty-day deadline. The essential agreement ended the fighting and set up a "temporary" demilitarized demarcation zone between North and South Vietnam. That demarcation would disappear when free elections would be held in July 1956 to unify the nation into one Vietnam.

Everyone believed then, with good reason, that Ho Chi Minh, conqueror of the French, liberator of the nation, would sweep those elections. They were never held. South Vietnam had not signed the Geneva accords nor had the United States, which had attended as an observer, not a full member of the conference. John Foster Dulles supported the refusal of the South to hold elections. The "temporary" demarcation line became a fixed line, partitioning the country between North and South.

The brothers Dulles, John Foster, at State, and Allen at CIA, along with the new chairman of the Joint Chiefs, Admiral Radford, all hard-line hawks, pressured President Eisenhower to give full support and military aid to the premier of South Vietnam, Ngo Dinh Diem, one of the few Southern nationalists who opposed French imperialism.

Eisenhower refused. He offered limited economic aid but only on condition that Diem would effect democratic reforms that could rally the people against Ho and the communists. Eisenhower, the man of peace, would not commit the United States to the defense of South Vietnam. Eisenhower was not responsible for the tragic, mindless American decision later to intervene in Vietnam. There are those who claim that Eisenhower took us a long step toward war in Vietnam. I do not believe this. From the end of the French war in 1954 to the beginning of large-scale American intervention in 1964 a full ten years went by. Eisenhower could not have taken us very far if it took ten more years to get there, two Presidents later.

Eisenhower had made peace in Korea, had refused French requests to intervene in Dien Bien Phu. He then became the first American President of the Cold War to propose a meeting with the Soviet leaders. Dulles and Republican senators fought hard against it, fearing a "new Yalta." Eisenhower assured them he would make no concessions to the Russians without consulting Congress. On July 18, 1955, I was back in Geneva for the opening of the first summit conference among the chiefs of government of the U.S., Britain, France, and the Soviet Union.

The conference produced nothing more than a good feeling about peaceful coexistence. Even that was a major accomplishment in the climate of those days. Above all, it was a tremendous personal success for the man of peace. Even France's influential paper *Le Monde,* most often critical of the United States, stated that Eisenhower had "emerged as the type of leader humanity needs today." The American media and the Congress cheered "the spirit of Geneva," and the Gallup poll showed an unheard-of eighty-four percent approval of Eisenhower's Presidency.

One month later, President Eisenhower was in the hospital, having suffered a massive heart attack. In another month, Eisenhower celebrated his sixty-fifth birthday and received the best present possible from his doctor, famed cardiologist Paul Dudley White, who found him well on the road to recovery. By the end of the year, Eisenhower was back in the Oval Office, on a full schedule, confounding everyone by planning to run for a second term. In January 1956, Dr. White gave him a rigid examination and announced that if Eisenhower ran again, he would vote for him with confidence.

The President had a number of explosive domestic issues to deal with. A brave black woman named Rosa Parks refused to give up her seat to a white passenger on a bus in Montgomery, Alabama. When she was put off, the blacks began a boycott of the bus system, in which they represented about ninety percent of the passengers. The system began to go broke. A young preacher came to help and his name made the headlines for the first time: Martin Luther King. That was the first crisis that hit Eisenhower when he came back to work in January 1956. The next month, another courageous black woman, Autherine Lucy, became the first black to enroll at the University of Alabama. A civil rights revolution was breaking out throughout the South.

There were foreign crises impending, too. John Foster Dulles first offered aid to Egypt's Colonel Nasser for construction of a High Dam on the Nile at Aswân. Nasser accepted. Then, in July, irritated by Nasser's talks with the Russians about Soviet aid for Egypt, Dulles high-handedly, and with little foresight of the consequences, canceled the Aswân project. Nasser, humiliated and furious, announced that he was nationalizing the Suez Canal, a direct threat to the lifeline of what was left of the British Empire and a move that could cost the French, who administered the Canal, many millions in revenue and lost prestige in the Middle East. Nasser also stated that he could no longer guarantee the safety of Israeli shipping through the Canal.

There was a welcome break in stories of demonstrations and war threats when a world weary of gloom and misery responded joyously to the news of a fairy-tale romance. Prince Rainier III, Son Altesse Sérénissime, would wed a Hollywood princess, Grace Kelly. Their marriage would be a happy union until Princess Grace was killed in a tragic car accident many years later. Rainier is the sovereign of a tiny principality, Monaco, with one small city, Monte Carlo, site of the world's most glamorous and famed gambling casino. Monaco is about the size of Central Park, located on the Mediterranean, inside France, near Italy. Small as it is, the wedding would attract some two thousand reporters, cameramen, and photographers, more than had covered the Normandy landings or any summit meeting. Journalists are not stupid.

I had known Rainier for many years. His father, Prince Pierre de Polignac, presided over the Monaco Lecture Forum and had invited me to speak in the late forties. I had made a short film of Rainier as a young man, training tigers and lions in cages on the palace grounds. We had met later in New York, at River House, and he had told me he had come to America to find a bride. I had written the story of a prince looking for his princess, for *Colliers* magazine.

Don Hewitt came to produce a half-hour program on the wedding, which I would write and narrate. After all the violence I had covered, in the Middle East, North Africa, Asia, and America, the wedding of Rainier and Grace was a welcome relief. It did have difficult moments. Rainier was infuriated by an ABC News TV commercial in which a brassiere was superimposed over the Grimaldi Palace and threatened to bar all reporters. I was named international press pool representative and negotiated a code of conduct to appease Rainier. It was good fun.

The fun did not last long. War clouds were forming up again over the Middle East during the Presidential election campaign. Eisenhower was then hit by yet another crisis. In October, there was an uprising in Warsaw and a Soviet threat to invade Poland. Dulles, who had been irresponsibly issuing empty threats to "roll back the Iron Curtain," was so alarmed that he announced that there would be no American military aid to the Poles. Having virtually made a career out of berating the Democrats for letting Russia enslave Eastern Europe, Dulles turned and ran at the first opportunity to do what he had been calling for.

A few days after the Polish strikes and riots, antigovernment demonstrations erupted in Budapest, Hungary, on October 23, just two weeks before the Presidential elections. One week later, on October 29, Israeli armed forces invaded the Gaza Strip and the Sinai.

The French defense minister, René Pleven, called me in and informed me that France and Britain, under the terms of the Tripartite Agreement of 1950, had the responsibility for intervening if international traffic were threatened on the Canal and if the stability of the area was endangered. He asked me to see his aide, Jeanne-Paule Sicard, and to make sure she knew where I was at all times. "We will soon be in touch with you on an important matter," the defense minister said.

As Americans prepared to go to the polls for another choice between Eisenhower and Stevenson—with the issue not the least in doubt—Soviet troops and tanks, which had pulled out of Budapest, suddenly turned around on November 4 and attacked the city in an all-out assault. Incredibly brave Hungarians, from teenagers to grandfathers, filled gasoline bottles and threw them at Soviet tanks. Thousands fell wounded and dead in a hopeless fight against overwhelming force. The Soviets installed a new Hungarian communist government and threw heavy guard units around all public buildings while armored vehicles patrolled the streets of Budapest. One of the Soviet commissars in Hungary that day was a man named Yuri Andropov.

The next day, November 5, at dawn, I received an urgent call to see Defense Minister Pleven. He informed me that French and British planes were bombing Egypt and that landing forces were moving to seize the Suez Canal. He said I had been selected as pool representative for the Anglo-American press. "We will put aside a plane for the world's press and have allotted ten seats for Americans. You will have to work out your own system for selecting the ten men. Tell them to pack one bag and come to the Ministry for instructions."

There was no way that I was going to select the men to go. Those left behind would tear me to pieces. I called the major bureau chiefs to meet at my apartment immediately. There were more organizations than the seats allotted so we agreed to draw names out of a hat. One network would pool dispatches for the three majors, one wire service for three, two dailies, one weekly, one photo magazine. Fortunately for me, NBC won the network draw. If CBS had won, they would have accused me of rigging it. The correspondents who won the draw rushed home to pack. They would never get into that plane to Suez which the French were forced to cancel by an Eisenhower ukase.

Meanwhile I was dashing back and forth to the studio, broadcasting all through the day reaction stories on Hungary and the American elections, and French dispatches on the fighting in Suez. I called Prime Minister Guy Mollet, who agreed to give me a television interview. George Markham, the CBS cameraman, and Paul Habans, the soundman, set up our equipment in Mollet's reception room. I was chatting with the prime minister about how the interview would be done when he was called in by a white-faced aide. It was November 6. Eisenhower had won the election by a landslide. The British and French had gained control of the Canal, the Israelis had seized the Sinai peninsula. It was a critical moment to interview the prime minister of France. I waited anxiously for him to come back to our camera position.

Mollet never came back. An aide, flushed with anger, came in and shouted at me: "Your President Eisenhower has betrayed his allies. He has ordered us to withdraw from Suez. We told him we would not. But Anthony Eden caved in. The British have been pulling out their fleet, our sole means of transportation and supply. We are finished and will have to pull out, too. It's a double betrayal. De Gaulle is right. The Anglo-Saxons are not to be trusted."

I left my crew, ran to my car, and drove to our broadcasting studio, at Press Wireless, behind the Scribe Hotel, Eisenhower's wartime headquarters. I called CBS and did a number of short broadcasts on various aspects of the crisis to be run through the day, plus a longer news report for Murrow, detailing the rage and frustration of the French.

There was angry confusion in the American media and in Congress where some voices condemned the French and British for an anachronistic nineteenth-century act of imperialism. Others were sharply critical of Eisenhower for betraying his NATO allies and saving the skin of the Egyptian dictator, making him the hero of the Arab world. Others defended Eisenhower, asserting that intelligence reports had revealed the massing of Soviet paratroopers and an invasion force on the Black Sea ready to intervene in Suez, claiming that Eisenhower had averted a world war.

I, myself, had not settled on any sure judgment. I sympathized with the Israelis, who could be hurt badly by losing shipping rights through the Canal, a violation of international law. They had also, as Eisenhower would later write in his memoirs, been suffering casualties and destruction for months from Egyptian attacks upon them from the Sinai. Eisenhower would state that in his view the Israelis had acted after considerable provocation. It seemed as though Eisenhower was hinting that he might not have acted against Israel if France and England had not come in. Many students of world politics still argue that the French and British made a grave mistake, that they should have let Israel do the job for them.

The issue is still being argued three decades later. One of America's most respected writers, Theodore H. White, asserted that Suez had been one of Eisenhower's most costly blunders. He argued, as many do, that our troubles in the Middle East began with the humiliation of the Western powers and the triumph of Nasser in seizing and holding the Suez Canal.

I have thought about this deeply and for long. All of my sympathies were with Israel and the West. I was distressed by Eisenhower's decision to stop the allies and force them out. I feared Nasser and his pan-Arab ambitions. I have, however, finally concluded that Eisenhower had to do what he did. The risk of a confrontation with the Soviets was real. More certain was the threat that the entire Arab world would turn definitively against the West if Eisenhower had supported the Anglo-French invasion.

I cannot believe that the rise of Arab nationalism stemmed from Suez. The Arabs did not react as a unified group after Suez nor when they were defeated by the Israelis in the Six-Day War of 1967. They did not boycott the West and turn off the oil until 1973. It was only then that OPEC, the Organization of Petroleum Exporting Countries, was formed. Our troubles are rooted in the OPEC trust and the sharp rise in prices that brought inflation to the West and transferred billions from the democratic industrial nations to Arab dictatorships and feudal regimes. Suez took place a full seventeen years before OPEC. It is not reasonable to blame Eisenhower for troubles we suffered almost two decades later.

I, like everyone else, do not know what would have happened if Eisenhower had not halted the allied advance against Nasser. Perhaps Teddy White and other critics might be right. Maybe that was the spark that ignited Arab nationalism and led to OPEC. The causes of Arab nationalism and of the creation of the oil trust are complex and deep. I am trying only to argue that those who blame Eisenhower are no more certain of their charges than Eisenhower's defenders are of theirs. The world is so complex and unpredictable that it is extremely difficult to understand what happened and why, without indulging in the futile speculation about what might have happened "if only . . ."

The Suez affair further weakened an already tottering Fourth Republic. Within eighteen months it would finally fall, and once again it would be a crisis in North Africa that would strike the fatal blow, not in the eastern Mediterranean but much closer to home, in Algeria.

Ever since the victory of the Vietnamese revolutionaries over the French, the indigenous peoples of French North Africa had been demanding independence. France yielded in Morocco and Tunisia, which had been ruled as protectorates, maintaining the fiction of a native government merely "protected" by the French. It was easy to give them full independence. For more than a century, however, Algeria had been incorporated into the French Republic itself, as a *département,* the equivalent of an American state. It was an integral part of the motherland in the same way as the United States would integrate into our Republic the far-off lands of Hawaii and Alaska. Independence for Algeria was unthinkable to most French citizens and, above all, to those called *colons* who resided in Algeria and whose parents and grandparents had created Algeria. "*Algérie française*" was not only their battle cry against Arab revolutionaries, it was their most passionate nationalism, their religion.

The indigenous peoples had formed a revolutionary movement called the FLN, the Front de Libération Nationale, the Algerian equivalent of the Vietminh in Vietnam. They had created mountain strongholds and urban terrorist commandos and were engaged in an increasingly violent clash with the French. I had covered that growing crisis in some twenty to thirty missions to Algeria. It had become so important that it was necessary to have someone there almost constantly. My colleague Lou Cioffi alternated trips with me. He was a good reporter and had made a name for himself in the Korean War. In May of 1958, Lou was in Algiers when the situation worsened.

He called me in the Paris office one morning and chatted about personal affairs, asking about his wife, Naomi, and his two sons, about Dorothy and my daughter, Lucy. I waited patiently, knowing he had a reason for the small talk. Suddenly I heard him say, "Well, by now, the censor must be bored. Stand by for a recording and throw your switch." My phone was wired up to record. Lou had our soundman, Paul Habans, with him, and Paul had wired Lou's Nagra tape recorder into his hotel phone.

Lou's voice came through again, this time on tape, telling of fighting in Algiers and the imposition of censorship. A censor was sitting in the broadcast studios and checking all scripts carefully. By patching through to me on the hotel phone, Lou was taking a big chance. He could be arrested by the military. We would be able to get him out, for there had been no declaration of war or official censorship by the French government. The locals were obviously taking authority into their own hands. But Lou might get roughed up in the process. I told him not to do it again. He insisted that he would. He was fighting mad and felt he would not let them obstruct his work as a reporter.

I kept getting his messages for the next three days, worrying constantly about him. He said they were a bunch of idiots and did not know what he was doing. I warned him that they were dangerous idiots and to stop playing Richard Halliburton. Lou just laughed me off.

The fourth day, the phone call from Lou did not come in. I was afraid he had been caught. As president of the Anglo-American Press Club in Paris, I had a lot of clout, and a number of leaders, Laniel, Bidault, Faure, Pleven, were in my debt. If Lou were in trouble I could get him out. I had first to find out why he had not called. Lou was safe but it took some time to find him because communications broke down.

I called the long-distance operator and asked how long it would take to get through to Algiers. She told me she could not put me through at all. I asked for the supervisor, one of the telephone sources I had cultivated for a long time, with perfume, cigarettes, and a Christmas bonus for special service. I had not abused my privileges with her and was sure she would give me a priority line.

Her voice was low and a little unsteady as she told me that she could not put me through to Algiers. I pressed. "A break in the line?" "No, sir." "Trouble on this end, censorship?" "No, sir." "Over there?" A pause, and then she said very slowly and with heavy emphasis, "Monsieur Schoenbrun, listen to me carefully. I cannot get through to Algiers, I CANNOT get through."

I thanked her and hung up. Something big must have happened in Algiers and communications had been cut to metropolitan France. I called General Ely, chairman of the French Chiefs of Staff. His secretary told me he was not in and she did not know when he would be. After a few probing questions, she finally told me the general was at the presidential palace in an emergency meeting. I called Jacques Duhamel who told me that Edgar Faure was at that same meeting. "All of them, Jacques?" I asked. "All of them," he solemnly replied.

I called the overseas operator and asked for a press priority call to CBS News in New York. It came right in and I heard our day editor, Bob Skedgell, asking me what was up. I told him to patch me into a recording machine, I had a hot exclusive for him.

A moment later, Bob said I was patched in and to go ahead in five seconds.

"Communications have been cut between Algeria and France. The top Cabinet ministers and military chiefs are meeting at this moment in an emergency session with President of the Republic René Coty. The long-feared coup d'etat by French civilian and military men engaged in a counterrevolutionary fight against the FLN, not trusting the weak governments of Paris, may well be in course at this moment. The Fourth Republic of France is in its death throes. I'll try to be back with more details as soon as possible."

Skedgell came on the circuit. "My God, David, there isn't even a hint of this on any of the wires. Are you sure of your sources on this? Is this absolutely reliable, or would you like to qualify it and tone it down?"

"Bob, go with it. I'm sure. I'll bet my job on it."

"Yes, indeed, Dave, you might well say that. Okay, I'll risk my neck but if it's wrong, yours is the head that will be chopped off. Get back fast if you can get any further details or confirmation. I'm putting a bulletin alert on the net right now. Good luck."

I hung up triumphant and terrified. If I were wrong, it would be my head, all right, not just from CBS but from a jittery French government. I decided to walk over to the presidential palace, just across the Champs-Elysées from my office. As I walked to the corner, I heard horns blasting away in a steady rhythm, two longs, one short, two longs—DAH DAH DEE DAH DAH. I then heard drivers and their passengers leaning out of the windows shouting "DE GAULLE AU POUVOIR" in the same cadence. The word must have gotten out by shortwave radio that there was a coup in Algiers, and people in Paris were shouting for de Gaulle to return to power.

I ran back to my office. The wire service teleprinter was already pounding out the news. People were massed at the presidential palace and at the Assemblée Nationale, main house of Parliament. The deputies were meeting and many were calling upon the prime minister to resign and call in de Gaulle.

My phone rang. It was Ed Murrow. He wasted no words, beyond a quick "Nice work, Buster." He began questioning me about what was going on in Paris and then asked me to record a five-minute piece for his program that night, giving the latest news and backgrounding it with the whys, the hows, and the what-nexts. I adlibbed off the top of my head for I had been living with the story for weeks.

The colons in Algeria believed correctly that the French government in Paris was too weak, too unstable to put down the uprising of Arab nationalists demanding independence. They made common cause with many French Army officers, still smarting from their humiliating defeat and withdrawal from Indochina. They began planning to seize Algeria and to call for a strong leader like General de Gaulle to take charge again.

De Gaulle, brooding in self-imposed political exile in his home in Lorraine, silently watched events, made no public pronouncements, but met at home and on the telephone with loyal friends who wanted him back in power. Finally, street demonstrations for de Gaulle in Paris, and the loss of control in Algiers, so frightened a defeatist, weak Parliament that its leaders finally asked the government to resign and asked the president of the Republic to call in de Gaulle to form a new government. Unwilling to serve as prime minister under the constitution of the Fourth Republic, which gave too much power to the legislature, de Gaulle was determined to come back only as the president of a new Fifth Republic with a constitution granting most power to the executive.

General de Gaulle finally left his self-imposed retreat in Colombey-les-Deux-Eglises and came back in triumph to begin a new life in his late sixties as president of the Fifth Republic of France. His wartime comrade General Eisenhower was entering the last two years of his public life as President of the United States. I had worked closely with both men, knew them well, and knew that there would be more French-American frictions with the prideful, nationalistic de Gaulle back in power.

It was fortunate for all that Eisenhower was the American President at that moment. He had been the only top American for whom de Gaulle had had respect and some feelings of friendship. If anyone could handle the prickly Frenchman it was Eisenhower. Events proved that this was a correct evaluation. There would be serious French-American conflicts but not until after Eisenhower had left office. While he was there, de Gaulle kept the lid on. Eisenhower had a unique ability among Western leaders to get along with de Gaulle. Perhaps his greatest quality was the fact that all through his Presidency he demonstrated over and over again that allied unity and peace were his top priorities, particularly peace.

Eisenhower defied his own party's war hawks time and again, not only on world peace but on civil peace and respect for the law at home as well as abroad. He supported the Supreme Court decisions against segregation and did not hesitate to use federal power against Orval Faubus, the lawless segregationist governor of Arkansas who tried to prevent black children from attending white schools in Little Rock. He refused to intervene at Dien Bien Phu and held American military aid and advisors for Vietnam to less than eight hundred unarmed men. At the height of the Cold War, Eisenhower sought détente and coexistence by attending a summit conference with the Soviets. When he invited Nikita Khrushchev to visit him in 1959, he became the first American President since the Bolshevik Revolution in 1917 to invite a Soviet chief of government to visit and tour America. He halted a war in the Middle East.

Eisenhower's record was not perfect. He was a President, not a saint. The United States wallowed in economic stagnation and suffered through three recessions. Eisenhower sent Marines on a brief and feckless intervention into Lebanon, and let the CIA overthrow the government of Guatemala. A Paris summit conference was aborted when a U-2 spy plane, overflying Russia, was shot down. Eisenhower took responsibility for the flight. He proceeded with production of more and more destructive atomic weapons, from the fission bomb to the fusion bomb, a thousand times more powerful than the first-generation bombs that destroyed Hiroshima and Nagasaki. There is much that can be criticized in his Presidency.

Yet Eisenhower was alarmed by the increasingly awesome power of the atom bombs and by the drainage of money, materials, and brains from the civilian sector to the military. This was the main theme of his farewell address to the American people. The advice he gave, which has been ignored, was even more important than the more famous farewell address of our first President, George Washington, and it was more accurate. Eisenhower saw the future more clearly than Washington had. Washington had advised us to avoid entangling alliances, not foreseeing how we would grow into a world power and be unable to live in isolation. Eisenhower warned us to beware of the military-industrial complex which, at worst, could lead us into a war that could destroy the world or, at best, bankrupt us in an uncontrolled arms race.

I believe that the last words he addressed to the American people as President were the most important ever spoken by any President. They cut right to the heart of a critical debate still raging in the 1980s. This is what the "man of peace" said:

". . . we have been compelled to create a permanent armaments industry of vast proportions . . . We annually spend on military security more than the net income of all United States corporations. This conjunction of an immense military establishment and a large arms industry is new in the American experience . . . Yet we must not fail to comprehend its grave implications. Our toil, resources and livelihood are all involved; so is the very structure of our society.

"In the councils of government, we must guard against the acquisition of unwarranted influence, whether sought or unsought, by the military-industrial complex. The potential for the disastrous rise of misplaced power exists and will persist.

"We must never let the weight of this combination endanger our liberties or democratic processes. We should take nothing for granted. Only an alert and knowledgeable citizenry can compel the proper meshing of the huge industrial and military machinery of defense with our peaceful methods and goals, so that security and liberty may prosper together . . .

"Disarmament with mutual honor and confidence is a continuing imperative . . ."

I wish that this farewell address were taught in all our schools, at every level, primary, secondary, college, and university. If humanity is to survive and if the United States is to regain its economic and fiscal health, it will only be when some President rereads his great predecessor's thoughts and acts upon the advice of the man of peace.

CHAPTER 16

WAS IT REALLY CAMELOT?

Eisenhower left office as the oldest President in American history, the last President to have been born and gone to school in the nineteenth century. Whoever won the election to succeed him would represent a symbolic centennial change, for the most likely candidates had been born and reared in the twentieth century.

Eisenhower himself could not seem to make up his mind whom he favored as his successor. Only one thing was clear at the outset of the run for the nominations, he did not like his own Vice-President, Richard Nixon. Eisenhower did not like Kennedy, either. He felt he was an overly ambitious, inexperienced young upstart not qualified to be President. That did not hurt Kennedy, for no one expected Eisenhower to support a Democrat. It was his failure to help his own man, Nixon, that became decisive.

At one point, Eisenhower was asked about possible successors whom he could support. The first name he mentioned was his secretary of the treasury, Robert Anderson. He then added other names and it took him time to mention, at the end of the list, Dick Nixon. He then hurt Nixon badly at the end of August when he was asked at a news conference what major decisions of his Administration Nixon had participated in. Eisenhower's highly inaccurate and quite inexcusable reply was: "If you give me a week, I might think of one."

It was an incredible indictment, even if true, and it was not true. Nixon had shown skill in settling a steel strike when Eisenhower was incapacitated in the hospital. There were many instances of Nixon's contributing to Administration decisions, and he had shown what many Americans considered to be Presidential qualities in his much admired "kitchen debate" with Khrushchev at the Moscow Fair. Eisenhower never publicly explained or retracted his remark. He would only campaign earnestly for Nixon at the last moment in the last week. Many observers thought that he had cost Nixon the election. It would be so close that a greater effort by Eisenhower could have made the difference.

The decisive event of the campaign took place on the night of September 26, in the first, all-network radio-television debate between Kennedy and Nixon. Some seventy-five million Americans, one of the largest audiences in radio-television history, watched that debate, enthralled by the tensions and the stakes. The debate was an outstanding success for Kennedy. It was not that he was better than Nixon but that he held his own against the more experienced and older Vice-President of the United States. Nixon's supporters could no longer charge that Kennedy was a callow youth with no grip on national or world affairs. By agreeing to debate with Kennedy, Nixon had lifted up the relatively little known young senator and made him his equal.

Nixon did not look his best, which is none too good, in the debate. He was exhausted from a twenty-five-state barnstorming tour. He had lost weight, was gray-faced and haggard, and looked sinister with Lazy Shave pancake makeup smeared over his dark beard which no amount of shaving could quite remove. Kennedy was tan, graceful, glowing with youth and self-confidence. Most of those who heard the debate on radio thought it was a standoff, but many thought that Nixon had won. On television it was also a standoff in debating points but not on the tube. The TV image of handsome, stylish Jack Kennedy triumphed over glowering Richard Nixon. It was a chilling thought that the way a candidate looked on television could decide an election.

By Election Day, all pollsters were saying it was too close to call. They were right. Kennedy's margin of victory was infinitesimal, barely one hundred thousand votes out of some sixty-eight million. With a number of observers reporting corruption in the count in

Texas and Cook County in Chicago, it was thought likely that Nixon had, in fact, won. Nixon finally decided not to test the enormously complicated and explosive issue of a recount, which could delay the installation of a President and leave the nation either ungoverned or the White House crippled.

Snow was falling heavily at dawn of Inauguration Day. It had been falling all night long, blanketing the capital. Ben Bradlee, the *Newsweek* correspondent, had been out partying until half past three in the morning and was in a deep sleep at seven o'clock when the bedroom windows of his Georgetown house rattled loudly. Ben groaned and turned over, burying his head beneath the pillow. Then the windowpane seemed to crack with the sound of a pistol shot. Ben shot up in bed. "Whatinhell?" He lurched out of bed and stumbled sleepily to the window. As he reached it, he saw a big snowball come arching up to hit it again. "Goddamkids," Ben muttered and reached to pull up the window.

As he looked out, another snowball hit above his head. He gaped at the guilty "kid." It was Jack Kennedy, President-elect of the United States, a few hours away from being sworn in as President. Kennedy was twirling a top hat. He saw Ben at the window and did a pirouette, shouting, "How do I look?"

Ben rubbed his eyes, and shouted back, "Right now I can't see anything through these bloodshot eyes. Please go back to bed, Jack, and let me get some sleep. I've got to cover the inauguration today."

Kennedy laughed. "Don't worry, Ben, I'll be there and I'll tell you all about it." He threw his hat high in the air and whirled around, catching it on the turn, then bowed to Ben and returned to his house for breakfast.

Bradlee would tell me that Kennedy and his friends were conscious of being young, with the world in their hands, and they were ready and eager to play football with it. Politics was a game and they had played it well and won the election. Now the stakes were bigger but they never doubted for a moment that they would succeed. They would never have believed anyone who had told them they were riding for a fall.

Graceful and slender, standing in the wind and bitter cold, hatless and coatless, the young and handsome PT boat commander stood at attention as the silver-haired Chief Justice, Earl Warren, swore him in as President of the United States. In a high-pitched voice, stretching out the broad *a*'s of Boston, the youngest President in our history proclaimed: "Let the word go forth from this time and place, to friend and foe alike, that the torch has been passed to a new generation of Americans." He went on to pledge that Americans would pay any price, bear any burden, for the preservation of freedom, and he exhorted his fellow Americans not to ask what their country could do for them but what they could do for their country.

There were many men of my generation, the ones to whom the torch was being passed, who thrilled to those words that day. I must confess that I did not. I had been buffeted too often by the winds of wars, hot and cold. I was allergic to high-flown rhetoric, having heard too much of it from Harry Truman and most recently from John Foster Dulles. The Truman Doctrine had led us into a massive rearmament program, the building of blocs and bases around the world. Jack Kennedy's "Haarvaard" accent may have sounded very different from the flat prairie tones of Harry Truman but it seemed to me both men were saying the same thing. The New Frontier sounded old and too familiar, however young and new the man who was making that speech.

I particularly resented the suggestion that Americans should not ask their country for anything but should instead ask themselves what they could do for their country. That struck me as demagogic and jingoistic. I loved my country, had fought for it, and was willing to do what I could for it. But I also had the right to ask my country what it could do for me. Democracy requires a two-way relationship between state and citizen. Anything less is statism, dictatorship. The Declaration of Independence proclaimed that Americans were forming a government to promote the general welfare of the people. We have a right to ask our country for jobs, for social security, for health insurance, just as the state has a right to ask us to pay taxes and to defend it against its enemies.

I admit that I was prejudiced against Kennedy at the outset and only began to appreciate his many qualities after I had met him and begun covering his Administration in Washington. My prejudice grew out of his undistinguished record as a congressman and senator, and his careless parroting of the China Lobby hawks who charged that inept American leaders had "given China to the Reds."

I had the impression that Kennedy was reckless. I was also

alarmed by the record of his brother Robert, who had been a lawyer on Joe McCarthy's Subcommittee on Government Operations. Later, when I met Bob Kennedy, I found a man maturing rapidly into a responsible official, with a first-rate brain, moral courage, and a compassionate concern for the poor, the hungry, the repressed minorities of America. But, during the election campaign, I was rooting silently for the Kennedys only because I could not abide "Tricky Dicky" Nixon.

President Kennedy appeared in a better light, as an heir to the Roosevelt tradition, when he issued Executive Order Number 1 on his first morning in the Oval Office. It called for the doubling of food rations for some four million poor Americans. The day before, during his inauguration, his keen eyes had noted that there was not one black face among the Coast Guard cadets who marched past the reviewing stand. He immediately asked his counselor and closest aide, Theodore Sorensen, to check on it and to correct what looked like discrimination in one of the armed forces.

Kennedy brought a number of Harvard alumni to Washington, men of outstanding ability and learning: McGeorge Bundy, Robert McNamara, and many scholars. There were so many Harvard men pouring into Washington that everyone took note when Orville Freeman, an outsider, a Minnesotan, was named to the Cabinet as secretary of agriculture. When asked why he was selected, Freeman replied with a straight face: "I suppose it is because Harvard does not have a school of agriculture."

Kennedy's very closest associate, however, was a man from Nebraska, a young lawyer of impressive brilliance, Theodore Sorensen. Some White House observers started to call him, to his distaste, the Deputy President. Sorensen was his speech writer, researcher, analyst, main source of judgment on national affairs. McGeorge Bundy was his National Security advisor, principal aide on foreign affairs, with more influence and access to the President than Secretary of State Dean Rusk.

The only member of his inner circle whom I knew well at first was his press spokesman, Pierre Salinger, a professional reporter, well read, intelligent, and a jovial fellow. In addition, Pierre, of Alsatian origin, spoke French and was a Francophile. He was therefore familiar with my broadcasts from Paris and that helped establish a good relationship between us. In early December 1960, a month before the inauguration, Pierre had been in New York with the President-elect, who was meeting with the powerful leaders of Wall Street, the banks, and New York's academic community, consulting on appointments that he would be making to his Cabinet and the diplomatic service.

I called Pierre and asked whether he could arrange a brief meeting with Kennedy. Pierre thought he might want to meet me to talk about de Gaulle, who fascinated Kennedy and with whom he would shortly have to argue out differences over NATO. A few hours later, Salinger called back to say it was okay and I was to come to Kennedy's suite at the Carlyle Hotel at about six. Kennedy would be leaving at about six-twenty to fly to Boston.

I turned up a little ahead of time and Pierre told me that Kennedy was running a bit late on his appointments. "Go down to the garage and ask for Sinatra's car. It's a white convertible, with a Secret Service driver. Here's a note to him telling him you'll be driving to LaGuardia with Kennedy. That way you can get your fifteen to twenty minutes with him alone in the car."

I was sitting in the back of the car, parked in front of the Carlyle, when cameramen and photographers came running out to catch pictures of Kennedy emerging from the hotel. Someone spotted a figure in the car and flattened his nose on the window to peer inside. I slunk down and pulled my hat over my eyes just as JFK walked into the car. He saw me and laughed. "Don't try so hard to hide, you're making yourself conspicuous."

I laughed in turn and told him how President Beneš of Czechoslovakia one day had told me not to make myself so small, I was not so big. Kennedy threw back his head and laughed loudly. He enjoyed true anecdotes with sharp and witty points and would often ask me in the brief years ahead to tell him de Gaulle stories or Churchill stories, both men whom he admired.

As the car turned east, heading for the Fifty-ninth Street bridge, Kennedy asked first about de Gaulle. Then he began to talk about the right kind of man to be his ambassador to France. I suggested a writer, a poet, an historian, a Foreign Service officer, an experienced diplomat like Charles "Chip" Bohlen, anything but a banker, industrialist, or a military man. Kennedy chose Bohlen, breaking my near perfect record on Presidential rejections of my advice. He then asked about the U.N. We ran through a long list of names.

He did not by so much as a flicker let on that he had already decided to appoint Adlai Stevenson. As our car drove out across the tarmac to his waiting plane, Kennedy shook hands, thanked me, and hoped he would see me in the White House. As we got out of the car and began walking toward the plane, the Washington reporters traveling with him spotted us. One of them, my CBS colleague Dan Schorr, a man with a sometimes caustic sense of humor, shouted, "Who's that fellow walking alongside Schoenbrun?"

Our talk in the car and Kennedy's frenetic pace showed that he was a man in a hurry, with no time to waste. Having won less than half the ballots cast, a minority President, Kennedy set about proving himself by frenzied activity. He was in the Oval Office at seven-thirty in the morning and did not leave it until seven-thirty at night. Any aide who did not come in before eight was in trouble because the President might call him at any moment from seven-thirty on. Unlike Eisenhower, who delegated as much as he could and did not want to be bothered by anything other than broad policy questions, Kennedy wanted to know every detail of every department and every issue. A day in which fifty visitors came to the West Wing was a slow day. The New Frontier was a nonstop track meet. He was trying to do too much, too soon, running at full speed, and a stumble could be disastrous. It was. Kennedy plunged headfirst into Cuba's Bay of Pigs in one of the worst fiascos in American history.

The plan to arm anti-Castro Cuban exiles for an invasion, based on the wishful thinking of a Cuban uprising against the communist regime, was quixotic, ill-conceived, incompetently managed. Thousands of brave men marched to their death and imprisonment in an affair that was bungled from start to finish by the CIA and the Joint Chiefs. Kennedy publicly took responsibility for the failure but in private he stormed against the "experts" who had misled him and the Cubans.

Ted Sorensen would tell me later that Kennedy wondered how he could have listened to "experts" of whose fallibility he had long been aware. I have always believed that he let them push him into the foolish venture because they were much older than he and more experienced, because they had told him, inaccurately, it had been planned by Eisenhower, and, finally, because he had been elected by less than one percent of the voters and felt he should not go against the advice of all the senior men who had worked with Eisenhower.

The humiliation of the Bay of Pigs pushed Kennedy even closer to a Cold War stance. He told the American Society of Newspaper Editors, meeting in Washington, that the United States was prepared to act "regardless of the cost and regardless of the peril" and "act alone, if necessary," to protect its security. He lashed out at Moscow in harsh terms, asserting that he would not brook criticism from those "whose character was stamped for all time on the bloody streets of Budapest."

Khrushchev, with a sharp eye on the new President, felt that he had revealed his inexperience and uncertainty in the Bay of Pigs. He had the opening he was looking for and prepared to strike and strike hard. A summit meeting between the Soviet and American leaders had been scheduled for June. Early in May, Khrushchev wrote to Kennedy asking for confirmation of their meeting. Kennedy, determined to show no signs of weakness or hesitancy, promptly confirmed an early June meeting in Vienna, on neutral ground. The news delighted me, for they would be meeting in Schönbrunn Palace, seat of the imperial Hapsburgs in the Viennese suburb of Schönbrunn. I had always dreamed of signing off a news report with "This is David Schoenbrun reporting from Schönbrunn, now back to CBS News in New York." I would get that opportunity later, but not at that summit meeting.

All Europe trembled whenever the two superpowers met face to face. More than any others, the French are ever fearful of "another Yalta." They are neurotic about Yalta. My editors wanted me to stay in Paris and report reaction to the summit. "Hold de Gaulle's hand," they told me, "and report every tremor."

I was disappointed to miss the summit but excited about Kennedy's decision to come to Paris and see de Gaulle before meeting with Khrushchev, a wise decision. De Gaulle was a statesman of unparalleled experience, a tough political fighter on the top levels after years of jousting with Stalin, Churchill, and Roosevelt. His advice and encouragement would be helpful and he would be pleased to be consulted by the new American President.

It was embarrassing for Kennedy to hold his first meeting with de Gaulle so soon after the disaster of the Bay of Pigs. De Gaulle, however, had just suffered an intense embarrassment of his own. Foreign Legion paratroopers, an elite unit of the French Army, had led a revolt against de Gaulle in Algiers. They joined forces with ultranationalistic French colons, who had vowed to keep Algeria French, had seized public buildings and arrested General Gambiez, commander of the French forces, in a coup d'etat. De Gaulle had made a radio appeal to the draftees who were loyal to the motherland, and to loyal officers. They refused to join the rebels and put down the coup. So both de Gaulle and Kennedy had suffered severe challenges to their leadership and were ready to help each other. Their meeting was mainly a "get-acquainted" session and no important agreements were sought.

Kennedy went on to his meeting with Khrushchev. He knew it would be rough. Khrushchev was a blusterer and a bully. He had shocked the world delegates at the United Nations by shouting, pounding his fists on the desk, and finally pulling off a shoe and using it as a gavel to emphasize his points. Averell Harriman, the American who knew the Russians best, the most experienced diplomat in Kennedy's Administration, advised the President to be cool and not respond to Khrushchev's tirades. Behind his bluster, Harriman said, Khrushchev would be as nervous as Kennedy. His was not a one-man dictatorship. He had a tough Politburo to report to and enemies who would like to bring him down. "Don't get into a shouting match," Harriman counseled. Eisenhower, who, on occasion, would resort to the crude barracks language of his army youth, liked to say, "Never get into a pissing contest with a skunk."

The meeting was even worse than Kennedy had feared. Khrushchev delivered an ultimatum which could lead to war. He told Kennedy that Berlin was "a bone in the Soviet throat." That bone must be removed. If the West did not withdraw from the divided city, the Soviets would sign a peace treaty with the East German communist government, a member of the Warsaw Pact. Thus any attack upon that regime would be considered an attack on the Soviet Union, a casus belli. "I don't want war, but if the United States wants to go to war over Berlin, so be it. The guilt for war will be on your head."

Kennedy came out of the meeting white-faced and exhausted. As they took leave of each other, Kennedy told Khrushchev, "It will be a cold winter." He then told Reston of the *Times* that Khrushchev had seen the Bay of Pigs as proof of Kennedy's inexperience and lack of guts. Kennedy concluded that he had to act and act in such a way as to demonstrate that the Bay of Pigs was an aberration and not reality.

All the world learned of Khrushchev's ultimatum on Berlin. It was then followed by a big increase of more than three billion rubles in the Soviet military budget. Kennedy countered by raising the American military budget by three billion dollars, quite a bit more than the ruble chips. It was a game of high-stakes poker. Khrushchev boasted that Russia had the most powerful nuclear bomb, fifty megatons. Then, in August, just after midnight on the thirteenth, Soviet tanks lumbered through the streets of East Berlin, while soldiers took up positions on the border of West Berlin and trucks unloaded workers with piles of bricks and bags of cement. When the sun rose, startled Berliners saw a wall being erected between the two sectors.

The Berlin Wall did no harm to the West. It became a symbol of the failure of communism. Tens of thousands of East Berliners had steadily been leaving and taking up residence in the West. The communist regime was losing its best educated, most professional people. The wall was built to stop the drain. East Berlin became a communist prison for its own people and a demonstration to the world that, given a choice, people would opt for the democratic, capitalist West, not the socialist state of the East.

The Voice of America ridiculed the Soviets and taunted them on imprisoning the East Germans. Kennedy rejected out of hand Khrushchev's demand that he control all Western flights into Berlin and let it be known that American fighter planes would accompany civilian flights if there were any interference. The West German Democratic Republic rejected vigorously Soviet demands that West German political leaders not fly into West Berlin. The German press began running retrospective stories about the Berlin airlift which had made Stalin back down and lift his blockade in the late forties.

Khrushchev got the message and began to back down. By the end of the year, he had waved away his own ultimatum and announced that he did not absolutely insist upon signing a peace treaty with East Berlin. He airily disposed of the Berlin issue by stating that two million Berliners did not count for much among a billion communists. The immediate crisis was over. There would be others. Far more serious crises were ahead.

I would be facing a personal crisis decision in the last weeks of 1961 as a result of a conflict between my former London colleague and close friend Howard K. Smith and top management in CBS. Bill Paley, once an admirer of Smith's, proud of his weekly radio news analysis from London on European affairs, which won awards and brought praise and prestige to CBS, had soured on him. Howard could say almost anything he liked from London about Europe, but when he replaced Eric Sevareid as chief Washington correspondent, and began appearing regularly on television as well as radio, Smith's sometimes biting commentaries provoked important people in Congress, the White House, and Wall Street.

CBS had once been a profitable but middle-sized corporation. In the early sixties, it was growing rapidly into a conglomerate closely watched by Wall Street. The richer Paley became the harder he had to work managing his money. I thought often of the financial advisor who had told Ralph Ingersoll that a man could control anything up to a million dollars but beyond that the money controlled the man. Paley proved his theory. He was no longer proud of his outstanding newsmen. He told Murrow, at one of their last meetings before Murrow left to take over the U.S. Information Service and the Voice of America for President Kennedy, that every time he heard about a new Murrow documentary, he felt a sharp pain in his gut. Murrow told me that Paley "had lost his guts."

Howard Smith had replaced Murrow as Paley's "pain in the gut." Paley was just waiting for the right moment and the right issue to get rid of him. It came in the making of a documentary on Birmingham, Alabama. Smith was there when a mob of bully boys, wielding ax handles and whips, stopped a bus and brutally beat up civil rights workers riding to a rally. Smith, born and reared in New Orleans, with a deep hatred of Southern racism, watched in horror as brutes clubbed unarmed, defenseless men and women. He saw the Birmingham police standing by watching, making no move to stop the beatings.

Smith was not only a Southerner ashamed of those racists who sullied the honor of the South, he had also been the CBS correspondent in Berlin. He had seen the rise of Hitler supported by Nazi street fighters. He was appalled to see what he felt were the same scenes in his own native land. In his closing commentary on Birmingham, Smith quoted Edmund Burke, saying, "The only thing necessary for the triumph of evil, is for good men to do nothing." Fred Friendly, the producer, and other CBS executives, certain that Southern stations would refuse to carry the program with a denunciatory commentary, asked Smith to kill his end-piece editorial. Smith refused.

Friendly exacerbated Smith by telling him that commentaries like his were not needed on the Birmingham report because the pictures were so dramatic that they told it all, no comments needed. This was and remains a typical producer syndrome: A picture is worth a thousand words. Friendly's point may have been well taken in this instance, but it hit Howard where he lived, telling him that his commentary was superfluous, that the cameraman had said it all.

There was a nasty expression coming into use in those days, still current today. Commentators and news analysts were called "talking heads." It is a term used by producers to express their disdain for men who deal in words and ideas when all they want are action pictures. The world of producers is overpopulated with yahoos and know-nothings who believe that thoughtful men slow up their "shows." The very best producers, men like Don Hewitt, respect their correspondents. Egomaniacs like Friendly put them down, as do the legions of mediocrities among the producers of news programs.

ABC, a bad third in the network competition in 1960, was looking for genuine superstars, men who had won awards and were highly respected newsmen. They took Howard Smith on at a generous salary and gave him his own news program on Sundays. It was a good move for Smith, for his days were numbered at CBS. Anyone who falls out of favor with the chairman will not be long with the company.

CBS News was in trouble. For a decade and more we had been more than number one, we were in a class by ourselves with no competition for the Murrow team. Then a huckster named James Aubrey, Jr., had been named president of the network. He made no secret of his disdain for the News Division. The big money in television was in entertainment. Paley, by then, was more interested in profits than prestige. News was kept under a tight rein.

It was at this critical moment in CBS developments that I was called in to learn that the executives had decided to name me as chief correspondent and bureau chief in Washington. I was startled. I had been certain that they would either recall Sevareid from London or name Charles Collingwood. I was flattered, honored, and disturbed. I had never forgiven the false security charge back in 1952, and had resolved never to work in Washington. I was well dug in in Paris, both personally and professionally. I was on top of my beat, with the most and best sources in town. I knew how to operate there. Washington was, for me, an alien place. I told CBS News President Richard Salant that I would talk it over with my wife and I asked for time to make a decision.

"Take all the time you need, David," said Salant grandly, "why, take as much as forty-eight hours."

I called Dorothy and gave her all the reasons why I would turn down the offer. She listened quietly, then said, "Fine. Now tell me why you are going to take the job."

I laughed and said, "Only if you agree, Dot."

The reason was simple and it overrode all the objections. Kennedy had said that the torch had been passed to a new generation of Americans—"born in this century, tempered by war, disciplined by a hard and bitter peace, proud of our ancient heritage . . ." That was my generation. I felt he was talking to me and about me. It was time for me to join those picking up that torch, time to go home, time to be an American reporter, not a foreign correspondent.

The most important news center in the world was Washington. By going there, I would share in the new adventure, in the city they were already calling Camelot, with Kennedy cast as King Arthur and the men around him the Knights of the Round Table, with Jackie as the beauteous Queen Guinevere.

Not since Roosevelt's first term had there been so many intellectuals, artists, poets, and writers working in Washington or invited to the White House. Kennedy's taste was eclectic, far-ranging, his friends including Frank Sinatra, Robert Frost, Norman Mailer, "Rosy" Grier, John Kenneth Galbraith, Theodore White, Ben Bradlee. His White House dinners were famous for their star-studded guest lists and his witty toasts. His brother Bob gave hilarious parties at his home in Virginia. There were hand-wrestling contests, push-up competitions (Teddy White almost had a heart attack after defeating Bob Kennedy by doing twenty-nine rapid push-ups). Upon occasion, a guest would be thrown or fall into the swimming pool. There were high-spirited, fun-loving, and also hard-working men and women in Camelot, and, as in the Arthurian legend, spicy tales of sexual adventures.

Above all, Kennedy and his Knights were determined to make good upon their promise to "get America on the move again." I wanted to be a part of that. I also knew, although it was less important, that my income would double and I would become a national face and name. I did not want to end my career as a specialist of French affairs. I wanted to become an American and world-affairs reporter. Washington was the place for that.

I knew it would be tough. Howard Smith had told me of the constant pressures under which he worked. Paley and Stanton had their own direct relations with members of Congress and with major lobbyists for business interests, including the interests of their advertisers. They were constantly afraid of provoking the commissioners of the FCC, who had supervisory and punitive powers.

Unlike Paris, where I was the acknowledged expert beyond challenge, Washington was overflowing with experts and politicians sensitive to any criticism of their favorite projects. I felt that my tenure would be limited but that if I could last through Kennedy's first four years I would have accomplished my goals. By 1964, I would have been a reporter for more than twenty-five years, in strong shape, ready for anything that might come next. I had no illusions about lasting longer and no desire to stay on beyond the first term. I was so certain that my tenure in Washington would be brief that I kept my Paris apartment and persuaded my housemaid to stay on for room and board and a weekly retainer to keep the rooms clean until our return.

My arrival in Camelot could not have been more pleasant. A beautiful and intelligent young woman, Nancy Hanschmann, was just beginning to break the male chauvinist prejudices against female reporters. She had been working for producers procuring congressmen and Administration personalities for our Sunday talk show, *Face the Nation,* and knew everyone in Washington. In addition, an aunt of hers owned the most exclusive club in Washington, the F Street Club. Nancy gave a "Welcome to Washington" dinner party for me at the club. Among the guests were Ed Murrow,

Defense Secretary Robert McNamara, General Maxwell Taylor. I felt like a Lilliput in the land of Gullivers, as all the men, well over six feet tall, towered over me. It was a glamorous evening and I was amused to see the secretary of defense tear around the dance floor in an exuberant rhumba. I wondered what the FBI would think of that, remembering their suspicions of my own rhumba passion.

Ben Bradlee, my old Paris buddy, gave a reception in the cramped garden of his Georgetown house. It seemed to me that all the Knights of the Round Table were there: McGeorge Bundy, Ted Sorensen, Pierre Salinger, Arthur Schlesinger, Ken O'Donnell. Finally, briefly, at the end of the reception, King Arthur made an appearance. The President smiled, shook hands, and left, but his coming was a tribute to Ben Bradlee.

The round of welcomes over, it was time to go to work seriously. I had learned in my years of reporting that success depended on two essentials: knowing your subject completely and accumulating a list of news sources, with office and home numbers. I had already read dozens of books about every aspect of American life. The first step, then, would be to establish relations with as many news sources as possible.

The first call I made was to Kennedy's alter ego, Ted Sorensen. We met for lunch at a small restaurant off Lafayette Square near the White House. I knew that the top New Frontiersman would not touch alcohol during a working day, so I suggested tomato juice and saw a small, knowing smile on Sorensen's lips. He cocked an eyebrow at me and said, "No apéritif?" I grinned back. "This isn't Paris, I'm a Washingtonian now." I knew I had to let him know I intended to get into the mainstream rapidly.

The New Frontiersmen were very macho, proud of their no-nonsense toughness. They were not Arthurian Knights. Camelot was a style, a charming fantasy, not an appropriate symbol. Sorensen demonstrated this at once. He fixed me with a cold eye and said: "It will be best for you to know right off that I am not impressed with the fact that you are the chief correspondent and bureau chief of CBS. Those are just titles, they are not the man. If you are going to get access to the White House, you'll have to prove yourself personally, earn your way. CBS has given you this first appointment with me. The rest will be up to you."

I returned his cold eye with a warm smile, but a bit of a tough counterpunch of my own. "Fair enough, Sorensen. I feel the same way about you, your colleagues, and the President himself. I'm going to keep a close watch on you. I'll judge you on your performance not on your style or your august titles. You'll get approval on the air if you earn it. If you foul up, you'll hear about it."

Sorensen's eyes gleamed. I had hit just the right note. He relaxed, stretched his hand across the table. "Okay, that's a deal. Now let's have a quick lunch, I've a lot to do."

I then had to go to the FBI office for fingerprinting and a color photo for my permanent White House identity and accreditation card. I shivered as I recalled my meeting with Lou Nichols. But that was all in the past. My accreditation came right through and it was time for a formal introduction to the President. Our meetings before his inauguration did not count. Protocol required a formal introduction. Salinger told me to report to the office of Mrs. Lincoln, the President's secretary, who sat at one of the entrances to the Oval Office. The other entrance was well guarded by Ken O'Donnell.

To my surprise, it was not Salinger who was waiting to bring me in, it was McGeorge Bundy, more affable than when I had met him in his own office. The President was buzzed and was getting up from his desk to greet me as we entered. Bundy said, "You know Mr. Schoenbrun, Mr. President." Kennedy smiled, put out his hand, and dazzled me by saying, "Oh, yes, I have read everything he has written. Even used some of it." Salinger must have tipped him off that I was prouder of my writing than of broadcasting. He had said exactly the right thing to win me over and I knew that I would have to be careful not to be captivated by him. There is nothing more dangerous to a free reporter than to come under the spell of a powerful and charming President. I would, by a conscious effort, keep free of Kennedy's charm and would never have to face that problem again with Johnson, Nixon, Ford, Carter, or Reagan.

Kennedy went to his rocking chair and waved me to a sofa near him. His first remark caught me off-guard. "Well, Schoenbrun, after all these wonderful years in Paris, how do you feel about coming to Washington?" I gulped and my mind raced. What in the world do you tell a President about his own capital? I knew that Kennedy was highly intelligent and would see through a phony answer at once.

"Well, Mr. President, it is of course a challenge and an honor to be here. I haven't been back long enough for any considered judgment. But, at first look, I would say that I like the people but not the food."

"Is that so?" Kennedy replied. "Hmmm. I would put it just the other way around."

We both laughed and the ice was broken. We chatted for about fifteen minutes, mainly about de Gaulle. Kennedy arose to end the talk and said politely that the door of the Oval Office would always be open to me. I knew that was just pro forma but it was nice to hear. In fact, it did prove to be more open than I had had any reason to hope. My experience around the world interested Kennedy and he would want to know about men and issues with which I was familiar. When, for example, King Hassan of Morocco was coming on a state visit, Kennedy asked me to tell him about the young sovereign whom I had known since he was a youngster of seventeen.

I had done many reports on Morocco's demands for independence when King Muhammad V was the sovereign, and Hassan the teenage heir to the throne. He revered his father and knew he had been friendly with me. On his father's death, Hassan, now king, invited me to the funeral and then the new coronation ceremonies, on which I did CBS news reports.

When King Hassan II gave a luncheon to honor President Kennedy at the Moroccan Embassy in Washington, I was one of two journalists invited, the other being Walter Lippman. The guests were among the top men in the President's Administration: Secretary of State Dean Rusk, Secretary of Defense Robert McNamara, along with National Security Advisor McGeorge Bundy, and Assistant Secretary of State Averell Harriman. I wondered who was running the government that day.

After lunch, we were served brandy and coffee in a reception room, while the king and the President sat down at a sofa at the end of the room, along with a State Department interpreter. I was standing, my back to them, at a distance, chatting with Dean Rusk, when the secretary said: "David, the President is signaling for you."

I turned in astonishment and walked to the President and the king. Hassan II said, "I asked the President if he would mind if you interpreted for us. I will feel more comfortable with you than an official interpreter." I looked at Kennedy, who had an amused smile on his face. He nodded his assent.

One exchange remains fixed in my memory. Hassan remarked that he and Kennedy were the two youngest leaders in the world. He confessed he had some anxiety about his youth and inexperience and asked how Kennedy felt. The President smiled and replied, "Because of our youth, we are not weighed down with all the baggage of history. We may have much to learn, but we have little to unlearn."

Everything went well for me on my reportorial rounds but not inside CBS. My colleagues in the Washington bureau had resented my appointment over their heads. I shrugged off their somewhat unfriendly attitude. They would learn that I was fair and generous and would help them when they needed help. If they wanted to cold-shoulder me, that would be their loss not mine. I had no time to waste on office politics and I had no intention of staying long in Washington.

More seriously, I was having problems with the top people in New York. I would learn that every Washington bureau chief would be in almost constant conflict with the home office. The *New York Times* men in Washington waged open warfare with their New York editors, even the publisher. We were all proud men, jealous of our prerogatives, guarding our turf, not letting New York second-guess us, fighting off pressures by Administration and congressional powers who would complain to New York when they did not like our critical reporting. Kennedy did not hesitate to use his power from time to time. It became intolerable later under Lyndon Johnson.

In Paris, I used to send cables offering news stories to Hewitt who produced the Cronkite show, or he would cable requesting news reports. There was rarely any conflict, for I was their man in Paris and they counted on me to explain the complex, often controversial policies of de Gaulle's government. They would not dream of questioning anything I said. Washington was totally different. There I would telephone Hewitt before noon and discuss an analysis piece for the evening. After writing it, I would telex it up to them. Cronkite, managing editor of his own program, would read it and discuss it with Hewitt. They would then set up an afternoon conference call about two hours before air and discuss my piece with me, sometimes suggesting changes or arguing about my point of view.

There was a day when I had done an important interview with

the French ambassador and it was canceled because Don Hewitt had just received some dramatic pictures of movie stars' homes going up in flames in a forest fire. There was no way I could explain to the ambassador why the interview had not been used. Every day was a hassle. I never knew what I was going to broadcast until a few hours before air, or whether I would be on or not. Friends, family, and news sources would ask me when I would be on and when I would use a story we had done, but I would never know. It was irritating and frequently embarrassing.

There was only one real solution to my problem. Like Howard Smith at ABC and Brinkley at NBC, I needed a show of my own. I was the only chief correspondent without a column in the papers or a news program on the air. I had many unpleasant sessions with Blair Clark, general manager, and Salant, president of CBS News, who told me that I was getting important national exposure on the evening news with Cronkite, even if I were not regularly scheduled. They accused me of egomania, a strange accusation in a medium peopled with egomaniacs.

I tried to explain to them that it was not just ego, although that was a part of it, but that I had learned that power resided in controlling air time. I could put leverage on important men if they knew I could put them on the air. The real power in television had moved from the reporters and even the on-air stars to the producers who controlled air time. I could not be an effective chief correspondent, or compete with David Brinkley, as they wanted me to, unless I had my own program. This battle raged on for weeks and I was becoming, as predictable, a "pain in the gut," not to Paley but to the news executives.

CBS Washington only had one program of its own under network President "Jungle Jim" Aubrey's close-fisted allocation of time to the News Division. It was the Sunday program *Face the Nation,* a showcase for Washington politicos. The anchorman was Paul Niven, accompanied by two or more bureau reporters to question the guests. It ran a poor second to NBC's *Meet the Press,* but ahead of ABC's *Issues and Answers.* New York asked me if I wanted to take over that program. I recoiled in horror. The very worst crime a bureau chief could commit would be to take over someone else's show. The whole staff would revolt. I refused firmly.

Meanwhile, there was my reporting to do and my learning process. I felt I could not be well versed in American affairs by sitting in Washington, so I made many trips across the country, from Bangor and Boston to Atlanta and Miami, across to New Orleans, then on to Oklahoma City and Dallas and Cleveland, not in one tour, but on weekend sorties. I gave lectures at universities and civic clubs in order to hear the questions my fellow Americans were asking and their criticism of television, which was sharp and constant.

I learned what I had already suspected, that people heard what they wanted to hear and were happy only when their own prejudices were aired. We were accused of being pro- and anti-Kennedy, soft on communism but also cold warriors. I remembered a radio commentary Murrow had once done: "I am a racist, nigger-lover, anti-Semitic Jew, a communist, a fascist, a great patriot, and a traitor, and I have letters from my listeners to prove it all." Obviously, the only tack was to ignore complaints and do the very best, most honest job one could do.

There were few gripping crises in the first six months of 1962, nothing that I could not handle without too much pressure. In mid-January, the Soviet tanks stationed at the Berlin Wall were withdrawn after Kennedy pulled out our emergency task force. That crisis was easing. In February, Kennedy ordered a ban on almost all trade with Cuba, after Cuba's membership in the Organization of American States had been suspended.

Kennedy then ordered the creation of a Military Assistance Command (MAC) for South Vietnam. I had a chance to talk with him that week and argued strenuously against it, warning that it would grow and get him involved in a dangerous trap. I knew it was bad form to argue with a President. A correspondent should use valuable Oval Office time to learn what he could from the President and not sound off on his own views. But I was thoroughly alarmed about the dangerous drift of Vietnam policy. I had talked with his top advisors and found them not well informed about Vietnam. War hawks like Walt Rostow and others were leading him into danger. Kennedy respected my knowledge of and experience in Vietnam but tended to dismiss it on the grounds that I had covered the French wars and that America was not the same as France, an arrogant assumption.

On February 14, Kennedy announced that U.S. troops in Vietnam were not "combat troops" but that they were authorized to fire to protect themselves if fired upon. His feet were on the slippery slope sliding to war in Vietnam.

In March, in retaliation for Soviet violations on a ban on testing atom bombs, Kennedy announced that the United States would resume nuclear testing. The arms race was heating up. The lovely fairy tale of Camelot was restricted to state dinners for important visitors with famous artists performing. I would attend some of those dinners, such as the one for the French Nobel laureate André Malraux, when, after dinner, we were treated to a concert by a most talented trio: Isaac Stern, pianist Eugene Istomin, and cellist Leonard Rose. Kennedy was in pain that night, his back hurting him as he sat in a small gilded chair and grimaced. The story went around that Malraux had seen his grimaces and had whispered to Jackie: "Doesn't the President enjoy music?" Jackie was supposed to have replied, "Only 'Hail to the Chief.' "

In April, Kennedy approved the explosion of a nuclear device near Christmas Island, the first such testing by the U.S. in the atmosphere in three years, definitely not an act of chivalry. Doctors and environmentalists began to complain bitterly about his irresponsible decision. The Soviets, the previous September, had conducted many more such tests, poisoning the air we all breathe, but that was no excuse for us to follow their evil lead. In July, defying more protests, Kennedy approved a thermonuclear explosion over Johnston Island, an explosion equal to 1.4 million tons of TNT. The arms race was on in deadly earnest and Eisenhower's farewell address forgotten.

Eisenhower said nothing. He sat silently on his Gettysburg farm. Later, his Cabinet secretary, Max Rabb, would tell me that a delegation of top brass from the Pentagon, including West Point classmates, had gone to see him to plead with him to keep quiet because his warnings had been hurting their rearmament programs.

In September important crises began to erupt. James Meredith was denied admission to the University of Mississippi by Governor Ross Barnett, in defiance of a federal court order. Kennedy promptly sent U.S. marshals to Oxford to escort him to the campus. Mob violence broke out and two men were killed before the police, with the aid of federal troops, restored order. On October 1, Meredith entered the university as an accredited student.

Just before the Meredith crisis, Kennedy had revealed that Russia had signed a treaty with Cuba to provide arms and technicians to Castro. The President warned publicly that if Cuba were to become an offensive military base for the Soviet Union, the U.S. would do "whatever must be done" to protect its security. That crisis occurred just as New York management gave in and let me have air time for my own news show. It could not have come at a more appropriate moment, for the most dangerous war threat since Korea was on the point of explosion.

We had agreed on a title for the program: *Washington Report with David Schoenbrun.* It was given a time slot in what was known as the "Sunday ghetto," noon, when people were coming out of church and going home for a big Sunday lunch. In the Midwest it would be 11:00 A.M., and in the Rocky Mountain zone, 10:00 A.M. Jungle Jim Aubrey was not exactly giving away prime time for my program. No matter, I had my platform and was determined to put on the finest news program in the country.

The format was simple enough: I would anchor the program and present the top news. Three or four of my bureau colleagues would appear to report special stories on their beats, generally George Herman covering the White House, Bob Pierpoint and Neil Strasser on the State and Defense Departments, Roger Mudd on Congress. I would do some "name" interview, other staffers would do inside-Washington stories or "brighteners," and I would close the program with my own news analysis.

On my first program in September I got off to a fast start with an exclusive White House interview with President Kennedy. It was a coup because the President rationed his television appearances carefully. He was ever mindful of the dangers of overexposure. No one understood television better than he or manipulated it better to his own ends. An earlier television special I had done with him on the occasion of the Trade Act of 1962 had been well received. Protectionists in Congress were hostile to the bill and he needed public support at that time. Kennedy had had Salinger tell me that I could have an exclusive with him if I could persuade former President Eisenhower to support the proposed bill on the same program. He had used us to get Eisenhower to support his legislation on the Trade Act.

Better than anything was the fact that almost every Monday

morning following my Sunday program, a news story presented on it was quoted in *The New York Times.* "Making the *Times*" was the supreme accolade that any television program could attain and very few ever did. My program began making the *Times* often. I could not have been happier. I was not worried about the ghetto time slot. As a journalist, I had what every ambitious reporter dreams of, my own byline, my own column on the air.

Barely a month after *Washington Report* had made its debut, it had to cope with the most explosive news development since Pearl Harbor, one which threatened to take the world over the brink and plunge it into nuclear war. I would find myself one Sunday morning looking right into the abyss.

The senator from my home state of New York, Kenneth Keating, a moderate Republican, an ordinarily quiet, responsible man, began to make unusual charges. At dinner in my house, Ken Keating startled everyone by saying in private what he had not yet said publicly, that he believed the Russians were preparing to put atomic warheads into Cuba. He told me he would let me know when he had information he judged reliable enough to make that charge publicly. Until then all he had been saying in the Senate was that a great number of Soviet cargo ships and freighters had been sailing into the Cuban port of Mariel, a deep-water port. The ships had very wide hatches and carried an unusually large number of Soviet technicians as passengers.

On October 10, Keating announced that reliable informants had reported to him that Soviet technicians were building six intermediate-range missile sites in Cuba. A week earlier, rumors were rife that Castro's personal pilot was purported to have boasted over drinks that Cuba had long-range missiles and atomic warheads.

On Sunday, October 14, on *Washington Report,* I carried Keating's charges and all the rumors about atom bombs in Cuba, as well as Administration denials that there was any proof of these charges. The Russians had never sent any missiles or atom bombs outside the borders of the Soviet Union, except under direct control of the Red Army. None of Russia's satellites in Eastern Europe, easily controlled by the Russians, had been given any. Cuba was not a member of the Warsaw Pact or even the communist bloc. Castro was considered unstable and unreliable and it seemed inconceivable that Khrushchev would entrust weapons that could incinerate the world to the posturing Cuban dictator. McGeorge Bundy,

Kennedy's National Security advisor, appearing on ABC's *Issues and Answers* that afternoon, asserted that Keating had been misled by the generally unreliable reports of anti-Castro refugees.

On that same Sunday, October 14, two U.S. U-2 spy planes were flying over Cuba photographing the island. That night Pentagon photographic analysts were painstakingly studying the pictures, centimeter by centimeter. By the next day they had discovered that Keating's charges were accurate. On Tuesday morning, October 16, McGeorge Bundy carried the photos into the President's bedroom and informed Kennedy that the experts had concluded beyond doubt that the Russians had smuggled offensive missiles and probably atomic warheads into Cuba.

The President directed Bundy to call key members of his Cabinet to a late-morning meeting. About a dozen key men were put on twenty-four-hour alert as members of an emergency Executive Committee of the National Security Council, to be known as Ex-Comm. I knew many of them extremely well and would be calling them and their staffs hourly trying to get bits and pieces of what was happening. Among them were: Charles Bohlen, newly appointed American ambassador to France; Douglas Dillon, former ambassador, with whom I had worked out the secret letter to Eisenhower on aid for Indochina; George Ball, under secretary of state, former lawyer to Jean Monnet, a steady hand and a disciplined mind; Presidential Counselor Ted Sorensen, with whom I had by then established an easy relationship. There were others more difficult to reach: McGeorge Bundy, Robert McNamara, Maxwell Taylor, Lyndon Johnson, Dean Rusk. It was a blue-ribbon panel of tight-lipped men who knew how to keep a secret.

Yet the very fact that a meeting of so many important men was held at the White House could not be concealed. We all knew that Keating's charges had been verified. By dint of constant telephoning and hard questions, the most experienced and knowledgeable reporters were able to fit together the bits and pieces of the story. I was on the phone with my sources, editors, and Cronkite all day long and far into the night. It was vital to know what was happening but even more vital to take care not to provoke a national panic. This was one story that we did not want to "break." We would no longer use rumors and would not go with anything that was not approved or stated by a top official.

Later we would learn of the discussions that were going on at

Ex-Comm. Bob Kennedy had become the chairman of the group, the discussion leader. The President, to show a front of calm, had left Washington for Boston Wednesday, the seventeenth, to campaign for Democratic candidates in the midterm legislative elections coming up in November. New U-2 photos shocked the Ex-Comm members, for missiles were now clearly visible and some two dozen sites were being rushed to completion and could become operational probably by the following week. The Soviets could be able to fire some forty to fifty nuclear warheads at targets throughout the United States. No one wasted time speculating about their intentions. It was their capability that gripped everyone's attention.

A majority of the Ex-Comm members, including normally prudent bankers like Dillon, secretary of the treasury, were calling for immediate air strikes. The secretary of defense, Robert McNamara, who knew more than Dillon about the horrors of nuclear war, was more cautious. Yet even he did recommend what was technically an act of war: a naval blockade of Cuba. A blockade would, at least, avoid bloodshed and would be less obviously warlike than bombing. Other options were put on the table: a U.N. Security Council meeting, an emissary to Khrushchev, an all-out invasion of Cuba.

By Thursday, October 18, the crisis had deepened. Intelligence estimates now put the missiles in Cuba at almost half the entire arsenal of the U.S.S.R. Were they all to be fired, as many as one hundred million Americans could be incinerated or killed by the blast and the fallout. The wild man of Ex-Comm, Air Force General Curtis Le May, demanded an immediate all-out attack on Cuba. Kennedy, remembering "expert" advice during the Bay of Pigs crisis, was not impressed by Le May's assurances. Someone remembered Roosevelt's "quarantine the aggressor" speech and proposed that we call the blockade a "quarantine," making it seem less an act of war.

The idea of a quarantine was leaked to a few reporters, and I was able to report it to Cronkite as a kind of trial balloon for the idea. Dean Rusk suggested that a deadline for action be set for Tuesday, October 23.

On Friday, October 19, the President flew off on another camouflage campaign in Chicago. It then became known that the Joint Chiefs had put the Atlantic and Caribbean commands on the alert, an operation so vast that it could not be concealed.

On Saturday, back in Washington, President Kennedy made the decision to order the Navy to blockade Cuba. B-52 bombers, fully loaded with atomic bombs, took to the air in a twenty-four-hour patrol. On Sunday, letters were drafted to more than forty heads of state and to Willy Brandt, mayor of Berlin. A special letter was prepared for Khrushchev. Urgent cables warned American ambassadors around the world to take measures to meet possible demonstrations and riots.

General de Gaulle, informed by former Secretary of State Dean Acheson of the details of the crisis and the measures Kennedy would take, asked Acheson to tell the President that he was behind him one hundred percent and would have done exactly what Kennedy was doing. De Gaulle might quarrel fiercely inside the family but stood firmly with us in time of danger. Not one of the forty-odd foreign ambassadors voiced any criticism. Congressional leaders grumbled that a blockade was not enough but gave their support to the President.

At 7:00 P.M. precisely on Monday, October 22, President Kennedy appeared before the microphones of all the networks, solemn, determined. He stated the facts simply and at once. He said that the Russians had put missiles into Cuba whose purpose was "none other than to provide a nuclear strike capability against the Western Hemisphere." He called the Russian move a "deliberate deception," and pledged that he would remove this nuclear menace. He described the naval "quarantine" as only the first step. Other measures would follow until the Soviet missiles and warheads had been removed from what he called that "imprisoned island." He asserted that any Soviet vessel that tried to run the blockade would be sunk and that any missile launched against any target from Cuba would be considered an attack on the United States that would bring a powerful retaliatory attack upon Russia. These were strong words, stopping just short of a declaration of war.

No one slept very well that Monday night. Dean Rusk would greet George Ball in the morning and grin at him. "Well, we are still alive." In truth, he had not been sure he would see that new dawn. More remarkably, the Soviets had not made a move anywhere, not in Berlin, not in the Dardanelles or against our bases near them in the Middle East. Moscow had been caught off-guard and was marking time debating its next moves.

The Organization of American States met on Tuesday morning

and unanimously endorsed the U.S. "quarantine" by a vote of 18 to 0 with only one state, Uruguay, abstaining.

Tensions mounted on Wednesday when some twenty American ships closed the blockade ring around Cuba, while about twenty-five Soviet vessels moved closer toward a confrontation, and a Soviet submarine was seen moving like a shark among them. U-2 photos showed round-the-clock work proceeding on the missile-launching sites and analysts informed the President that more than twenty jet bombers could be uncrated and in action in a day or two.

The first break in the tension came in midmorning when most of the Soviet merchantmen stopped advancing toward the ring of steel and a dozen of them suddenly took sharp turns and began heading away from Cuba. It was then that Secretary of State Dean Rusk made a remark that would be quoted often and become part of American history: "We were eyeball to eyeball and the other fellow blinked."

Early Thursday morning, the twenty-fifth of October, the Navy made its first interception of a Soviet vessel. The ship was known to our naval analysts. It was the oil tanker *Bucharest.* Our captain signaled him to proceed through the blockade. Then an East German passenger ship was waved through. No weapons-carrying freighters had yet challenged the blockade. Workers were still scurrying like ants around the missile sites and the jet bombers were being uncrated. Soviet Ambassador Valerian Zorin foolishly challenged our U.N. ambassador, Adlai Stevenson, to prove his charges about missiles in Cuba. The secrecy in Washington had been so tight that Zorin was not aware of the massive photographic evidence we had gathered.

Stevenson pounced like a tiger against a tethered goat. He challenged Zorin to deny that the missiles were there. "Yes or no?" he shot at Zorin. "Don't wait for the translation, yes or no?" Zorin snapped back, "This is not an American courtroom." Right, Stevenson retorted, this is "the courtroom of world opinion and you can answer yes or no." Zorin backed away. "You'll have your answer in due time." Stevenson moved in for the clincher. "I am prepared to wait for your answer until hell freezes over . . . and I am also prepared to present the evidence in this room."

The amphitheater of the United Nations was hushed and expectant as Stevenson strode confidently to covered easels, pulling off the sheets around them like a magician about to make a stunning apparition. He revealed giant blowups showing the Soviet missile sites in Cuba. Zorin slunk in his seat, defeated. We had clearly won the diplomatic battle. The real test was still ahead.

Just after dawn on Friday, October 26, a U.S. destroyer, appropriately named the *Joseph P. Kennedy, Jr.,* after the President's older brother (who had been shot down and killed in a bombing raid in World War II), ordered a Soviet freighter to heave to. It did, and an armed boarding party of Americans clambered aboard and began a search. There were no weapons on board and the freighter was waved on its way. The blockade had won its first test. Moscow had ordered its captains not to resist search parties and not to try to force the ring.

The deep gloom in the Oval Office did not lift, however. More photos revealed that the missile sites were on the verge of becoming operational. They might be ready to fire off their missiles within hours or another day at most. Pierre Salinger released this information at his White House press briefing. Tensions were at a peak and we were teetering on the brink of war.

That afternoon there was a strange development in the crisis. John Scali, who covered the State Department for ABC News, received an urgent phone call from Alexander Fomin, known to be a high-ranking KGB, Soviet Secret Service, officer, at the embassy. He pleaded with Scali to meet him within ten minutes at a nearby restaurant. At the meeting Fomin asked Scali to find out if the State Department would negotiate an agreement with three provisions: the removal of the missiles under U.N. supervision; a pledge by Castro to forego any future offensive weapons; a balancing American pledge not to invade Cuba. Scali, his mind boggled by being made intermediary on a crisis threatening to explode into war, told Fomin he would check it out with Rusk and get back to him.

While Rusk was still studying the Fomin proposals and reporting them to the White House, a long letter arrived from Khrushchev, disjointed, rambling, highly emotional. For the first time, the Soviet leader admitted that there were Russian missiles in Cuba. He offered to pull them out and take a pledge to send no more if Kennedy would agree not to invade Cuba. It was essentially the same proposal Fomin had passed on to Scali and Rusk. For the first time in almost two weeks the tension eased. The President rubbed his red eyes, stretched his weary and aching back, and prepared for a night's sleep, certain he would see a better dawn. His Soviet experts would be up all night studying the Khrushchev and Fomin proposals and deciding how to reply.

Suddenly, a bolt of lightning struck from the East. A second letter from Khrushchev arrived just as White House experts were drafting a positive reply to the first one. The second letter was not at all conciliatory. It was tough. It demanded that the United States dismantle its missile bases in Turkey as a condition for the withdrawal of Soviet missiles from Cuba. This was, the White House men knew, a perfectly valid demand but one that would embarrass the President, weaken our NATO credibility, and balance the books as though we were as guilty as the Soviets. It would let Khrushchev off the hook.

The Ex-Comm was in session. The President, stunned and furious, turned to Secretary of State Dean Rusk and snapped, "Didn't I ask you weeks ago to get those missiles out of Turkey?" Rusk hung his head and mumbled something about having been occupied with other affairs of state. The President froze him with a subzero stare, his blue eyes two chips of ice. Robert Kennedy later described the scene in his book *Thirteen Days.*

Bad news tumbled in on bad news. The tough new letter was followed by FBI reports that Soviet diplomats were preparing to destroy their documents, a traditional move on the brink of war. An American photo plane had been shot down over Cuba by a Soviet SAM antiaircraft missile. The Joint Chiefs of Staff, in emergency session, recommended that the President order a massive air strike on Monday to be followed by an invasion of Cuba. The recommendation came to the Ex-Comm meeting. Everyone, with one exception, approved the recommendation. The one exception was President Kennedy. He told his committee, as Lincoln had once done with his Cabinet, "All Ayes and one No. The No carries it."

Robert Kennedy, who had emerged as Kennedy's strong right arm, came up with a genial solution to their dilemma. He suggested that they simply ignore the second letter and reply only to the first letter. He said it was clear that the first letter had been written by Khrushchev. The style was definitely his and the proposals were reasonable. The second letter had just as surely been written by a committee of hard-liners in the Politburo who were either trying to stiffen Khrushchev or were challenging him. We could strengthen him and avoid the harsher terms of the second letter by answering the first. And pray that Khrushchev was still hanging on.

Robert Kennedy and Ted Sorensen drafted a reply which the President endorsed. Robert Kennedy called the Soviet ambassador and told him that an affirmative response had to be received by the next day, October 28.

I awoke at six o'clock that Sunday morning, the thirteenth day of the Cuban missile crisis. In America, 13 is held to be an unlucky number. In France, however, 13 is lucky. I told myself that after all my years in France maybe some French luck had rubbed off on me and we would get through that thirteenth day alive. I jumped out of bed, showered, made myself a glass of orange juice, toast and coffee, taking care not to disturb Dorothy who had suffered through the crisis with me, nerve-jangling day after nerve-jangling day.

I walked into my deserted newsroom just before seven o'clock, made my way to my private office and tuned in to a morning newscast. Nothing but yesterday's news rehashed. The producer and associate producer of my *Washington Report* were in the cutting room editing pieces for our noon show. I would have to write the opener on the missile crisis. I began leafing through the Sunday *Washington Post,* marking off some background material that could be useful in fleshing out the bare bones of the story. I was still reading, finding little, when suddenly all the bells in the newsroom went off.

An office boy came running in, shouting, "Look at this, look at this!" I grabbed the teletype copy out of his outstretched hand. It had been ripped off the Reuters, the British news agency, machine and was marked BULLETIN BULLETIN BULLETIN. "Radio Moscow announces an important message to be broadcast at 9:00 A.M." I jumped up and ran to the teleprinters and stared fixedly at them until they all began clattering out their next bulletins. "Moscow announces decision dismantle missiles, crate them and return them to the Soviet Union."

By God, Kennedy had won! Khrushchev had caved in. The missile crisis was over. We were saved! I let out a primal scream that brought my producers running white-faced to the newsroom.

I pointed to the machines and shouted, "Tear up the show. Let's put together a new one. Read this and get going!"

I ran back to my office and put through a call to Salinger's home. It was about nine-fifteen. His wife answered and protested that he was fast asleep for the first time in almost two weeks and she would not wake him. "Wake him, don't argue, it's great news, we've won." She shouted, "We did? I'll get Pierre." A few minutes later a sleepy bear growled at me, "David, this better be good or I'll beat the hell out of you."

I laughed. "Pierrot, K has backed down. He's pulling out the missiles. Your boss has won. Listen to this." I then read him the lead paragraphs on Reuters, the AP, and UP. There was a half-sob, half-groan and I felt that Pierre was choked up, fighting not to cry with joy. I asked, "Where's the President? Does he know?" Salinger shouted back, "Hell, no, he can't know, he's at morning mass at church." "Well, God surely heard his prayers this morning. Can you get to him?" "Yeah, I can get through to the Secret Service detail on their car phone. Hang up, Dave, I've got things to do." "Just a sec, Pierre, I gave this to you first, and I've got a show coming up at noon. Promise you'll get back to me and give me what you can before noon?" "You've got it, ole buddy. I'll be back. And, Dave? Thanks for waking me up, you bastard."

I began calling every official I could. George Ball was home after days of sleeping on a cot at the State Department. He promised me a comment but said he could not come to the studio. Nick Katzenbach, number two man to Bob Kennedy at Justice, said he would be in the studio at quarter to twelve and discuss what had happened.

I put in urgent calls to Paris, Bonn, and Moscow. Marvin Kalb answered his phone in Moscow. He had been trying to get me but all outgoing calls had been delayed. I told him I wanted him to do a situationer from Moscow at the top of my show. Never mind about time, we would wing it and I would question him. I could not reach the Paris or Bonn bureau but Moscow was the important one.

My producers were in the film library pulling out file film of people in the streets of Moscow, of the Kremlin walls, of missiles on Red Army Day and the October Revolution parades in Moscow. Our show was being hammered out as airtime neared. I would go on with only a little more than half the program nailed down and have to make up the rest as I went along, with a Katzenbach interview and a senator, whoever showed up, and ad-lib a brief closing commentary.

I had not been so keyed up, with so much adrenaline flowing, in any of the most exciting news events I had ever covered. This was the one big one, the one I would remember for the rest of my life. My ghetto time had worked to my advantage. No one had wanted that time, so my program was the only news report on any network in America that incredible morning. Anybody who wanted to know what had happened would be listening in. What an audience! What a chance to make or break! What a joy to be alive with a clear, brisk October sky and not a mushroom cloud in sight!

At 12:00 noon the opening title and billboard shots rolled, and at 12:00 noon plus 30 seconds the floor man, his hand at the side of the camera, pointed at me as the red light came on and I was on the air. In a calm voice, belying the raging passions inside me, but with a big smile, I announced that the missile crisis had come to an end, that the Soviets were pulling their offensive weapons out of Cuba. I ran through the details of the first bulletin on the Moscow Radio announcement, then switched to a recording we had made of the Moscow announcer reading the message, then back to me. "Our correspondent in Moscow, Marvin Kalb, is standing by. Marvin, what's happening in Moscow at this moment?"

We had no direct satellite pictures in the sixties, so we ran a still portrait of Marvin as he began to broadcast on a radio circuit, then cut back to me at my desk, listening to Marvin on the telephone and taking notes on his report. Kalb gave his rundown on how the news broke in Moscow and went on to say that people were congregating around the Kremlin, talking in low tones, with grim faces, digesting the Soviet defeat.

Within some ten seconds, a little bulb next to my telephone began flashing a red light, a signal to me from the control room that something was wrong and that I should interrupt and go to a commercial break to get an urgent message. My heart beating wildly, I interrupted Marvin and said that we had to take a short break and I would get right back to him, please stand by. The tube began showing one of our standard noncommercial appeals for funds for some disease, the Cancer Fund or the Arthritis Fund, some public service film.

I picked up my phone and heard Salinger's voice, crisp and conveying a sense of urgency. "David, I'm speaking from the Oval Office during an Ex-Comm meeting. The meeting adjourned to watch your show. The President is right next to me. Please do not let Kalb run on about a Soviet defeat. Do not play this up as a victory for us. There is a danger that Khrushchev will be so humiliated and angered that he will change his mind. Watch what you are saying. Do not mess this up for us."

I was elated, flying high, my admiration for Kennedy at a peak. It never occurred to me for even a microsecond that a President ought not to be cutting into a live news program to tell a broadcaster what to say. This was so far beyond the issue of unfettered reporting, of freedom of the press, that it was not until four days later, when someone raised the issue, that I even thought about it. The stakes for everyone were enormous. The President's judgment was perfect. He would not gloat or taunt the Russians or claim a victory for himself. This was bigger, infinitely bigger than any television program, bigger than the President himself. The chances for peace could be impaired by any careless talk. He had a right to warn me, and I was happy to comply.

Salinger's message did not take more than fifteen seconds and the public service appeal was still running when I put down the phone and called out to the floor man, "Okay, get Kalb back on when the commercial ends."

"Marvin, I wonder if people in Moscow are getting some of the thoughts I'm hearing here in Washington today? That this is not a defeat or victory for any power, it is a victory for all mankind, a victory for peace."

Kalb, as bright a man and as fine a reporter as I have ever worked with, caught on at once. "Well, not generally, David, not yet, but there are a few people at the top who understand what a great moment this is for everyone. It will get through to the masses of the people quickly. The Russian people value peace as much as any people. They will rejoice when the realization sinks in that this is a great day for everyone."

I breathed a deep sigh of relief and then went on to breeze through the rest of the program, repeating, in a brief closing comment, the thought I had expressed earlier, that we could celebrate a victory for all mankind, for peace. As I gave the signature and the credits began to roll, my red light flashed again. I picked it up with a smile. I knew who it would be. "Dahveed! *Merci, mon brave.* Thanks, ole buddy."

I closed my eyes and saw the Oval Office, the President, Bob Kennedy, Rusk, McNamara, Dillon, Bundy, Ball, Sorensen, Salinger, and company beginning to sip their daiquiris, the President's favorite drink. I would have loved to have heard their toasts and congratulations. I knew that I had made a lot of friends in that office and that *Washington Report* had earned some laurel leaves.

After the Cuban missile crisis there was a blessed period of calm in world and in home affairs. Kennedy announced the end of the controversial series of atomic tests in the atmosphere. The U.S. terminated military aid to India, given when a border war with China had erupted. The President signed an executive order prohibiting racial discrimination in federal-financed housing. Just before Christmas, 1962, Castro began releasing Cuban prisoners captured in the ill-fated Bay of Pigs expedition. The gayest New Year's Eve parties in many a year celebrated a peaceful year-end.

In mid-January, Soviet and American diplomats began nuclear-test-ban talks and Ted Sorensen was hard at work preparing a budget message for Congress. He had accepted a dinner invitation at our house on the seventeenth but called to say that he was polishing up the budget message and would be late. He asked Dorothy to keep a plate warm for him in the oven. Ted showed up finally at quarter to midnight, long after all the guests had left. There is a tradition in Washington, an early-rising town, that at the stroke of 11:00 P.M. a woman of senior rank would arise, give thanks for the evening, and leave. That was the signal for everyone else to follow. I wished we had had the same system in Paris where there were times I thought the guests would never leave.

Ted was exhausted but happy. "The President gave me the strictest orders not to break through the psychological barrier of one hundred billion dollars. I cut and pruned and shaved and I finally held the budget down to 98.6 billion. We'll have a deficit of about twelve billion but we can handle that." A total national budget for all operations including defense for under one hundred billion! Those were the good old days. But they were by no means all that good. There was not a day without a major problem.

On January 31, the Soviets abruptly broke off nuclear-test-ban talks. Then a U.N. Disarmament Committee convened in Geneva to begin a series of talks which would go on, break off, reconvene, get nowhere, and then start in all over again. They were still talking disarmament in a variety of forums right up through 1983, while arms and atoms proliferated in ever increasing numbers all around the world.

After the missile crisis, *Washington Report* had solidly established itself and had become the talk of Washington. I had reached the top and was second only to Cronkite in rank and prestige at CBS. That proved to be a very important "only." There is very little room at the top in any organization and the higher you get the more people are trying to chop off the rungs from under you. It happens in every human enterprise. French poet Jean Cocteau had observed that "The statues to great men are made of the stones thrown at them in their lifetime."

The more successful my Sunday show became, the more trouble I had with New York. One day, Ernest Leiser, a correspondent who had turned producer, called to tell me he had just spoken with the French ambassador, Hervé Alphand, and had asked him for an interview with Cronkite. Alphand had replied that he would love to but he had already promised Schoenbrun to appear on *Washington Report.* Leiser asked me to call off Alphand and hand him over to the Cronkite show.

There was no doubt at all that an appearance on the Cronkite news program would give Alphand a much bigger audience than my Sunday-morning-ghetto program. I had to admit that Cronkite's program, the most important and profitable of all news programs, had priority over mine. Had they called me first and asked me to invite my French friend to be interviewed by Cronkite, I would gladly have done so. As chief correspondent and bureau chief it was my duty to report to Cronkite's program and help them get anyone they wanted.

I reminded Leiser that they had not called me, they had gone over my head in my own territory, and had done so after I had already made arrangements for my own program. To call Alphand at that point and ask him to be interviewed by Cronkite instead of by me would be a humiliation that would seriously undermine my position in Washington. It was too late for such a switch. We had a shouting match on the phone, followed by a call from Hewitt.

I liked and admired Hewitt and never fought with him for he was always competent and fair. He heard me out and said I was right but warned me that the conflicts of interest between my role as bureau chief and my role as anchorman of my own program would become intolerable.

Hewitt was right. It all came to a head soon enough. Cronkite, Hewitt, and Leiser came to visit me in the Washington bureau. They were all smiles and told me they had great news for me. I was deeply suspicious. Great news is conveyed by telephone or by letter. Only bad news, or an anticipated controversy, could bring that powerhouse New York trio to see me in Washington. I was right and wrong. There was bad news but first there came the good news.

They informed me that top management, after a year of study and argument, had finally decided to increase the time of the evening news with Walter Cronkite from fifteen minutes to a half hour. Anyone under forty today will find it hard to believe that the major news program covering national and world affairs was ever as limited as a quarter hour. In fact, with commercials counted, the program had barely twelve minutes to cover the world, an absurdity. Even today's half-hour program is inadequate. Cronkite himself has admitted publicly on several occasions that television news is only a brief summary of headlines and cannot deal substantively and satisfactorily with any important issue. There was a joke current in the newsroom in those days that if there had been television when Moses came down from Sinai, the lead sentence would have been, "Moses came down from the mountain today with Ten Commandments, the two most important of which are . . ."

I was, of course, pleased to hear about the doubling of the time available. They went on to say that I would be the news analyst on the program and would be given a substantial raise in salary. I was properly grateful but cautiously waiting for the other shoe to drop.

It did. Leiser had obviously been designated to be Mr. Bad Guy, permitting Walter and Don to be the Good Guys, which, in truth, they were. I knew that they were doing what they had to do and that there was no personal animus against me. Cronkite and Hewitt are two of the most talented, decent gentlemen with whom I have been privileged to work. There just was not room enough on the limited CBS schedule for two stars, not even a small one with the big sun. There was room for only one. I would be asked to hitch my wagon to Cronkite's star and not try for any luminary status of my own, other than on his program.

Leiser gave me the bad news. He claimed that Jungle Jim Aubrey had only consented to give the News Division the extra fifteen minutes a night on condition that they return other airtime to the network. And what was the other airtime to be returned? Why, David Schoenbrun's *Washington Report,* of course. It was humbug. They were canceling my program to force me to work full time for the evening news. At one point in the discussion, which grew more and more heated between Leiser and me, Ernie pounded his fist on my desk and shouted, "Goddamn it, you're an employee of CBS. CBS pays your salary and CBS tells you what to do. Take it or leave it."

Cronkite and Hewitt were embarrassed. I knew that Don would give Leiser hell later. That was no way to talk to me. It was totally uncalled for. I got up, ending the discussion, and told Ernie, "Shove it. Now get the hell out of here. I've heard more than enough from you." I turned to Don and Walter and expressed my regrets and told them that I would think about this. It was a major change and I needed time to digest it. We shook hands, as Ernie, fuming, waited outside.

When they left, I sat down, crushed and depressed. Deep down, I had known from earlier conflicts that this was bound to happen, just as a hypochondriac fears a disease, finally gets it, and cannot believe it. I went home to tell Dorothy. She was calm, cheerful, and supportive as always. "You must have known this was coming," she said. "Just quit and get it over with. We have money saved, your reputation is excellent. You are a good writer and do not need television. I would prefer that you devote yourself to books anyway."

I tried to smile but could not quite make it. "Dot, maybe I should not react hastily. What is wrong with appearing regularly as the analyst on the Cronkite show? It's a lot of money and national exposure. Not easy just to throw away."

Dorothy has always been wiser than I and always knew me better than I knew myself. "You'll be swallowing bile every day. They'll tell you what to do and how to do it. That's why you fought for your own show in the first place. You'll be miserable and it will poison our lives. Don't do it, it isn't worth it."

I flew up to New York to see the news director, Blair Clark. He told me there was nothing to be done. My show would be canceled. He urged me to go on with it until the time came for the schedule change. It could take a few months. I asked if I would appear nightly on the evening news, although I knew as a professional that they could not guarantee it. The news alone would determine the frequency of appearances. I asked again, foolishly and hopelessly, if I could have a regularly scheduled appearance, say, Monday, Wednesday, Friday, so that people would know when I would be on. I knew it made no sense but I kept pressing a sore tooth.

The crunch came when Clark and Salant called me in to offer me the post of chief correspondent in Europe, and a promise that they would find time for a half-hour weekly "European Report." I did not believe for a moment that they had any intention to find such time or that Aubrey would give it to them. I refused and went on to see Frank Stanton, president of CBS, who had sent me congratulatory telegrams almost weekly after each *Washington Report* program.

Stanton told me confidentially that the News Division was in a turmoil and that both Clark and Salant were in trouble for having badly mishandled Howard Smith and now me. He asked me to take a leave of absence on full pay and go back to Paris to write a biography of de Gaulle that I had been planning. "Be patient. Clark and Salant are going to be pulled out. Then we can talk again."

Recently, I saw Stanton and he told me that Paley had never liked Salant. Salant was Stanton's man and Stanton saved his job by putting him back into the corporation counsel's office from which he had taken him originally. Clark was simply fired. Fred Friendly would briefly replace Salant as president of the News Division before he, too, broke with CBS. Top jobs at CBS do not last long, except for two remarkable survivors, Cronkite and Hewitt. Stanton himself, under the illusion that he was Paley's partner, his brother, fell under the ax. He would tell me later that "I discovered after a quarter of a century of devotion that I was merely an employee, too."

Friends came to counsel me. Art Buchwald pleaded with me

to be patient. Arthur Goldberg cut short a fishing vacation to rush back to Washington and tell me that I was needed and must not leave. Angier Biddle Duke, the aristocratic, elegant chief of protocol of the State Department, came to tell Dorothy and me that if I left CBS, I should leave Washington, too. "You think you have a lot of personal friends and standing in this town. Let me warn you that your friends will disappear overnight, except for a few true ones. Your house will be empty, no one at your dinner parties, and your invitations will stop coming. You are not David Schoenbrun in this town. You are David Schoenbrun of CBS. Without CBS, the brutal truth is that you are nothing." He was not being unkind. He was one of the finest gentlemen I have ever known. He was simply telling me the truth about Washington.

Dorothy's face flushed red and she was furious. She is slow to anger and is a gentle person but if anyone tries to hurt me, Dorothy is an enraged tiger mother protecting her cub. She never forgave the people who asked her, "What will happen to David without CBS?" and would always love the French who, when we returned briefly to Paris, came rushing over to ask, "What will become of CBS without David?" America is supposed to be the country that values the individual above all else. Not true. We have become the country of the corporate symbol. France is where the individual still stands on his own ability and value.

I finally rejected Stanton's generous offer and decided to try the Salant-Clark proposal to be chief correspondent in Europe. It did not work. They did not give me the promised program. They did not even give me an office. I was located in my own old Paris bureau which was then run by Blaine Lytell, who would later reveal to me that Blair Clark had called him and told him not to let me step on him and make it clear that any facilities I wanted had to go through him. Some chief European correspondent. I called my agent, Nate Bienstock, and told him to negotiate a separation agreement. I had decided, with Dorothy urging me on, to quit CBS.

Many friends failed to understand how I could have refused the chance to be the commentator of the new half-hour Cronkite evening news, at a six-figure salary and with national fame. They knew nothing of the tight editorial controls, nothing of the irritations by men who did not know the story as I did, telling me what to cover and how to say it, nothing about the maddening frustrations of analyzing world news in depth for ninety seconds between an underarm deodorant and a postnasal drip.

I flew to New York and took a suite at the Algonquin. Bienstock told me that he had received many offers from newspapers, syndicates interested in a column, from magazines for articles, from independent radio stations wanting commentary, and, above all, an urgent message from Jim Hagerty, my old friend from the Eisenhower campaign, who was now chief of news for the ABC network.

Nate and I conferred with him at the Algonquin. He had an exciting idea, a chief correspondent on American and world news, a man to cover the top story wherever it was, whatever it was, for the evening television news and specials. He was talking big money and strong promotion. Best of all, he would base me in Washington and ask me to compete directly with CBS. Howard Smith would do the analysis pieces and anchor some of the evening news, I would be the senior correspondent doing "in-depth reporting." By that he meant combining analysis with the hard news story. It was an excellent offer and we agreed to meet again and firm it up within a week.

Before the week was up so was Hagerty. He was "kicked upstairs" in a general reorganization of ABC's top command. I was relieved at what I realized would have been an error. The sudden reassignment of Hagerty, who had had no inkling of it when he was negotiating with me, reminded me dramatically what life at the top was like in the networks. I had worked for the best, CBS, and seen it slip because of executive shifts. I had watched Howard Smith and Murrow leave and had left myself. Why tie myself to another network, which would not be any different and, at the moment, was not even as good? I vowed I would not take another salaried position, no matter how glamorous it sounded, no matter how much money was offered. I would be nothing but an employee, subject to the whims of unreliable hucksters. I told Nate to make contract arrangements for articles, books, and broadcasts as an outside contributor, not a staff member.

Fortunately, ABC would eventually decide to use several contributing commentators to get variety and different names on their programs. They chose William Buckley and me to start it off. Jack Sullivan, general manager of one of New York's top radio stations, WNEW, called Bienstock, told him he was a fan of mine, and asked whether I would do a five-a-week analysis for their news program. He also said that it would be carried by all the Metromedia stations, some of the most powerful transmitters in the nation. He offered a generous fee per broadcast and absolute freedom.

My old OWI and Algiers buddy, Mike Bessie, for whom I had written my book on France when he was an editor at Harper's, had founded his own publishing house, Atheneum, in partnership with Pat Knopf. Mike came through with an excellent advance for a biography of de Gaulle. *The New York Times* Sunday Magazine, for which I had done many articles from Paris, called to ask for articles. So did *Colliers,* the *Saturday Evening Post,* the *Reader's Digest, Harper's,* and the *Saturday Review.* With university lectures added to broadcasting and writing, my plate was overflowing. I had more than a year's freelance work contracted in advance for a total income higher than the CBS job I had just quit. In addition, I managed to obtain a generous separation payment from CBS. Dorothy was ecstatic. I was not exactly down in the mouth.

I was now David Schoenbrun, standing on my own name, received warmly by all, without a logotype branded on my forehead. I could pick my assignments, go where I wanted to, when I wanted to. I would still, of course, have to deal with editors and producers but on a totally different basis. I was not their wage slave.

I decided to headquarter in New York, my native city. New York is the city that makes everything happen in the communications and literary world, the city of the networks and the publishers, the great national magazines. The newly scheduled Eastern Shuttle service made it easy to fly to Washington at eight in the morning and fly home at five, giving me a full working day there several days a week, keeping alive my news sources in the Kennedy Administration and the Congress.

The pressures shifted that spring from foreign crises and confrontations to the home front, with an explosion of civil rights conflicts. President Kennedy was able to put down his warrior lance and appear in the role of protector of the oppressed, a noble cause more fitting to the Camelot image.

Young black Americans were losing patience with the slow progress of integration and job opportunities. To those who told them not to rush things, they bitterly replied that they had been waiting for one hundred years for emancipation to become a reality. Violence broke out in Birmingham, the city that Martin Luther King said was the most segregated city in the nation. The police chief, Eugene "Bull" O'Connor, was a huge bully who hated blacks and reveled in terrorizing and brutalizing them. He laughed at federal regulations and laws and ran Birmingham as his personal fief.

Dr. King, refusing to be intimidated, launched a series of sit-ins and marches in Birmingham. Hundreds of blacks were beaten and arrested. Thousands more came out to be met by white thugs. "Bull" Connor led his troops personally and attacked the blacks with dogs and then turned powerful fire hoses on them. On May 4, papers and TV stations around the nation and the world showed a picture of a terrified black woman cringing before the fangs of a dog. The President was sickened. Blacks were enraged, and a week later many thousands more came out, too many even for "Bull" Connor to control.

Blacks rioted, smashed shops, set fires, overwhelmed police lines. Bully-boy Connor appealed for help to the governor of Alabama, an almost unknown racist named George Wallace. His name would become known around the world and he would astonish the White House and the media by touching a raw nerve in millions of Americans. We would learn that segregationists did not live exclusively in the South and were not all rural red-necks. Racism would erupt everywhere in the United States, in New England, the Midwest and Far West, as well as in the Deep South. Wallace would replace Joe McCarthy as the Ugly American with a strange ability to draw the worst out of his fellow citizens.

President Kennedy sent troops to an air base near Birmingham and announced that he would do "whatever must be done to preserve order, to protect the lives of citizens and to uphold the law of the land." Wallace denounced the President as a "military dictator" and filed suit with the Supreme Court, calling his action unconstitutional. Bob Kennedy's Justice Department replied firmly that the Commander in Chief of U.S. armed forces could send troops to any base he chose.

Marches were held in a dozen Southern cities and in Chicago. Flames swept across the country. More than fifteen thousand blacks were arrested in the South. In a memorable comment, Ken O'Donnell predicted it would be "a long, hot summer." Medgar Evers, field man for the NAACP in Mississippi, was shot down and murdered by a sniper as he was returning to his home in Jackson after a church rally. The high point of the summer came at the end of August when the largest number of demonstrators ever to assemble for one event, two hundred thousand men and women, whites arm in arm with blacks, marched to Washington to hear Martin Luther King speak at the Lincoln Memorial.

I had come to Washington to cover that story. Ed Murrow, then director of the Voice of America, had called me and asked me to anchor a panel of celebrities who wanted to speak out against racism. He would then make hundreds of copies of that remarkable program and send them all around the world. I led a discussion among the following men: James Baldwin, Burt Lancaster, Charlton Heston, Marlon Brando, Harry Belafonte, and Sidney Poitier. They were intelligent, articulate spokesmen for integration and equal rights for all Americans. Their fame gave added weight to their words. It was one of the most moving television programs I had ever done.

Murrow's people had set up a television viewing room so that we could all see and hear Martin Luther King. When King proclaimed, "I have a dream that one day this nation will rise up, live out the true meaning of its creed . . ." I saw Belafonte and Poitier, tears streaming down their faces, reach out and clasp hands. Then Brando stretched his hand out to them, then Baldwin, and soon we were all sitting on the floor before the set, in a circle, holding hands and vowing to fight for a decent and lawful America.

When King's rich, baritone voice hit his peroration and he proclaimed, like a black Moses, holding outstretched arms to the people, "Free at last, Great God Almighty, free at last!" the entire panel began to applaud and cheer. Belafonte's husky voice rose in a lilt as he sang the words "Great God Almighty, free at last." His closest friend, Poitier, embraced him. Those of us present there were bound together thereafter by the experience. Whenever I see Poitier or Belafonte, I get a crushing bear hug. We felt we had been to the mountain with King and would never forget it.

John F. Kennedy was at the height of his popularity that summer of 1963, admired around the world, even in the Soviet Union. On June 20, at American University he delivered an address which Khrushchev would later tell Averell Harriman was the greatest speech by an American President since Roosevelt. Kennedy rejected the counsel of those who were saying it was useless to pursue peace until the Soviets had proved by their actions that they wanted peace. Kennedy said we should do everything to persuade the Russians to join us for peace. He then stated that we would be well-advised to reexamine some of our own attitudes, that we were not without fault.

Camelot was in full flower. The three Kennedy wives, Jackie, Ethel, and Joan, young, vital women, all active in a number of causes, were all pregnant, as were the wives of other Administration officials. It was one of the youngest Administrations in our history, and playpens were as much in evidence as desks. Kennedy had just turned forty-six on May 29. I congratulated him and told him he had one quality that I did not appreciate at all. He was the first President of the United States who was younger than I, and I did not like being even a little older than a President. There were delightful evenings, good food, good conversation, and dancing until dawn. Washington glittered with handsome men, beautiful women, and a scintillating collection of brains. The Camelot image was brighter than ever.

I flew back to Paris in the late fall to begin a series of European reports. I came home one night to dress for a dinner party at the home of Alain and Marjorie Bernheim. Alain was a leading theatrical and movie agent for Hollywood studios. I was late. Dorothy had already dressed. She went to the living room to tune in the evening news at eight, while I jumped into the tub for a quick, refreshing dip before dressing. Suddenly I heard Dorothy and my daughter, Lucy, shouting, "Oh no! Oh no!" I jumped out of the tub and dashed into the living room. Dorothy, weeping, said, "The President has been shot in Dallas. They are hinting that he is dead."

I groaned, dressed hastily, and drove wildly to the presidential palace across the Seine. As I rushed through the double glass doors of the entry, the usher, who knew me, was startled to see me rush to the marble staircase leading to President de Gaulle's office. A security guard moved to stop me. I shouted at him, "Kennedy has been shot, does de Gaulle know?" He came up the steps with me and we went into the anteroom of de Gaulle's aide. I told him the news. He was shocked and said that he was sure de Gaulle did not know. I asked him to check with de Gaulle. He hesitated and said: "He is in his private quarters with his children and grandchildren. It is de Gaulle's birthday and they are giving him presents. I don't know if I dare interrupt."

He straightened up, made up his mind, and went to inform de Gaulle. A few minutes later he came out. "The president will make an official comment later. He is calling Washington now. He did not know. It was thoughtful of you to come at once. It is terrible news."

I drove home and Dorothy told me that Jack Sullivan of WNEW had called. He asked that I take the very first plane to Washington and begin broadcasting developments. The next morning, I was on the first plane out. As I came into the cabin I saw Jean Monnet at a window seat. I sat next to him and we began talking about the tragedy. "A terrible loss for the entire world," Monnet told me. Then he asked what I knew and thought about Lyndon Johnson. I had no encouraging words to tell him. At that moment, the mayor of Berlin, Willy Brandt, came on the plane. He looked around and found a seat in the rear. I knew he was a close associate of Monnet in the European unity movement and that the two leaders would want to talk. I signaled Brandt to come over and yielded my seat to him.

The rest is all a blur in my memory: the extraordinary funeral cortège which Jackie had planned; the truly heroic performance of all the television broadcasters, ad-libbing their way through a heart-wrenching tragedy; the address to Congress by President Lyndon Johnson; the sadness and the fear that gripped America but the magnificent way the country held together, its unity restored, the succession orderly and lawful, demonstrating the basic strength and soundness of the American polity.

After some ten days of reporting the succession, when it was apparent that the crisis, if not the tears, had passed, I flew back to Paris and decided to take a brief break to clear my mind and to think through what the Kennedy Administration had really been like, its accomplishments and failures, and where it had been going when a bullet from a mail-order gun had brought it down.

Was it really Camelot? A good and brave king surrounded by noble knights? No, not that. Camelot was an image conjured up by the media, enchanted by the youth and beauty of Jack and Jackie and all the intellects they had gathered in Washington. It was style, not substance. Yet the style itself did have its own substance. We were proud of our President and First Lady and they were admired throughout the world. Men like Ted Sorensen, Ken O'Donnell, Arthur Schlesinger, McGeorge Bundy, and Pierre Salinger were among the brightest, most attractive, dedicated young Americans to serve at high levels since Roosevelt's first Administration. Yet they were not pure and noble knights in a storybook romance. To call it Camelot is to distort the reality of Kennedy's Administration.

Kennedy's promise was greater than his performance but I believe that, had he lived, he would have given the nation a period of prosperity, peace, and civil progress. He had a potential for greatness. It is tragic that he achieved a special place in history only as a martyr.

CHAPTER 17

LYNDON JOHNSON'S LOST DREAM

Overnight the White House changed from a fairy-tale castle to a rowdy Texas rodeo, whose star performer was a six-feet four-inch cowboy wearing size 14 boots, with a bullhorn voice, and the power of a longhorn steer. Lyndon Baines Johnson was the kind of man whom the French call *une force de la nature,* an elemental force.

Kennedy had been a thoroughbred, with fine lines, touched with grace. His wit was dry and subtle, his style understated. He was well-educated and even more well-read. He had style and manners. Lyndon Johnson was crude and coarse. He had attended a high school in East Texas which was not accredited even in those easygoing days in that easygoing state. In two qualities, however, he did match Kennedy. Johnson was highly intelligent and had limitless energy. He was also just as dedicated as the Kennedys to civil rights and the succor of the poor and hungry. Johnson had a big heart; unfortunately he also had a big mouth which he could not control. Everything about him was outsize. If Kennedy was King Arthur, Johnson was King Kong.

Lyndon Johnson terrified me. From the moment I met him, I sensed a potential for cataclysm. He had come to Paris as Senator Johnson, Vice-President-elect, to head an American Congressional delegation to a NATO meeting, in December 1960. I had been alerted to his coming by a letter from CBS President Frank Stanton. Only later would I learn to what extent Johnson used and dominated Stanton, as well as NBC's president, Robert Kintner.

Johnson was fiercely possessive of colleagues and friends. He spoke grandly of "my Cabinet, my Army, my Navy, my Air Force," stopping just short of saying "my America." Once, after having met with a half dozen foreign leaders, he referred to them as "my prime ministers." In Paris, on meeting me, he immediately took me over and called me "my boy." Sometimes he would shorten it to just "boy."

Stanton asked me to take care of Johnson and his "party," and bid them welcome to Paris. Only after he arrived did I discover that his "party" was a kind of royal retinue of courtiers to King Johnson: his personal physician, a strange character wearing a black opera cape lined in red silk, looking like Count Dracula, and a number of Texans and their wives. The wives kept Dorothy busy all day long shopping for dresses, perfume, and Paris costume jewelry at discount stores.

Johnson took me over as though I were his personal batman and recording secretary. Within minutes he began a monologue about the new Administration. I pounded my ear to be sure it was functioning correctly when I heard him make the incongruous statement: "This Administration is going to do more for the niggers than any since this Republic was founded."

Johnson said he would like to go out that night for some good food and dancing. "Frank Stanton said you knew the best places. And he'll okay your expense account, so don't zip up your pockets." I did not at all like to hear a politician, especially a Vice-President, telling me about my expense account. It would have been extremely rude if it had not been said with a cheerful bonhomie that dulled its cutting edge. Johnson seemed utterly unaware of his crudeness and vulgarity.

I called Maxim's and spoke with its Directeur de la Salle, Roger, handsome and more elegant than any of his guests. I told him I wanted to bring the Vice-President of the United States for dinner and needed a table of fourteen. I should have known it does no good to namedrop with Roger. He has received most of the kings, princes, millionaires, and other royalty of the world for years. A mere Vice-President is small potatoes. Roger smoothly replied: "We are very full tonight, Monsieur Schoenbrun, but I will find room for you and your friends."

At midnight-thirty, Lady Bird said she had a headache and would like to go home. Dorothy quickly asked if she could go with her. The Secret Service was standing by with a limousine and escorted them. Lyndon bellowed at me across the table. "Now don't y'all go party pooping too, boy. Ahm just beginnin' to enjoy mahself."

It was three o'clock and even the night people were leaving before I could get Lyndon to call it a night. I had been told that he had suffered a massive heart attack, but that week in Paris he was a wild bull threatening to give us all heart attacks.

I could not imagine what his relationship must be with Kennedy. The cowboy and the Brahmin were clearly a poor match. We Americans really have a strange system of government. A Presidential candidate chooses a running mate to appeal to a different constituency from his own. As a result, there is almost always a sharp difference between the President and his potential successor. John Nance Garner, the whiskey-swilling, poker-playing Texan, was no match at all for the aristocratic Franklin Delano Roosevelt of New York. Nor Harry Truman, small-time, small-town member of a corrupt political gang. Now Lyndon Johnson and John Fitzgerald Kennedy. When I met Kennedy in Paris after meeting Johnson I could not believe that the two could work together. I would discover that they did not.

President Kennedy did try to give Johnson some useful and important assignments. He appointed him to head committees on space exploration, a major goal of Kennedy's Administration, with the announced intention of putting a man on the moon within ten years. It was spectacular but it diverted many billions badly needed here on earth. We lived ankle-deep in garbage in the streets of New York, one of the world's greatest and dirtiest cities, while gleaming, spotless missiles carried men into space.

Kennedy would also send Johnson on a mission to Southeast Asia, a tremendous error, for Johnson knew nothing about the area but could not resist portentous statements and commitments after a day's "investigation." Virtually on arrival in Saigon, he hailed Ngo Dinh Diem, the Catholic, nationalist dictator of South Vietnam, as the "Winston Churchill of south Asia," hyperbole to the point of lunacy. When reporter Stan Karnow then asked him whether he really believed what he had said about Diem, Johnson hitched up his trousers, jammed his thumbs in his belt, and snapped, "Shit, man, he's the only boy we got out here."

Johnson retained Kennedy's principal aides but he was constantly troubled by comparisons in the media between Kennedy and himself, almost all unfavorable to him. He had deep resentment of the intellectuals and Harvard men and used to argue that he would never get full credit for anything he did because he had not gone to Harvard. This enormously self-confident man had an inferiority complex about Eastern liberals and scholars, magnified by their open contempt of him. He was deeply wounded, justifiably, by an odious play called *MacBird* which depicted him as an assassin. Every mean, cruel political joke of the past thirty years was revived and made Johnson its butt. Robert Kennedy despised him and did not keep it secret in his seminars in his home, Hickory Hill. New Frontiersmen had snubbed and isolated him in the Vice-Presidency and many would turn against him as President.

When I arrived in Washington, one of the first invitations to dinner came from Johnson. He had bought Perle Mesta's famed home, once the center of Washington social life. When Dorothy and I arrived for dinner, we discovered that the other guests were Johnson's secretary, Mary Margaret; and his aide, Jack Valenti, who would later marry Mary Margaret; Liz Carpenter, Lady Bird's P.R. spokesman, an intelligent, witty writer; and her reporter husband, Les Carpenter, all members of Johnson's staff and immediate family, no one else.

Liz Carpenter would call me on Saturdays or Sundays after *Washington Report* and ask me over to her house in Silver Springs, mentioning casually that Lyndon would be there and glad to see me. He was, in fact, lonely, with almost no one but his own people to talk with and he was drawing me into his orbit to have a network man available to listen to him. It was almost pitiful, for, as a senator and majority leader, Johnson was one of the most powerful, sought-after men in Washington. As Vice-President in Camelot, he was an ugly Cinderella who never got to go to the ball.

The Kennedys continued to dominate him even after he became President. It is almost automatic for opinion polls to show that the First Lady is the most admired woman in the world. In the spring of 1964, a Gallup poll put Jacqueline Kennedy, the former First Lady, number one on the list, ahead of Lady Bird Johnson, the incumbent First Lady.

Yet, Lyndon Johnson, the consummate politician, had the Democratic Party well in hand and would turn the nomination at the convention into a coronation. The Republican Party, on the other hand, was wide open, with no one in sure control at the start of 1964. President Kennedy had been certain that his opponent in 1964 would be Barry Goldwater, and he looked forward to an easy reelection against the senator from Arizona.

Barry Goldwater was a strange paradox of a man. A major general in the Air Force Reserve, an experienced and able jet pilot, an expert radio ham, he was the compleat twentieth-century Technological Man. Politically, however, he was a nineteenth-century anachronism. A current joke pictured Goldwater faced with a Russian threat and ordering his generals to put their tanks in a circle.

Goldwater did not seem to have even a glimmer of an understanding of where most people stood on the major issues. At a time when Americans had become alarmed at reports of the atmosphere being poisoned, when President Kennedy won a big majority for a nuclear test ban, Senator Goldwater had voted against the test ban. During one public appearance, he airily proposed that we ought to toss an atom bomb "into the men's room at the Kremlin."

As a result of his thoroughly irresponsible and frequent proposals to use nuclear weapons, the Democrats would twist a Republican campaign slogan, "In your heart you know he's right," and make it read "In your heart you know he might." Then Goldwater virtually assured his defeat by saying that he favored making Social Security contributions voluntary. This was the equivalent to ending Social Security payments, a fact he did not understand but which the media did, headlining across the nation: "Goldwater Calls For End To Social Security." The message was read by tens of millions of American voters counting on future Social Security checks in their old age. One of Goldwater's own friends called him "honest but dumb."

Goldwater was playing right into Johnson's hands. Johnson would not only guarantee the integrity of Social Security, he would bring it up-to-date and put through the Congress a Civil Rights

Act, originally drafted by President Kennedy, extending federal laws against many forms of discrimination. Then he would declare, with great fanfare, a "War on Poverty." He did not believe that there had been the national swing to the right proclaimed by ideological Republicans. It would take the excesses of Lyndon Johnson himself to sap the American economy, divide the American people, and provide that swing just in time for Ronald Reagan. In a strange way, Goldwater was a man of the past and of the future, but not of his own times.

All this was already clear when the Republicans assembled at their national convention in San Francisco. There, Goldwater won the nomination but lost the election when he declared that "extremism in the defense of liberty is no vice." And then, to sink the shaft all the way into the hearts of any liberals still left in the Republican Party, he proclaimed that "moderation in the pursuit of justice is no virtue."

I was in my broadcasting booth over the floor listening to that incredible speech. When Goldwater finished and the arena exploded into a Walpurgisnacht of extremist revelry, I observed, "Well, there goes the election." Later, Barry Goldwater would confirm that judgment himself, by admitting, "If I had had an ounce of common sense I would have known the election was lost in San Francisco."

Lyndon Johnson went to the Democratic Convention in Atlantic City in August, well after the Republicans had already revealed all their weaknesses to him. He was determined to put on a dignified and responsible show in contrast to the Republican disgraceful performance. Americans would not soon forget the way the extremists had shouted down and reviled Nelson Rockefeller, with little old ladies in tennis shoes screaming "Lover Boy! Lover Boy!" to drown out his speech. Nor would they forget Goldwater's endorsement of extremism.

Johnson had carefully scripted the Democratic Convention and kept almost total control, except for one incident that caught him by surprise. A group called the Mississippi Freedom Party, mainly young people, both black and white, challenged the credentials of the all-white Mississippi delegation and set up a picket line. Lyndon Johnson, an inveterate television viewer, was watching the tube and saw the demonstration, a stain on "his" convention.

Johnson picked up a phone and called his good friend NBC

President Robert Kintner. NBC was the only network showing the demonstration at that time. When Kintner got on the phone, he heard the President of the United States screaming, "Get those goddamned cameras off those niggers! Get them off right now!" Before such an order could be carried out, causing a horrendous precedent in television reporting, the cameras had already moved on to other scenes.

There was another television upheaval at Atlantic City which did win wide public attention. CBS News had fallen badly in the ratings, and its new president, Fred Friendly, a talented producer but an insecure and inexperienced executive, panicked. He removed Walter Cronkite from his anchor position and replaced him with a duo to compete with the NBC twosome Huntley and Brinkley.

He chose two excellent men if one judges them by their individual talents in the right spot. Unfortunately they did not play off each other as Huntley and Brinkley did and they were in the wrong spot. Robert Trout had anchored conventions going all the way back to Herbert Hoover in 1928. That was going back too far. Roger Mudd was a first-rate political reporter but he was not yet ready to anchor a national convention. The ratings fell into the cellar. Cronkite had been needlessly humiliated.

Johnson was crowned king by the convention. A special documentary film was shown in memory of the martyred President Kennedy. Bob Kennedy and the New Frontiersmen were unhappy men but there was nothing they could do. They had no use for Johnson but were genuinely afraid of Barry Goldwater. They had no choice but to support Johnson, in the spirit of a Chinese foreign minister in World War II who told a reporter, "China welcomes Russia's entry into the war, on our side, with a heavy heart." Bob Kennedy would support Lyndon Johnson with the heaviest of hearts.

The campaign was one of the most disgraceful and vicious in American history. Eisenhower had accepted the one-minute television commercial, selling a President like a piece of soap. Johnson and the Democrats in 1964 would break new ground, inventing the adversary commercial. Until then, American advertising was always positive. The sponsor's brand of soap was the best ever made. Never did it say that the rival brand was no good. Today, television commercials do not hesitate to present alleged tests that show the sponsor's product beating out the rival brand, by name.

Johnson breached that barrier with savage attacks on Goldwater. This has now, regrettably, become a standard low practice in commercials and politics.

The most effective but outrageous television spot showed a little girl pulling petals off a daisy when suddenly the whole idyllic scene dissolved into a giant mushroom cloud. There were a number of these "atomic" commercials, including one of a darling child eating an ice cream cone when . . . BOOM! All of them exploited Goldwater's careless, repetitive references to nuclear war and his apparent readiness to "push the button."

It was extraordinarily inept of Goldwater and his people to allow Johnson to play the role of Angel of Peace and portray Goldwater as the Demon of War, for the Democrats were vulnerable on the peace-and-war issue. Some twenty thousand American military men were in Vietnam, a huge escalation from Eisenhower's eight hundred advisors. Yet Johnson took over the peace issue as his very own.

He barnstormed the country after the convention, making the most solemn and unqualified pledges never to get involved in a shooting war in Asia, promises that would later be thrown back in his face by angry antiwar demonstrators. "We don't want our American boys to do the fighting for Asian boys." "Vietnamese boys must fight for Vietnam. We will advise them. We will equip them. But they must fight for their country." "We are not going to send American boys nine or ten thousand miles away from home to do what Asian boys ought to be doing for themselves." "I promise peace for all Americans."

As Johnson was posing as the Apostle of Peace, some two hundred Americans had already been killed in Vietnam, a small number but the handwriting on the wall, just asking for a Republican riposte, which never came, for the Republicans were kept busy denying that they were going to atomize the world. Furthermore, Goldwater dug his own grave when he proposed that more American soldiers and airmen be sent to Vietnam, giving the vulnerable Johnson the chance to accuse Goldwater of warmongering.

It surprised no one when Lyndon Johnson and his Vice-President, Hubert Humphrey, swept the polls on Election Day. They won 486 electoral votes to Goldwater's 52. The Democrats virtually took over the Congress, winning 28 out of 35 senatorial seats, giving them a majority of 68 to 32, and better than a two-thirds majority of the House, 295 to 140, plus 33 Democratic governors against 17. It was a wipeout.

There had been a number of memorable events that had taken place during the campaign. In Philadelphia, Mississippi, law-enforcement officers were arrested and indicted by a federal grand jury for conspiring to violate the rights of others. It was, in fact, a murder case, not a civil rights case. Three civil rights workers had been killed, Michael Schwerner, age twenty-four, of Brooklyn, New York, white; Andrew Goodman, twenty, also of New York and white; and James Chaney, twenty-one, black, a native Mississippian. Schwerner and Goodman had been shot dead but Chaney had been badly beaten before being executed. Seven men were eventually found guilty and sentenced to prison. It was the first time in history that a federal jury of white Mississippians had convicted white defendants in a civil rights case.

In September, the Warren Commission issued its report on President Kennedy's murder, concluding that the assassin, Lee Harvey Oswald, had acted alone and that there was no basis for believing in any conspiracy. In October Martin Luther King was awarded the Nobel Peace Prize and Nikita Khrushchev was deposed as leader of the Soviet Union. Khrushchev's downfall, appropriately enough, came on October 15, exactly two years after he had sent missiles into Cuba.

The most important act of that Presidential election year, and one of the most duplicitous in our history, occurred in August and made a mockery of all President Johnson's pious declarations of peace and promises never to get tied down in a land war in Asia. It has become known as the Tonkin Gulf incident.

It became public on August 2 when the White House announced that North Vietnamese communist PT boats had attacked the U.S. destroyer *Maddox* on a noncombat cruise through international waters in the Gulf of Tonkin. On August 4 came a second announcement that the destroyer *Turner Joy* had also been fired upon by communist ships, without provocation. President Johnson bellowed his outrage, wrapped himself in the flag, and ordered American planes from our aircraft carriers to bomb North Vietnamese vessels, torpedo boat bases and other targets. Without a declaration of war, the President ordered acts of war, in an atavistic return to nineteenth-century gunboatism, using lethal twentieth-century weapons.

The President called in his good friend, Senator J. William Fulbright of Arkansas, chairman of the Foreign Relations Committee, and asked him to manage a resolution authorizing the President to take whatever action he deemed necessary to deal with aggression by the communists of North Vietnam. He went on television to rail against "aggression" toward the armed forces of the United States. Fulbright rushed to put through the resolution which would give the President a blank check to make war without consulting the Congress, a violation of the spirit and the letter of the Constitution.

It would take years before Fulbright and the senators would learn the whole truth. Johnson had hoodwinked them into a most dangerous precedent and plunged them into a war he had sworn never to fight. The simple truth, which had been suppressed by the Pentagon and the White House, was that our destroyers were not engaged in a peaceful cruise and had not been fired upon without provocation and had not, in fact, been hit by any communist fire. They were working in tandem with South Vietnamese commandos attacking North Vietnamese islands, near the coast, and not out in international waters. These armed raids had been going on for some time.

The *Maddox* was sailing close to shore to probe the communist radar installations in order to destroy them by shelling. That took place on August 1. No one really knew what happened on August 4. The *Turner Joy* commander reported to the Pentagon that his radar operator had reported blips but could not identify them. It could have been a covey of ducks. The *Turner Joy* promptly opened fire, not knowing what it was shooting at. Nothing had appeared on the *Maddox* radar screen. Its captain reported that it was doubtful that any torpedos had been fired. He felt his sonar men had been nervous. That was the terrible "aggression," the "piracy" which had outraged the President and which he claimed justified sweeping powers to meet this communist "challenge" to the United States.

By exploiting the Gulf of Tonkin incident, Johnson was able to put down one of Goldwater's themes, that the Democrats were "soft on communism," had done nothing against the Berlin Wall, as though there were anything to do about it. Reason is often absent from election campaigns. Only two senators refused to be hoodwinked, Wayne Morse of Oregon and Ernest Gruening of Alaska, who both voted against the Tonkin Gulf Resolution. Both would be defeated in their bid for reelection. All others, including leading liberals who would later criticize the war in Vietnam—George McGovern, Birch Bayh, Gene McCarthy, and company—voted for the legislation. It breezed through the House without a single dissenting vote. The Congress behaved like Johnson's pet beagle and let him pull it up by its ears.

A week after President Johnson's inaugural address, Buddhist uprisings broke out in South Vietnam and an Army general seized the opportunity for a coup d'etat. General Khanh talked about a "neutralist" policy and the withdrawal of U.S. forces. It was a unique opportunity for Johnson to disengage without any loss of face. Instead, he announced he was determined to resist communist aggression and make American aid "more effective." He sent his National Security advisor, McGeorge Bundy, to Saigon to investigate the crisis there. At that moment, Soviet Premier Kosygin flew to Hanoi. It was an ideal time to explore a possible negotiation. Kosygin had informed Johnson of his mission and suggested that they meet after his trip to Hanoi. Johnson had agreed to do so.

Guerrillas then struck against the American barracks at Pleiku, killing 8 and wounding 126. Instead of striking back at guerrilla camps and bases, Johnson ordered American jets to strike deeply into North Vietnam, in the first major air raid inside that country. The raid took place on the very day, February 8, 1965, when Kosygin was in Hanoi conferring with Northern leaders. Soviet spokesmen told reporters that Kosygin at first had refused to believe the news of the American air raid. His peace exploration was blasted away by the bombs, his prestige was directly challenged, and Kosygin was made to look foolish in his talks with allies who were being bombed by Americans whom he had just offered to meet seeking peace.

On February 12, U.N. Secretary-General U Thant, dismayed by what had happened, publicly appealed to all parties to "move from the field of battle to the conference table." Moscow warned that it would take measures to defend Hanoi. Kosygin called for an international conference on Vietnam. On February 24, U Thant repeated his call for diplomatic negotiations. In an unusual statement, that usually cautious diplomat implied that the American people were not being told the truth. He said: "I am sure the great American people, if only they knew the true facts and the background to developments in South Vietnam, will agree with me that further bloodshed is unnecessary." He then added: "As you know, in times of war and of hostilities, the first casualty is truth."

Few Americans paid attention to Thant's warning, indeed, very few had heard it or read it, for it had not been prominently carried on radio, television, or in the press. It had been buried by the clamor over the shooting of Malcom X during a Black Muslim rally in Harlem on February 21 and the burning of Black Muslim headquarters on the twenty-third.

Two weeks later, thirty-five hundred Marines landed in South Vietnam to guard the U.S. air base at Da Nang. A deadly cycle was underway: First you send unarmed advisors; then they are threatened and are issued arms with orders to shoot back; then they are shot, so you send in troops to protect the advisors; the troops are ambushed, so you send in helicopters, gunships, and planes to protect the troops and bomb enemy bases; then you build warehouses to stockpile arms and ammo for the troops and the airmen; then you send in the Marines to defend the warehouses and the air bases; then more troops are needed to protect the Marines, and, before you know it, you are in full-scale war, without planning it, without declaring it, unable to disengage for fear of being accused of losing another country to the communists.

The dispatch of the Marines in mid-March 1965 did not attract much attention because of continuing civil rights demonstrations. On March 21, Martin Luther King, with some 3,000 followers, began a five-day, fifty-four-mile march from Selma to Montgomery, Alabama. By the time the march ended, his followers would number 25,000, many of them white, from many states in the Union. People paid a bit more attention to Vietnam in April when Defense Secretary McNamara announced that the costs of fighting there had risen to $1.5 billion annually. Anxiety mounted, along with the first public opposition, when the President announced in July that he would increase U.S. armed forces in Vietnam from 75,000 to 125,000 men, and would double the draft from 17,000 to 35,000 men monthly.

Riots broke out in Watts, the black ghetto of Los Angeles, and raged from August 11 to 16. Hundreds were injured and thirty-five killed, with some $200 million in property damage. The day the riots ended, the Pentagon released casualty figures on Vietnam: 561 killed, 3,024 wounded, 44 missing in action since the first advisors had been sent by Kennedy in 1961. These were relatively small figures but mounting ominously with the increase of U.S. forces. The next communiqués would show casualties doubled, then tripled. More public protests were heard, along with the first tentative questioning editorials. Until the summer of 1965, there was no important opposition to Johnson's buildup in Vietnam. Before the year would end, however, strong opposition would erupt.

In mid-October 1965, public antiwar demonstrations spread across the nation, from the campus of Columbia University in New York to Berkeley in San Francisco. A great many draft-age young men wanted no part of what they had begun to call "Johnson's war." Draft cards were publicly burned and Johnson struck back with a law making destruction of draft cards a crime. The first youngster was arrested under that law on October 16.

On November 27, between twenty to twenty-five thousand men and women, young and old, marched toward the White House in the first major antiwar rally. William Fulbright, now aware of the fact that his good friend LBJ had hoodwinked him, struck back at the beginning of the new year, 1966, by scheduling the first hearings on Vietnam at the Foreign Relations Committee, and he called in television cameras to cover those hearings. I was one of the witnesses that Fulbright would call. He was aware of my many years of reporting in and about Vietnam.

The outsize President overreacted with predictably outsize acts. The U.S. Air Force began massive bombing raids on North Vietnam. They were retaliations for American casualties but camouflaged as raids to "interdict infiltration" into the South, as though bombs could interdict jungle trails through thick green cover. Johnson sent more and more troops. By the end of 1966, he had escalated up to 375,000 Americans, supporting 614,000 South Vietnamese, armed by us, a total allied force of some one million men, more than quadruple the size of the enemy forces.

Despite the growing draft and casualty lists and the emerging opposition, the overwhelming majority of the American people and their representatives in Congress, as well as the press, supported the war in Vietnam. Those of us who publicly opposed the war were charged with being defeatists, undermining the war effort, with being something less than patriots. I was one of the first, early in 1965, to speak out against the war, just as I had privately argued with President Kennedy against any involvement in Vietnam.

At many universities, students would cheer my appearances, but at public lectures or civic clubs, I would get a chilly reception, even boos and catcalls. In one meeting, in Paramus, New Jersey, the police had to protect me from a belligerent group of some two hundred American Legionnaires who stood up, waved the flag, and sang the national anthem when I began to speak. I sang along with them and then challenged them to send one of their leaders up to the platform to debate me and to match combat records in war with me. They declined the invitation and a few made to rush the stage when a burly police captain stepped forward and offered to break a few heads.

Every generation of man has known war and people have come to expect war and to prepare for war. With such deeply rooted psychological acceptance, it is easy for governments to make war, and, in the absence of any kind of world system of control, rival power forces are bound to clash. In the special case of the American people, there was still prevalent in the sixties an added syndrome that makes it very difficult to negotiate peace once war has broken out. Americans, unique among the peoples of the world, not only expect war, they expect, indeed demand, that they win any war they enter. That is why Korea was such a shock, such a break in tradition. We did not win the Korean War, we accepted a stalemate and only a national military hero like Eisenhower could have gotten the people to stand for it.

Despite the example of deadlock in Korea, perhaps because of it, Americans were not prepared to accept a deadlock in Vietnam. And a larger-than-life Texan like Lyndon Johnson could not abide the thought. In his typically Texan style, he would boast that "We're gonna nail the coonskin to the wall." He was not only the President, he was the Lone Ranger, and he was going to get those varmints in black pajamas waving red flags. He would not negotiate. Hell, no, he was going to win and he instructed his generals to tell him he was winning. They obliged, with ludicrous reports of "body counts" and enemies killed. They tried to defoliate jungles and did destroy much land and burn tens of thousands of people with napalm and chemical agents, but this was not winning the war.

American planes dropped as much tonnage on Vietnam by 1968

as they had dropped on Japan or Germany in World War II. After 1968 increased tonnage of explosives dropped surpassed all the bombs loosed on both Japan and Germany. And they called it a "limited war." It is true that no atomic bombs were used. Had they been, all Asia and much of the world would have turned against the United States. It is true, too, that war had not been declared, Americans were not totally mobilized. But Johnson did send 525,000 men to fight in Vietnam and virtually wiped out all of its northern cities except the capital, Hanoi, and the port, Haiphong, although both were hard hit. It was not all-out war but it was not very limited, either.

By 1967 Johnson and his advisors knew it could not be won, despite the absurd claims of military spokesmen in Saigon, whose daily briefings were ridiculed by reporters as the "Five O'Clock Follies." Tragically, Johnson could not concede that he could not win, so he lumbered along, lost in the jungle. It was a reenactment of the French tragedy which Ho Chi Minh had foreseen at our dinner in Paris twenty years earlier, a war between a tiger and an elephant. The elephant was being clawed and losing his lifeblood slowly, unable to corner the tiger and crush him with his sharp tusks and powerful body.

I tried to tell this to my fellow Americans in broadcasts, articles, and lectures. Many heard me and joined the antiwar movement. Many more did not. Then I wrote an article for the *Columbia University Journal.* A word in the title would become common usage and play its part in the national debate: extrication. The article was entitled "The Case for Extrication." Many writers and speakers began to combine "extrication" with another word, one from David Halberstam's book on Vietnam, "quagmire." How to extricate ourselves from the Vietnam quagmire was the question of the day.

The article from the *Journal* was reprinted, with my permission, by the antiwar Quakers, who sold almost two million copies at a quarter apiece to finance their projects. I had waived all royalties.

Toward the end of 1966 I received a call from a distinguished scholar, John Seely, Dean of the Center for the Study of Democratic Institutions, headed by one of America's finest journalists, Pulitzer Prize winner Harry Ashmore. Seely invited me out to their place in California to discuss a project they had in mind. They wanted me to go on a trip through Asia, particularly the fighting fronts in Indochina, beginning in Japan, then on to South Vietnam, North Vietnam, if I could get in, Laos and Cambodia, Thailand, Singapore, Malaysia, and Indonesia.

A retired dentist, Irving Laucks, had offered to finance the trip. We spent a week working out details. Dorothy was with me and made a number of suggestions, the most determined and startling of which was her decision that she would go with me.

"You've gone off to many wars and revolutions, leaving me home to worry about you. No more. This time, I'm going. I can take photos, make sketches, and take notes. In any case, I'm going or you are not." It was very much like the speech she had made back in 1947 when, pregnant, she insisted on going to Prague. Dorothy is a considerable person, a believer in equal rights for women, and not at all willing to play the role of the little lady knitting at home. I agreed at once.

The first big problem would be to clear our passports for North Vietnam. In those days, all passports were stamped "Not to be used in North Vietnam," and a number of other communist and embattled places. We flew to Washington to see the assistant secretary of state for Asia, our old friend Averell Harriman. Harriman was enthusiastic about the prospect of getting an experienced TV foreign correspondent into the communist North. The only man to get into Hanoi had been Harrison Salisbury of *The New York Times.* He had been restricted to Hanoi itself.

Harriman was anxious to get more observers in, and above all, he asked me to make a special effort to find out what was happening in the prisoner of war camps. He hoped, too, that I could get out of Hanoi and try to see what the rest of North Vietnam looked like after our massive bombing raids. Aerial photos were not enough. They could not tell anything about public morale or how people were living in the bombed areas. He sent us to a woman in charge of the Passport Office and she struck out the restrictions in our passports. So our trip was officially endorsed by the government. This would protect us from critics who would want to charge us with consorting with the enemy. Dorothy and I went as reporters, not as "peaceniks" or dissidents. This was professionally of the utmost importance.

From Honolulu we flew to Tokyo for a week. I obtained interviews with the prime minister and finance minister. Dorothy accumulated more useful information by checking the department stores, shops, and factories. She said that Japanese industry had made incredible strides. Their workmanship was of the highest quality, and Dorothy predicted that the Japanese would become a redoubtable commercial rival. Dorothy is a keen-eyed, tough-bargaining comparison shopper. I have watched her haggling with Arab merchants in the alleys of the Djemaa-El-Fna in Marrakesh, Morocco. I did not doubt her prediction about the Japanese.

From Tokyo we flew on to Saigon, resisting the temptation of a brief holiday in Hong Kong—with regret, but a sense of mission. Saigon had not changed much since my visit in 1954, except that the uniforms in the street were American and that the city was bursting with violence and corruption, rape, theft, and drugs. I could not get anyone, American or South Vietnamese military or diplomatic officials, to drive me outside of Saigon. They went everywhere by armed helicopter, flying over villages I wanted to visit, to land in heavily fortified places. It became obvious that the Vietcong, the communists, controlled the area around the capital and, in fact, the entire delta.

News sources from the past told me that it was the same as the last years of the French, with the Americans controlling the South by day, the Viets controlling it by night. Village chiefs would pay taxes to Saigon officials and then to the communists. They administered their villages under orders from both contending sides. When I tried to discuss this with military officers, they told me harshly to "get on the team or get out of Saigon." I got out of Saigon, for there was no way I would get on their deaf-and-dumb team.

We flew to Phnom Penh, Cambodia. It looked like a sun-drenched French provincial town in the Midi. We checked into an unexpectedly luxurious hotel, the Royal, with a big swimming pool surrounded by palm trees, and with the scent of orange and lemon blossoms in the air. We were greeted by Paul Johnson and his wife, Jean, running the Quaker mission in Cambodia, and by one of Japan's leading reporters, Kyoichi Sawada. They were all waiting for visas to Hanoi. Sawada would be killed in an ambush years later when the war swept over Cambodia.

I checked in with the embassy of North Vietnam and filled

out visa applications. There was a line about people we might know in Hanoi and I wrote down "President Ho Chi Minh." The consular official, who spoke excellent French, asked me how I came to know President Ho. I told him about meeting Ho in Fontainebleau and Paris and that the president had dined at my home. He whistled silently and made a notation on my application form, assuring me it would get prompt attention.

While waiting, we hired a car and guide and went to visit one of the great archaeological and art treasures of the world, the ancient temple of Angkor Wat. We bought pressings of the lovely frieze carvings on the temple walls. As we drove through lush tropical jungle we saw a profusion of brilliantly colored flowers and the bent backs of peasants, knee-deep in the water and mud of rice paddies. We stopped in many small villages and were offered cool lemonade, bright red slices of watermelon, orange mangoes, and a fragrant fruit we had never tasted before, mangoustines, a kind of perfume-scented, astringent but luscious litchi nut. Everyone was kind and hospitable. Years later, Dorothy and I would suffer as we heard the news of the torture and slaughter of those gentle people by a monstrous communist leader, a madman named Pol Pot, more bloodthirsty and cruel than Idi Amin, an Asian Hitler.

We returned to Phnom Penh and were invited to the palace by King Norodom Sihanouk, the saxophone-playing monarch, a tubby, jolly fellow. He was very fearful of the war in Vietnam spilling over into his country. The North Vietnamese were already infiltrating down jungle paths, called the Ho Chi Minh trail, to attack South Vietnam, and Americans were shelling the trail inside Cambodia. I knew from press statements that our people were denying any shelling of Cambodian territory. Sihanouk shrugged. "They are lying, you know."

We dined on the lawn of the British ambassador's estate and heard rumblings far-off. When we asked about it, he said, "Oh, it's your boys dropping some of their eggs in the jungle." Everyone in Cambodia seemed to know about our shelling and bombing despite official denials. We would learn, years later, that one of the men who plotted out targets for American bombing under Nixon, and who consistently lied about it, was Thomas Enders. He became later a key American official in charge of policy in the Caribbean, particularly Nicaragua and El Salvador.

At four-thirty in the morning, my bedside phone rang. I was still woolly-headed with sleep when I heard a voice ask me to come to the embassy of North Vietnam, on Mao Tse-Tung Boulevard, to see Nguyen Van Bich, who had an important message for us. I slipped out of bed, careful not to disturb Dorothy, pulled on cotton slacks, a light, open-necked shirt, and sandals, and went through the cool marble lobby of the Royal Hotel to hail a pedicab boy. It was dark, the sky was deep blue velvet, glittering with a billion stars, the air cool. In two hours, the sun would rise and melt the pavements. That is why I was called before dawn, when it was still cool enough to move about.

Nguyen Van Bich was waiting for me, dressed in a whiter-than-white shirt, a black tie, and black trousers, small and slender like most Vietnamese. He served me a cold beer while he drank boiling hot Chinese green tea. "Where is Mrs. Schoenbrun?" he asked as his first question. When I told him she was with me, but still asleep at the Royal Hotel, he smiled and said, "Good. I have your visas and I was instructed by Hanoi not to give you yours unless she accepted hers." When I asked why, he replied, "We put great faith in women. They are more peace-loving and commonsensical than men. Our women play a most important role in our war effort. President Ho was most anxious that you come with your wife. Besides, she was his hostess in Paris and he wishes now to receive you in his home."

At breakfast back in the hotel, the Johnsons and Sawada congratulated us on getting the visas so quickly, admitting a little jealousy, for they had been waiting for more than six weeks. "When did you first apply for the visa?" Paul Johnson asked. I smiled at him and said, "Twenty-one years ago." When I told them the story of how we had met Ho in Paris, they understood why our visas had been granted so swiftly.

Paul generously helped me through the horrendous red tape of the journey. We had to get exit visas from the Royal Cambodian police and security forces, as well as Royal Air Cambodia, the airline. We needed transit visas through Vientiane, Laos, and then a priority number for our reservations on the plane. There were a dozen categories of officials who had higher priorities than we, but the Indian travel agent smiled and said, "Don't worry, you'll get your seats. The others are all International Control Commission officials and the ICC does not pay. You are the only paying passengers, so they'll take you."

I could not believe my eyes when we walked across the tarmac to our plane. Although it had been painted white and had civilian outfitting, its configuration brought me back some twenty-five years to Camp Ritchie and our class in airplane identification, enemy and friendly. It was a B-17, "Flying Fortress," the main bomber of our Air Force in World War II. It must have been the only Flying Fortress extant outside the Smithsonian Institution. I said nothing to Dorothy about flying that ancient crate through Asia's summer squalls and typhoons. It was not pressurized or air-conditioned. We would boil on the ground, freeze over mountains, and would be almost deaf for three days after our flight to Hanoi.

We got to Vientiane without any difficulty. But when we took off from Laos to Hanoi, we were ordered to turn back because of American warplanes in the air between us and Hanoi. The next day we took off again in thick gray fog. The plane began to bump and twist like a belly dancer. Our ears snapped and then went dead when the pilot tried to fly over the weather. The old Fort groaned and creaked against a strong headwind. Suddenly we dropped like an elevator out of control, a few hundred feet, our stomachs in our throats. Then the plane bucked like a bronco. The pilot announced that a typhoon had swept into our flight path and he was turning around and heading back to Vientiane again. Back we went and were grounded in Vientiane for three days.

This gave us a chance to attend some diplomatic receptions and meet Prince Souvannah Phouma, the head of the government, and William Sullivan, the American ambassador. We saw "Air America" planes parked at the field. The local reporters told us that it was a phony CIA company, running arms and smuggling opium. Sullivan denied that there was any American bombing of Pathet Lao rebel positions. Later we would discover that, like Thomas Enders, Sullivan himself was selecting bomb targets in conferences with the Air Force every morning. There was no end of barefaced lying by our officials in Indochina.

We finally took off again and made it to Hanoi. But the day we landed, the U.S. Air Force had bombed Hanoi. Our planes had knocked out the Long Bien Bridge and we would have to ferry across the Red River. The temperature at the Gia Lam Airport was one hundred, and it was nighttime. Daytime was a furnace. Monsoon rains did no good. They only raised steam from the burning sidewalks. The heat and humidity of North Vietnam in the summer were the worst burden of our trip, worse than the six to eight air raids daily, for the bombers went by quickly while the oppressive, suffocating heat never ceased. We would shower, dry ourselves off, and be soaking wet again in a minute. Bad as Hanoi was, the jungle was much worse, for we would drive through swarms of insects that would burrow into our noses, mouths, ears, and eyes. One day, our guide took us to a mountain base. There the air was cool, an escape from the oven. But we slept on wooden slats, without a mattress, in a cave, and we washed in ice-cold mountain water piped in from a nearby stream.

We had been given permission to see Hanoi and its air defenses and then go south toward the demarcation line and the area of the heaviest bombing. Hanoi looked like a porcupine, with spiny steel snouts of antiaircraft guns bristling all around the city. I could believe American pilots who reported the thickest flak since Berlin in World War II. We then took the ancient Route Mandarine, a plumb line north to south, the principal supply route of North Vietnamese forces and their guerrillas operating in the South.

As we drove down Route 1 in the dark, the road was suddenly lighted up as bright as daytime. American Pathfinder planes were dropping flares over the road to light the way for bombers and fighter-bombers coming in for an attack on the highway. Our command car pulled off the road and into the cover of the jungle. We dismounted and were pushed deeply into bamboo by our guide. He tried to shove Dorothy into a hole dug in the ground for protection against shrapnel but when she directed her flashlight into the hole and saw spiders and other crawly things, she pulled back. So did I. We huddled on the ground against bamboo roots as the bombs began falling on the highway.

Within five minutes the bombers had veered off and away. When Dorothy and I walked back to our command car out of the bamboo thickets, we saw an astonishing sight. Long antlike lines of men, women, and children were out on the road busily shoveling dirt and gravel into huge craters blown out by our bombers. There had been thousands of bicycles on the Route Mandarine. The riders all were carrying shovels, lashed to the sides. Apparently they had a lot of experience coping with bombs. In little more than an hour, every crater was filled in and the riders remounted their bikes, or walked alongside them, pushing them along.

Across the front and back wheels of each bicycle, a wooden plank had been bolted on, and on it were tied baskets. My guide explained that each basket carried fifty pounds of weight, a total of one hundred pounds of food, ammunition, and spare parts per bike. Twenty bicycles carried one ton of materiel. There were tens of thousands of bicycles moving constantly up and down the highway day and night. It was awesome. The Vietnamese people could move as many supplies as our famed Red Ball Express. Our bombing was futile. It could not stop the flow of materiel to the fighting areas. Vietnam was not a great industrial power with six-lane highways dependent on being able to move trucks. There was no dense concentration of factories. Our bombers had no vital targets. We were trying to swat a swarm of mosquitoes with sledgehammers.

Our car got moving again and within an hour we found ourselves at a river crossing. Here our bombers had found a valid target, a bridge, which they had knocked out. It had been an utterly useless exercise. The Vietnamese simply floated six flat-bottomed sampans down to the bridge site, lashed them together with pontoons made of empty gasoline drums, and then laid over them a carpeting of wooden planking. It was not an army engineer's idea of a bridge, but it worked. The bicycles, a few army trucks, and our command car moved slowly over the "bridge." It creaked and squeaked as we rolled over it but it held and we were across. The U.S. had lost hundreds of planes costing hundreds of millions, and lost many of their pilots in our constant bombing of North Vietnam, yet all to no avail. It was a senseless, tragic waste. I thought of the men in the Pentagon grinding out their communiqués of air raids, dutifully reported by the media. I would have to report the truth to the American people. I wondered how many would believe me or curse me for blasting their illusions.

We drove deeper south and the terrain began looking like a lunar landscape. The millions of tons of explosives had, indeed, torn up a huge part of North Vietnam. The devastation was almost total. Yet we saw peasants who had converted bomb craters, filled with water, into a fish nursery. They were working the rice paddies which bombs could not destroy.

We were almost killed on a collective farm when three Navy planes, heading back to their carrier, came out of the sun, dived down, and began strafing the field. Luckily, we were near the dairy shed at the time and we jumped into a cow's stall with bullets whistling all around us. I hugged Dorothy tightly when she got up uninjured, and was proud of her when she smiled at me ruefully and said, "Well, it seems that we are military objectives." She was referring to Air Force claims that our planes did not bomb or shoot at civilians or peaceful villages, only at "military objectives."

We had seen enough. We asked our guide to take us back to Hanoi, to be there in time for the celebration of Independence Day. We had been invited and would see Ho Chi Minh. The ride back was ghastly, under a merciless sun. We had a case of lemonade in our car but when we opened a bottle to drink it, it was boiling hot like tea from a kettle. The car bumped on the roads and then slithered in the mud on top of dikes, with a thirty-foot drop on either side. The lemonade slopped and sloshed out of the bottles, covering us with sticky liquid. Flies, mosquitoes, and bees immediately swarmed on us, attracted by the sugar in the drink and our hot blood. It was torture night and day.

When we got back to our hotel room, which we had looked upon as the Black Hole of Calcutta, it looked like a suite at the Ritz. Dorothy should be in the *Guinness Book of World Records* for a nonstop fourteen-hour shower. Her body was covered with bruises and insect bites, her hair wildly tangled and snarled. She told me she was ready to play one of the three witches in *Macbeth,* "all three," she added.

We spent the next day transcribing notes of our journey through North Vietnam. We described what happens in a hamlet of some thirty huts when the air-raid sirens sound, each inhabitant scurrying to do a special task, tots of four and five gathering up chicks and piglets, older children rounding up goats, teenagers racing to the field to the bullocks to drive them into deep slit trenches, mothers and babies dashing to other trenches, the men grabbing guns and sending sons out as spotters. We saw this first in the hamlet of Phu Xa, in the village of Phu Thuong. In a raid a year earlier, before they were prepared and drilled, twenty-four villagers had been killed and twenty-two wounded in a raid.

It was a Catholic hamlet but many of the Catholics had joined the Communist Party since the war. The communists provided arms, training, seed, food, medicine. The villagers huddled around the local communist agent for protection. I recalled Ho Chi Minh's assertion twenty years earlier: "Right now," he had said, "only ten percent of our people are communist, ninety percent nationalists and Catholics or Buddhists or other religions. By the time we have been at war four or five years, those figures will reverse and ninety percent of the people will be communists." He had been correct. The French and then the Americans, in their zeal to fight communism, did the very opposite. They made the country communist, for they permitted the communists to wear the mantle of nationalists defending independence against white, Western intruders in their country.

That night, as we dined at the hotel, our guide suddenly arrived at about nine-thirty, his face beaming. "Come with me quickly. Your application to visit a prisoner of war camp has been approved." We were delighted and surprised. We had made the request on arrival more than a month earlier and had been told that there was little hope, so we had forgotten it.

We went out to a waiting car with two army officers in it. Dorothy had run up to our room to get a little sack she clutched as though it were a jewel case ever since we had left Phnom Penh. It contained a special skin lotion given to her by the Quaker Jean Johnson, who had gotten it from a Mrs. Hughes back in the States. Her husband, an Air Force pilot, had been shot down over Hanoi. He had earlier sustained severe burns on his arms and needed the lotion for the scar tissue, which would dry up, crack, bleed, and itch to the point of torture if not treated. Jean had given it to Dorothy, asking her to try to get it to Colonel Hughes. Dot had been badgering every official we saw, challenging them to prove their humanity by letting her deliver the lotion to the colonel. She was determined to do so that very night.

Our car drove through the darkened Hanoi streets, twisting and turning until it drove through the gates of a French colonial mansion much like a foreign embassy. It had been converted into an army barracks and prison. We knew at once that we would be shown a showcase prison, nothing like the real POW stockades where our men were being held. Later we would learn that the prisoners called it the "Hanoi Hilton," set up to impress foreign visitors. The officer in charge, Commandant Bui, received us in a pleasant living room with well-stuffed armchairs covered in cool white linen. He told us straight off that Colonel Hughes was not being held in this camp but had been brought here just for us.

We were then taken to a reception room where tables were laid out with lemonade, tea, cakes, and cigarettes. A camera team was waiting to film the event. A door opened at the rear of the room and a tall man, thin and stooped, came in blinking at the bright camera lights. Hughes had been told who we were. He thanked Dorothy as she handed him his lotion. He was about forty years old, with black trenches under his eyes. He said he was not ill but suffered from the heat. He wanted his wife to know that he was all right so he rolled back his sleeves and rolled up his trouser leg to show the camera his scar tissue.

"You see," he said, "no bleeding, no cracking." There was virtually no skin at all on his arm and leg, just scar tissue. He had been told that he could give us a written message to his wife and could also record one directly on the camera microphone. As he started to talk, he choked up and began to cry. He finally pulled himself together and recited a brief message obviously taught to him but which he seemed to believe. He expressed his remorse at what he had done as a pilot and asked his wife to do what she could to persuade our people to end the bombing. Dorothy fought to hold back tears. The colonel was clearly deeply troubled and I was surprised that the Vietnamese had let us see him, for he was no showcase prisoner. I suspected that Dorothy's vehemence had frightened them and they were afraid all their efforts to persuade her of their cause would be lost if she had not been permitted to deliver the lotion to him.

We were then led across the courtyard to a low, shedlike building that must have once been servant's quarters. The commandant told us that the prisoners had not been apprised of our coming. We knew they would be startled. We were led into a narrow hallway and the commandant opened a door. We could see, as the door opened, three men in purple-and-red striped pajamas jump up from their beds to stand at rigid attention. They had surely been under strict military discipline. As we came into the room, they gaped at Dorothy as though she were a ghost, and one of them asked hesitantly, "You Americans?" When we said we were, and the commandant had not made a move to interfere, they began laughing and cheering and crowding around us, shaking hands and shouting out a barrage of questions. We got them calmed down and told them we were not government people but reporters. They introduced themselves: Air Force lieutenants Robert Abbott, age twenty-five, from Deckerville, Michigan; James Shively, twenty-five, from Spokane, Washington; and Loren Torkelson, twenty-five, Crosley, North Dakota.

All had been shot down and slightly wounded but they told us they had been given adequate medical care and food. They complained about the lack of letters from home, their need for books and recreational materials. They got enough exercise and were in good physical shape, and were clearly showcase prisoners in a showcase camp. When I asked to visit other camps, we were sharply refused. The "Hanoi Hilton" was the only Potemkin façade that we were going to be shown. We were grateful even for that little and the men were delighted to meet fellow Americans even so briefly. We took down their home phone numbers and promised to call their families when we got home. Meanwhile their families would learn they were alive and well from their local newspapers, which would receive my dispatches on the wires.

We had a surprise waiting in the next room (they were rooms, not cells). When the door opened, we saw a husky, good-looking youngster sprawled out on a cot. He did not jump to attention. He slowly arose with a lazy grin on his face. His name was Doug Hegdahl and he told us he was an apprentice seaman. I gaped at him. "What in the world is an apprentice seaman doing in a POW camp in Hanoi?" Doug grinned again and explained that he was standing at the rail of the U.S.S. *Canberra,* a guided-missile ship, when coast artillery opened up and the captain took sharp, evasive action, pitching Doug overboard into the South China Sea.

"I was out there, twenty miles from land, with sharks all around, saying my prayers, when suddenly a hand grabbed my hair and I was yanked aboard a fishing boat." Hegdahl laughed loudly. "Mister, prison camp is no vacation resort but it's got the South China Sea beat by far. I'm lucky to be alive. No complaints. I'm living on borrowed time."

We went back to our hotel and transcribed our notes on the visit. In the morning, a security officer came by to take us to the

National Assembly Hall for Independence Day ceremonies. Along the way we saw giant posters showing an ugly, big-nosed, scowling Uncle Sam, wearing spectacles and a red, white, and blue stovepipe hat and striped jacket. The captions on the poster in bright red block letters proclaimed: DA DAO GION XON GIAC MY—DOWN WITH JOHNSON THE AMERICAN PIRATE. All along the road, there were graffiti with the two most hated words in the Vietnamese language, GION XON.

Some two thousand people were in the hall, carrying flowers and the national flag. The Cabinet and general staff were on the stage and everyone stood and cheered when two men walked out of the wings to center stage. One, fairly tall and slender (I don't think I ever met a fat Vietnamese), walked arm in arm with a small man, so frail he must have weighed only eighty pounds. The old man's hair was snow white, as were his long chin whiskers. With a start I recognized Ho Chi Minh. He had aged greatly in the twenty years since I had last seen him. I was certain that he was seriously ill. I became convinced of it when the other man, his prime minister, Pham Van Dong, led him to an armchair and helped him sit down.

Pham Van Dong delivered the traditional Independence Day speech, normally made by Ho himself. When he had finished, Ho arose and made his way slowly to the rostrum. The hall exploded with applause and cheers. In a feeble voice, Ho said he hoped that there would be peace before the next Independence Day. He spoke for only about fifteen seconds and seemed to be having difficulty getting the words out. My suspicions were confirmed when I was led backstage later to shake his hand. His hands were bony and brittle. I could see a distinct droop on the right side of his mouth. Ho had clearly suffered a stroke and had not fully recovered.

Pham Van Dong told me that President Ho would have liked to dine with us to repay our hospitality in Paris but that he could not stand the hot weather in Hanoi and would be taken to a favorite mountain retreat immediately. Dorothy and I were ushered out at once. We would lunch with Pham Van Dong and attend receptions by General Giap, the famed conqueror of Dien Bien Phu, and other ministers. Pham Van Dong would grant me a two-hour interview just before we left Hanoi.

My agent, Nate Bienstock, had done wonders arranging for dispatches from Hanoi, which I cabled to a Paris newspaper, and which were syndicated throughout Europe, Asia, Canada, and the United States. My dispatches received very wide circulation around the world. There would be much more to be done after I left Hanoi and its military censorship. The next stop on our journey would be Bangkok, Thailand.

Waiting for us at the airport there was my former CBS, Paris colleague Lou Cioffi, who had become a close friend of ours. Lou was then working for ABC News. We embraced. He handed Dorothy a bouquet of orchids, with colors we had never before seen. He then whisked us away in an air-conditioned Mercedes limousine to a palatial hotel suite.

Lou was excited and wanted to know all about our trip. He told me he had seen my dispatches and that they had provoked a lot of comment. John Scali would be flying in the next day to do a series of interviews with me. Then, when we had finished our trip through Southeast Asia, down to Indonesia, and had flown home, ABC News wanted to do a series of reports for the evening news show and one or two half-hour specials. He gave me a letter from Bienstock informing me that the *Saturday Evening Post* wanted a four-thousand-word cover story, which would also be syndicated worldwide. The trip would be a sensational success and a big money earner.

We spent a week of Rest and Recreation in Bangkok, Dorothy buying up all the beautiful Thai silk robes, scarves, neckties, and bolts to bring to friends, dressmakers, and tailors in New York and Paris. We sent it all home air freight, addressed to dear old Uncle Nate Bienstock who would get it through customs and hold it for us, one of his many invaluable services. I went to the U.S. Embassy while Dot was shopping and spent hours reading through back copies of the American newspapers and magazines to catch up on all we had missed while sweating through the jungles of Vietnam. We had missed a lot.

Stalin's daughter had come to New York and then astonished officials by requesting asylum. Hundreds of thousands of antiwar protesters had gathered in Central Park, New York. Seventy thousand counterdemonstrators, led by hard-hat construction workers, staged an eight-hour parade in New York in support of American troops in Vietnam. Our poor country was being torn apart in a political civil war.

The Israelis, in six days, had won one of the swiftest, most triumphant victories against greater Arab forces. Cassius Clay was fined ten thousand dollars and sentenced to five years imprisonment for refusing to be drafted. He would come back to the ring as Muhammad Ali, burying his "slave name," Cassius Clay. The worst race riots in American history erupted in Detroit on July 23, taking 43 lives, hundreds injured and 5,000 homeless before it ended. Property damage exceeded $200 million. Arab leaders meeting in Khartoum on August 28 declared a policy of "Triple No": "no peace, no negotiations, no recognition of Israel." The Israeli government failed to come up with any peace proposal to exploit its military victory. Both sides had lost an important opportunity for peace. Their hatreds and wars would continue right up to today.

We finished our tour and flew home, where I sat down and worked hard for two weeks compiling a one-hundred-eighty-page report for the Santa Barbara Center. I made my scheduled appearances for ABC News and was flooded with requests for lectures and personal appearances. One of them delighted me, a debate in Phoenix, Arizona, against William F. Buckley, Jr., a formidable opponent on most subjects.

The debate had two distinguished sponsors, Peggy Goldwater and Clare Luce. The audience was black-tie and dinner gown, the conservative Establishment of Phoenix, one of the most far right centers in the nation. I will resist the temptation to recount what happened other than to say that it did not quite work out the way the sponsors and the audience had expected.

I was then appointed senior lecturer at the Graduate School of International Affairs of Columbia University to teach the first course on contemporary Vietnam, one of the first in the country. I was made welcome by students who rushed to sign up for the course, and by members of the faculty, several of whom came to audit, that is, observe, my class. I had a public heated debate with a professor named Zbigniew Brzezinski, head of the Center for Communist Studies, who became prominent in government some years later, and conveniently forgot he had at first supported the war in Vietnam. Dean Acheson, in his haughty, elitist style, had once said of him, "Never trust a man with three *z*'s in his name."

In the fall of 1967 and winter-spring of 1968 there was some spectacular movement on the civil rights front, as it erupted in the North, with rioting in Spanish Harlem, Rochester, Milwaukee, New Haven, and Cambridge. Martin Luther King called for civil disobedience in Northern cities to force the federal government to carry out President Johnson's promises. Johnson was losing both his wars, the war on poverty and racism and the war in Vietnam.

There were, however, some victories. Thurgood Marshall took his oath as Supreme Court Justice on October 2, the first black man to do so. Walter Washington was sworn in as commissioner of the District of Columbia, the first black to head a major city government in American history. He was followed quickly by Carl Stokes, elected mayor of Cleveland, and Richard Hatcher, elected mayor of Gary, Indiana, both black, both Democrats. These singular victories served mainly to underline the miserable existence and continued repression of millions of their fellow black Americans.

Johnson's ham-fisted grip on the nation, so tight, so sure at the outset of his term, had begun to slip and then, rapidly, he lost control. Defense Secretary Robert McNamara resigned. Health, Education, and Welfare Secretary John Gardner, opposed to Johnson's policy, followed suit. Johnson had lost, in turn, the men leading his two wars, the war in Vietnam, the war on poverty. Arthur Goldberg, his ambassador to the United Nations, quit, making it three Cabinet members, in a short time, walking out on him.

A B-52 plane, carrying four deadly hydrogen bombs, crashed near Greenland and spewed radioactivity around the area. Two days later, on January 23, 1968, North Korean patrol boats seized a U.S. spy ship, the *Pueblo,* the first time in more than one hundred fifty years that a U.S. Navy vessel had been captured by an enemy. And on January 30, the Vietnamese communists, whom Westmoreland had promised at Christmastime were going down in defeat, the end of the war in sight "at the end of the tunnel," struck back in their most powerful, widespread offensive of the entire war.

The attack came on Tet, the Vietnamese celebration of the lunar New Year. Enemy forces hit some thirty-five to fifty cities and towns. They captured the ancient imperial capital at Hue and drove hard at the big base of Khe Sanh. The war in Vietnam became the longest ever fought by the United States, longer than the War of Independence. General Westmoreland, who had reported so many enemy dead that it would seem there was hardly any enemy left, was aghast when some twenty thousand Vietcong attacked the Marine base at Khe Sanh. The base was under siege, taking heavy casualties, for more than two and a half months. So much for the light at the end of the tunnel.

More than fifty thousand communists hit dozens of cities and towns for almost a month in the Tet offensive. Walter Cronkite, who had been dutifully reporting the fantasies of the Pentagon, finally got off his anchor seat and went to Vietnam himself. He got caught in the biggest battle of the war, the battle of Hue. From then on, he would take a more critical line on the war. When the offensive ended and the American officials had counted many communists dead, wounded, and prisoners, clearing the enemy out of every place they had attacked, the Pentagon and the White House naturally claimed a great victory, asserting that the communist Tet offensive had failed to achieve its objectives.

In fact, the Pentagon did not at all know what North Vietnamese General Giap's objectives really were. He certainly knew that he could not capture and hold main cities and bases against American firepower. That was not his objective. His objective was more psychological than military. He wanted to demonstrate the falseness of Westmoreland's claims that the war was winding down and that the communists had been badly beaten. He wanted the American people to know that at the moment the war had become the longest war in their history, and it was due to go on much longer. In that, he certainly achieved his objective, for Tet was an ice-cold shower for war-weary Americans and for angry youth facing greater draft calls in an unending struggle. Senator George Aiken, a conservative from Vermont who had loyally supported the war effort, showed his disillusion in a cynical comment on Pentagon claims. "If this is failure, I hope the Vietcong never have a major success."

American casualties passed the twenty-thousand mark. Westmoreland's credibility was shattered and he was replaced by General Creighton Abrams. The biggest casualty was President Johnson himself. He had blustered, boasted, and lied. He was politically dead. The death sentence was pronounced by voters in New Hampshire on March 12, 1968. Senator Eugene McCarthy, fed up with the lies and the futility of the war, had decided to run against the incumbent President of his own party. He was little known outside Washington and his home state of Minnesota and given no chance. At the very best, experts felt he might win as much as twenty percent. The experts were wrong. McCarthy won forty-two percent against Johnson's forty-eight percent. He had come close to defeating the President.

Robert Kennedy, who had said he would not split the party by running against the President, changed his mind hastily. McCarthy had already split the party and Kennedy saw his chance. He infuriated McCarthy, one of the earliest supporters of John F. Kennedy, by coming in to steal his near victory from him. Ted Sorensen, Arthur Schlesinger, and Ken O'Donnell, staunch New Frontiersmen, joined Kennedy's team, along with Larry O'Brien who resigned as postmaster general. Johnson was through and he knew it. On March 31, Johnson, a broken man, appeared on national television to announce: "I shall not seek, and I will not accept, the nomination of my party for another term as your President."

Johnson had lost the war in Vietnam, and, because of it, he had also lost the war on poverty, with billions drained away to Asia. He had made progress on his pledge to advance the cause of black Americans but his efforts had been aborted. More blacks than any other Americans were, in proportion, fighting in Vietnam. Martin Luther King, who had at first felt that Vietnam was not a concern of blacks, had come to realize that there would be no progress while the war was being fought and had become a vocal opponent to the war.

At a meeting of the California Democratic Council, I was a speaker, along with Dr. King. Andrew Young introduced me to him before lunch in the greenroom. Dr. King astonished me by saying, "You're the man who got me into a lot of trouble." He smiled at my startled reaction and added: "It was your article on 'The Case for Extrication,' in *The Columbia University Journal,* which turned me around and made me see the need to oppose the war in Vietnam." My wife, daughter, and son-in-law were there and heard the exchange. The pride and love in their eyes gave me strength to continue the struggle.

Johnson, not clearly comprehending the connection between his two wars, at home and abroad, felt betrayed by the blacks for whom he had done so much. He could never accept anything less than total allegiance. Lyndon Johnson had truly dreamed of becoming a modern Lincoln, emancipating the blacks and the poor from economic depression and political repression. Tragically for him, for the blacks and the poor, and for all of us, the Vietnam nightmare had blasted his dream.

CHAPTER 18

THE UNMAKING OF AMERICA

Much of what we are suffering today in the eighties finds its roots in both the successes and the errors of Lyndon Johnson, particularly the war in Vietnam, compounded by his successors but created by him. Sociologists had already been writing about the phenomenon they called the Revolution of Rising Expectations. They pointed out that revolutions are rarely caused by downtrodden people without hope, but rather by repressed peoples who are stimulated by hope and moved to revolt when they see opportunity arising. Johnson's greatest achievements, his civil rights legislation, above all the Voting Rights Act of 1965, stimulated hope for the blacks and other deprived people of America.

The blacks, seeing progress and the chance for true equality, would not settle for a slow spoon-feeding of freedom. Dr. King told me one day that he was furious with those who told blacks to be patient, not to press too hard, too fast for full rights. He said, "The struggle of the American blacks for full and equal citizenship is the only case in history of a one hundred year dash." The advances engineered by Kennedy and Johnson did not satisfy the blacks, it spurred them on to obtain more and to obtain it in reality, not in laws that were more often honored in the breach.

Black ghettos exploded across America in the late sixties, in the North and the South both, from Harlem to Watts, cutting a swath through New Haven, down to Washington, Baltimore, and Atlanta, across the Middle West through Dayton and Toledo, Detroit, Chicago, Milwaukee, Minneapolis, and on to San Francisco and Los Angeles. Dr. King marched peacefully, preaching, like Gandhi, passive resistance, but Rap Brown, Stokely Carmichael, the Black Muslims, and the Black Power movements shouted, "Burn, baby, burn."

More than a decade had gone by since the landmark Supreme Court decision "Brown vs. the Board of Education," rejecting the segregationist argument of "equal but separate" schools for whites and blacks. Racism was still rampant in segregated schools throughout the land. The blacks now wanted rights to be enforced, not merely passed by Congress and the Supreme Court.

As we moved toward the seventies, rising expectations proved to be infectious. There were poor whites as well as poor blacks in America, oppressed women, rebellious students. Tens of thousands of Americans refused to be drafted, preferring prison or exile to the war in Vietnam. The fever spread to all youth in all social classes but was particularly virulent among the affluent, who had become increasingly alienated by a society they did not like or trust. Wealthy youngsters were easily identified, for they wore the dirtiest, scraggiest jeans, had the longest hair, filthy fingernails, and a vocabulary composed mainly of four-letter words. The Free Speech movement, started in Berkeley, had little to do with freedom and mostly was devoted to dirty words. Unlettered, largely ignorant freshmen told their professors what they wanted to study. The word "relevance" became a revolutionary slogan.

I was teaching at Columbia University when it exploded in 1968. Grayson Kirk, the president, did not know how to cope with an unprecedented challenge to authority. He called in the New York police to clear unruly students from occupied buildings. They did so with a brutality that would have been inexcusable even against hardened criminals. Yet most New Yorkers cheered the police. The generation gap had split children and parents, old against young. Like the wave of black violence, student violence flooded across the nation even in the most conservative centers.

The largest, most underprivileged class in America, women, were infected by revolutionary zeal. A Women's Liberation Movement exploded in a kind of spontaneous combustion. It was serious and long overdue but it caught American men by surprise and they reacted in anger. A few minor and silly incidents, such as bra-burning, were exaggerated out of all importance by the media and served to discredit the women's movement. There were endless linguistic arguments about the proper form of address for female professionals or officials. Is a woman poet a poet or a poetess? Is a presiding officer a chairwoman or a chairperson? Male wits had fun with such words as "manhole cover." Is a female entering college a freshwoman or a freshperson? Gloria Steinem, one of the brightest, most intelligent leaders of the feminist movement, insisted that the linguistic issue was a genuine one. I was not convinced but felt I would not allow such an argument to weaken in any way my own dedication to the cause of equal rights for women. The final defeat of the Equal Rights Amendment in the summer of 1982 is not final. The amendment will be put forward again and it will eventually pass when men come to realize that their own rights are not endangered by equality for all.

As Lyndon Johnson's term wound down in the spring of 1968, America was coming apart everywhere and all at once, like the wonderful one-horse shay. On March 28, just three days before Johnson, confused, bitter, and frustrated, announced he would not accept nomination for another term, violence exploded in Memphis during a march in support of a sanitation workers strike. One black man was killed, hundreds of blacks and whites injured. The National Guard was called in. On April 4, in a Memphis still trembling from the violence, a sniper shot and killed Martin Luther King.

Riots exploded in black ghettos throughout the country and many whites joined blacks to vent their anger and sorrow. It was as though some evil demons had set about to tear America apart. We seemed to be witnessing the unmaking of America as the sixties came near the end. We could not know that it would get worse in the seventies, when our most precious institutions, including the Presidency itself, would come near breaking down.

Riots erupted in Chicago on April 15, and Mayor Daley, a hard case, gave orders to his police "to shoot to kill" anyone engaging in arson, looting, or rioting. In effect, that meant that a teenager stealing a television set during a riot could be killed. There was no law in the land making looting a capital crime but Mayor Daley personally instituted such a procedure by fiat. Most Chicagoans, angered and frightened by lawlessness in their city, cheered the mayor's order. Americans had been provoked beyond reason. More than anger, it was fear that motivated their harsh cries for "law and order," code words for unrestricted brutality by the forces of public safety.

Even liberals screamed for revenge when Robert Kennedy, after winning the California primary, a big step forward toward the nomination and the Presidency, was shot down by Sirhan Sirhan in a Los Angeles hotel. I, myself, resolutely opposed to the death sentence, would have, in grief and fury, accepted the execution of Sirhan. The murders of Martin Luther King and Robert Kennedy, within two months, were more than one could bear. Cleveland erupted in four days of ghetto riots and sniper attacks upon the police. Three policemen died of their wounds. It was a long, hot summer and was about to become hotter as the two major parties prepared for their national conventions to choose a Presidential candidate in the month of August 1968.

The Republican front-runner, from the first primary in New Hampshire, was Richard M. Nixon, with the longest record of public service, as representative, senator, and Vice-President. Nixon got off to a running start when he swept the New Hampshire primary with an overwhelming seventy-nine percent of the votes.

Nixon went on to sweep primary after primary, knocking off all opponents. He was the man of the day in Miami where Republican delegates to the convention acclaimed him as their candidate. For running mate he chose a man unknown to the public outside his own state, Governor Spiro Agnew of Maryland. Headlines across the land asked, "Spiro Who?" We would soon find out.

Nothing that Nixon and Agnew did to advance their own cause could match what the Democrats did to give the election to them by a disgraceful performance at their convention. It was held in Chicago, an appropriate setting, for the stockyards, redolent of blood and broken bones, were symbolic of what would happen at that worst convention in the history of the Democratic Party. Party leaders knew in advance that there would be public protest demonstrations against the war in Vietnam. Dissident groups, ranging from serious citizens to the wildest of radicals, had trumpeted their plans well in advance. A coalition of peace groups had formed the Committee to End the War, under the chairmanship of David

Dellinger, claiming they would rally some fifty thousand people to demonstrate around the Democratic Party convention hall. They would be joined by a motley band of hippies, Yippies, dissidents of all kinds, amounting, they asserted, to a total of some one hundred thousand demonstrators.

Chicago's Mayor Daley, stage manager of the convention, responsible for security, law, and order in his city, the man who had not hesitated to instruct his police to shoot to kill looters and arsonists, was not to be challenged by a collection of "peaceniks and kooks." He turned the convention hall into an armed fortress. Daley put his 12,000 city policemen on emergency alert, working twelve-hour shifts. He sealed all manhole covers in the area and threw a seven-foot-high chain link fence, topped with barbed wire, around convention hall. Some 6,000 National Guardsmen were put on the alert and another 7,500 federal troops received standby orders directly from the White House. Lyndon Johnson may have withdrawn from the race but he still was President and he was not going to let wild-eyed radicals take over his party's convention.

Johnson was, however, humiliated when the Secret Service told him it would be too dangerous for him to attend the convention. Nothing could more starkly illustrate the unmaking of America than the sight of a proud President, isolated in the White House, unable to appear publicly at his own party's convention on the occasion of his birthday.

The Secret Service fears were almost certainly exaggerated but nonetheless very understandable after the assassinations of Martin Luther King and Robert Kennedy. Even the Republicans, with candidates much less controversial than the Democrats, had put in place the tightest security cordon in their history, around the convention center in Miami. The most cautious security was certainly in order. What was not in order and what led to a catastrophe was Mayor Daley's belligerence and readiness to enter into combat with any who would challenge his authority in Chicago. Daley had many fine qualities but his dictatorial rule over Chicago and his pugnacity were not among them.

There is no doubt that the police were severely provoked and attacked by savages who had infiltrated the peaceful protesters. Policemen were pelted with steel ball bearings, rocks, bricks, and assaulted by baseball bats studded with nails and razor blades when they moved to push back the demonstrators. Both sides were primed for confrontations which could have been avoided by security lines instead of police charges into the crowd.

Inside the hall, the party machine worked smoothly to nominate Hubert H. Humphrey on the first ballot with only token opposition from the liberal candidates Eugene McCarthy and George McGovern. While the business of the convention was proceeding, delegates were watching on television the violence erupting in the streets outside the hall. Many were sickened by the brutality.

One of the most distinguished of the Democrats, Abraham Ribicoff of Connecticut, stood at the rostrum and looked down directly at the Illinois delegation seated in front of him and shouted at Mayor Daley that he was using "gestapo tactics" in Chicago. Daley jumped to his feet, his face scarlet with rage, and began screaming profanities at Ribicoff. Television viewers, watching the close-up camera shots, could read the four-letter words spouting out of Daley's lips even if they could not be heard in the uproar as Daley's claque rose to shout Ribicoff down. Anyone watching the spectacle sensed that the Democrats were destroying themselves and throwing away the election.

Richard Nixon watched this spectacle on television with very special interest and satisfaction. He felt that nothing could now stop him from winning the election. However, it proved to be a cliff-hanger, much closer than anyone had imagined.

The tide began to turn after a Humphrey speech in Salt Lake City calling for an end to the war in Vietnam, breaking with Lyndon Johnson. Liberals, who had been sulking on the sidelines, not contributing efforts or money to the campaign, suddenly realized that their most hated enemy for twenty years and more, Richard Nixon, "Tricky Dickie," was on the verge of becoming President. Frightened Democrats came back to support the party's candidate. On the day before the voters went to the polls, Gallup showed Nixon at forty-two percent, Humphrey at forty percent, George Wallace at fourteen percent, with four percent undecided. It could go either way between the top contenders. In fact, the Lou Harris poll had Humphrey at forty-three percent over Nixon at forty percent.

Tuesday night when the polls closed, the television networks put on a thrilling cliff-hanger of changing results. The electric tally boards went swiveling through changing leads every quarter of an hour, Nixon jumping off to a slight lead, Humphrey passing him, Nixon creeping up to a new lead. As the new day came in after midnight, Humphrey had a thirty-thousand lead, insignificant in the millions of votes, showing no definite trend. Nixon's electoral college votes began to outdistance Humphrey, who still held a somewhat widening popular-vote lead. With votes coming in for Wallace, it began to look in the early morning hours as though no one would win an electoral college majority. That could throw the election into the House, which the Democrats controlled. Nixon had lost a squeaker to Kennedy and it seemed as though he was again going to be nipped at the tape.

Then the West and Far West, whose polls closed latest, began to send in votes. The West is now almost as solidly Republican as the Democrats' once solid South. Nixon's electoral lead jumped and it became clear that he would win by a comfortable electoral college majority. That is the way it finally ended: Nixon 301 delegates, Humphrey 191, Wallace 45. The electoral college tallies are, however, a most inaccurate reflection of how the people voted. In the popular vote, it was one of the closest elections in history, almost a dead heat: Nixon 31.7 million, Humphrey 31.2 million; a margin of less than .7 percent. At the same time, the Democrats won the majority of the Senate and House seats. Nixon would be the first President in more than a century to enter office with the opposition controlling both houses of Congress.

Democratic leaders and liberals were in a state of shock. They got little pleasure from the Congressional victory. Most of them feared and hated Nixon. Worst of all, they wallowed in guilt at their own errors which had cost Humphrey the election. Humphrey was coming on so strong in the last three days of the campaign that had the election taken place three, even two, days later, he would surely have won. The Democrats had cheated themselves of campaign time by delaying their convention to coincide with Johnson's birthday. Many believed that the lost time resulted in a lost election. They were furious, too, with many of the Kennedy and McCarthy voters who were so angry with Humphrey for loyally supporting Johnson and the war in Vietnam until too late that they had stayed home and not voted.

Most scholars of American politics and our most astute political journalists were convinced that the late Democratic Convention and the police brutality in Chicago had given the election to Nixon. Suddenly those who had said there was no valid choice between "the evil of two lessers" realized that there were a number of old and sick men on the Supreme Court and that Richard Nixon would probably get the chance to appoint more Supreme Court Justices than any President since Roosevelt. Supreme Court appointments were for life and Nixon would be setting the judicial climate of America for many years.

It was too late for regrets. Tricky Dickie, the witch-hunting comrade of Joe McCarthy, the man who had accused the Democrats of twenty years of treason, the advocate of get-tough policies with China and Russia, was now the President of the United States. For liberals, it was a chilling thought. For most Americans, it was a gamble.

The popular vote was so close that it is difficult to generalize the reasons for his victory, for it was not a clear-cut victory, not the mandate he had asked for. Still, he had won, so the question was posed: Why did almost thirty-two million Americans choose as their leader a man with the nickname Tricky? Why did they vote for Eisenhower's Vice-President when Eisenhower himself had made it clear enough that he did not think Nixon had the qualities to be President?

No comprehensive, authoritative studies were made to ascertain why Nixon voters had voted for him. There is, of course, a predictable, traditional block of Republican votes, but it is far smaller than the almost thirty-two million who had voted for Nixon. Nixon won independent votes, swing votes, and some Democratic votes. He also profited from Democratic abstentions. Where did the majority margin, however small, come from and why?

One can only speculate on the basis of admittedly narrow and controversial evidence. I asked this question at a great many lectures in the following year. That is not, of course, a reliable sample of opinion. But it did give me a clue. Many people, even liberals, said that they had been thoroughly alarmed and angered by all the multiple rebellions breaking out everywhere in the sixties: the violence of the blacks, the defiance of youth, the demands for women's rights. Many Americans wanted someone who would put down the blacks, the kids, and the women, someone tough enough to stand up to their demands and discipline them all. Humphrey, a lifelong liberal, was not the man to do that. Nixon, a lifelong hard-liner, looked like he could and would take action, not only against radicals at home but against communist enemies around the world.

One cannot say that Americans wanted a tough guy in the White House since almost as many voted for Humphrey as for Nixon. But perhaps one can say that this was the issue that provided the margin and that the issue had been highlighted by the television pictures of rebellion in Chicago. Never since the Civil War had Americans been so torn, had laws been so flouted and morals laughed at.

Magazines published diagrams on how to make bombs. Topless waitresses, their breasts bouncing, wiggled their rumps as they moved between tables, while so-called decent housewives wore mini- and microskirts and see-through blouses formerly seen only in brothels. Our daughters and wives looked like call girls. Our sons looked and behaved like tramps, smoked "shit," and popped their veins with poison bought openly from street pushers. The government was spending money as though there would be no tomorrows, piling up deficits for future generations. All values were being demonetized. There was, unquestionably, a yearning for a government that would balance the budget, uphold the law, bring back old virtues. Whether Nixon was the man to accomplish this was another question. He had, in any case, become the man whose responsibility it would be.

I was determined to keep an open mind on Nixon and his Administration, for reasons of professional integrity, out of respect for the Presidency, and because I had learned in some three decades of covering Presidents in many countries in the West how unpredictable are the actions of a man or woman once elevated to the summit of responsibility. I had never liked or trusted Nixon from his first campaign for the House when he smeared his opponent Helen Gahagan Douglas as a "pinko." He had been a dirty fighter throughout his career, a hawkish Cold Warrior, the kind of man who might lead our country into a real, shooting war beyond Vietnam, a war he fully supported. Yet experience had taught me not to judge a President on his record before entering that magic mansion, the White House. The White House is a mysterious crucible that can turn big men into midgets and midgets into giants.

One of America's most revered Presidents, Abraham Lincoln,

was a small-town lawyer of no great achievements before he entered the White House. John Adams was a famed leader of American political thought, a Founding Father of our Revolution, but his temperament was irascible and revolutionary. Adams had little faith in or liking for democracy. One can argue endlessly about the wisdom of Harry Truman but almost everyone might agree that he entered the White House a very little man and grew to giant stature in that magic mansion. I was willing, therefore, to judge Nixon day by day and month by month, by his performance rather than on his previous record. I was certain we would all be in for many surprises.

His Cabinet was not much of a surprise at first view. It was, in his own image, white, Western, Middle America, middlebrow, conservative. Nixon did try to appoint some Democrats and blacks but his choices all turned him down. Key jobs went to old friends: William Rogers, State Department; John Mitchell, attorney general; Robert Finch, HEW. What the eye did not yet see under the surface were three White House aides who would wield enormous power: H. R. Haldeman, John Ehrlichman, and National Security Advisor Henry Kissinger. They would surface soon enough.

In February, a month after Nixon's inauguration, the North Vietnamese launched a new offensive against our troops, giving the lie again to Pentagon claims, one year earlier, that the "failure" of the Tet offensive had cost the communists so many casualties that they no longer were a coherent fighting force. Nixon struck back, as Johnson had done, with intensive bombing, although the futility of bombing in Vietnam had been clearly demonstrated. There was a twist this time, and very Nixonian. There was intensive bombing of Cambodia, not North Vietnam. Reporters would only discover much later that the bombing of Cambodia had been secretly ordered by Nixon himself, while he publicly denied any knowledge of U.S. bombing in Cambodia. That seemed to be the old Nixon, in keeping with his record for duplicity. In the first few months, the White House crucible did not work any magic on Nixon.

In the Mideast a new leader emerged at the head of an embattled state. Lev Eshkol, Israel's prime minister, died and was succeeded by one of the great personages of our times, Golda Meir, who took over responsibility for the Jewish state on February 26, 1969. No giant of our times stood taller, straighter, wielding power with greater firmness, sensitivity, or compassion than that universal grandmother, pride of the Jewish people, admired by the world, even by the enemies of Israel. When I heard of Golda's appointment (everyone called her Golda, and those of us who knew her loved and revered her), I thought of the day in Paris, at a reception in the Bois de Boulogne, when she had come as Israel's foreign minister to see de Gaulle.

Golda had accompanied the "Lion of Judah," Prime Minister David Ben-Gurion, in a mission to seek French aid for Israel. It was during the period of close French-Israeli cooperation when the French were fighting Arab rebels in Algeria, who were supplied with military materiel by Egypt, so France was inclined to help Israel in her struggle to survive. De Gaulle admired Ben-Gurion and the people of Israel. All that was before the break between de Gaulle and Israel when France discovered that oil was more important to her national interests.

After Ben-Gurion's meeting with de Gaulle, a story made its way around Paris that de Gaulle had asked Ben-Gurion why, in a country fighting for survival against dangerous enemies, he had given the important portfolio of foreign minister to a woman. Ben-Gurion had laughed heartily and replied, "Golda? A woman? Why, Golda Meir is the very best man I've got."

I had not believed the story for a minute. It was just the sort of thing that Parisian wits loved to invent. De Gaulle was always scrupulously polite in his dealings with foreign statesmen, particularly those he admired. I doubted that he would have put such a question to the prime minister of Israel. Still, it was an amusing story with a valid point in it, for there was no doubt that Golda was the most valuable, competent minister in the Cabinet. I wondered if Golda had heard it, so when I had a chance to converse with her at the garden party, I asked her if she had heard what Ben-Gurion had said about her to de Gaulle.

Golda smiled her sweet, sad smile and said: "You mean that he said I was the best man he's got?" I nodded. Golda took a deep drag on her cigarette, shrugged, and said, "Men think that's a compliment." I laughed, but she made a gesture to cut me off and said, "So, there are more serious things to talk about. What have the French been saying of our mission? Are they well disposed?" She fired off questions about the Mirage plane, about the possibility of low-interest credits. I knew she had already been well briefed by her ambassador, one of the best informed diplomats in Paris. But Golda had an insatiable appetite for information and opinion and checked and rechecked everything she heard.

I would not have believed that day that the United States would replace France as Israel's principal supplier of arms or that wise, beloved Golda would become one of the most enthusiastic supporters of Richard Nixon. We would argue later when Golda toured America telling Jewish audiences to vote for Nixon. I thought she was being dangerously indiscreet and, as a foreign leader, should not be interfering in the American electoral process. She brushed aside my remonstrance and said sharply, "Nonsense, I am not worried about diplomatic niceties. Israel is in a life-and-death struggle for survival. Nixon and Kissinger are our friends, they provide the arms for our defense. Without them, we might fall. Don't talk to me about indiscretion. I am concerned only with survival." She was responsible for a large Jewish vote for Nixon.

In March, Dwight D. Eisenhower died, James Earl Ray was sentenced to ninety-nine years in prison for the assassination of Martin Luther King. In April, American dead in Vietnam reached a grim total of 33,641, exceeding the total number killed in Korea, 33,629. Nixon proposed an eight-point peace plan for Vietnam, including withdrawal of all foreign troops within a year and elections supervised by an international body. He then flew to Midway Island in June to meet South Vietnamese Premier General Thieu. He announced that 25,000 American troops would leave Vietnam by August 31.

Later, he would spell out a new "Nixon Doctrine" for Asia. The people of Asia, he declared, must "lead the way to peace" and not look to the United States to do it for them. Nixon warned Asians that "too much dependence on a protector can eventually erode its dignity." This sounded very much like Lyndon Johnson's 1964 campaign pledge not to send American boys to do what Asian boys should do for themselves.

Nixon was duplicitous and mendacious. His supporters would argue that Lyndon Johnson had also deceived and lied to the American people. Indeed he had, but that seems a weak defense of Nixon. There is no principle that a President can cheat and lie because others did. Typical of Nixon twists in the early months was his talk of halting tests on the controversial new weapon the MIRV, multiple bombs that could be carried by an intercontinental missile, then released, with each targeted to hit a different city. That would mean one missile could deliver bombs on six cities instead of only one city, "a bigger bang for a buck." While Nixon was publicly saying it would be wiser to delay testing of the MIRV, the Pentagon was secretly letting the first contracts for production, as Nixon certainly knew.

The first signs of a "new Nixon," of White House alchemy at work, came on his return from his Asian trip. En route home, Nixon stopped off for a visit to Rumania. Although Rumania would proclaim its independence from Moscow and refuse to be a member of the Eastern Bloc, it was, nonetheless, one of the most heavy-fisted, ruthless communist police states behind the Iron Curtain, the kind of red dictatorship that Nixon had built a career on denouncing. Yet, he shook hands most cordially with the dictator and rode through the streets of Bucharest as an honored guest of the communist regime.

Nixon smiled and waved when, to his surprise and delight, tremendous, excited crowds cheered him and waved American flags. The oppressed peoples of Rumania could not protest against their government publicly. They could not march or demonstrate, but the occasion of Nixon's drive through the streets gave them the chance to vent long pent-up emotions and applaud a president whose office was the most respected symbol of freedom in the world.

Perhaps it was that first cheering contact with the peoples of the communist world, rather than any special White House magic, that transformed Nixon, the red-baiter and anticommunist warrior, into Nixon the conciliator, Nixon the peacemaker. In his inaugural address, President Nixon had asserted that "The greatest honor history can bestow is the title of peacemaker." He was not then referring to peace with foreign adversaries but rather peace at home in America's civil strife. He had made that clear by saying that "We are torn by division, wanting unity."

In clear, strong rhetoric, worthy of a Kennedy, Nixon told his fellow Americans, "We cannot learn from one another until we stop shouting at one another—until we speak quietly enough so that our words can be heard as well as our voices." Coming from a man with the most raucous of voices who had spent a lifetime shouting at, cursing out, those who disagreed with him, this inaugural address was an occasion of instant White House magic, if he meant and would practice what he said. In his cunning way, Nixon did decide to play the low-key, soft-spoken role but to use Agnew to spit venom and spread hatred among Americans. He did, however, break with all precedent in his own record when he became the peacemaker seeking détente with China and Russia.

On February 21, 1972, Richard Nixon, who had accused the Democrats of giving China to the reds, flew across the Yangtze River in his plane, the Spirit of '76, and then came down to land in the ancient capital of Peking, which he had denounced as the evil fomenter and supplier of the communist war in Vietnam. No Democrat could possibly have walked through open gates to the old Forbidden City and embraced the dictator of China, Mao Tse-Tung, so often portrayed by Nixon as an evil Fu Manchu. Just as it took a conservative military hero like Eisenhower to make peace in Korea, for which an Adlai Stevenson would have been denounced, so did it take the scourge of the communists, Richard Nixon, to seek peace in Peking, and then, three months later, walk smilingly into the Kremlin, arms outstretched in greeting to the hated red dictator, Leonid Brezhnev.

I had seen startling reversals of form and ideology often, in many lands. It took a crusty old Tory like Winston Churchill to accept and consolidate the welfare benefits introduced to Britain by the socialist Labor Party. It took a socialist like French Premier Guy Mollet to play the role of Napoleon and send an armada to Egypt. The left could most successfully implement policies of the right, and the right could best consolidate the projects of the left, and only Richard Nixon could open the gates of Peking and Moscow.

The fact that Nixon would choose to do so, and abandon positions he had hotly championed for a quarter of a century, was an indication that, deep down, Nixon was not an ideologue. He had no passionate belief in his own doctrines, his own rhetoric. He was, rather, a pragmatist, aiming at targets of opportunity. In the forties, he had sensed that America's hatred of communism would turn to fear during the Cold War, and that he could play upon those fears to advance his own political career. In the seventies, with Russia having broken America's atomic monopoly, engaged in an arms race, the dangers of war had become awesome, and American fears now demanded not war but peace. By offering his hand in peace in Peking and in Moscow, Nixon was bidding for his place in history as the "Great Peacemaker."

Nixon's popularity was high and grew higher after he had flown to Peking and Moscow. Ed Muskie had cracked up. Ted Kennedy had eliminated himself, perhaps forever, as a Presidential candidate by his incredible behavior at Chappaquiddick, failing to report a fatal accident for some eleven hours. Nixon had, however, suffered some setbacks. His Cambodian "incursion" was discovered, infuriating the Congress and setting off the worst student riots, more widespread and violent than the 1968 riots. Four students were shot dead at Kent State in Ohio, and two were killed by the police at Jackson State, in Mississippi. The massacre at My Lai blackened America's name in the world and increased opposition to the war in Vietnam. The publication of the Pentagon Papers exposed the lies and distortions of official communiqués on Vietnam.

Nixon had moved to counter some of these problems by announcing on January 25, at the outset of the electoral year, that Henry Kissinger had held twelve secret negotiating sessions in Paris with North Vietnam officials Le Duc Tho and Xuan Thuy, holding out new hope for peace. He signed a treaty outlawing the use of biological weapons in April, and in May he became the first American President to visit Moscow. He negotiated an agreement to sell $750 million worth of grain to the Soviets. He laughed when the Democrats nominated George McGovern as their candidate on the first ballot at their Miami Beach convention. Nixon knew that McGovern was too far to the left, too radical for America in the seventies. To compound McGovern's troubles, his Vice-Presidential running mate, Thomas Eagleton, resigned in July when the media discovered he had a history of treatment for nervous disorders. There was no doubt in the minds of political reporters and pollsters that Nixon would have an easy victory in November. He did not need the dirty tricks or dirty money that would eventually lead to his disgrace.

On November 7, Richard Nixon swept to one of the most decisive victories in American history, winning the electoral votes of 49 of the 50 states. McGovern was almost totally rejected. Nixon was at the peak of his popularity and prestige. Flushed by victory, he announced, just before New Year's Eve, that he had halted all bombing north of the twentieth parallel in Vietnam and promised peace in the new year ahead.

On January 11, Nixon lifted most of the controls he had imposed on wages and prices. The controls had been another strange aberration in his strange career, breaking with traditional Republican opposition to any wage and price controls. The biggest New Year's present of all was offered to the American people on January 27, a four-party agreement in Paris to end the war in Vietnam and restore peace to that war-ravaged nation.

It would, however, take a long time before the shooting stopped and peace came to Vietnam. It was, in fact, not so much a peace as a face-saving mask for American withdrawal and defeat, as the communists moved to take over the entire country. By then, it was a question of no great concern to a defeated Richard Nixon who had destroyed himself and furnished much of the evidence against himself from tapes he had made of his White House conversations. There is no doubt at all that his own name should have been at the very top of his enemies list. Watergate and his cover-up brought him down. His enemies did not do him in. He did it himself.

To make matters worse for the Administration, Vice-President Agnew was being investigated on charges he had received illegal kickbacks as Baltimore's County Executive. Agnew went on national TV to deny the charges. Two months later, Agnew resigned as Vice-President, pleading "no contest," the equivalent of a plea of guilty. Nixon appointed Gerald Ford to succeed Agnew as Vice-President.

While this internal upheaval was shaking America, the outside world exploded once again, as so often, in the Middle East. On October 6, the holiest of Jewish days, Yom Kippur, the Day of Atonement, when the devout spend the day fasting and praying in their synagogues, the armies of Egypt crossed the Suez Canal, while some two thousand Syrian tanks thundered down the Golan Heights against some two hundred Israeli tanks, many of whose commanders and crew were wrapped in prayer shawls, oblivious to the attack.

For the first time, Arab troops forced the Israelis back. Israel was grievously wounded, staggering, and almost fell. At the last moment, the men and women, boys and girls of Israel closed their ranks, fought back, stabilized the battle lines and then began to strike back. Golda Meir sent urgent messages to her friends Richard Nixon and Henry Kissinger. They were embattled themselves, wounded, bleeding and falling, their leading political aides indicted or about to be, some spilling their guts to investigating committees. Yet they responded to the pleas of Jerusalem and sent urgently needed arms and planes, a fact never to be forgotten by Israel's leaders and by the people of Israel, many of whom still value Nixon and Kissinger as true friends.

A brilliant tank commander, an Israeli General Patton, Ariel Sharon, "Arik," slashed through Egyptian lines, crossed the Suez Canal, encircled an entire Egyptian Army and opened the road to Cairo. Other units smashed the Syrian assault and were within a half hour's drive from Damascus. Out of a threatened defeat, the troops of Israel had again fashioned another victory over Arab armies many times their size. Before the victory could be consolidated, however, the United Nations, which had done nothing when the Arabs had attacked Israel, met to demand an immediate cease-fire. That is the way of the world: When the Jews are under attack, the world takes no action; when the Jews are winning, the world becomes peace-minded.

Washington has played the same game. Golda's friends there joined in the demand for a cease-fire and an Israeli withdrawal. Washington is committed to the survival of Israel but not to the triumph of Israel, for Washington fears the wrath of the Arab oil sheiks who control the spigots that hold the lifeblood of the American and allied industrial machines. On October 17, eleven Mideast oil countries declared an embargo on oil exports to the United States. America saw itself in deadly economic and industrial peril. It ordered Israel to cease and desist. Five days later, Israel and Egypt agreed to a cease-fire.

The very next day, October 23, 1973, eight resolutions calling for Nixon's impeachment were introduced in the House. Leon Jaworski was appointed Watergate Prosecutor and made it clear that he intended to see the investigation through without tolerating any "stonewalling" by the White House. On November 21, the White House confessed that there was an eighteen-and-a-half-minute gap in the subpoenaed Watergate tapes. The noose was closing around Nixon's neck.

Still fighting back, on January 4, 1974, Nixon said he would not comply with subpoenas of his tapes and documents, claiming an "executive privilege" that is not inscribed in the Constitution and had never been recognized by the Supreme Court or the lawmaking bodies of the Congress. On February 6, the House Judiciary Committee opened impeachment inquiries against Nixon. Patty Hearst was kidnapped and Henry Kissinger persuaded seven Arab states to lift their oil embargo. There was not one day in the winter-spring of 1974 without some sensational news. Americans crowded around their television sets every evening. Never before had television networks enjoyed so consistently large an audience night after night. Television became, without rivals, the leading source of news for Americans. Polls showed that some fifty-five percent of Americans received their news from television. I was very busy as the news analyst of Channel 11, WPIX–TV, in New York. Channel 11 later syndicated our news program and formed an important new national network, called INN, Independent Network News. I have been their news analyst for more than a decade.

Nixon, escaping from internal turmoil, flew to the Middle East to urge peace on all parties, then flew on to Moscow for another summit with Brezhnev, Summit III. It was ironic to see Nixon turning to Russian communists to improve his image under fire at home. No novelist could have written a plot that would be acceptable to any editor if he had just copied down the twists and turns in Nixon's career and in American politics.

On July 24, the House Judiciary Committee threw open its impeachment hearings to the national television networks. Now the whole country could look in, see and hear the evidence against Nixon and his cohorts. It was piling up like manure at the stables. Nixon himself had said earlier that mistakes, even wrongdoings, occur in heated campaigns, but what was worst was not the wrongdoing but the lying in an attempt to cover it up. No enemy of his could have put the case against him better.

On the day the televised hearings began, the Supreme Court upheld the Special Prosecutor's subpoena of White House tapes. A week later, grudgingly, President Nixon began turning over the subpoenaed material. On that day, July 30, the House Judiciary Committee voted three articles of impeachment. It was clear that it would vote more and that when the final decision would pass to the Senate, Richard Nixon would become the first American President in history to be thrown out of office by impeachment, unless he first resigned.

Nixon was doomed, not by his enemies, not by the "impudent snobs" and the "self-elected elite" of the media, to use Agnew's accusatory words, but by the long record of misdeeds, of violations of the law, his own lies and cover-ups. He and his cohorts had burgled, wiretapped without judicial approval, raised money illegally, hid it and then "laundered" it, had drawn up enemy lists and used IRS agents to harass critics, and had the CIA create a file of ten thousand citizens and engage in secret, illegal domestic espionage against dissidents and antiwar activists. Nixon had drawn up a plan of attack upon critics which J. Edgar Hoover himself had rejected as a move to turn America into a kind of police state. Nothing could save him from impeachment but resignation. On August 8, 1974, Richard Nixon surrendered to reality. He announced that he would resign. The next day, Gerald Ford was sworn in as President of the United States and Nelson Rockefeller as Vice-President.

On September 8, President Ford, in a decision that provoked a national controversy and diminished his own reputation for integrity, pardoned Nixon for all crimes he may have committed or participated in during his Presidency. Many Americans believed and still believe that Nixon had made a deal with Ford to name him Vice-President on Ford's promise to pardon him. There is no proof of such a deal and I doubt that any such bargain had been explicitly struck. Ford simply could not face up to the possibility of an American President being put into prison and, I suspect, most Americans would not have wanted it to go that far. Nixon had been disgraced. Enough was enough.

What is remarkable has been the slow but steady rehabilitation of Richard Nixon ever since his disgrace. The man is really a living human version of the legendary phoenix bird, falling in flames, then arising anew from its own ashes. Many Americans were shocked when Nixon was named as an official American government representative at the funeral of Anwar Sadat. Many asked: Is this the kind of man, who had betrayed the highest office in our land, who had admitted publicly in his interview with David Frost that he had lied and had "let the American people down," to name as the representative of those same people? One can accept his being pardoned and not sent to prison. Enough certainly is enough, but naming him as an American official is just as certainly too much.

If he has slowly been rehabilitated in America, he has never been found guilty in the rest of the world. There is no political phenomenon in the world today more remarkable than the esteem in which Nixon is held in many countries. I travel often through Europe, North Africa, the Middle East, and Asia, and wherever I go, Nixon's name is sure to come up at some lunch, reception, or dinner, with people asking me just what he had done to have been thrown out of office. It is not that they are not informed on every item in the many indictments against Nixon. They know the entire story. They do not, however, seem to understand that these crimes were intolerable when committed by a President. Europeans, Africans, Asians simply do not understand the reverence Americans have for the Presidency. There is no other system of government exactly like ours anywhere in the world, so it is perhaps not surprising that we are not understood.

I saw an example of Nixon's special place in the hearts and minds of Europeans on a balmy July day in 1982, when my wife and I were visiting Budapest, Hungary. We were walking down Vaci Utca, the shopping street in the heart of Pest, just off the Danube, when, near the end of the Vaci, at the little park in Vörösmarty Square, police cars came screeching around the corner, sirens wailing. Four black limousines followed the police car, braked, and a number of thick-necked "gorillas" jumped out. Dorothy and I stopped, startled, wondering if a raid was being carried out, when, suddenly, right in front of us, Richard Nixon stepped out of one of the cars.

He had aged, his back was rounded and stooped. He carried his head, as always, slanted down, jaw jutting forward, as he looked up out of thick black brows, now flecked with gray. He has begun to look like a Rich Little caricature of himself. He looked around as people stared and some began timidly to applaud. Street demonstrations are not usual in communist countries, although Hungary is certainly the most free and prosperous of all the lands in the East. Most of the people did not recognize or react to Nixon. I stood and watched this man who had been a principal actor in world affairs, out of power, but still seeking its trappings in his visits around the world.

Nixon remains popular in many places around the world because he had been the man of détente, the "Peacemaker," and because other peoples do not expect as much from their leaders as we do. What they like best about Nixon is that he is remembered as the man who went to Peking and Moscow and sought to advance the hopes of peace. That is more precious to the peoples of the world than the niceties or evils of American politics.

Gerald Ford, after the controversy over the pardon died down, came on as Mr. Clean. Nixon's darkly sinister face on TV gave way to Ford's all-American open freshness, blond as a wheat field, steady as the center of the Michigan football team that he had been. He was clumsy, and helped comedian Chevy Chase become famous in his imitations of Ford falling over his own feet. We all smiled warmly as Ford appeared in golf tournaments and hooked his ball into the crowd, while Bob Hope hid behind his golf cart, hamming it up. It was the best way to exorcise the demons of Watergate and help the nation laugh its way out of the jitters.

We all owe a debt to Jerry Ford for being the picture of an honest, well-meaning, decent man. And most of America fell in love with his handsome, brave wife, Betty, who talked frankly of problems millions of Americans were facing: alcoholism of nervous wives; drugs and abortions; extramarital sex; parental loss of control over their children. Jerry Ford's Presidency was brief, a mere footnote in American history, but just what was needed after Nixon.

In November 1974, at the midterm elections, the Democrats, as might be expected after Watergate, scored big gains, winning forty-three additional House seats to take a commanding majority. Ford then flew to Vladivostok for a summit meeting with Brezhnev and signed an agreement to limit the number of missiles that carried MIRV's. Ford unveiled a new WIN program, Whip Inflation Now, which got nowhere. Sugar jumped from 18 cents a pound in January to 65 cents a pound in November. The Senate finally ratified a 1952 Geneva Protocol on the prohibition of biological and chemical weapons.

In February 1975, Nixon's principal aides, Haldeman, Ehrlichman, and Mitchell were sentenced to prison for their role in the Watergate cover-up. John Mitchell became the first attorney general in American history to go to jail. In May, Ford faced his first foreign crisis when the merchant ship *Mayaguez* was seized and charged with spying in Cambodian waters. A domestic scandal shook his otherwise tranquil regime when the director of the FBI, Clarence Kelly, admitted that illegal break-ins and burglaries had been carried out by FBI agents, but defended them by claiming that national security had been involved.

In September, two deranged women tried to assassinate Ford, Lynette Fromme, in Sacramento, and Sara Jane Moore in San Francisco. It was ironic. No one had ever taken a shot at the hated Nixon, but there were two attempts against innocent, likeable Jerry Ford. Henry Kissinger resigned in November. Defense Secretary James Schlesinger quit on the same day, and so did William Colby, head of the CIA. All three had become highly controversial and it was known that they did not have a high regard for the current Administration. After much hesitation, and under heavy fire, Ford decided to support legislation to lend $2.3 billion annually to save New York City from bankruptcy. He then toured Asia in December and announced, as all Presidents do, a new "doctrine," the "Pacific Doctrine," which recognized Japan as a "pillar of U.S. strategy and security."

1976 was again a Presidential election year. Ford announced his intention to seek the Republican nomination so that he could win the Presidency in his own name and be President in his own right. Normally, the Republicans do not like to challenge an incumbent President of their own party. However, Ford was not a genuine incumbent. He was Nixon's handpicked, unelected Vice-President and had become the unelected President on Nixon's resignation.

A well-liked Republican, who had collected many political due-bills by loyal campaigning and successful fund-raising, the former governor of California, Ronald Reagan, threw his hat in the ring to challenge Ford. It would be Reagan's second run for the roses and he would fail again. Just as Nixon was written off after he had failed to win the governorship of California, so then was Reagan written off in 1976 when the Republicans rejected his bid and chose Ford. So much for writing off politicians while they are still breathing.

The Democratic race was wide-open with a baker's dozen of aspirants. Watergate had so destroyed the Republican image that all observers agreed that the Democratic nomination was tantamount to election. No one gave the Republicans a chance. Public opinion polls showed that only twenty percent of Americans considered themselves to be Republicans, the party's lowest showing ever. Every Democratic congressman and governor began dreaming about becoming President.

Henry "Scoop" Jackson, a perennial dreamer; George McGovern, a defeated dreamer; Frank Church; Hugh Carey; every day a new name popped up on the list of potential candidates. The newest was a man unknown outside his native state, the governor of Georgia, Jimmy Carter. If ever there was a man who did not have an outside chance to be nominated and elected, it was Jimmy Carter. He had more handicaps than assets. His family alone would seem to be good reason to kill his candidacy. His mother was an old hippie, hopping around the world, joining the Peace Corps when most grandmothers were knitting on the front porch. His brother was a beer-guzzling, foul-mouthed red-neck, his sister a Bible Belt circuit-riding evangelist and faith healer, while he described himself as a "born-again Christian." America is a Christian nation and wants its leaders to be good church-going men, but not zealots. On top of everything, Carter's mouth was fixed in a permanent smile showing more teeth than human beings are supposed to have, while his eyes were cold and never reflected the smile on his lips.

Not only was Jimmy Carter an unknown, with a weird family and a controversial, high-toned religiosity, he was from the Deep South, from Dixie, without a chance of winning Northern and Midwestern votes. Every expert knew that. Moreover, he made some bad mistakes in his campaigning. He granted an interview to *Playboy* magazine in which he confessed to lust in his mind for women other than his wife and admitted that he had actually "committed adultery in his heart." How in the world could this inept clown think he could become President of the United States?

The experts were made to look foolish. Jimmy Carter won seven of the first nine primaries that he entered. His biggest early win came in April when he triumphed in Pennsylvania, his first victory in a major Northern, industrial state. He went on to victory upon victory, and, on July 14, smiling Jimmy Carter was acclaimed as the nominee of the Democratic Party. How had he done it? Simply by sensing that the Watergate scandals, foreign crises, domestic rioting, and rising inflation had disgusted the American people with all those in Washington who had been in power during the unmaking of America.

Carter's program had only one real plank in it: He had never served in Washington. Jimmy Carter was the outsider asking the American people to turn away from all those tired, corrupt old politicians and try someone new, clean, and Christian. That did it. On November 2, 1976, in the year of America's celebration of two hundred years of independence, Jimmy Carter was elected President by a narrow but clear majority.

Wearing his widest smile and leading his family, his devoted wife on his arm, Jimmy Carter marched on foot to the White House after his inauguration as President on January 20, 1977. At the White House, Jimmy Carter rolled up his sleeves and went to work, his desk in the Oval Office piled high with documents and folders marked "Urgent." Carter was going to be an activist, hardworking President, with a tight hand on the reins, checking and re-checking everything himself, as though sheer personal effort would solve the nation's problems.

Carter, though elected as an outsider, was faithful to the philosophy and traditions of mainstream Democratic Party thinking, from Roosevelt through Truman, Kennedy, and Johnson, particularly on issues of economic and social justice at home and human rights in the world. In his very first act as President, on January 21, Carter pardoned most Vietnam draft evaders who had not been charged with other crimes. He instructed his secretary of state, Cyrus Vance, to reduce American aid to Argentina, Uruguay, and Ethiopia because of human rights violations, with threats to cut aid off completely if repression continued.

On March 9, Jimmy Carter announced that U.S. ground forces in Korea would be withdrawn over a period of five years. He then ended travel restrictions to Cuba, North Korea, Cambodia, and Vietnam. U.S. and Vietnamese negotiators began meeting to discuss "normalizing relations." Carter was anxious to move away from the hostilities of the war and to make it clear to Asian nations that they would have to take over primary responsibility for their security. When a major general, John Singlaub, publicly criticized Carter's policy of troop withdrawal from Korea, the President, determined to let the military know who was in command, promptly removed him from his assignment as Chief of Staff for U.S. forces in Korea. Carter was not going to tolerate any imitations of MacArthur. He further challenged the Pentagon chiefs by ordering a halt to production of the B-1 bomber, stating that the development of the cruise missile made it unnecessary.

Carter's top priority project in the first year of his Administration was conservation of energy. The Arab oil embargo, the formation of the OPEC cartel, and a quantum jump in the price of oil had fueled the flames of inflation. Soon after his inauguration, he began studying plans to deal with the crisis. On April 18, 1977, President Carter called for energy conservation and characterized the urgency of the project as "the moral equivalent of war." The crisis was certainly real and urgent but Carter's rhetoric was hyperbolic and would come back to embarrass him, for the measures he called for were short of what war would require. His grave weakness was to announce heroic measures and then abandon them.

If Jimmy Carter failed to make headway on the problems of the American economy, if inflation mounted to a horrendous double-digit level, while the prime rate exploded to a frightening twenty percent, he did, however, realize one historic success in the turbulent Middle East. He owed this opportunity for success to one of the most remarkable men ever to rise to leadership in the Arab lands, Anwar Sadat of Egypt. Sadat's emergence as a statesman, a man of peace, holding out his hands in friendship to Israel, is further proof, if any is needed, of the alchemy of power that can turn a once bitter, hateful man into a visionary of peace and friendship.

In his youth, Sadat, a junior officer, was anti-Semitic and an admirer of Hitler. He lusted for war with Israel and cheered Nasser's threats to drive the Jews into the sea. Yet, as President of Egypt, Sadat came to realize that his people's real enemy was not the Jews of Israel but the murderous poverty, illiteracy, and disease that were rampant in Egypt, the largest and poorest of all the Arab nations. Sadat had come to understand that war with Israel was futile and simply increased the misery of his suffering people. He understood that his oil-rich Arab "brothers" were always ready, as Sadat expressed it to a number of intimates and reporters, "to fight to the last Egyptian."

Egypt has the largest Arab army and had carried the heaviest burden in all the wars against Israel. Egypt had lost each war, but, in the Yom Kippur War, for the first time, Egyptian arms had won striking victories, had swept across the Suez Canal and deep into the Sinai. The tide finally turned and Israel had won the final victory, but Egypt could boast of its own victorious battles. This gave Sadat the opportunity he had long held under consideration: an honorable peace with Israel.

History was made when Anwar Sadat, the modern Pharaoh of Egypt, flew to Jerusalem, a holy city of the Jews and Arabs both, sweeping aside all the Arab objections to visiting Jerusalem under contested Jewish sovereignty. Sadat defied history itself, thousands of years of hostility and hatred, and defied all the other Arab governments, which had sworn never to recognize Israel or deal with the leaders of the Jewish state. It was one of the most daring exploits in Middle East history, in the history of the world.

The scenes throughout Israel were unforgettable, one of those rare glorious moments of hope and joy in a cruel world and in the lives of desperation that most people live. Jewish and Moslem citizens of Israel sought each other out, embraced, joined hands, and danced wild horas, hand in hand in widening circles through the night, until the first rays of sun lighted up the golden stones of Jerusalem and the ancient hills of the not so holy Holy Land. In Jerusalem itself there were moments that gripped one's heart and brought tears of happiness, such as the poignant scene when Anwar Sadat advanced with open arms to embrace Golda Meir, and said, "I have often dreamed of meeting you," and Golda opened up her own arms, softly replying, "What took you so long?"

As I watched this incredible, miraculous drama being played, I thought of other remarkable scenes in the City of David, that bloody place so incongruously named City of Peace. In May 1948, David Ben-Gurion, whose adopted Hebrew name means "Son of a Young Lion," was sitting in his kitchen hastily scribbling the first draft of Israel's Declaration of Independence, the renascence of a Jewish state after two thousand years of exile in the world's diaspora. As he scribbled on sheet after sheet, he ran out of paper and shouted to his devoted wife, "Paula, Paula, more paper, please." Paula, making coffee, as always, began searching through all the cupboards but could find no writing paper. Israel's cupboards were bare in 1948. Finally, she ran over to David, chewing his pen impatiently, and said, "So, here is paper, it's all I've got," and threw a roll of toilet paper on the kitchen table. David grinned, grabbed her and kissed her and said, "After what has been thrown at us through the years, it is most appropriate, no?" Ben-Gurion finished the first draft of the historic document on sheets of toilet paper. Later, he laughed heartily as he described the scene during an interview at his house in Jerusalem.

I remembered the dark morning, just before dawn, when I stood on top of the hill overlooking the valley of Armageddon. It was bitter cold and I was trembling in my light cotton, khaki short-sleeve shirt and slacks. Later, in Jerusalem, it would be hot and I had mistakenly dressed for later. I looked at the president of Israel, the prime minister, and members of the Cabinet. They, too, were blue with cold. Only the honor guard of soldiers and the security police were dressed in warm woolens. We stood in a huddled group, looking up at the sky for the first sign of the warming, rising sun, and also to the east at the gap that had been cut into a barbed-wire fence that marked the hostile Arab border, waiting for the visitor to arrive and come through.

An hour passed, the mists lifted, the sky in the east turned from black to rose. Just as the first rays of sun hit the top of the barbed wire, cars drew up to the gap, and out of one of them, dressed in white, wearing the white skullcap that the Jews call a yarmulka, came the Pope of Rome. Paul VI walked through the gap in the wire, along the ridge overlooking Armageddon, arms outstretched, and pronounced the most beautiful word in the Hebrew tongue, "Shalom," as he advanced to be greeted by the president of Israel. Suddenly I was warm, my blood pulsing through my heart, a lump in my throat, all very unprofessional for a reporter supposed to observe with cool, clear eyes. Reporters are human, not machines, and react emotionally to a rare event bringing promises of hope and peace. I have not seen many such events in fifty years of watching and hoping.

Tears of happiness filled my eyes that morning and again on the evening of Sadat's arrival in Jerusalem. Jews and Egyptians had killed each other in wars in 1948, 1956, 1967, and 1973, to say nothing of the murderous "war of attrition," the constant bombardments across the Suez Canal, down from the Golan Heights, and the banks of the Jordan in the years between the all-out wars. To hear Sadat say with the intensity of true conviction, even passion, "No more war! Never again war!" was to hear the trumpets of the angels of peace over the Holy Land. I had once thought that nothing could exceed my joy the day I sat in the little schoolhouse in Reims, France, and watched the arrogant Nazi generals bow their heads in abject, unconditional surrender to the Allied commanders. Yet even that great moment, a triumph of force, could not match Sadat in Jerusalem, a triumph of peace, freely offered to end the most ancient of hatreds.

The palm leaves of peace are fragile and are most often chilled by the winds of war. They need to be nurtured and sheltered in this violent world. It seemed for a moment, in the new year 1978, that the hopes engendered in Jerusalem were again imperiled, when President Carter, in a highly controversial decision, seized the opportunity of Sadat's offer of peace to Israel, to propose the first arms shipments to Egypt since the 1950s.

On February 14, Carter proposed sending 50 F-5 E fighter planes to Egypt and 50 F-15 fighters to Saudi Arabia, attempting to placate Israel with a bigger shipment of 75 F-16's and 15 F-15's. The Pentagon had urged the sale on the grounds that Egypt was threatened by its radical neighbor, Libya, while Saudi Arabian oil fields needed protection from the pro-Soviet radical states of Syria and Iraq.

Israel protested bitterly that the Saudis were not the so-called moderates that Washington feigned to see, but were the most virulently anti-Semitic as well as anti-Israel of the Arab states. Sending arms to the Arabs was not the way to bring peace to the Middle East, Jerusalem argued. Washington paid tribute to our dependence on oil, using the Soviet menace as an additional excuse to bow to Arab demands. We also needed to pay for oil by arms sales. America had become the premier arms salesman of the world, far exceeding even the Soviets who were in second place as merchants of death. Our biggest customer was the arrogant Shah of Iran to whom we had sold billions of the most modern weapons.

The danger of selling so many deadly weapons to dictators hated by their own depressed and tortured peoples became acute on February 18 when widespread antigovernment riots broke out in Iran, the most strategically important nation in the Middle East, dominating the Persian Gulf on its southern borders and fronting on the Soviet Union in the north. Menachem Begin, alarmed at the course of events, flew to Washington to see Carter and to call for American help in implementing Sadat's offer of peace which still had to be translated from a gesture to a treaty. Begin arrived in Washington on March 1, and the very next day, obsessed by fears of Soviet expansion, Carter publicly warned the Soviet Union against any attempts to subvert and infiltrate the Horn of Africa.

There was one bright spot in the African scene. On March 3, the warring factions in Rhodesia signed a peace agreement that provided for the establishment of majority rule by the black peoples of the nation by the end of the year. America's U.N. ambassador, Andrew Young, a black activist, flew to Rhodesia to meet with Patriotic Front black leaders, promising sympathetic American support for their goals. Three black leaders were sworn in, for the first time, as members of the Executive Commission, ending eighty-eight years of exclusive white rule in Rhodesia.

President Carter, determined to be the President of peace, and to dedicate America to support for human rights in the world, had put his prestige and power on the line by agreeing to turn sovereignty over the Panama Canal to the people of Panama by a gradual process to be completed by the year 2000. Despite that moderate procedure, with many safeguards, and despite the fact that even military authorities conceded that the Panama Canal was no longer the vital, strategic link it once was, the idea of pulling down the American flag over "our canal" ignited raging fires of nationalism and superpatriotism. It was not just a blow to pride, it was a challenge to American hubris, to the excessive chauvinism from which all nations suffer. There was a furious debate in the Senate that raged on for months until, finally, on April 18, by one vote, a key vote by Republican Senator Howard Baker, courageously staking his own political future on the decision, the Senate ratified the Panama Canal treaties.

The following week, Carter found himself faced with another dangerous challenge from the Soviets. There was a coup d'etat in Afghanistan. The Afghan president and several ministers of his Cabinet were killed on April 27, and on the thirtieth, the Soviet Union recognized the new communist regime. The old regime had also been communist and supported by the Soviets, so the change did not bring about the transfer of a noncommunist state to a Soviet satellite. But that fact was overlooked, generally because it was largely not known by the public, and principally because any Soviet-supported coup was seen at once as an example of Soviet expansion in Southwest Asia, uncomfortably near to the Persian Gulf. The

Soviets, of course, immediately denied any role in the Afghan coup but Washington brushed aside its denials. Later, Carter decided to embargo American grain sales to the Soviets, a move generally popular politically but one that angered the farmers who counted on their sales to Russia.

Throughout the summer came news of more and more rioting in Iran and of more Cuban troops pouring into Angola and Ethiopia. Carter accused Castro of being the Soviet proxy in Africa. The Senate called upon the President to order production and stockpiling of neutron bombs, subject of a national controversy, the bomb that only killed people but did not damage property. On the home front, Howard Jarvis and his California tax revolt held the headlines and began to spread to other states. The House passed a bill to curb federal payments for abortions, the subject of another major national controversy. America was pursuing the unmaking of its unity, tearing itself apart in class, sexual, regional, and social struggles, interest groups against interest groups, not all for one and one for all but "Me first, and to hell with you."

Carter's chance for greatness came early in September 1978, when Israeli Prime Minister Menachem Begin and Egyptian President Anwar Sadat flew to Washington and then, with Carter acting as the friend of each, conferred at Camp David on plans for a stable, substantive peace between their countries. The Camp David talks began on September 5 and ended in accord on September 17.

The two parties agreed that they would work together to tighten the ties between their peoples, through diplomatic, trade, communications, and cultural exchanges. Planes would fly freely between Cairo and Tel Aviv. There would be appointments of ambassadors and trade commissioners. These were practical steps to convert Sadat's symbolic gesture into a real peace process. Israel made the most important concession of all, demonstrating Menachem Begin's commitment to peace. He agreed, despite considerable opposition in his own government, to return, in stages, all of the Sinai to Egypt.

Begin and Israel never have received the credit they deserved for this real sacrifice in the cause of peace. By returning the Sinai, Israel was giving up one of the biggest, most modern airfield complexes in the world, which the Israelis had built there. In a world in which oil was king, oil that Israel did not have, they were giving up oil wells in the Sinai, wells they had drilled and developed. Those who do not like Israel and Jews were quick to say that it was no sacrifice, that the Sinai after all belonged to Egypt and Israel should give it up.

Egypt's claim to the Sinai was a shaky one at best. Egypt had never colonized the Sinai. It had been a no-man's-land, traversed only by nomads throughout history. Besides, how many of Israel's critics, like the Soviets, gave up what they won in war? How could senators, who insisted that we owned the Panama Canal because we built it, criticize Israel for claiming the Sinai won by blood? Begin's concessions in the cause of peace were precious. Sadat knew it and said so, even if critics of Israel did not.

Begin also agreed to negotiate autonomy for the Palestinians living in the West Bank and the Gaza Strip. He pronounced words that would lash back at him later when he accepted the principle of "self-rule," in all but military and foreign affairs, for those territories. Begin kept using the ancient biblical designations for those lands, Judea and Samaria. His government began a policy of expropriating land for Israeli settlements in the West Bank which Carter would assert were violations of the spirit if not the letter of the Camp David Accords. The settlements did not violate the agreements but were highly controversial and have been roadblocks on the road to peace, disputed by Cairo and Washington and even by many Israelis. But the Camp David Accords were a giant step forward, one of the great events of our times.

Two days after the Camp David Accords were announced, Saudi Arabia and Jordan, the so-called moderate Arab states, denounced them. One by one, all the Arab states refused to accept the accords and further announced that Sadat was a traitor to the Arab "nation," as though such a nation existed. There have been more wars among the Arabs themselves, Syria against Jordan, Iraq against Syria, Libya against Egypt, more wars and revolutions between, among, and inside the Arab states than between Arabs and Israel. The phrase "Arab nation" is only rhetoric. The Arab states are not united in brotherhood or politics. "Moderate" Saudi Arabia promptly cut off its monetary subsidies to Egypt. Jordan, mainly a Palestinian state itself, refused any participation in negotiations on the status of Palestinians living in the West Bank.

It was a triumphant moment, however, for Jimmy Carter. I had heard high praise of Carter from Begin, Sadat, and officials in both delegations. The Israelis and the Egyptians said they could never have reached an accord without the good offices and guarantees of the American President. "We are small countries, living in insecurity, with a heritage of hostility, hatred and mistrust. Every time we ran into a snag, Carter would be there to encourage us, to make helpful suggestions, to reassure us. Jimmy Carter is the true architect of this peace agreement." Every official confirmed that this was the opinion of Begin and Sadat themselves. Carter had won a special place in history with those Camp David Accords.

American political leaders, except for victory in wars, do not, however, win a permanent place in the hearts and minds of their countrymen by triumphs in foreign affairs, particularly when affairs at home are going badly. The American economy was in deep distress, inflation mounting to a fever pitch, balance of trade and of payments showing billion-dollar deficits every month. The Japanese were taking over the markets for radio and television sets in addition to cars. Our steel plants were inefficient and unable to compete with European steel plants, many of which we had built or financed in the days of the Marshall Plan when we were on top of the world. Meanwhile, in addition to domestic crises, foreign affairs began to turn against Jimmy Carter, and would finally wreck his Presidency.

All through the fall of 1979, rioting increased in Iran. In November, the Shah imposed military rule over his country. Richard Nixon, returning to public life, called on Carter to support the Shah, our "faithful friend" in the Middle East. On November 30, President Carter publicly expressed his sympathy and support for the Shah but weakened the impact of his statement by hastening to add that America would not intervene in Iranian affairs, making it clear that the Shah would have to stabilize his state himself. More riots broke out. On December 31, as 1978 came to an end, Washington asked all American dependents in Iran to leave the country immediately.

On January 16, 1979, the Shah was forced off the ancient Peacock Throne of Persia and fled Iran with his family. On February 1, the fundamentalist Moslem leader Ayatollah Khomeini ended a fifteen-year exile in France and returned in triumph to Iran, acclaimed by millions of the Shiite faithful. On February 14, Iranian demonstrators stormed the U.S. Embassy in Teheran. Carter flew to Cairo and Jerusalem to confer with Sadat and Begin and to make arrangements for them to return to Washington formally to sign their peace treaty. Begin ordered the evacuation of Israelis from the Sinai town of Al Arish after twelve years of settlement there.

At the end of June, Carter flew to Japan and, after his return, took the unusual step of asking his entire Cabinet to resign. As he put together a new Administration, word came in from Teheran that the Ayatollah and his supporters had won a massive victory in the first general election in Iran since the revolution. Many opposition parties had refused to participate in the elections which had been dominated by the mullahs, the Moslem clergymen of Iran.

The fatal blow was struck on November 4, when hundreds of Iranian students, or alleged students, broke through the thin line of Marine guards at the U.S. Embassy, seized some fifty hostages, and demanded that the Shah, under treatment for cancer at an American hospital, be returned to Iran and tried on criminal charges. The Iranian government resigned and turned over all power to the Revolutionary Council on November 6.

On November 7, Senator Edward Kennedy said he would oppose Carter's renomination and run against him for the Presidency. Carter announced a halt in the import of oil from Iran. Then, the day after Christmas, Washington was rocked by news of a massive Soviet invasion of Afghanistan. Carter denounced the Soviet aggression as a grave threat to world peace. The secretary-general of the U.N., Kurt Waldheim, flew to Teheran in an unsuccessful effort to negotiate the release of the American hostages. Public opinion in the United States reached fever heat in demands for action against the Iranians and Soviets.

America and, it seemed, the whole world were flying apart and there was little that Jimmy Carter could do. It could not have happened at a worse time, 1980, a Presidential election year. Carter called the Soviet invasion of Afghanistan "the greatest threat to peace since World War II," an exaggeration that made his own impotence worse. A U.N. Commission flew to Teheran but was not permitted to see the hostages. Archbishop Oscar Romero was shot dead while celebrating mass in El Salvador. Vietnamese invaders were driving deeply into Cambodia. New York was paralyzed by a subway and bus strike. Palestinian terrorists infiltrated an Israeli kibbutz near the Lebanese border and took children hostage. Israeli troops attacked and killed the terrorists. Carter broke diplomatic relations with Iran, while the Iranians laughed and called America "Uncle Satan." Our allies were appalled by our impotence. President Tobert was assassinated in a military coup in Liberia, and thirteen of his associates, friends of the U.S., were publicly executed.

Carter, under tremendous pressure to take some action, sent a helicopter-borne commando to rescue the American hostages in Iran. It was not only a failure but a humiliating fiasco. Eight Americans died in the botched rescue effort. Cyrus Vance resigned as secretary of state. Carter appointed Senator Ed Muskie to replace him, in a clear bid for party support for his renomination.

Sadat, angered by Begin's actions in the West Bank, refused to resume negotiations on Palestinian autonomy. Carter's greatest triumph was breaking down along with everything else. And, as though nature was affected by human crises, Mount St. Helens, in Washington State, erupted. Nothing worked. Faulty computers, twice in one week, put American nuclear forces on the alert, reporting, in error, an imminent Soviet attack. It was hallucinating.

On July 14, in a Detroit hit hard by recession, the Republican Party, by acclamation, nominated Ronald Wilson Reagan to be its nominee for President of the United States. Reagan had finally made it on his third try. He named as his running mate a man who had run against him in the primaries, George Bush, a New Englander, who had moved to Texas and made his fortune there.

On August 11, despite the nation and the world exploding all around him, Jimmy Carter was nominated by the Democrats for reelection. Senator Kennedy had badly misjudged the mood of the media and the people. He thought that Chappaquiddick was a dead issue. It was not. The media had not let up on him and his behavior there all through the campaign. Reporters, who had been accused of being stooges for the Kennedys, demonstrated that they were not. They simply tore Ted Kennedy to pieces.

Carter agreed to debate Reagan on national TV. It was no contest. Reagan won the debate easily, not by any substantive arguments but by Carter's nervousness and stiffness and Reagan's easy, relaxed charm. When Carter attacked him, Reagan would smile and shrug and say, without rancor, "There he goes again." At the end of the debate, the veteran actor looked right into the eyes of millions of Americans and asked them whether America was stronger and more respected in the world, whether they were better off than four years ago. That did it. Carter was beaten.

On November 4, Ronald Reagan was elected fortieth President of the United States. Moreover, the Republicans had won control of the Senate for the first time in twenty-six years. Yet, half the eligible citizens did not vote and Reagan won less than fifty percent of the votes and less than twenty-five percent of the eligible voters.

For the first time since Franklin Roosevelt, the Americans had a President of the right, who promised a counterrevolution against the New Deal philosophy which had dominated American politics for almost fifty years. Eisenhower and Nixon were Republican Presidents but one was a moderate conservative, the other a pragmatist. Neither one thought to undo the New Deal. Neither one thought we should "unmake" the system that had prevailed for almost a half-century. Ronald Reagan did plan to do exactly that and would set about it from the first day of his Presidency.

CHAPTER 19

THE REAGAN DEVOLUTION

All through the early months of the Reagan Presidency, despite a number of explosive foreign crises in Poland, the Middle East, and El Salvador, the main drive of the new Administration was to put across a new budget with huge cuts in social spending, the biggest tax cut in history, and a tremendous increase in military spending. Each of these projects had been specifically pledged by candidate Reagan and he was going to be one President who did carry out his campaign promises.

As President, Reagan would be the same man he was as candidate. Reagan, unlike Nixon or other predecessors, is not a pragmatist, he is an ideologue, a true believer in his own political and economic philosophy. His opposition to welfare and his dedication to the needs of business go beyond theory, they are a theology, and any departure from his Commandments is blasphemy, except where he would argue that the diversion could not be helped.

The major diversion would occur when it became apparent that cutting taxes and increasing military expenditures would cause a far greater loss of government revenue than could be made up even by butchering social programs. His budget would not be balanced, as he had pledged, but would, on the contrary, give us the biggest peacetime deficits ever, triple the deficit of his predecessor, Carter. A wildly unbalanced budget and giant deficits are violations of his sacred law, but Reagan would argue that Presidents before him had made such a mess that, in the process of correcting their errors most urgently, he was obliged to take steps that, regrettably, caused deficits. It was not his fault, it was the fault of "decades of profligacy and mismanagement."

On February 18, one month after his inauguration, President Reagan called for drastic budget cuts affecting eighty-three major programs, mostly in the sector of human services, the environment, and safety regulations for highways and industries. At the same time, he asserted that the United States had fallen behind the Soviet Union in weapons production and called for massive increases in military expenditures. He sent Budget Director David Stockman to Capitol Hill to round up Congressional support. Stockman had compiled a three-inch-thick "Black Book," his Budget Bible, to flood Congress with facts and figures demonstrating that the impossible was attainable. It was clear even then that something was seriously wrong with Reaganomics. In fact, it had been clear during the election campaign, even to leading Republicans. George Bush called Reagan's tax cuts and military increases "voodoo economics." That, of course, was before he became Reagan's Vice-President.

Despite criticism, Reagan won a comfortable victory for his budget. Congress gave him everything he wanted. He kept telling the American people to be patient, that he could not in a few months correct decades of errors. Every public opinion poll showed that the people were ready to give him time. His personal popularity and the approval of his conduct of the Presidency were very high, more than sixty percent in his first two months. Of course, most Presidents rate high in the springtime of their Presidency, the honeymoon of their first hundred days.

Then, during the honeymoon period, on March 30, President Reagan, sauntering slowly out of a Washington hotel, waving and smiling at cheering crowds, was shot down by a madman's bullets.

The nation went into a kind of deep self-analysis. Papers ran editorials asking, "Are we a sick people?" Not only had five Presidents been shot, so had Presidential candidates and national leaders Robert Kennedy, George Wallace, Martin Luther King, not to forget the attempt by Puerto Rican nationalists to shoot Harry Truman and the two women who sought to shoot President Ford. On news analysis for Independent Network News, I strongly rejected the notion that we are a sick society. As a reporter in France I had covered a half-dozen assassination attempts against President de Gaulle. Rome was a shooting gallery for the Red Brigades and Germany a hunting ground for the Baader-Meinhof terrorists. America was no more violent than other nations.

Absolute security for a President cannot be achieved if he is to function properly. No President wants to live inside a bulletproof bubble. What is most important is not the security of a President but the security and health of our institutions. So far, they have functioned superbly well, providing orderly change swiftly after each attack upon a President. Television is not to blame for the violence which existed long before television was invented.

After an initial reaction of shock and horror, the American people rallied around the President with thousands of letters, telegrams, and get-well cards. Public opinion polls had given President Reagan a high rating of sixty-three percent for performance before the shooting, about as high an approval rate as a President can win. After the shooting, the polls soared to seventy-three percent, the highest ever.

No President can maintain an approval rate that high for long, faced with inflation, high interest rates, unemployment, and an unstable, explosive world. Reagan's own policies were too controversial to escape wide criticism once the tides of sympathy had ebbed. His foreign as well as domestic policies came under fire.

Reagan, Alexander Haig, Caspar Weinberger, and U.N. Ambassador Jeane Kirkpatrick were all longtime anti-Soviet hard-liners. They seemed to be obsessed with the Soviet danger more than any previous Administration. It is one thing to recognize the Soviet challenge, as Harry Truman did, and take measures to meet it and contain it. It is very different to see world affairs exclusively through the prism of the Soviet menace, a prism with only one color in it, red. The world is more fragmented and complicated than that, with gradations of political colorations from red to black, from communist to fascist and many other isms in between. Reagan and his principal aides and spokesmen had a Manichaean view of the world, seeing it as a struggle between the forces of darkness and the forces of light, with Leonid Brezhnev as the Black Baron and Ronald Reagan as the White Prince. It was an unrealistic, Hollywoodian view of Bad Guys and Good Guys, of Black Hats and White Hats, a view not shared by any of our allies, or by many American observers of world affairs.

Controversies inside the United States and with our allies would break out over policy in the Caribbean basin. Reagan and the radical right in America had been critical of President Carter for not having supported the dictator Somoza in Nicaragua, permitting the communist-led rebels of the Sandinista Party to seize power. Refusing to acknowledge the basic causes of rebellion, the poverty and police-state tyranny under the dictator, conservative experts on Latin and Central America, like Georgetown University professor Jeane Kirkpatrick, insisted that Cuba, financed and supplied by the Soviets, was behind the communist Sandinistas, and that the Soviets were trying to destabilize the Caribbean.

Rebel insurgents were fighting against another military dictatorship in Central America's El Salvador. Once again, the cry was heard: The communists are responsible for the insurgency. Nicaragua, Cuba, Russia were fomenting rebellion. Washington refused to acknowledge the real reasons for the insurgency: the fact that the most fertile land was owned by a small group of multimillionaires living in Miami, while landless peasants worked the fields as peons for starvation wages; illiteracy, disease, ruthless police, and military suppression of human rights. These were the underlying causes of rebellion, not fomented by, but easily exploited by, communists. The United States supported the tormentors of the Salvadoran people while the Cubans and Soviets offered them sympathy and help. To whom would they turn?

On February 19, 1981, a month after Reagan's inauguration, the State Department sent a memorandum to the embassies of friendly and allied governments in Washington, calling the insurgency in El Salvador a "textbook case of indirect armed aggression by the Soviets." Many of the foreign diplomats who received that memorandum were distressed by it. Allied ambassadors told me and all reporters privately but frankly that the United States would not find an efficient way to cope with rebellion in the Caribbean until it first recognized the prime causes of that rebellion. No doctor can cure a disease if he has not diagnosed it correctly. Many of our allies, particularly the French, who had made their own mistakes often enough, were quick to tell us that the U.S. was heading toward disaster in Central and South America.

President Reagan and his principal aides all warned of impending disaster in Central America. They revived the discredited domino theory of the Vietnam War, arguing that if El Salvador fell to the communist rebels, Guatemala would then be toppled and, after Guatemala, Mexico. The President went so far as to proclaim that "they" would then swarm into the United States, just as Lyndon Johnson had once claimed that the Viets would be landing in Hawaii. This is the ultimate theater of the absurd.

If the domino theory were valid in Central America, then Mexico would be an early fallen domino. Yet the president of Mexico seemed unafraid and told President Reagan that support for the Salvadoran junta was not a wise policy.

The controversy over our Caribbean policy reached a crisis peak in October 1983 when U.S. Marines and Rangers, followed by a small force of a few hundred policemen from tiny neighboring islands, invaded the island of Grenada. The President gave no less than three reasons for the invasion in the first few days: 1) to restore law and order and democratic institutions in Grenada; 2) to rescue about one thousand American residents and students at the St. George Medical School; 3) to prevent a Cuban-Soviet takeover that would make the island a base for terrorism and a threat to sea lanes vital to our security. Each of these reasons was highly challengeable and seemed, in turn, like afterthoughts.

There was an immediate uproar in the United States and around the world. Members of Congress, Republicans as well as leading Democrats, accused the President of violating the Constitution by making war on his own initiative. Critics charged that force should be a last resort not a first resort to cope with challenges, assuming that the alleged threats to our security and the safety of Americans were valid. There was an even greater uproar and denunciation heard around the world, including sharp criticism from our allies and some of President Reagan's closest friends and admirers.

Margaret Thatcher, prime minister of England, a hard-line conservative like Reagan, who had not hesitated to send British fighting forces into the Falkland Islands, surprised him by rejecting his invasion of Grenada as an unwise, unjustified aggression. The leaders of France and Italy, who had held hands with Reagan on deploying new American atomic missiles in Europe, and who shared with Americans peacekeeping duties in Lebanon, broke with him in denouncing his adventure in Grenada.

The reasons that he gave at the moment of invasion, and those projected afterward, were, to say the least, highly controversial. On restoring law and order, critics asked: Who gave the U.S. a mandate to restore law and order in other countries? And if we are so concerned about law and democracy, why do we not invade Chile, South Korea, or the Philippines or South Africa where we support lawless, cruel dictatorships? Or, for that matter, why don't we invade Cuba and Russia, the source of the threat?

As for the safety of Americans, most observers who were there claim that the students were in no danger from the communist coup. The communists in Grenada, before the invasion, invited the State Department to send officials to assure themselves of the safety of Americans and to arrange their departure if they wished. State did send officials who found no danger. There was danger after the invasion, when fighting broke out between Grenadians and the Americans. American officials then revised their argument and talked of a "potential" danger, arguing that we could not wait until it was too late, as in Iran. That is a good debater's point but not a convincing argument. Why didn't we get them out earlier when we could have, and why didn't we launch a rescue operation instead of an invasion?

Finally, there is the argument of the Navy that the ten-thousand-foot airport runway and Grenada's position in strategic waters made it necessary to prevent it from becoming a Cuban-Russian base. There are many more and bigger runways in Cuba, ninety miles from our shores not nineteen hundred miles away as in Grenada. There are at least three bigger runways in other islands. The British firm which designed the runway in Grenada said it had no antiaircraft emplacements and no underground storage for ammunition and fuel. It was purely civilian for the tourist trade, not military. As for the waters, Grenada is not on strategic waterways, and if it did try to interfere with our shipping, our bombers and warships could blast it out of the Caribbean. Grenada, after all, is only the size of Martha's Vineyard, with a population of only 110,000 people. It's a gnat and we won a mere flyswatter victory there, at best.

But, there is no arguing against a quick, cheap success. Public opinion polls showed an overwhelming majority of seventy-one percent in favor of the invasion, or, as President Reagan likes to call it, the "liberation" of Grenada. That is why Speaker O'Neill of the House, Senator Moynihan, and other Democrats hastily reversed their earlier criticism and finally "admitted" that perhaps Reagan had been right. They are politicians and politicians do not oppose seventy-one percent of the voters.

Most Americans, frustrated by our humiliation in Iran, by a series of perceived setbacks in Vietnam, Angola, and Nicaragua, alarmed by reports of Soviet advances in Afghanistan, Ethiopia, and the crushing of Solidarity in Poland, were delighted to learn that, at last, a President had hit back and crushed even a tiny Cuban-Soviet penetration in the Caribbean. No matter what the rest of the world said, President Reagan certainly won a big political victory at home. Critics are eating sour grapes. One of the anomalies of politics is that you can't be right if everyone tells you that you are wrong.

There is no doubt that Reagan is a lucky man. Grenada came about within days of a terrible defeat for Americans when a suicidal terrorist drove a truck, filled with two thousand pounds of TNT, into the American barracks at the Beirut airport. The final toll was 239 Marines killed. That same day another Kamikaze terrorist blew up the French barracks, with about 60 casualties, and a few days later, farther south, the Israeli barracks, with another heavy loss of about 80.

This terrible bloodletting and our apparent impotence to contain terrorist attacks were a severe blow to all Americans and provoked opposition to the President from Republicans as well as Democrats, who began questioning the wisdom of our involvement in Lebanon. However, the invasion of Grenada diverted attention from the tragedy in Beirut and strengthened the President in his struggle with Congress over his authority to use our armed forces.

Reagan was lucky, too, on another controversial issue: our support for the bloody, ruthless military dictatorship in Argentina. Some twenty thousand Argentinians had been arrested and never heard from again. Jews have been brutalized there and swastikas painted on prison walls in Argentina. Dissidents have been taken up in planes and thrown out. Reagan's tolerance of this dictatorship had come in for heavy criticism. But, in November 1983, Argentina held an election to replace, with civilians, the cruel and inept generals who had failed so miserably in their attempt to seize the Falkland Islands. A kind of miracle occurred. The radical Peronista Party was soundly defeated by a centrist party which set about trying to form Argentina's first democratic government of modern times. They took Reagan off the hook.

The President has long been in trouble not only in the Americas but throughout the Third World. He ran into a series of scoldings and a rare moment of education when he agreed to attend a summit meeting on Third World problems at Cancún, Mexico. The President deserved to be applauded for risking what his predecessors had feared, becoming the target for criticism by most of the poor countries in the world who are angry at America's failure to appreciate their problems and to aid in solving them. The Soviet Union, invited to the meeting, refused to attend. The Soviets are not at all interested in Third World problems or in aiding them in their struggle against poverty and disease. Russia only gives "aid" to revolutionary "wars of liberation," it cares little for problems of the developing nations.

Reagan told the other nations that he had come to listen and to learn. He had no sweeping proposals to make, no great promises of American aid. He startled them, however, with one proposal, to send an agricultural task force to show them how to become self-sufficient, with the cost borne by private business rather than by government. This was consistent with his philosophy of shifting responsibility downward from central government to state and county governments to private business.

There is no historical precedent for believing that private business would take on the burden of aid. Private business is deeply engaged in international affairs but its only purpose, its legitimate purpose, is to sell its products and make a profit. No one could expect vast and costly initiatives to be administered and financed by the oil companies, ITT, or IBM. Corporations are not created for such purposes. Executives are not trained or mandated for it.

President Reagan heard speeches that must have reminded him of some of the criticism hurled at him back home. President Julius Nyerere of Tanzania told him: "The Third World is not asking for charity. We are asking for a chance to earn our own living. We are asking for an end to the system which now causes wealth to flow automatically from the poor to the rich. We are asking for implementation of the commitment to attack the poverty which endangers all of us."

The speaker was a socialist but Reagan heard similar complaints from one of the richest countries in the Third World, Nigeria, the second largest supplier of oil to the United States. Nigeria's foreign minister, Ishaya Audu, said he could understand the value of private initiative in some enterprises. But he denounced Reagan's task-force proposal as "private sector voodoo." He must have been following the rhetoric of the American electoral campaign. "Nigeria," he said, "had tried that route and it simply did not work." Third World development is largely agricultural, and private business will not take the risks of investing in agriculture. Nigeria had invited a major multinational company to help them and the company had built a factory to process food but did nothing to help them grow food.

Reagan had replied that the young U.S.A. had been an underdeveloped nation and look how far it came through economic freedom. The Third World delegates rolled their eyes and controlled themselves not to laugh in his face. How could he possibly compare the early United States with its vast, rich continent, its forests and rivers teeming with game and fish, its plains a fertile stretch of tall grass, to the parched countries of Africa and Asia, or the rain forests teeming with insects and predators? America had been founded and developed by Englishmen of an advanced culture and high education. Africa and Asia had been conquered, colonized, exploited, riddled by disease, crippled by illiteracy. What does America's free-enterprise system and natural wealth have to do with them?

More than three billion peoples in the Third World live near the poverty level or, at best, in mediocre conditions. At the very bottom of the heap are some eight hundred million people whom the World Bank describes as "living in absolute poverty." These people live beneath any reasonable definition of human decency. The average per capita annual income in the thirty-five poorest countries is less than three hundred dollars. Some economists call this group the Fourth World. It contains fifty-three percent of the world's population. To talk to them about the virtues of free enterprise is grotesque.

There was one lesson the President could have learned if he had studied the documents of world trade carefully. The developing world, despite its problems, is a major export market for the U.S., accounting for thirty-nine percent of American goods shipped abroad. One out of twenty American workers has a job directly related to trade with less developed nations. These nations are also a source of raw materials and low-cost products that help keep down inflation. Third World debts are owed heavily to U.S. banks which could be endangered if they defaulted. We cannot afford to ignore the problems of the developing world, for our own economy and well-being are involved.

Shortly after Reagan returned home from Cancún, he found himself plunged into the most serious crisis of his Administration, one that threatened his entire economic and budgetary program. On November 10, an article by William Greider in the *Atlantic Monthly* revealed that the Reagan budget, prepared by David Stockman, was based on deliberately fraudulent data. David Stockman himself in an incredible public confession told this to William Greider. Stockman had fed his basic budget data into a computer and asked it to estimate the impact on the economy of Reagan's planned tax cuts. Stockman confided to Greider that the results were "absolutely shocking." The Reagan program would produce the highest peacetime deficits in history—$82 billion in fiscal 1982 and $116 billion in fiscal 1983. Stockman said that if those figures were made public the financial markets would panic, interest rates would shoot sky-high, and inflationary psychology would soar. Stockman thereupon simply changed the figures, reprogrammed the computer to produce the forecasts he needed to sell Reaganomics. He perpetrated a fraud of Nixonian dimensions, a kind of economic Watergate.

Not content with stacking the deck and doing injury to the economy, Stockman proceeded to insult Reagan's major contributors and constituents in the business world. Describing the lobbying that went on in Congress on the Reagan tax bill which was passed in August, Stockman asked, "Do you realize the greed that came to the forefront? The hogs were really feeding. The greed level, the level of opportunism, just got out of control."

Reagan and his cohorts all but repealed the corporate income tax. President Reagan gave business the largest tax cuts in memory, capping a long-time trend to reduce income tax on business. Thirty years ago, under Eisenhower, the government took in one tax dollar in four from business profits. Today it is down to only one dollar in ten.

It might well be justifiable to give business and industry big tax breaks to build new plants, but only if they are required to do so. What has happened in Reaganomics is that the big companies get big tax cuts but they do not put it into new plants. They buy other big companies. U.S. Steel's plants are largely obsolescent, but Big Steel took its tax-cut money and bought up Marathon Oil, going into the oil business instead of improving its steel plants. Dupont and others carried out similar multibillion-dollar purchases that do nothing to improve our economy.

In news analyses on INN I pointed out the weaknesses in Reagan's tax program, predicting that it could hinder the promised recovery, that the cuts were excessive, untargeted, and ran directly counter to the Federal Reserve's tight money policy which Reagan supported. White House and Treasury officials kept forecasting a strong recovery by the fall of 1981, then for the spring of 1982. I found myself, as I had during the Vietnam War, in a debate with government spokesmen both on the facts and the analyses of Reaganomics.

A White House admission of failure finally came on a very high level, James Baker III, White House Chief of Staff. On August 15, Baker conceded that last year's supply-side tax cuts had not stimulated the economy. The cuts and the recession had caused soaring deficits. Reagan had had to reverse himself and, after granting the biggest tax cuts in history, had gone back to Congress in the summer of 1982 to ask for a $98.3 billion tax *increase,* the largest in memory. This was exactly the kind of flip-flop for which Reagan had chastised Carter. The Republican's leading financial expert in Congress, Robert Dole of Kansas, chairman of the Senate Finance Committee, admitted that "The economy has not recovered." He then went on to say, "I never really understood all that supply-side business." It is infuriating to think back to the way Republicans and Reaganauts maligned critics who said exactly the same thing a year before. It is always satisfying to find one's arguments finally confirmed but it never quite makes up for the abuse suffered in the process of disagreeing with a President.

One of Reagan's most controversial moves was to instruct the Internal Revenue Service to grant tax exemptions to schools that were openly, defiantly racist, deliberately maintaining segregation in violation of existing laws and regulations. *The New York Times,* in an editorial entitled "It's Still Tax-Exempt Hate," sharply criticized President Reagan for granting exemptions to notoriously racist institutions—Bob Jones University and Goldboro Christian School. The *Times* wrote: "Contrary to tax law, against the grain of every civil rights achievement in a generation, at odds with three prior Administrations, Ronald Reagan voluntarily permits tax benefits to flow to segregated institutions, even to those that don't even deny their racial bias. However obfuscated, however perfumed, that is still tax-exempt hate."

A storm of protests hit the White House. Senator Moynihan of New York denounced the decision as "surely immoral, and in my view, illegal as well." The Council for American Private Education, which claims to represent organizations that enroll some eighty-five percent of private-school students, called the move "a highly regressive step." The Anti-Defamation League charged that "The state has no right to reward discrimination and, in effect, with taxpayers' money. This is the wrong signal, encouraging the wrong people and discouraging the people who are victims of discrimination."

Alarmed, two of Reagan's principal White House aides, Ed Meese and Michael Deaver, arranged for him to talk with two black aides and the only black Cabinet member, Sam Pierce, secretary of housing. Out of the meetings and staff studies came a call from President Reagan to Congress to pass legislation that would "lay down the law" on this issue. Many observers and editorialists charged that this was an attempt to "weasel out" of a bad hole. No new legislation is required. There is already on the record a number of legal decisions on this issue. Three previous Presidents had ordered the IRS to bar exemptions.

President Reagan was trying to shift his own responsibilities to Congress. To make matters worse, he instructed the IRS to continue to grant the disputed exemptions until Congress passed new legislation. White House spokesman David Gergen read a statement to reporters in which President Reagan said he was "unalterably opposed to racial discrimination in any form." President Reagan is certainly not a racist, but he is permitting important benefits to be paid to racists. For many Americans, white and black alike, it is almost irrelevant to say that Reagan is not a racist when he puts through instructions that finance racist schools.

The argument was finally decided in May 1983, by the Supreme Court in an 8 to 1 decision to deny federal aid to schools practicing discrimination. Reagan's own appointee, Sandra O'Connor, voted against his policy.

There was one bright light for the Reagan Administration as he approached his midterm test in the November 1982 Congressional elections, in which the Democrats would make great gains in the House. Inflation, which had been the number one concern of Americans in 1980, had come down from its frightening double-digit peaks to seven percent by 1982. Even that success was contested, not only by Democratic critics but by his natural constituents in Wall Street. Reagan was dismayed when the Street and its top financial analysts remained skeptical of his economic-recovery claims. The market did not rise, it was depressed or sluggish until, without warning, or economic recovery, a bull market exploded in October 1982, sending the Dow over 1000. The main reason was that falling interest rates made stocks a more attractive investment.

Analysts would argue that inflation came down partly because of an oil glut that had reduced prices, but mainly because of widespread unemployment and a recession that kept demand low. Millions of Americans had little money to spend above minimum necessities. The drop in demand brought about a drop in prices and in interest rates. President Reagan had not reduced inflation by any positive policies but by the most painful method of all, unemployment and recession. Official figures in October revealed the highest unemployment rate, 10.1 percent, since 1941, with more than eleven million unemployed. These figures do not reveal the grimmer fact that for every man or woman unemployed there are at least three dependents who suffer their loss of income. Eleven million unemployed means at least forty to fifty million economically depressed and emotionally distressed Americans. The unemployment figures shot up to fourteen million at the midterm mark.

Despite these crises, President Reagan never for a moment appeared to have lost confidence in his programs. In his news conferences, television addresses, public appearances of all kinds, he remained the tall, athletic, graceful, good-humored Ronnie that so many Americans loved. His adoring wife, Nancy, always at his side, pretty and chic, slim and elegant, had her admirers, too. They certainly are a handsome couple, a much needed symbol of devoted married love in an era where that is becoming a rarity. The Reagans are surely the handsomest First Family since Jack and Jackie and many Americans like what they see.

As the Reagan Administration came to its halfway mark, it

could still count on the goodwill and patience of many fellow citizens.

The most explosive flash point for Reagan, as it has been for every Administration for more than thirty years, is the Middle East, which exploded early in his Administration.

Savage Palestinian shelling of Israeli villages in the northern Galilee in the spring of 1981 met with immediate Israeli bombing of PLO artillery positions and terrorist camps in south Lebanon. The death toll mounted to four hundred. Arab states called on the U.N. to order Israel to stop its bombing and demanded that the United States put pressure on Israel. The U.N. never protested the PLO shelling of Israel or the Palestinian armed raids on Israeli settlements in the Galilee, which had been going on for years, yet every time that Israel took action against its tormentors there would be a storm of protests against Israel.

Israel and its many friends in the United States, non-Jews as well as Jews, were becoming alarmed by the first signs of declining support for Israel in the Congress. One of the reasons was the tough talk, including sharp criticism of American policy, by Israel's feisty prime minister, Menachem Begin, and his even tougher and more outspoken defense minister, General Ariel Sharon. Sharon warned repeatedly that he was prepared to wipe out the PLO in Lebanon and did not care what anyone thought about it, and by "anyone" he clearly meant the American government. American-Israeli relations were deteriorating rapidly, a cause for concern among American Jews and all friends of Israel.

The situation became more tense in June 1981, when Israeli warplanes carried out a raid deep into Iraq and destroyed a nuclear reactor under construction and nearing completion. The reactor had been built by the French and there was an immediate howl of anger from Paris. There was a new government in Paris. One month earlier, on May 10, François Mitterand, leader of the Socialist Party, had been elected president of the Republic, while his party, in an electoral alliance with the Communist Party, had won a majority of seats in the Parliament. In that victory, it was Mitterand and the Socialists who emerged on top. The Communists had lost strength. It was the first time since World War II that the democratic Socialist Party had become the first party of France.

Mitterand had been known, even more than Reagan, as a close

friend of Israel, but France, much more than America, was dependent upon the import of Arab oil. The French felt they had to protest the Israeli action as violation of international law, an aggression against Iraq. The French government spokesman announced that France would rebuild the destroyed reactor. Israelis shrugged and told us reporters, "Let them. We'll blow it up again." Meanwhile, Washington also felt obliged to join the chorus of protests. More importantly, President Reagan ordered the Pentagon to postpone delivery of planes scheduled to be sent to Israel.

I was asked in May 1981, by Independent Network News and by PBS, the Public Broadcasting System, to fly to Israel to cover two important news events there, the first World Assembly of the survivors of the Holocaust and Israel's national elections. Before flying out, I went to Washington to talk with members of Congress and fellow reporters. I kept my distance from the Reagan people, knowing there was no way we would find common ground. I recalled the fury of our government back in 1962 when the Soviets sent missiles to Cuba. President Kennedy was ready to bomb, even invade Cuba. We were on the brink of World War III. Everyone in Congress, all Americans, fully supported the President. We could not and would not tolerate an atomic threat so near our borders. I asked everyone I could in Washington: "If it was all right for us to risk a world war over nuclear missiles in Cuba, why is it wrong for Israel to bomb a nuclear reactor in Iraq, a radical, pro-Soviet state that had vowed to destroy Israel?" I never did get a satisfactory answer.

I flew off to Israel and found the country in a state of agitation and division I had never seen since the state had been founded in 1948. Israel was split asunder between left and right, between the Ashkenazim, Israelis of European origin, and the Sephardim, Israelis of African-Asian origin, the so-called Oriental Jews. Among these Oriental Jews were thousands of teenagers, children of Jews who had fled Morocco, Algeria, Iraq, Syria, and the Yemen, who believed that they were being discriminated against by the better educated Ashkenazim. It was an ugly, almost racist issue dividing embattled Jews who needed national unity more than ever. Among the Sephardic youngsters there was a minority that was extremely militant, some of them little better than hoodlums. They supported Begin and his right-wing coalition and I watched with dismay as they began attacking Labor Party electoral meetings, throwing bottles and stones, setting fires. It would be intolerable in any country. In Israel it was outrageous, totally out of keeping with the moral tone and traditions of the Jewish state.

Leading intellectuals of Israel were heartsick. I have never heard Begin denounced more bitterly anywhere than in Jerusalem in June 1981. When his Likud coalition of conservative, rightist, and ultrareligious parties won the narrowest of majorities in the Knesset, and Menachem Begin was reelected prime minister of Israel, I saw some of Israel's leading writers, artists, journalists, and scholars break down and cry. One famed writer, whose name it would be kinder not to mention, for it was an emotional outburst, shouted, "I'm getting out of here. This is not Israel anymore." He did not mean it and he did not leave his beloved land. He has stayed on in the opposition to Begin.

I was disheartened by what I saw and heard but I was determined not to let it affect my devotion to Israel and its struggle for survival in a hostile world. I found myself often opposed to Begin, Sharon, and their policies but it in no way influences my support for Israel, any more than my anger at Lyndon Johnson, Nixon, the Vietnam War, and Reaganomics affects in any way my love and loyalty for the United States. Israel's present government may commit many errors, even sins, but Israel is still the best friend America has in the Middle East, an oasis of democracy in that vast desert of autocracy, feudalism, racial hatred, and rampant fundamentalism.

On July 1, I flew to Cairo and spent some time with the press chiefs of the Egyptian government. Late at night, in an open-air restaurant looking out upon the floodlit pyramids, we began to open our hearts and minds to each other. I admitted that I was worried about the hard-line policies of Begin and Sharon. They admitted that they did not blame Israel for bombing the Iraqi reactor. They further admitted that despite Arab rhetoric there was little or no support throughout the Arab world for Yasser Arafat and the PLO. They told me that the PLO had threatened the stability of every state in which they had resided and were destroying Lebanon. The Egyptian officials said they had been telling other Moslems that Sadat had proved that the only way to get concessions and territory from the Israelis was not by war but by peace.

I had asked for a meeting with Sadat in Alexandria. He had

told them his schedule was filled up but that, if I could stay on for two weeks, he would then receive me. If not, he would grant me an interview on his visit to Washington and New York in the fall. We agreed that I would call the Egyptian Embassy the first week in October. I never did, for on October 6 Anwar Sadat was assassinated. It was a tragedy for everyone and above all the Israelis. The Israeli-Egyptian peace negotiated at Camp David has since deteriorated to a static no-war situation, rather than a progressive development of a friendly cooperation in peace.

Israel was then shocked when the Senate voted 52 to 48 to permit the sale of AWAC's to Saudi Arabia. It was the first major defeat of Israel in the Congress. It was, however, a Pyrrhic victory for Mr. Reagan who lost considerable credibility as a good friend of Israel. The last word has not necessarily been said on this issue, for it will take three or four more years before those AWAC's can be delivered and there could conceivably be a new situation in Washington and in the Middle East before that time arrives.

On the eighteenth of December, more trouble with Israel. The Israelis, who had suffered for years from Syrian shelling of their farms from artillery positions atop the Golan Heights, and who had occupied those positions after they had stormed them in the Six-Day War, suddenly announced that they would annex the Golan Heights and never return them to Syria. There was a worldwide uproar against Begin's "piracy." The Israelis, inured to criticism, shrugged it off.

President Reagan ran into fierce controversy on some domestic proposals as well as foreign crises. One of the most disputed of his proposals was offered in his first State of the Union message, on January 26, 1982, when he unveiled his plan for a "New Federalism." He had already sent an advance signal of what he had in mind, on January 20, when he proposed that the federal government assume the costs of state Medicaid programs in exchange for the states' assuming full responsibility for food stamps. Governors and mayors gasped when they heard his full proposal for shifting many welfare programs from Washington to the fifty state capitals. The first reaction was an uproar of protests.

The New Federalism proposal was the brainchild, if that is the proper description, of David Stockman, the self-confessed wheeler of Trojan horses up to the gates of the Capitol. Many of Mr. Reagan's own allies and enthusiasts in the Congress joined with alarmed governors in vigorous denunciations of the scheme. One of their main arguments was that the President was changing the nature of government's functions without changing the course of an economic policy that had not worked and which had no immediate prospect of working. The country was plunged into the worst recession since the thirties, business paralyzed by high interest rates, labor by rising unemployment, the poor and near poor distressed by deep cuts in welfare, students without loans wondering whether they would have to drop out of school. Was this the time for a radical new policy, a sweeping change in federal responsibilities?

Some cynics thought that the proposal to shift many federal services to the states was occasioned precisely because Reaganomics was not working. The President had promised, without qualification, that the budget would be balanced by 1984. New estimates, by his own economists, admitted that in 1984 the budget would not only not be balanced but that there would be a deficit of one hundred billion dollars or more. It would actually soar to two hundred billion dollars. Therefore, critics held, Stockman's New Federalism was just a Machiavellian plan to reduce the deficit by transferring federal costs to the individual states.

President Reagan presented the plan as part of his "dream" of streamlining the federal government and returning more authority to those closest to the people, their state, county, and city officials. This version was meant to appeal to conservatives who have long complained about "Big Government," inefficient, wasteful, and distant from the people. Suddenly, however, it was a question of dollars and cents, not theory or rhetoric. State and city governments were already having a hard time balancing their own budgets and paying for local services. They had already lost some thirteen billion dollars in federal cuts the preceding year. Almost all cities had had to reduce the number of police, fire, and health services. With the President cutting the federal budget and federal taxes, states and cities would have to raise their own taxes or endanger public safety by drastic cutbacks in public services.

In Kansas City, Missouri, elimination of one federal grant meant that 12,000 elderly and infirm citizens would not receive their free flu shots in the middle of one of the coldest winters of this century. In New York City, which had lost 460 million federal dollars in the past year, welfare benefits would be eliminated for 104,000 people. In Baltimore, 40,000 people were awaiting public housing. The new cut in funds would leave them waiting. Five big health clinics were faced with closing down in Chicago. A quarter of a million municipal employees had already lost their jobs and more would follow.

States would face a calamity in October 1983, when they would be scheduled to take over Aid to Dependent Children and food stamps. At first glance it seemed possible, for the added costs of some $48 billion would be offset by the government taking over $47 billion in other costs, including the grant of a trust fund financed by excise taxes and windfall-profits taxes on oil. But the trust fund would only run through 1990. Then the states would lose it and be on their own.

If ever programs were properly the responsibility of the federal government, they would necessarily be food stamps and Aid to Families with Dependent Children (AFDC). AFDC and food stamps were originally designed as federal programs for the very good reason that states varied widely in their ability or their willingness to help the poor. The discrepancies show the danger of leaving these programs to the states.

Even with matching federal grants and federal supervision, we find that Hawaii provides a family of three with $468 a month while Mississippi provides only $96. These differences do not arise necessarily out of a state's inability to pay, but also out of its unwillingness to help the poor. Texas is a rich state but it pays one of the lowest benefit levels in the nation and has not seen fit to increase its AFDC levels for almost a decade, despite rising inflation. The federal government has been picking up a greater percentage of AFDC costs for the poorest states—77 percent in Mississippi and Arkansas, only 50 percent in California. Under the shift proposed in the New Federalism, the poorest states would thus lose the largest amounts of federal help. The result could be another massive migration of Americans from poor and tight-fisted states to richer and more generous states.

Federal policies have already discriminated among the states. Energy-rich states, in a kind of golden arc from Texas to Alaska, have also profited greatly from the defense buildup, receiving billions in military contracts. Texas, Oklahoma, and Louisiana are among the rare states with surpluses running to hundreds of millions of dollars, although they are not among the most generous states as providers of welfare benefits. The Frost Belt states deeply resent the favors given to the Sun Belt states. Our United States is in the middle of an undeclared but real social and economic civil war. President Reagan's assurances that private business will close part of the gap and pick up some of the tab for the needy are not borne out by studies on this issue. A survey of four hundred corporations by the Conference Board, a New York research group, revealed that only six percent of corporations plan any increase in philanthropic spending in 1982 in response to federal budget cuts.

The New Federalism was still being hotly debated when there erupted another innovation that was even more controversial. It was the proposal for an amendment to the Constitution that would make a balanced budget obligatory. These two proposals together, the New Federalism and the Balanced Budget Amendment, led me to look upon Reagan's term of office as the Reagan "Devolution," a turning inward and downward of American government, shucking responsibility on the federal level and moving it to the states or hiding behind the Constitution when officials are unable or unwilling to carry out their mandated responsibilities.

The New York Times attacked the Balanced Budget Amendment in an editorial on August 19, 1982, that expressed many of the arguments hurled at the proposal by the nation's leading law scholars and economists. The *Times* charged that the proposed amendment was "ignorant economics, destructive law, foolish administration and cynical politics." It is ignorant because it is more important to balance the economy than to balance the budget. In a recession it could be necessary to spend to fight unemployment and even run a deficit. If the amendment were in effect now we would have five million more unemployed. It is destructive law because, wrote the *Times,* it "would stuff the Constitution with baloney." A balanced budget is not a philosophical question of fundamental rights and does not belong in the Constitution. It is as frivolous and unenforceable as the Prohibition Amendment. A budget is composed of a number of assumptions, on tax collection, on business activity, on world crises. A budget can be presented as balanced on paper, but, eighteen months later, produce a big deficit. Who will be punished for violating the Constitution? This amendment is essentially an admission by the President and the Congress that neither can perform the functions for which they were elected. The Senate passed the bill but it was defeated in the House. It is a bomb still ticking away.

Despite the controversies at home and crises abroad, President Reagan, for most of his first two years, maintained a high rating of public approval in the opinion polls. He was particularly strong in the South and the West, still personally popular in parts of the Midwest, except in the centers of high unemployment in Detroit and other cities which depend on auto production. The President was least popular in the Northeast, which had been hardest hit by the depressed economy and his social-benefit cuts. Overall in the nation, the polls held steady at high levels through the summer of 1982 and then began to plunge in the fall and winter 1982–83. Inevitably, the erosion of crises had taken its toll. No one, not the most charming and likeable of men can long survive at peak popularity when every act, every word he speaks, is examined and magnified in the Cyclopsean eye of television.

One of the most controversial issues of Reagan's Administration was the military budget and the plan to fight a "protracted nuclear war." Criticism was targeted on Defense Secretary Caspar Weinberger and the Pentagon. Millions of men and women from every class and every political sector, mainly, however, middle class and moderate, paraded and protested across the nation. In New York City alone, seven hundred and fifty thousand demonstrators marched carrying banners calling for a nuclear freeze.

I covered that march in New York in June 1982 for WPIX–TV. It was different from any public demonstration I had seen in more than forty years. These were not the angry young men and women who had demonstrated against the Vietnam War. This was not the left on parade, not a group of political militants. These were the so-called ordinary people of America. There were as many middle-aged and elderly as young protesters. These were white-collar and blue-collar people, welders and accountants, school teachers and butchers, a cross section of the American people.

I talked with hundreds of them over an eight-hour stretch of marching and speech-making. Most of them told me they had never marched before for any cause. Most were not political militants of any party. There were as many Republicans as Democrats and

Independents, although the number who said they were politically independent seemed larger than I had ever observed. The nuclear freeze "movement" had burst forth almost spontaneously and without national organization, not from the top down, as most movements grow, but from the people up, with no leaders and no followers, just masses, hundreds of thousands of people. A few, who were not leaders but were articulate and knowledgeable, spoke to them and for them. It was the largest and most orderly crowd in history, some seven hundred thousand gathering in Central Park, New York, without any violent incidents, without an arrest. It seemed that even the muggers and the purse-snatchers were caught up in the demand for a freeze on nuclear weapons.

President Reagan could not ignore the force of this nationwide, grass-roots movement. He tried hard to argue that a nuclear freeze would leave the United States at a disadvantage, for it would automatically freeze "the Soviet lead over us." The marchers laughed away this argument. Those who spoke for them replied that there was no such thing as Soviet nuclear superiority and that an American attempt to build our own superiority was a chimera, for the plain fact, that even the least informed citizen knew, was that each side had more than enough nuclear-armed missiles to destroy the other. The issue of superiority is a fantasy.

President Reagan was forced to propose urgent U.S.-Soviet talks for control of nuclear arms and to insist that he had always been ready for a summit meeting with Leonid Brezhnev, that he would go anywhere, any time for peace. Yet, despite Brezhnev's frequent calls for a meeting at the summit, President Reagan had somehow not found the time or place for the meeting.

One of the best informed and wisest authorities on this nuclear issue is Dr. Jerome Wiesner, long-time president of the Massachusetts Institute of Technology (MIT), one of our most prestigious science and engineering universities. I had first met Jerry Wiesner in Washington when he had been science advisor to President Kennedy. He was one of the voices of sanity in the country on issues of military spending and atomic testing. Wiesner had been instrumental in recommending a test-ban treaty, one of the major achievements of the Kennedy Administration. He had opposed spending multibillions on useless Antiballistic missile and civil defense programs. Dr. Wiesner regarded those programs as useless because there is no defense possible against an atomic missile attack, no way to shoot down all the missiles blasted off a nuclear offensive; no way to build shelters for millions of people in our crowded cities; no way to evacuate them.

Without a nuclear attack, traffic in New York City is semiparalyzed all day long. How could New York ever be evacuated? And where would people go, with a thirty-minute advance warning, all the warning one would get in this missile age? In thirty minutes it would be impossible to get beyond the area of the blast, of scorching, killing wind and fallout. Dr. Wiesner went beyond the appeals for a nuclear freeze in an Op-Ed Page column in *The New York Times* in which he proposed that the United States take the first steps toward a unilateral moratorium on production of nuclear missiles, to challenge the Soviets to a peace race instead of an arms race. We have more than enough weapons to permit us to halt production or even to dismantle a great many in such a challenge, while still retaining enough to deter the Soviets with the threat of total destruction if they launched a first strike against us. Dr. Wiesner's moratorium would win world acclaim and give the U.S. a peaceful instead of aggressive image.

The fears of a first strike, the heritage of our Pearl Harbor sneak-attack syndrome, have been used by the military and the arms lobby to justify spending up to a hundred billion dollars on developing and producing a mobile missile, the MX. President Carter at first considered approval of the MX missile but then opposed it. President Reagan approved development plans for a kind of shell game in which the missiles would be shuttled around in deep trenches so that the Soviets would never know exactly where they were and therefore would not dare attack. This phantasmagoric "strategy" was abandoned when the Pentagon could not find a state, even in the wide-open spaces of the West where the President is most popular, which would let him dig trenches across their ranges. Other plans were proposed, including a "dense cluster" system, about which there was no enthusiasm outside the Strangelovean laboratories of the Pentagon. It soon faded away. The Pentagon finally decided to put the "mobile" MX into fixed-position silos, the ultimate travesty of transforming a mobile missile into a fixed, vulnerable missile, cancelling out its justification but proceeding nonetheless with its production.

All of these schemes deliberately ignore the reality of our "triad" of nuclear forces, on land, in the air, and under the sea. There is no way that the Soviets can launch a first strike that would wipe out all those weapons, particularly the truly mobile submarine and bomber forces. The MX never was needed in the first place since we already had enough mobile sea and air missiles to deter the Soviets.

In the course of the MX debate, there were strong protests, even from some Republicans, about the vast cost of the project, estimated to exceed more than one hundred billion dollars. For the first time since Eisenhower's Farewell Address, warning us all against the military-industrial complex, there were critics who protested the waste of the taxpayers' money on useless projects, to say nothing about the cost overruns and the outrageous gouging of the too-willing Pentagon by greedy suppliers.

The bulletin of the Center for Defense Information in Washington, *The Defense Monitor,* in its 1983 issue Number 7, asserted that "the Reagan Administration will spend 450 billion dollars on projects over the next six years. . . . In the next decade, the U.S will build about 17,000 new nuclear weapons." We already have something between 15,000 and 20,000 atomic warheads, enough to destroy Russia about 40 times over. Why spend $450 billions more?

This kind of criticism comes not only from former Pentagon officials but even from the Right. One of the most hawkish newspapers, a fervent supporter of the President, the *New York Post,* protested shocking Pentagon waste in its editorial of November 16, 1983. The *Post* listed the following scandalous expenditures:

- General Dynamics billed the Pentagon $9609 for a wrench sold for 12 cents to a local hardware store

- It tried to charge $7147 for a steel pin the same hardware store was giving away free

- The Pentagon bought a $5 cutting tool for $1158

- Boeing charged the Air Force $1118.26 for a plastic cap to protect the stool in a radar plane

- The Navy has been paying $511 for 60 cent lamps and $100 for simulator parts that cost Sperry 5 cents

President Reagan tells stories, often imaginary, about welfare cheats and food-stamp frauds. Even if this kind of cheating were prevalent, it would be peanuts compared to the billions wasted by the Pentagon, but Americans have not heard the economy-minded President denouncing excessive spending and cheating in military procurement. Supporters of huge military expenditures find all kinds of ingenious arguments to justify a budget that has already, by early 1984, grown beyond $200 billion and is projected to reach $1500 billion over the next five years.

One sophistry is to take the Soviet budget and convert rubles into dollars to prove how much the Soviets are spending. This is a meaningless figure, for the ruble is not freely traded as an international currency, so the dollar conversion value imposed by the Soviet government is a figure without any validity. Moreover, even if we accept the meaningless figure, does it follow that Americans must automatically spend as much as or more than the Soviets? Are we in a dollar race as well as an arms race? If the Soviets are bankrupting themselves to build their military and draining off from their deprived civilian sector scientists, skilled workers, and materials, must we do the same?

Another justification for the military budget is the percentage game. The defenders of military spending point to the percentage of the budget or of the Gross National Product that goes to the military and demonstrate that it is at the same levels or is even declining. Ipso facto, the military budget should not be cut. This argument presumes that the military is entitled to a guaranteed, constant percentage of the budget. The pertinent question, however, is not What is the percentage, but Do we have enough to defend our nation and help defend our allies and interests in the world. Even defense-minded Richard Nixon once said as President: "Enough is enough."

The most hallucinatory military doctrine to emerge in the Reagan Administration, surpassing the blackest visions of Kafka or Orwell, is the "doctrine" of fighting and winning a "protracted nuclear war." Even more nightmarish was President Reagan's proposal in March 1983, revived again in October, to put missiles into space, able to intercept and shoot down enemy missiles. The media dubbed this as his "Star Wars" plan. Hardly anyone thought it was a serious proposal until it surfaced again in the fall. It is becoming a major issue for debate.

In the fifties, the basic American doctrine for the nuclear age was the doctrine of the balance of terror, based on each side's having enough nukes and missiles to destroy the other side, so that this mutual deterrent would assure the peace. To rely on mutual terror for peace is Orwellian enough. The balance of terror has worked so far but is showing dangerous signs of breaking. All through 1983, for the first time since the atomic Pandora's box was opened, new demons flew out. At the highest levels of government in Washington, in the Pentagon and in the White House, men began talking about a nuclear war that would not wipe out the combatants in one fiery Armageddon, but which could aim at specific, "limited" targets and be fought for as long as six months or more. Caspar Weinberger and the Chiefs of Staff even talk airily about "winning the nuclear war," a concept that no other American Administration for thirty-five years has ever considered.

The secretary of energy, James Edwards, said, as early as August 1982, "I hope we never have to get into another war. If we do, I want to come out number one, not number two." Edwards apparently is unaware of the judgment of most atomic scientists that everyone would come out of a nuclear war as number 0. Until now, the consensus of the best informed, most knowledgeable specialists of nuclear war has been that, after a nuclear exchange, civilization as we have known it would have been obliterated and that "the living would envy the dead." No longer is that the wisdom in the Reagan Administration. Spokesmen for Defense Secretary Weinberger have told reporters that "one side could emerge victorious, with enough of its resources and population to begin again."

Air Force General David Jones, who has served as chairman of the Joint Chiefs of Staff under both Carter and Reagan, does not believe it possible to wage a limited nuclear war. In his statement upon retirement in June 1982, General Jones said he could not imagine a nuclear exchange between Russia and America that would not escalate. Preparations to fight a limited or protracted war would, he said, be throwing money into a "bottomless pit." Admiral Gene LaRoque, who could not speak on active duty, has also been sharply critical of Pentagon plans since retirement.

Despite opposition, President Reagan has been moving ahead toward adoption and implementation of this new "strategic doctrine." His appointment of Colin Gray to the advisory board of the Arms Control and Disarmament Agency is yet another example of his granting authority to men who are opposed to the very institution to which they are named. Gray favors more production of nuclear weapons, not disarmament and control. Two years ago, in the very Establishment magazine *Foreign Affairs,* Mr. Gray wrote that "Washington should identify war aims that in the last resort would contemplate the destruction of Soviet political authority and the emergence of a postwar world order compatible with Western values." I wonder just how many people there are who would agree with Colin Gray that a world of humanistic Western values could emerge after an atomic war? Very few, I suspect, although those who do exist already seem to be working for President Reagan. The President finally ended lunatic talk of winning nuclear war by declaring during a visit to Japan in November 1983: "A nuclear war cannot be and must never be fought."

Even the most unthinkable, nightmarish ideas sometimes have their lighter moments. There are some dangerous men talking about nuclear doctrine in government today, but there are also some delightful clowns whose comic antics serve as relief. The great Grock, at the height of his career, never came near the performance of Ralph H. Jusell, the civil defense coordinator of the Post Office. Mr. Jusell, a clearly inspired man, told the Congress that the postal service had plans for delivering the mail after a nuclear holocaust. This cheering news was released in mid-August 1982. At a House subcommittee meeting, Post Office officials outlined plans for delivering the mail after a nuclear war. When Representative Edward Markey of Massachusetts wondered aloud whether there would be many people left to read and write letters, Ralph Jusell replied with calm and assurance, "Those that are left will get their mail." The congressmen were, unfortunately, too kind to ask him and other postal officials why they did not have a plan for accurate and swift delivery of the mail now, before a nuclear holocaust.

When challenged, the Post Office actually did unveil details of its plan for postholocaust mail delivery. It calls for moving postal operations to remote areas to provide fallout protection for postal executives and mail handlers. The Post Office would, presumably just before the bombs dropped (although it was not explained how they would know this), pass out emergency change-of-address cards, help censor international mail, and register federal workers and enemy aliens. It confessed that it would not be able to handle food stamps, passports, or migratory-bird collector's stamps. Damn! There really are horrors in a nuclear war. Representative William Clay of Missouri looked at the postal authorities testifying and said, "This idea is lunatic."

There is some hope for long-suffering citizens, however. Gary Robbins, a tax analyst at the Treasury, sent around a memo pointing out that in a nuclear disaster many government and private tax records would be destroyed. A postholocaust government, wrote Robbins, a clear thinker, would have to scrap the income tax. Before you cheer too soon and too loudly, however, know this: Mr. Robbins is not going to let you off the hook just like that. To make up for lost income-tax revenue, he proposes a national sales tax of twenty percent after a nuclear war. These are the "forward-thinking" projects being planned for us by dedicated government workers these days.

There have been, alas, no lighter moments, no clownish antics to relieve the gloom and tragedy of the one development that horrified the world for more than two months, from June through August 1982, and again in the fall of 1983 in Lebanon. Only a decade ago, Lebanon had been the most successful, most beautiful, gayest of all the Arab states. It was the one place where East met West, in Oriental bazaars and swinging discotheques, on sunny beaches and in luxury hotels. Lebanon was sometimes called the Paris of the Middle East, and sometimes, because of its thriving, efficient banks, the Switzerland of the Middle East. By whatever metaphor, its capital, Beirut, was the most glamorous, chic, fashionable, modern Arab city. By August 1982, Beirut was a mass of rubble, stained with blood, its sandy beaches torn up by tank treads, its hotels and high-rise apartments ghostly skeletons trembling from bomb hits, its streets a vast hospital emergency room, with few doctors or medicine.

The destruction of Beirut, the fragmentation of Lebanon, was inevitable. Its success and glamour were all on the surface. Underneath, fiery passions, political, social, religious, and military, were bubbling like lava. The volcano had exploded several times in the past quarter of a century, ever since France had given up its League of Nations mandate over the "Protectorate" of Lebanon. Lebanon's population was divided among Maronite Christians, Druse Moslems, Shiite Moslems, Sunni Moslems, Greek Orthodox, and other, smaller sects. It was agreed that they would share power, a Christian president of the Republic, a Sunni prime minister, and a Shiite speaker of the Parliament, with some Cabinet posts for a Druse and smaller sects. It was a fragile structure, particularly since it was not possible to share economic and social influence as one could share political office. The Christians tended to be the upper classes, best educated, holding the most important and highly paid positions. They ran the banks and international trade. The Moslems were shopkeepers or laborers, a lower-middle and underclass. This provoked jealousy and resentment and occasionally boiled over into riots.

A foreign element was then injected into the body politic of Lebanon, the PLO and its guerrillas. The PLO had originally been based in Jordan, ruled by King Hussein, grandson of the Hashemite tribal chieftain the British had put on the throne when they created the kingdom. Hussein, uneasy on his throne, threatened by the armed guerrillas of the PLO, sent his Arab Legion of loyal Bedouins against them in September 1970, in a bloody fight in which thousands were killed. The PLO called it Black September.

Driven out of Jordan, the PLO leaders and their guerrillas sought a new base in Syria. The Syrians did not trust them, either. No government feels safe with a large, armed alien force within its borders. Syria, like Jordan, wanted the PLO to conduct operations against Israel, but was unhappy about having them based in Syria. The Syrians forced them out, without an armed battle, persuading them to go to Lebanon, promising them military aid and political support. In Lebanon, the PLO soon became a state within a state. The weak, divided Lebanese government could not control them. Yasser Arafat, George Habash, and other PLO chieftains dug in and created their own enclaves of power, dominating the peaceful citizens of Lebanon who are mainly merchants, not guerrillas, not fighting people.

The Palestinian guerrillas' proclaimed goal is to create a Palestinian state where they assert it always existed, that is, in the land that is now the state of Israel. Palestinians did live there for centuries, and some five hundred thousand still live there as citizens of Israel, but there never was a Palestinian state as such in the territory that once was ancient Israel, where Israel now lives again. One of the tragedies of the Palestinian demand for statehood is that they cannot seem to understand that they cannot build their home on the ashes of the home of the Jewish people.

There are only two places where a Palestinian state could come into existence, the West Bank of the Jordan River and the Gaza Strip. Its only hope for economic viability would be some kind of attachment to the kingdom of Jordan. There is no hope at all for any agreement on a Palestinian state until the Arabs at last follow the lead of the Egyptians and make peace with Israel. Israel has a right to live as a Middle Eastern nation, recognized by its neighbors, behind secure and peaceful frontiers. President Reagan has confirmed this view in his "Peace Plan" proposing a Jordanian-Palestinian "linkage" and acceptance of Israel.

There is a consensus in the world today that there will never be peace in the Middle East until the legitimate aspirations for nationhood of the Palestinian peoples are achieved. That may well be true, but it is not, as almost every government proclaims, the core of the problem of the Middle East. The core of the Middle Eastern problem today, as it has been since 1948, is the Arab refusal to recognize the state of Israel. That was the problem that provoked wars before the PLO came into existence. That is the core problem today, the very first, essential step to peace, peace with Israel.

The Israelis cannot for a moment consider the creation of a Palestinian state on their borders just so long as the Palestinians and the Arabs threaten the destruction of Israel. Those who urge Israel to recognize the PLO and agree to a Palestinian state would never do it themselves if faced with a similar threat. How would the United States react if armed guerrillas, demanding the return of Texas, would operate out of Mexico, lobbing shells into El Paso, making raids into Texas and southern California, seizing schools and holding children hostage? That is what the PLO has been inflicting upon Israel for the past decade. Israel has warned many times that it would be obliged to invade Lebanon and crush the PLO if it continued to use Lebanon as a sanctuary for raids on Israel. The time finally came in June 1982.

The trigger that set off the explosion was the assassination in London of the ambassador of Israel. The Israelis had had enough of murder, terror, and raids on the Galilee villages of Israel by the PLO in Lebanon. Prime Minister Begin gave his tough defense minister, General Sharon, the signal to send the Israeli armies into Lebanon. The initial explanation of the invasion was that it was a drive to wipe out the PLO artillery positions that were conducting almost daily pounding of Jewish settlements in the northern Galilee. The Israelis at first announced that they would clear out an area some twenty-five miles deep, so deep that Palestinian guns could not reach Israeli territory again. The Israeli troops penetrated swiftly, successfully investing the PLO strongholds and camps, driving the guerrillas back, with heavy casualties to the PLO. The Israelis were greeted as liberators by many of the Lebanese people, who told reporters how they had been tyrannized by the PLO.

There were the usual demands for a cease-fire and an Israeli withdrawal, ignored by the Israelis. The U.N. met and voted sanctions against Israel. The Israelis were infuriated when France joined the Arabs to vote sanctions against Israel. They were pleased that President Reagan, while calling upon them to halt their invasion, vetoed the U.N. sanctions. They had thought the French president, François Mitterand, an avowed friend of Israel, would have at least abstained, but they underestimated the pressures on Mitterand to vote with the Arabs. France is more heavily dependent on Arab oil than the United States. Moreover, France had been the "Protector" of Lebanon for some thirty years and was still nostalgic about its power role in the world. The Gaullist dreams of French grandeur and of France as one of the "Big Five" of the world are shared even by the socialist François Mitterand. In the course of the fighting in the summer of 1982, this would lead to an ugly confrontation between Prime Minister Begin and the French.

The Israeli troops did not stop when they reached the original goal of a twenty-five-mile penetration and "cleanup" of Lebanese territory. They kept on fighting and driving northward. Prime Minister Begin would later claim that they had wanted to stop, having attained their objective, but that the PLO guerrillas and Syrian army troops, which had earlier moved in to occupy the Bekaa Valley, kept firing upon the Israelis. No one, not the American negotiator Philip Habib nor President Reagan, the only real friends Israel has in the world, accepted Begin's claim. Everyone assumed that Israel's real aim was to destroy the PLO as an armed force.

Whatever the original plans had been, the fighting in Lebanon moved north against the PLO, with flank combat on the eastern front against the Syrians dug in in the Bekaa Valley. The Syrians were particularly proud of their latest Soviet weapons, giant tanks and the most modern SAM antiaircraft guns. The Israelis hit the advanced Syrian lines, destroyed the Soviet tanks, while overhead the Israeli pilots in American-made jets pounded the Syrian encampments, knocking out the Soviet SAM's. Military observers from around the world were impressed with the superiority of the American weapons over the Soviet. Some of that superiority was attributed to the higher skills and motivations of the Israeli soldiers and airmen but there was no doubt about the technical superiority of the American weapons themselves. This has emerged as one of the most interesting lessons of the Lebanon fighting.

Another most important, most revealing lesson was the fact that it could no longer be denied that the Arab states, despite their verbal support of the PLO, are not genuine enthusiasts for its cause. Not one Arab state made a move to come to the rescue, even to offer help to the PLO as the Israelis drove them back, inflicting heavy casualties upon them. Nor did the Soviets make a move or voice any real protests. Not only did the Arabs not help the PLO, but when the Palestinians were crushingly defeated and had to agree to leave Beirut, where they had been entrenched, few Arab states would agree to accept them as refugees. Finally, grudgingly, under severe pressure and embarrassment, they did agree to take in the remnants of the PLO and its leadership, but they split them up into small packages among a half-dozen nations: Syria, Iraq, Jordan, the Yemens, Saudi Arabia, Tunisia, and Algeria, making certain that no nation would have to take a large contingent of Palestinians, striking proof that they were not trusted.

In the last stages of the conflict in August 1982, the PLO guerrillas fought out of their bases in West Beirut, located in residential districts and office buildings, using the Lebanese civilians as a shield between them and the Israeli guns. They expected that the Israelis would hesitate to fire upon them and kill civilians in the cross fire. They underestimated the toughness of General Sharon and Prime Minister Begin. The Israelis had come too far, had lost too many men themselves, to stop at the brink of victory. Their artillery and planes hit the Palestinian positions with devastating bombardments. They said they regretted the civilian casualties but called on the PLO to surrender and withdraw from their civilian hideouts. Israel blamed the PLO for the civilian casualties. Then, the Israelis permitted Christian militia to enter Palestinian camps, and the militia, in cold blood, shot down and killed some three hundred fifty men, women, and children. The Israelis disclaimed responsibility.

The world did not agree with Israel. It never does. This time, however, even the United States expressed its outrage at the Israeli offensive in Beirut and the Phalangist "massacre" of Palestinians. The American media, which the Arabs claim is owned and controlled by Jews and biased in favor of Israel, castigated the Israelis in a flood of critical reports and editorials. Never had American-Israeli relations been so strained. President Reagan repeatedly called upon Israel to accept a cease-fire.

On the very day that the Israeli government had finally accepted a peace plan negotiated by Philip Habib, General Sharon ordered the fiercest bombardment of the war, ten hours of artillery and bombs turning West Beirut into a flaming hell. President Reagan was properly "outraged." That is the word his spokesmen used to describe his angry telephone call to Prime Minister Begin, no longer appealing but demanding that the bombing stop. The President could not understand how such fierce bombardments could be launched after the PLO had already agreed to be evacuated and Israel had accepted the plan.

The answer came with the revelation that General Sharon had ordered the bombardment himself, without consulting the prime minister and the Cabinet. The Cabinet met in Jerusalem, and several ministers stormed against Sharon demanding his resignation. Prime Minister Begin refused to order him to resign but he did denounce the cruel last-minute bombings. He ordered Sharon to halt them immediately and not to give another offensive order of any kind without obtaining prior Cabinet permission. Israel had been badly split by this controversy between those who regarded Sharon as an Israeli hero and those who felt he was a dangerous and irresponsible hothead who should not be in command of Israel's armies. Lebanon was the conflict in which Israelis were not fighting for survival, in self-defense, but fighting to destroy an enemy. Many Israelis did not want to see their men bleed and die for such an objective. They demanded and obtained an official inquiry into the Lebanon war, a tribute to Israeli democracy.*

* The Israeli Commission of Inquiry came to the conclusion that Sharon was guilty of not taking steps to prevent and then to stop the massacre. The Israeli Cabinet voted to fire him as defense minister but keep him in the Cabinet without portfolio.

One of the most unfortunate consequences of the fighting in Lebanon was the outbreak of anti-Semitic violence in France and a vicious attack upon France and its president, François Mitterrand, by Prime Minister Begin, who went beyond all bounds in calling the French racists and anti-Semites.

French Jews, who are deeply assimilated into French culture and are loyal, patriotic French citizens, were furious with Begin. Alain de Rothschild, head of a Jewish community group, rejected the notion of any Jewish self-defense vigilantes, expressing his total confidence in the French government to take necessary actions to defend all its citizens without regard to race or religion. Most French Jews made it clear that they did not regard Begin as a kind of Jewish Pope responsible for Jews everywhere. One of the most eminent Jews of France, former Prime Minister Pierre Mendès-France called Begin a "madman" and denounced him as "thoroughly irresponsible."

Shimon Peres, Begin's main political rival, head of the Israeli Labor Party, came to France to make it clear that he and most Israelis did not agree with Begin. France is not an anti-Semitic country, Peres declared. There are anti-Semites in France, to be sure, just as there are, regrettably, in every country in the world, including the United States. Peres made it clear that criticism of Israeli government policies is not the equivalent of anti-Semitism. It is true that many anti-Semites use the mask of "anti-Zionism" to hide their hatred for Jews. But criticism of Mr. Begin is not criticism of Israel, and criticism of Israeli policies is not anti-Semitism. If it were, almost half of Israel would be anti-Semitic because it opposes Begin.

In May of 1983, however, Begin and the Israelis again became popular and admired in Washington. Secretary of State George Shultz had gone to the Middle East to try to bring peace to Lebanon. In two weeks of brilliant "shuttle diplomacy" he achieved the greatest foreign-policy triumph of the Reagan Administration: an agreement by Lebanon and Israel to end their thirty-five-year state of war. The most important clause in the arrangement was an Israeli agreement to withdraw its army from Lebanon and leave only small units to join Lebanese troops in patrolling the southern border sector to prevent PLO terrorists from infiltrating back in. The Israeli concessions and cooperation with the U.S. secretary were cheered in

Washington, raising hopes that the two traditional friends would find a warm reconciliation after two years of disastrous deterioration of relations in the Begin and Reagan regimes.

The agreement with Lebanon was fragile, for Israel's withdrawal was dependent on a simultaneous withdrawal of all Syrian and PLO forces. Syria and Arafat rejected the agreement. Israel did begin a partial withdrawal in the fall of 1983, pulling its forces out of Beirut and the Shuf mountains to a new line on the Awali River in the south, some twenty-five miles from Israel's border, the area the PLO had used to shell Israel's villages in the Galilee. Israel's unilateral withdrawal was not only not matched by the Syrians and the PLO; on the contrary, their troops moved forward into positions around and inside Beirut.

The entire Middle East power equation was shaken up in November 1983 when dissident PLO forces, under a PLO rebel named Saeed Moussa, a Syrian mercenary, led his men on an attack upon Yasser Arafat's troops in the north of Lebanon, near Tripoli. They poured shells at the rate of seventy a minute into two refugee camps and into the city of Tripoli itself. These shells hit areas heavily populated by civilians, some one thousand of whom were killed, thousands more wounded and made homeless. The "massacre" far surpassed the earlier "massacre" for which Israel had been excoriated, but this time there was no U.N. meeting, no Washington howls of outrage, no world protests against the savagery and ruthlessness of the PLO troops responsible.

The anti-Arafat rebels are men financed and armed by and under control of Syria. Assad is using them as tools to carry out his own design to conquer Lebanon. His actions have already destroyed Arafat as the leader of the PLO and the "sole spokesman" of the Palestinian people. This may open the way for new negotiations between Palestinian residents of the West Bank and King Hussein of Jordan. The power balance in the Middle East has shifted dramatically. Arafat is finished as the leader of a split PLO. Assad of Syria is now one of the most powerful and dangerous men in the Middle East.

The crisis in the Middle East, in full eruption as 1983 drew to an end, was matched by an angry crisis in American-Soviet relations. Soviet fighter planes shot down a commercial plane of South Korean Airlines, flight 007. The Soviets claimed, without any evidence, that it was a spy plane. Even if it had been, it could have been forced down by Soviet fighters instead of being shot out of the air, killing all civilian passengers and crew members, more than two hundred and fifty innocent people.

There was an outburst of protest around the world and bitter invective from Washington. The incident was just what President Reagan needed to confirm his militant anti-Soviet stand, his denunciations of Russia as an "evil empire." It gave him a chance to tell Congress that Soviet behavior required passage of his requests for greatly increased military expenditures. It assured funds for the controversial MX missile and the biggest Pentagon budget in history, more than two hundred and fifty billion dollars.

President Reagan's popularity on the eve of election year 1984 bounced around 50 percent. It was most favorable on the issue of the invasion of Grenada, but he suffered a strong disapproval rating of 48 percent, against 41 percent on his handling of American involvement in Lebanon. The polls will undoubtedly shoot up and down all through the election campaign of 1984 as circumstances provide successes or failures for American policies. The conventional wisdom in early 1984 held that Reagan would win reelection.

Republican Howard Baker, the Senate majority leader, asserted on the David Brinkley Sunday morning newscast that he did not know what area or issue, Lebanon, Central America, arms control, or some other flash point in the world, would be the major issue in the election, but he did insist that foreign policy itself would be hotly debated. He felt, and so do most political observers, that if the economy continues to recover, the President's chances for reelection are good.

President Reagan can boast about impressive economic recovery gains. When he came into office the prime rate exceeded 20 percent. By March 1984 it was at 11½ percent. That is a real achievement, but it is not exactly healthy to still have a double-digit prime rate. Unemployment has fallen from a peak in 1982 at 10 percent to 7.2 percent in the spring of 1984. That is progress but not, by far, where it ought to be. It is still higher than the rate when Carter was President. Housing starts and auto sales are all the way up.

More than four million men and women have been added to the nation's payrolls. Excellent, to be sure. But there are still nine million unemployed, and the number of Americans living at or below the poverty level has increased under Reagan, from some twenty-eight million to thirty-five million. Every shiny apple the President shows the voters has worms in it. His "recovery," while real, is not unblemished. And there is a big black thunderhead looming over the American economy: annual deficits of some $200 billion. Every economist, including the President's own advisors, is fearful of those storm clouds and most say they will burst, flooding the recovery. But the break will probably come in 1985, too late to affect the outcome of the 1984 elections. There again, Reagan's luck seems to be holding out.

Two years ago, in the depth of the Reagan recession, the Democrats felt that 1984 would be their year. They did well in the midterm elections, recapturing many congressional seats lost in the Reagan landslide of 1980. The Democrats, sensing a chance to win, came up with no less than eight contenders for their nomination: former Vice-President Walter "Fritz" Mondale; Senators John Glenn, Alan Cranston, Gary Hart, Ernest Hollings, former Senator George McGovern; former Florida Governor Reuben Askew, and a late, controversial entry into the field, the Reverend Jesse Jackson, a former associate of Martin Luther King. The candidates soon came down to three: Mondale, Hart, and Jackson.

Jackson has no chance of winning the nomination but that is not his main goal. He is seeking to register large numbers of black voters, enough to provide a margin of victory over Reagan or any other Republican candidate. This would give him a voice in the councils of the Democratic Party, perhaps even a Cabinet post. He says he is fighting for the poor of all colors, black, brown, and white. He is undoubtedly personally ambitious but since when is ambition a vice in American politics? If Jackson is loyal to the Democratic Party and supports their nominee, he may well help the party win and gain the influence he seeks not only for himself but for the have-nots of the nation.

As we finish our journey from 1933 to 1984, the future directions of America could swing further to the right with a conservative Republican victory or back toward the center where Americans are generally more comfortable. The 1984 elections will determine whether the basic principles of the New Deal remain rooted in American society or whether America will continue its move toward oligarchy, splitting our union into hostile rich and poor citizens, blacks against whites, with women in militant protest. Will we continue to rearm despite our present costly overkill capacity? Will we enter into a dialogue with the Soviets to reduce the menace to all humanity of the atom bomb? These are the most important questions crying for answers in 1984.

This journey through fifty years of the American experience from Roosevelt to Reagan has seen enormous changes in America and the world. Our population has doubled, the population of the world has broken all bounds. More than a hundred new nations have been born, proud of their new sovereignty after centuries of colonial domination. They are not in awe of the great powers and cannot be coerced. It is difficult even to persuade them. It is largely a hostile world, with people jealous of American strength and wealth, while still, deep down, admiring America and seeking refuge here.

We have not yet adjusted to this new world or evolved a consistent policy for a new world order. Russia and America are dangerous, heavily armed rivals for world power, capable of destroying the world, concentrating more on their rivalry than on the search for peace and world order or a better society for their own people.

At the outset of this saga, the United States lived in isolation. The great powers were the empires of Britain and France. Over the years war destroyed those empires and projected America into a world role. For a brief period after the Second World War, the United States was the supreme power of the world. We had an atomic monopoly and the only factories still standing and operating in a world of rubble. We could sell anything we made. This led us to believe that we were the very best in everything. We had forgotten that some of our greatest strength and wealth had come from European inventors, including the atom bomb. European and Asian factories may have been destroyed but not the creativity and the brains of other peoples.

We got lazy, fat, and used to automatic prosperity. Others around the world went to work, often in factories that we had rebuilt for them. No nation on earth has ever been so generous a victor as the United States. Soon, vanquished Germany and Japan began to make better cars, radios, and television sets at better prices than

American industry could produce. Yet, we have not lost the skills that once made us a leader of the world. We can regain our eminence, if not our preeminence, by hard work, by productive investments, by restructuring our economy to meet current needs.

We are rapidly becoming a service economy as well as an industrial economy, white-collar and blue-collar workers, electronics and computers instead of mainly smokestacks. That is the wave of the future and we can stay abreast of that wave by retraining our workers and children to new skills in new industries—particularly the high-tech industries in which we excel. I do not believe for an instant that Americans have lost their abilities. We are still a highly productive people and an inventive people. We must stress education for the technological revolution that is following the industrial revolution.

Labor and management must learn to cooperate instead of fighting each other. We must end the pernicious class and social struggles that are not a part of the American dream: rich against poor and both against the middle classes; male chauvinists against women's libbers; the children of European immigrants against the new immigrants from South America and Asia; cities against farms; the employed against the unemployed; the young against the old; and the Frost Belt against the Sun Belt. These are divisions that sapped older civilizations and should not be permitted to sap ours.

None of this will be easy. But I remember the horrors of the Great Depression: one out of four Americans out of work and money; our factories idle and rusting; our military neglected, even despised. My generation of Americans went to work and built one of the greatest societies in the world. We were so hungry, so eager to build, that we did not realize we were polluting the air, poisoning our streams, eroding the land. We made mistakes, grave mistakes, but we pulled ourselves out of a catastrophic condition.

I cannot believe that the new generation of Americans cannot bring our country back to good health as my generation did. I cannot and will not believe that we will turn our society into a jungle where only the fittest survive. The principle, now fifty years old, that the federal government is responsible for the victims of free-market Darwinism, is still valid. We cannot permit the weak to rot and die. Social services may have gone too far and been too loosely administered. The faults need correction but the system must not be and will not be eliminated. That would be like a doctor killing his patient because the cure is costly and takes too long.

I said at the outset that I was an optimist, albeit a disenchanted optimist. I know that these are not good times. I also know that there never have been any "good old days." The good old days were not our yesterdays. They could still be our tomorrows.

EPILOGUE

A PERSONAL CREED

Ed Murrow had once told me that he saw CBS News as a national teaching institution, the biggest classroom in the world. He confirmed my own belief that newsmen should be teachers. This meant to me, having studied to be a teacher, that news people must first be the most diligent of researchers, scholars in their own field. Reporters must master their field if they are to enlighten the public.

Murrow told all of his correspondents: "Dig down deeply into your story, get fully into it and let it get fully into you. When you know what you want to say, say it as clearly and briefly as you can. When you reach a conclusion, put it forward, even if it runs counter to the prevailing wisdom. Do not seek to be different or contentious but do not flinch from it."

This has been my personal creed in a career now well into its fourth decade. I have seen the media fall into disfavor, rating low in the public esteem. The press, radio, and television have certainly been erratic and have made their share of mistakes. I believe, however, that the level of reporting and the integrity of reporters overall are much higher than the public thinks. Most people are angered by reporters who do not tell them what they want to hear. Or confuse the messenger with the message. Governments, and a good part of the public, would like us to be the cheerleaders of society.

That, I am convinced, is not a proper role for newsmen. Society has all the cheerleaders it needs, among the politicians, the churchmen, and the self-appointed superpatriots who believe that only good should be said of the nation.

That is not an enlightened view of a reporter's role. A reporter must first be a teacher but must also view his function as that of a diagnostician. To expect news people only to say good of the nation, to endorse its government and agree with the President, is not patriotism, it is foolish and dangerous blindness. If someone you loved was ill, you would want a doctor to make the most intensive examination. Would you say: "Doctor, this is my father and I love him dearly and am loyal to him, so do not tell me anything bad about him." No, you would beg the doctor to take every test possible to find out what was wrong and then find a cure for the malady. Well, then, is it not reasonable that a reporter who loves his country and is loyal to it, should want to dig down deeply and find out what is wrong or right and attempt to propose remedies? Doctors are not infallible, so it is not surprising that reporters are not, either. All we can do is our very best, our most honest best, to find out what is happening.

Long ago, I gave up worrying about what the public or officials thought about my reports. I never gave up wanting them to think well of me but I did stop worrying about them giving me hell, as they have done a number of times, notably during the Vietnam War. As a friend of mine said to me one day, "David, if you are right when everyone else is wrong, you might just as well be wrong." I do not agree with that view. I would rather be right, all alone, than wrong with everyone else. I cannot, of course, be absolutely certain that I am right when I reach a conclusion. All I can do is to put it forward clearly and honestly, without fear, and wait to see what happens. Eventually, we find out what was right or wrong.

I am, after many troubled years, now at peace with myself, a big step toward being at peace with others. I owe that peace of mind to one of the finest teachers, one of the wisest men among the many remarkable men and women that I have met in my career. He is dead now, but his teaching is still alive. His name was Abraham Heschel, a scholar of the Bible and of comparative religions, one of the lights of the Theological Seminary of Columbia University. I met Dr. Heschel at Columbia and at a number of meetings of protest against the war in Vietnam.

One day in 1968, the Quakers invited a number of specialists to a study session at their headquarters in Philadelphia. The purpose was to find new ways to present the views of the peace opposition. John Kenneth Galbraith was there, and so, too, was Dr. Heschel. I had, a few months earlier, returned from a tour of the fighting fronts in North Vietnam and seen first-hand the futility as well as the bloody cruelty of our bombing. I sat and listened to Galbraith, a brilliant man but occasionally a gabby gadfly showing off his wit but contributing little of substance to the discussion. I was angry and depressed. I got up during a coffee break and walked down to the street for a breath of air, hoping to cool down. As I stood in the doorway, I felt a tap on my shoulder. It was Dr. Heschel.

"David, you're all the way down. Come, let's go to the coffee shop. Get it off your chest. I am a good listener."

I admired Dr. Heschel and was grateful to him for his kind, humane concern. Seated in the coffee shop, I told him why I was in a black mood. My first experience with the Vietnam issue had come very early, in 1946, when I met Ho Chi Minh and watched my French friends betraying their promises to him and preparing to use military force in an imperial strike to win back their colony. I had gone to friends and officials, up to President de Gaulle himself, to beg them to abandon an impossible colonial policy. They brushed me off, often in anger. I had then gone to the American ambassador and been almost thrown out of his office. Later I would learn that one of his aides had sent a report to the State Department calling me a communist and suggesting that they tell Murrow not to hire me.

For eight years, I watched the French bleed in Vietnam, killing tens of thousands, all in a hopeless cause. Then, to my despair, I had to watch my own beloved country repeat all the mistakes of the French, all the horrors and killing, the death on all sides. That day in Philadelphia we were at the peak of the lunacy, and I knew it would end badly. For all my pains, I was being subjected to intense pressures. President Johnson had publicly called me a liar and had stopped just short of calling me a traitor. Others had not stopped at that vile denunciation. I had made hundreds of broadcasts, written dozens of articles, barnstormed the country in speeches against the war. And I had not by any significant measure slowed up the war or won over enough fellow Americans to stop it.

Dr. Heschel sat and listened quietly to my lament, running his fingers through his beard, occasionally pinching the bridge of his nose and rubbing his eyes. He was tired and under strain himself but he heard me out patiently. Then, when I had finished he leaned over, squeezed my hands, and patted my shoulder. "Yes, yes," he sighed, "you have reason to be depressed. But do not give way to despair. This terrible war will end and you must go on fighting against it, whether you think you are being effective or not." He stopped, pinched his nose again, and said, "Let me tell you a story that may help you."

He sipped his coffee and then spoke in a soft voice.

"Some three centuries ago, there was a rabbi in Poland who was revered as the wisest scholar of his time, a brilliant man. Students competed to be accepted by him for their final studies toward ordination. One of his students was the most brilliant young man who had ever come to him. When the day arrived for his ordination into the rabbinate and the old rabbi had performed the final ceremonies, he invited his student to come home with him for tea. He told him that he was no longer a student but a colleague and, undoubtedly, there were questions he had never dared ask in his student days that he could now ask as a fellow rabbi.

"The young rabbi unburdened himself. 'Revered Reb, you are the wisest scholar and the greatest, most eloquent orator of our times. You have spent the past forty years fighting against racism, intolerance, injustice. Yet, I look around me and that is what I see, virulent as ever, racism, intolerance, and injustice. If you have been unable, with your wisdom and eloquence, to eradicate these evils, then to what can I look forward, who do not have your wisdom or your gift of oratory? I am fearful and depressed as I get out on my rabbinate to think that you, the great man, have not succeeded. Tell me, honestly, Reb, have you been able to make a change in the world?'

"The old Reb looked at the young man. He pulled at his beard, sipped his tea, and thought carefully. Then he replied. 'No, my friend, I have not been able to change the world. But I have not let the world change me.' "

I looked at Dr. Heschel, with a wide, happy grin on my face and tears in my eyes. We got up. I embraced him. We went back up to the Quaker meeting. I have not given way to despair ever again.

ACKNOWLEDGMENTS

In a career spanning fifty years, I have met thousands of people in many professions and walks of life and have learned something from each of them. A full list of acknowledgments to all who have made a contribution to this book would run longer than the index of names that follows.

There are, however, a special few who made most valuable contributions to the writing of the manuscript. Always first is my wife Dorothy, who makes important editorial suggestions long before the manuscript reaches the professional editors. We have been together for all of the fifty years covered in the book, as teenagers and marrieds for forty-six years.

My warmest thanks go to Amy Clampitt, who has been an invaluable research associate since 1968. In that period I have watched her grow into one of America's foremost poets. Her book of poems, *The Kingfisher,* published by Knopf, 1983, is brilliant and I am proud that this fine writer continues to work with me on my books.

My thanks go to Channa Taub, too, who did a thorough job of page-by-page line editing. Above all, I am indebted to Gladys Justin Carr, Editor-in-Chief and Chairman of the General Books Editorial Board of McGraw-Hill, for her highly professional structural and stylistic editing.

Finally, thanks to Shirley Sulat, who typed the manuscript several times, deciphering the hieroglyphics of scribbled corrections and handling every emergency, real and imagined, with efficiency and never-failing patience.

INDEX

ABOUT THE AUTHOR

David Schoenbrun has had a distinguished career as a journalist and scholar. In journalism he has served as the CBS News chief correspondent in Paris, Europe, and Washington. He is currently news analyst for the national syndicate I.N.N., Independent Network News. As a scholar he has taught French in New York City schools, been a fellow of the Columbia School of Journalism and Senior Lecturer of the Columbia School of International Affairs. He is currently Senior Lecturer of the New School for Social Research. Mr. Schoenbrun is the author of many articles and books on politics, history, and world affairs. He has won some twenty awards from his peers in journalism and more awards in more categories than any other journalist, including: the Overseas Press Club Awards for best radio reporting from abroad, best television reporting from abroad, best magazine article, and best book (*As France Goes*).